Silver Burdett Ginn
MATHEMATICS
Exploring Your World

AUTHORS

- Ruth I. Champagne
- Herbert P. Ginsburg
- Carole E. Greenes
- Larry P. Leutzinger
- William D. McKillip
- Lucy J. Orfan
- Fernand J. Prevost
- Bruce R. Vogeli
- Marianne V. Weber

Problem Solving Team

- Lucille Croom
- Gerald A. Goldin
- Stephen Krulik
- Henry O. Pollak
- Jesse A. Rudnick
- Dale G. Seymour

Multicultural Advisory Group

- Jackie Baston
- Lucille Croom
- Winifred Deavens
- Carl Grant
- Pamela Howard
- Earl Ingram
- Willie May
- Charlene Parker
- Josephine Scott

Silver Burdett Ginn

Morristown, NJ ■ Needham, MA

Atlanta, GA ■ Deerfield, IL ■ Irving, TX ■ San Jose, CA

ISBN 0-382-28204-3

CONTENTS

THEME **Inventions: Ideas Whose Time Has Come**

TIME • DATA AND GRAPHS

74

THEME **Amazing Animals**

UNDERSTANDING MULTIPLICATION AND DIVISION

110

HotPages are also showcased in the INTERACTIVE MATHEMATICS CD-ROM Program, where they "come alive" with the click of a mouse.

Do we have enough equipment for our team?

You got 4 hits in 8 times at bat— that's great!

THEME At the Seashore

CUSTOMARY MEASUREMENT

410

I can't wait
for our next game!

WELCOME to the exciting world of mathematics!

This year you will learn by *doing* mathematics. You may enjoy writing about your activities in a Math Journal. Try recording your experiences as a decision maker and problem solver.

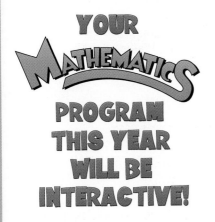

YOUR MATHEMATICS PROGRAM THIS YEAR WILL BE INTERACTIVE!

- You will learn how to find the best way to solve math problems.

- You will discover what different cultures have contributed to mathematics.

- You can use a computer and special math tools with certain pages in your textbook.

- You can share your math experiences with other students and your family.

This year's program will involve many activities beyond the printed page. Materials such as geoboards, space figures, pattern blocks, spinners, calculators, and computers will make math exciting.

TURN TO THE NEXT PAGE
and discover what lies ahead for you in *MATHEMATICS: Exploring Your World*.

ACTIVITY

Investigating Division

You can use base-ten blocks
to play Divvy Up.

Working together

Materials: spinner, base-ten blocks, Workmat 7

A. Spin the spinner two times and use the numbers to form a two-digit number, for example, 26.

B. Model the number, using the fewest possible base-ten blocks, for example,

C. Spin again to find the number of groups. Share the blocks equally, using the number shown by the spin, for example, 4. When necessary, exchange tens blocks for ones blocks.

D. Record your results on the

You will use pattern blocks, spinners, and geoboards
to **DO** mathematics. You might graph information,
explore unit costs, or investigate geometry in motion.

If your classroom has our CD-ROM package, you can
interact with special pages on a computer screen. Sound
and QuickTime™ video make the HotPages come alive.

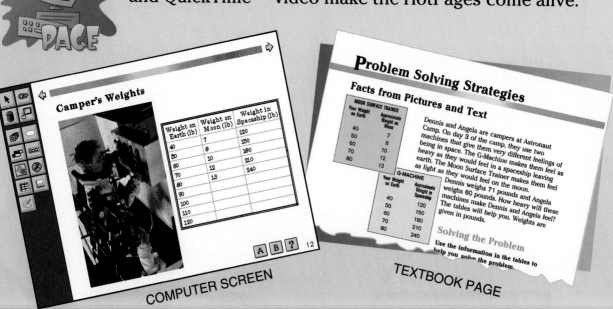

Camper's Weights

Weight on Earth (lb)	Weight on Moon (lb)	Weight in Spaceship (lb)
	7	120
40	8	150
50	10	180
60	12	210
70	13	240
80		
90		
100		
110		
120		

A B ? 12

COMPUTER SCREEN

Problem Solving Strategies

Facts from Pictures and Text

MOON SURFACE TRAINER	
Your Weight on Earth	Approximate Weight on Moon
40	7
60	8
70	10
80	12
	13

Dennis and Angela are campers at Astronaut Camp. On day 3 of the camp, they use two machines that give them very different feelings of being in space. The G-Machine makes them feel as heavy as they would feel in a spaceship leaving earth. The Moon Surface Trainer makes them feel as light as they would feel on the moon. Dennis weighs 71 pounds and Angela weighs 60 pounds. How heavy will these machines make Dennis and Angela feel? The tables will help you. Weights are given in pounds.

G-MACHINE	
Your Weight on Earth	Approximate Weight in Spaceship
40	120
50	150
60	180
70	210
80	240

Solving the Problem

Use the information in the tables to help you solve the problem.

TEXTBOOK PAGE

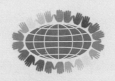

You will examine the mathematical contributions of different cultures over the years.

Math Around The World

ANCIENT EGYPTIAN NUMBERS

The Egyptians represented the numbers 1 through 9 with a form of tally marks.

1 2 3 4 5 6 7 8 9

Here is how they represented other numbers.

10 100 1,000 10,000 100,000 1,000,000

When the Egyptians wrote large numbers, symbols were written next to each other in a row. For example:

CHOICES

You will make choices about *how* to solve problems.

Do you need an exact answer or an estimate?

What is the best way to find an answer?

- manipulatives?
- calculator?
- mental math?
- paper and pencil?
- computer?

JOURNAL WRITING

By recording your experiences this year, you'll see how you've progressed. The textbook has suggestions for journal entries like the one below.

Now might be the time to start your Math Journal. Use the **JOURNAL WRITING** suggestion to begin your record. Or, create your own topic to start! After all, *YOU* are the mathematician exploring your world! Enjoy your excursion!

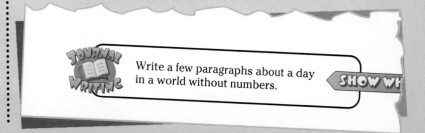

JOURNAL WRITING

Write a few paragraphs about a day in a world without numbers.

SHOW WH

1 Building Number Sense:
Place Value and Patterns

THEME   Beyond the Clouds

Sharing What You Know

How does Halley's Comet look different from a star? Do you know anyone who saw Halley's Comet when it passed near Earth in 1986? Not everyone gets to see it in his or her lifetime. It passes near Earth about every 76 years. How can mathematics help you know when Halley's Comet will visit Earth again?

Using Language

When Halley's Comet passed near Earth in 1986, there were many changes that had taken place since its previous visit. One difference was that in 1986 spacecraft made it possible for people to get a closer look at the comet than ever before. In this sentence the word **difference** means "not the same." In mathematics, when you compare values or amounts, you find the **difference.** Why do you think we use the word **difference?**

Words to Know: add, addends, sum, subtract, difference, order, compare, about

Be a Problem Solver

Think of the oldest person you know. Will you be at least that age when Halley's Comet passes near Earth again? no

Imagine you are traveling on the tail of Halley's Comet during its next visit. Look down at Earth. Describe some changes that may have taken place since 1986.

Addition Properties

The Order Property The order in which numbers are added does not change the sum.

$$4 \leftarrow \text{addend}$$
$$\underline{+5} \leftarrow \text{addend}$$
$$9 \leftarrow \text{sum}$$

$$5$$
$$\underline{+4}$$
$$9$$

$$4 + 5 = 9$$
$$5 + 4 = 9$$

addend addend sum

The Grouping Property The way in which addends are grouped does not change the sum.

$$4 \searrow 9$$
$$5$$
$$\underline{+3}$$

$$\underline{+3}$$
$$12$$

You can add down.

$$4$$
$$5$$
$$\underline{+3} \searrow \underline{+8}$$
$$12$$

You can add up.

$(4 + 5) + 3 = \square$
$\quad 9 \quad + 3 = 12$

$4 + (5 + 3) = \square$
$4 + \quad 8 \quad = 12$

Work inside the ( ) first.

What is the sum when you add the numbers in this order?

$(4 + 3) + 5 = \square$

The Zero Property The sum of any number and 0 is that number.

$$4$$
$$\underline{+0}$$
$$4$$

$4 + 0 = 4$

$$0$$
$$\underline{+7}$$
$$7$$

$0 + 7 = 7$

Check Your Understanding

Add.

1. $0 + 9 = \square$
   $9 + 0 = \square$

2. $8 + 6 = \square$
   $6 + 8 = \square$

3. $(4 + 2) + 3 = \square$
   $4 + (2 + 3) = \square$

Share Your Ideas Describe 3 ways to add $3 + 6 + 2$.

Add.

4. 1   6   5. 3   8   6. 7   8   7. 9   5
   +6   +1   +8   +3   +8   +7   +5   +9

8. 4   9. 8   10. 6   11. 9   12. 5   13. 3   14. 7
   +8   +2   +9   +9   +6   +5   +4

15. 5   16. 9   17. 7   18. 6   19. 8   20. 3   21. 9
    +7   +4   +7   +7   +8   +7   +8

22. 1   23. 2   24. 3   25. 2   26. 4   27. 5   28. 1
     3   0   3   3   2   3   7
    +6   +4   +3   1   0   6   2
                                +5   +6   +1   +3

29. $(3 + 2) + 7 = \square$

30. $4 + (4 + 1) = \square$

31. $2 + 0 + 1 + 7 = \square$

32. $5 + 2 + 0 + 1 + 5 + 4 = \square$

Use the clues. Find the mystery number.

33. The number is less than
    $9 + 5$. It is greater than
    $4 + 4 + 3$. It is an odd number.

34. The number is less than
    $8 + 9$. It is greater than
    $5 + 0 + 7$. It is not a number
    you say when you count by 4's.
    It is an even number.

Think and Apply

35. In China the ninth day of the
    ninth month is set aside as Kites'
    Day. At one town park there were
    3 dragon kites, 2 fish kites, and 5
    butterfly kites. How many kites
    were there in all?

36. One kite collector owns 2 blue
    kites. He has 2 more red kites
    than blue kites. He also has 3
    more black kites than red kites.
    How many black kites does he
    have? How many kites does he
    have in all?

Use the addends 6, 4, and 3. Write
two different addition sentences.
Solve each. Explain what you did.

SHOW WHAT YOU KNOW

Add 1 to itself. What is the sum? Add 2 to itself. What is the sum? Do the same for the numbers from 3 through 10.

Mental Math: Addition Strategies

There were 6 astronauts on the *Columbia* shuttle that took off in November 1983. There were 5 different astronauts on the *Discovery* that took off one year later. How many astronauts were on the two shuttles?

$6 + 5 = \square$

▶ Knowing sums of doubles can help you add mentally.

$5 + 5 = 10$

$6 + 5$ **is one more.**

So $6 + 5 = 10 + 1$
$6 + 5 = 11$

There were 11 astronauts on the shuttles.

▶ Finding sums of 10 can help you add mentally.

$3 + 6 + 7 = \square$ $\qquad$ $9 + 2 + 8 = \square$

$10 + 6 = 16$ $\qquad$ $9 + 10 = 19$

Check Your Understanding

Tell which double would help you find the sum. Then find the sum.

1. $4 + 5 = \square$ $\quad$ **2.** $5 + 6 = \square$ $\quad$ **3.** $7 + 6 = \square$

Tell which of the addends add up to 10. Then find the sum.

4. $4 + 1 + 9 = \square$ $\quad$ **5.** $3 + 2 + 7 = \square$ $\quad$ **6.** $4 + 8 + 2 = \square$

Share Your Ideas Explain how knowing the double $4 + 4 = 8$ can help you add $4 + 6$.

Find each sum. Write the double that helps you.

7. $4 + 3 = \square$ **8.** $8 + 9 = \square$ **9.** $4 + 5 = \square$ **10.** $9 + 10 = \square$

11. $5 + 6 = \square$ **12.** $6 + 7 = \square$ **13.** $7 + 9 = \square$ **14.** $5 + 7 = \square$

15. $9 + 11 = \square$ **16.** $8 + 10 = \square$ **17.** $4 + 6 = \square$ **18.** $6 + 8 = \square$

Add mentally. Look for sums of 10.

19. $4 + 6 + 5 = \square$

20. $8 + 2 + 6 = \square$

21. $8 + 5 + 5 = \square$

22. $3 + 3 + 7 + 7 = \square$

23. $1 + 5 + 3 + 9 = \square$

24. $4 + 3 + 7 + 6 = \square$

Write an addition fact for each sum. Use three addends.

25. 11   **26.** 14   **27.** 15   **28.** 18

Estimate to compare. Use >, <, or = for ●.

29. $8 + 6$ ● $6 + 7$

30. $12 + 8$ ● $8 + 12$

31. $15 + 20$ ● $30 + 15$

Think and Apply

32. Some planets have moons. Earth has 1 moon. Mars has 1 more moon than Earth. How many moons does Mars have?

33. Jupiter has 16 moons. Mercury and Venus do not have any moons. Write an addition sentence to show how many moons these three planets have in all.

Logical Thinking

34. Copy the triangle shown. Use the numbers 4 through 9 to fill in the circles. Write each number only once. Each row of four numbers must have a sum of 17.

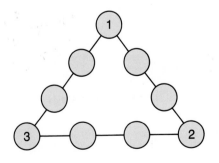

Which double would you use to find these sums? Explain your choice for each.
$6 + 8 = \square$ $9 + 11 = \square$

SHOW WHAT YOU KNOW

5

What number do you add to 7 to get a sum of 10? What number do you add to 6 to get a sum of 11?

Subtraction

A constellation is a group of stars that form a shape. The Lion is a constellation that has 17 stars. The Ram has 9 stars. How many more stars are there in the Lion than in the Ram?

17 − 9 = □

You can subtract to compare.

$$17 - 9 = 8$$

difference

$$\begin{array}{r} 17 \\ -\ 9 \\ \hline 8 \end{array} \leftarrow \text{difference}$$

Use addition to check subtraction.

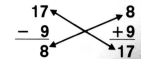

There are 8 more stars in the Lion than in the Ram.

Knowing about zero in subtraction can help you do some problems mentally.

▶ When 0 is subtracted from any number, the difference is that number.

$$\begin{array}{r} 5 \\ -0 \\ \hline 5 \end{array} \qquad 5 - 0 = 5$$

▶ When a number is subtracted from itself, the difference is 0.

$$\begin{array}{r} 9 \\ -9 \\ \hline 0 \end{array} \qquad 9 - 9 = 0$$

Check Your Understanding

Subtract. Check by adding.

1.	**2.**	**3.**	**4.**	**5.**	**6.**	**7.**
2	10	9	8	15	9	18
−2	− 6	−8	−8	− 6	−0	− 9

Share Your Ideas Explain how you know the difference of 32 − 32.

Subtract. Check by adding.

8.	9.	10.	11.	12.	13.	14.
7 − 0	8 − 2	6 − 6	13 − 9	10 − 3	9 − 6	17 − 8

15.	16.	17.	18.	19.	20.	21.
13 − 4	14 − 7	10 − 7	12 − 8	14 − 5	13 − 7	18 − 9

22.	23.	24.	25.	26.	27.	28.
12 − 7	17 − 9	15 − 6	16 − 7	13 − 6	9 − 5	16 − 9

29. $16 - 8 = \square$ **30.** $9 - 9 = \square$ **31.** $15 - 8 = \square$ **32.** $13 - 5 = \square$

33. $12 - 6 = \square$ **34.** $14 - 8 = \square$ **35.** $10 - 4 = \square$ **36.** $11 - 8 = \square$

Use each input number. Follow the rule to find each output number.

Rule: Subtract 4.

	Input	Output
	6	2
37.	8	
38.	9	
39.	11	

Rule: Subtract 2.
Then add 2.

	Input	Output
	5	5
40.	8	
41.	7	
42.	9	

Think and Apply

43. There are 6 stars in the Crab constellation. There is 1 more star in the Little Dipper. How many stars are in both constellations?

44. The star with the longest name is Shurnarkabtishashutu. How many more consonants than vowels are in the name?

45. The sum of two numbers is 14. Their difference is 4. What are the numbers?

46. The sum of two numbers is 18. Their difference is 0. What are the numbers?

JOURNAL WRITING

Write a different question for **43** and **44**. Give your new problems to a friend to solve.

SHOW WHAT YOU KNOW

THINK AND SHARE

What number do you add to 6 to get 10?
What number do you add to 3 to get 10?

Fact Families

The planetarium has 10 sky shows each day.
There are 4 shows in the morning and 6 in
the afternoon.

You can use the numbers 10, 4, and 6 to write
four related facts.

$$
\begin{array}{cccc}
4 & 6 & 10 & 10 \\
+6 & +4 & -\ 4 & -\ 6 \\
\hline
10 & 10 & 6 & 4
\end{array}
$$

▶ Related facts can help you find missing numbers
in a number sentence.

$13 - \square = 9$

One way to solve this subtraction sentence
is to write an addition sentence.
Then find the missing addend.

Think $\square + 9 = 13$
          $4 + 9 = 13$
So $13 - 4 = 9$

Check Your Understanding

Find each missing number.

1. $8 + 2 = \square$
$2 + 8 = \square$
$10 - 2 = \square$
$10 - 8 = \square$

2. $13 - 7 = \square$
$13 - \square = 6$
$6 + \square = 13$
$\square + 7 = 13$

3. $15 - \square = 8$
$\square - 7 = 8$
$7 + \square = 15$
$8 + \square = 15$

4. $9 + \square = 12$
$\square - 3 = 9$
$12 - 9 = \square$
$3 + \square = 12$

5. $\square + 8 = 13$
6. $8 - \square = 5$
7. $9 + \square = 18$
8. $\square - 4 = 8$

Share Your Ideas Explain how to use a related
addition fact to subtract $16 - 9$.

8

Find each missing number.

9. $7 + \square = 10$
$3 + 7 = \square$
$\square - 3 = 7$
$10 - \square = 3$

10. $9 + \square = 11$
$2 + \square = 11$
$11 - \square = 9$
$\square - 9 = 2$

11. $\square + 6 = 11$

12. $14 - \square = 6$

13. $\square - 5 = 7$

14. $\square - 6 = 9$

15. $14 - \square = 5$

16. $\square - 6 = 7$

17. $\square + 4 = 12 - 3$

18. $12 - \square = 11 - 7$

Write the related facts for each.

19. 1, 7, 8

20. 3, 8, 11

21. 4, 9, 13

22. 0, 5, 5

23. 7, 7, 14

24. 6, 9, 15

Think and Apply

Write an addition or subtraction question for each story. Then answer the question.

25. There are 9 children and 4 adults using telescopes in the planetarium.

26. Each week at the planetarium there are 14 shows about the planets and 9 shows about the stars.

27. Each visitor to the planetarium is given a hand telescope. When the telescope is closed, it is 7 inches long. When the telescope is open, it is 12 inches long.

JOURNAL WRITING

Put the same number into each $\square$.
Explain how you found the number.
$6 + \square = 8 + \square - \square$

Mixed Review

1. $\begin{array}{r} 6 \\ +7 \\ \hline \end{array}$

2. $\begin{array}{r} 16 \\ -8 \\ \hline \end{array}$

3. $\begin{array}{r} 9 \\ +8 \\ \hline \end{array}$

4. $\begin{array}{r} 14 \\ -8 \\ \hline \end{array}$

5. $\begin{array}{r} 6 \\ +9 \\ \hline \end{array}$

6. $\begin{array}{r} 10 \\ -5 \\ \hline \end{array}$

7. $\begin{array}{r} 7 \\ +7 \\ \hline \end{array}$

8. $\begin{array}{r} 17 \\ -9 \\ \hline \end{array}$

9. $\begin{array}{r} 5 \\ +3 \\ \hline \end{array}$

10. $\begin{array}{r} 13 \\ -7 \\ \hline \end{array}$

11. $\begin{array}{r} 8 \\ +9 \\ \hline \end{array}$

12. $\begin{array}{r} 18 \\ -9 \\ \hline \end{array}$

13. $3 + 7$

14. $10 - 4$

15. $6 + 6$

16. $4 + 9$

17. $8 - 8$

18. $1 + 9$

19. $6 + 0$

20. $15 - 6$

SHOW WHAT YOU KNOW

CHECKPOINT

Add. pages 2–3

| 1. | 5 +4 | 2. | 4 +5 | 3. | 7 +0 | 4. | 5 3 +2 | 5. | 4 5 +3 | 6. | 7 5 +2 | 7. | 7 2 +0 |

8. $6 + 0 + 9 = \square$　　**9.** $8 + 3 + 2 = \square$　　**10.** $9 + 2 + 3 = \square$

Find each sum. Look for doubles and sums of 10. pages 4–5

11. $6 + 7 = \square$　　**12.** $3 + 4 = \square$　　**13.** $8 + 5 + 2 = \square$

Subtract. Check by adding. pages 6–7

| 14. | 6 −6 | 15. | 15 − 7 | 16. | 8 −0 | 17. | 13 − 2 | 18. | 7 −0 | 19. | 12 − 3 | 20. | 9 −9 |

21. $13 - 7 = \square$　　**22.** $8 - 8 = \square$　　**23.** $11 - 7 = \square$　　**24.** $9 - 0 = \square$

Find each missing number. pages 8–9

25. $9 + 7 = \square$　　**26.** $12 - 8 = \square$　　**27.** $11 - \square = 4$　　**28.** $\square + 6 = 11$

29. $12 + 7 = \square$　　**30.** $16 - \square = 9$　　**31.** $\square - 8 = 9$　　**32.** $\square + 6 = 15$

Choose the correct word to complete each sentence.

33. In $5 + 3 = 8$, 5 is called an _____.

34. The answer in addition is the _____.

35. The answer in subtraction is the _____.

Words to Know
addend
difference
sum

Solve.

36. In 1959, the United States started its space program with 7 pilot astronauts. Another 9 were added in 1962. How many astronauts were there in all?

37. In 1963, 14 pilot astronauts were added to the space program. In 1965, 6 scientist astronauts were added. How many more pilot astronauts than scientist astronauts were added to the program?

10

INVESTIGATING
PROBLEM SOLVING

THINK
EXPLORE
SOLVE
LOOK BACK

How Many Sessions?

Astronaut Camp has become very popular. The graph shows the number of sessions offered by the camp.

Thinking Critically

How many sessions should the camp offer in Year 5? When should the camp offer 30 sessions? When you explore problems like this, keep a written record of your work so you can share your thinking. You may want to work in a small group.

Analyzing and Making Decisions

1. How many sessions were offered each year?

2. How many more sessions were offered each year than the year before?

3. Do you think the number of sessions will continue to increase? Why or why not?

4. Study the pattern in the graph. How many sessions might the camp offer in year 5?

5. Predict when there might be a need to offer 30 sessions. Explain.

Look Back   Why might the camp not be able to increase the number of sessions every year?

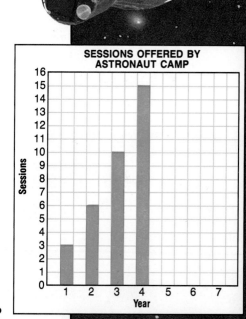

SESSIONS OFFERED BY
ASTRONAUT CAMP

MOON SURFACE TRAINER	
Your Weight on Earth	Approximate Weight on Moon
40	7
50	8
60	10
70	12
80	13

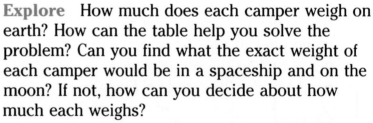

G-MACHINE	
Your Weight on Earth	Approximate Weight in Spaceship
40	120
50	150
60	180
70	210
80	240

Facts from Pictures and Text

Dennis and Angela are campers at Astronaut Camp. On day 3 of the camp, they use two machines that give them very different feelings of being in space. The G-Machine makes them feel as heavy as they would feel in a spaceship leaving earth. The Moon Surface Trainer makes them feel as light as they would feel on the moon. Dennis weighs 71 pounds and Angela weighs 60 pounds. How heavy will these machines make Dennis and Angela feel? The tables will help you. Weights are given in pounds.

Solving the Problem

Use the information in the tables to help you solve the problem.

Think   What is the question?

Explore   How much does each camper weigh on earth? How can the table help you solve the problem? Can you find what the exact weight of each camper would be in a spaceship and on the moon? If not, how can you decide about how much each weighs?

Solve   How heavy will each of these campers feel when using each of the machines?

Look Back   Which chart is easier to use? Explain.

Share Your Ideas

1. **What if** you wanted to throw a ball into the air? Would it be harder to throw it on the moon or inside a spaceship leaving the earth?

Solve. Use a calculator where appropriate.

CHOICES

Apples	Bag of 6	$2.00
Oranges	Bag of 3	$1.00
Canteloupe	1	$1.00
Watermelon	1	$3.00
Lemons	Bag of 4	$1.00

Use the information in the table to help you solve 2–5.

2. Which fruits are sold by the bag?

3. Which fruits are sold by the piece?

CREATE
YOUR OWN

Write a problem using the information about the grocery items.

4. Chris bought a bag of apples, 2 cantaloupes, and 1 watermelon. How many pieces of fruit did she buy?

5. Stu bought lemons, oranges, and watermelon. He has 9 pieces of fruit. How much of each fruit does he have?

6. How many even numbers are between 0 and 20?

7. How many odd numbers are between 0 and 20?

Use the information in the sign to solve 8 and 9.

8. How many days in a week is the planetarium open?

9. Reggie said that if the planetarium is closed, it must be Monday. Do you agree? Explain.

AMERICAN MUSEUM-
HAYDEN PLANETARIUM

PLANETARIUM
Closed Monday
Open Tuesday
Through Sunday
9:00 - 5:00

13

How many different three-digit numbers can you write that have a 2 in the tens place and a 5 in the hundreds place?

Numbers to Thousands

One of the world's longest scheduled non-stop airline flights is 6,901 miles long.

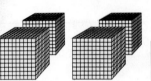

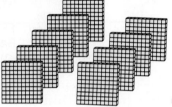

6,901 miles

Hong Kong

6 thousands   9 hundreds   1 one

- standard form   6,901
- read   6 thousand, 901
- word name   six thousand, nine hundred one
- expanded form   6,000 + 900 + 1

THOUSANDS			ONES		
hundreds	tens	ones	hundreds	tens	ones
		6,	9	0	1

↓ 6,000   ↓ 900   ↓ 0   ↓ 1

The comma separates the thousands and the ones. It helps you read the number.

The value of a digit depends on its place in the number.

Look at the place value chart. Why is there a 0 in the tens place?

Check Your Understanding

Read each number. Give the value of the digit 2.

1. 276   **2.** 402   **3.** 1,523   **4.** 2,009   **5.** 8,280

Share Your Ideas   Write 9,000 + 40 + 5 in a place value chart. Did you use any zeros? Explain.

Write the value of the underlined digit.

6. 7<u>6</u>8   7. <u>3</u>05   8. 6,90<u>7</u>   9. <u>9</u>,743   10. 5,<u>1</u>28

11. 8,5<u>4</u>3   12. 5,78<u>9</u>   13. 2,<u>8</u>00   14. <u>3</u>,400   15. 7,0<u>9</u>0

Write each number in standard form.

16. 100 + 30 + 9   17. 800 + 2

18. 4,000 + 60 + 7   19. 6 thousand, 12

20. four hundred twenty-nine   21. three thousand, three

22. fourteen hundred   23. twenty-one hundred thirty-six

Write the numbers in standard form.

24. In nineteen hundred three, Orville Wright flew the first successful airplane. He flew a distance of one hundred twenty feet.

25. Charles Lindbergh made the first solo flight across the Atlantic Ocean. He flew a distance of three thousand, six hundred ten miles.

Think and Apply

26. **Write the number described below in standard form. Then write its word name.**

- The thousands digit is a 7.
- The tens digit is 2 more than the thousands digit.
- The hundreds digit is 6 less than the tens digit.
- The ones digit is 3 more than the hundreds digit.

Common Error

27. Derek said "Write the number two thousand, three hundred six."

Janet wrote 2,306.
Eric wrote 236. ← Incorrect

Explain what Eric did wrong.

What number is 3 hundreds more than two thousand, four hundred seventy-five? Explain.

SHOW WHAT YOU KNOW

THINK AND SHARE

Count by ones to 10. Count by tens to 100. Count by hundreds to 1,000. Use patterns to predict what to count next.

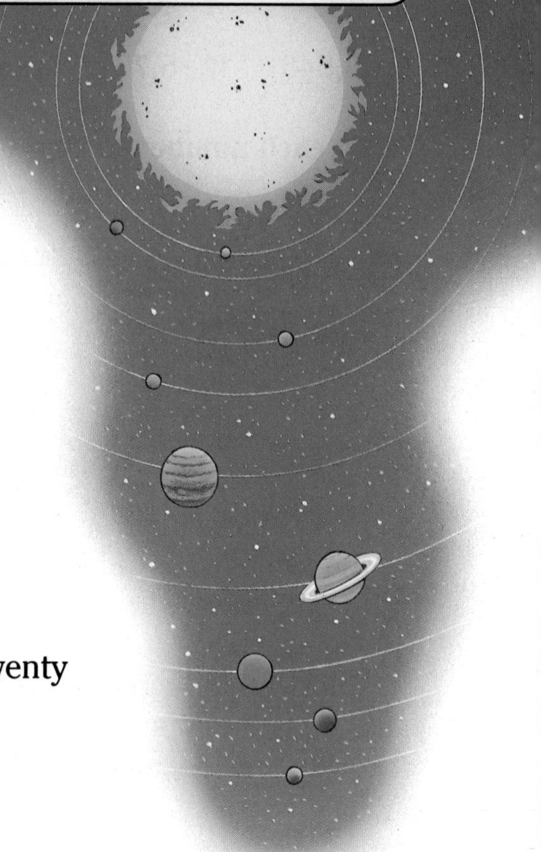

Ten Thousands, Hundred Thousands

The farther a planet is from the sun, the slower it moves. Pluto is the farthest planet from the sun. Pluto moves at a speed of 10,620 miles per hour.

THOUSANDS			ONES		
h	t	o	h	t	o
	1	0,	6	2	0

The place value chart shows the value of each digit. What is the value of the 1?

- standard form   10,620
- read   10 thousand, 620
- word name   ten thousand, six hundred twenty
- expanded form   10,000 + 600 + 20

Another Example

- standard form   107,100
- read   107 thousand, 100
- word name   one hundred seven thousand, one hundred
- expanded form   100,000 + 7,000 + 100

Make a place value chart for 107,100. Why is there a 0 in the ten thousands place?

Check Your Understanding

Read each number. Then write the number in expanded form.

1. 6,520   **2.** 38,901   **3.** 394,035   **4.** 250,879

Share Your Ideas   How many digits in all do you need to write three hundred thousand, two?

Write each number in expanded form.

5. 8,405   **6.** 4,793   **7.** 20,204   **8.** 49,673

9. 16,290   **10.** 904,509   **11.** 320,916   **12.** 480,002

Write each number in standard form.

13. five thousand, two hundred seventy-nine

14. eight hundred thirty thousand, thirty-eight

15. 20,000 + 4,000 + 600 + 30 + 1

16. 70,000 + 300 + 5

17. 10,000 + 4 + 6,000 + 700 + 400,000

18. Use the clues to complete this number.

6 □□,□ 1 □

- The digit in the ten thousands place is half the digit in the hundred thousands place.

- The digit in the hundreds place is three more than the digit in the tens place.

- Another name for the digit in the ones place is 4 + 5.

- The sum of all the digits is 23.

Think and Apply

Use the table to identify the planet.

19. Its speed has a 5 in the ten thousands place.

20. Its speed is twenty-nine thousand, two hundred thirty-two miles per hour.

21. Its speed is about 13,000 miles per hour faster than Mars.

Planet	Speed (miles per hour)
Mercury	107,100
Venus	78,336
Earth	66,636
Mars	53,964
Jupiter	29,232
Saturn	21,564

Tell how to write the number that is 10,000 less than six hundred fifty thousand, thirteen.

SHOW WHAT YOU KNOW

What is the greatest three-digit number?
What is the least three-digit number?

Numbers Through Millions

The world's busiest airport is the
Chicago-O'Hare International Airport.
In one year 56,280,545 passengers
traveled through it.

MILLIONS			THOUSANDS			ONES		
h	t	o	h	t	o	h	t	o
	5	6,	2	8	0,	5	4	5

▶ Commas separate the three periods:
millions, thousands, ones.

Each period has 3 digits: hundreds,
tens, ones.

- standard form   56,280,545
- read   56 million, 280 thousand, 545
- word name   fifty-six million, two hundred eighty thousand, five hundred forty-five
- expanded form   50,000,000 + 6,000,000 + 200,000 + 80,000 + 500 + 40 + 5

Check Your Understanding

Read each number. Give the value of the digit 3.

1. 7,930,712   **2.** 23,419,865   **3.** 347,200,501   **4.** 836,002,482

Share Your Ideas Put commas in the number
8060402. Then read and write its word name.

Write the value of the underlined digit.

5. 1,375,963

6. 4,529,765

7. 35,019,468

8. 86,600,009

9. 100,004,923

10. 904,772,000

Write each number in standard form.

11. 19 million, two hundred thousand

12. 500,000,000 + 40,000,000 + 7,000 + 90

13. six hundred million, seven hundred thousand

14. seventy-two million, ninety-nine thousand, two hundred four

Think and Apply

Write the number in standard form.

15. In one year, eight hundred three thousand planes landed at Chicago-O'Hare International Airport.

16. In one year, forty-four million, eight hundred seventy-three thousand, one hundred thirteen passengers traveled through Los Angeles International Airport.

17. MATH PROCESSOR Use Frames to help you complete the chart. Stretch the frame to the right to show the number of columns. Pull the frame up to show the number of rows. Complete the chart. Use frames to check your answers. What number patterns can you find in the completed chart?

Number of Columns	Number of Rows	Product
1	2	2
2	3	6
3	4	12
4	5	20
5	6	
6		
7		
8		

How many zeros do you need to write the number seven hundred million, seven?

SHOW WHAT YOU KNOW

Investigating Millions

A special stamp was made to honor the Apollo 11 space flight. What if the stamps were printed on sheets of paper with 100 stamps on each sheet? How many sheets of stamps would you need to have a million stamps?

Working together

Materials: Workmat 1 cut into 10 centimeter by 10 centimeter sections.
(Each section of paper stands for 100 stamps.)

A. Decide how many sheets of stamps you need to show 1,000 stamps. Tape these sheets together to make a rectangle, 1 sheet wide and as many sheets long as necessary. Write *1,000* on the rectangle.

B. Decide how many rectangles you need to show 10,000 stamps. Combine your rectangles with those from another group. Then make more rectangles until you have enough to show 10,000 stamps. Tape the rectangles together to form a square.

Sharing Your Results

1. How many sheets of 100 stamps show 1,000 stamps?

2. How many 1,000's show 10,000?

3. How many squares of 10,000 stamps would you need to show 100,000?

4. How many 100,000's would you need to show 1,000,000?

Extending the Activity

Work in pairs to explore one million. Use a calculator when needed.

Imagine a book that shows a million dots. Suppose there are 100 dots on each page of the book.

5. Discuss with your partner a way to find out the number of pages in the book. Then find the number of pages.

6. **What if** there were 200 dots on each page? How many pages would there be in the book?

7. **What if** there were 1,000 dots on each page? How many pages would there be?

All dollar bills weigh 1 gram.

8. How many one-dollar bills do you need to have a million dollars?
   How much would they weigh?

9. How many hundred-dollar bills do you need to have a million dollars?
   How much would they weigh?

Show What You Know

10. Your heart beats about 100,000 times a day. Beginning with January 1 of this year, on what date will your heart make its one-millionth beat?

> What number is 4 thousand more than one hundred thirty-two thousand, six hundred?

Comparing and Ordering

Compare 252,711 and 221,456.

▶ To compare two numbers, start at the left. Compare the digits in each place.

THOUSANDS			ONES		
h	t	o	h	t	o
2	5	2,	7	1	1
2	2	1,	4	5	6

same   5 > 2

So 252,711 > 221,456 and   > means is greater than
221,456 < 252,711   < means is less than

Order these numbers from least to greatest.

713,508   713,564   73,518

▶ To order numbers, compare them two at a time.

   73,518 < 713,564   The whole number with fewer digits is less.

713,508 < 713,564

   73,518 < 713,508 < 713,564   The numbers are in order from least to greatest.

Check Your Understanding

Compare. Use >, <, or = for ⬤.

1. 1,476 ⬤ 1,746   **2.** 949,753 ⬤ 945,300   **3.** 327,465 ⬤ 327,654

Share Your Ideas Describe how to order these numbers from least to greatest.   123,456   123,345   234,654

Compare. Use >, <, or = for ●.

4. 378 ● 392

5. 1,275 ● 1,275

6. 4,832 ● 8,432

7. 813 ● 98

8. 72,516 ● 70,159

9. 3,945 ● 30,945

10. 432,801 ● 399,999

11. 88,888 ● 100,000

List these numbers in order from least to greatest.

12. 946   1,013   928

13. 840   480   4,825

14. 16,592   24,435   21,683

15. 26,384   28,634   26,834

16. 235,012   235,002   234,999

Fill in the least digit to make the sentence true.

17. 4,382 > 4,3☐2

18. 3,662 < 3,☐62

Think and Apply

Choose any six digits on the sign.

19. What is the greatest number you can write?

20. What is the least number you can write?

21. What is the greatest number you can write with all digits less than 6?

22. What is the greatest number you can write with a 7 in the hundred thousands place?

Look back at **20.** How did you decide where to place the digits?

Mixed Review

1. 7
  $+8$

2. 17
  -8

3. 2
  $+8$

4. 13
  -6

5. 2
   4
  $+5$

6. 7
   1
  $+9$

7. 2
   3
  $+6$

8. 8
   5
  $+4$

9. 3
   4
   0
  $+5$

10. 8
   2
   4
  $+2$

11. 4 + 7

12. 16 − 7

13. 6 + 6

14. 12 − 9

15. 15 − 6

16. 8 + 9

17. 14 − 5

18. 3 + 0 + 9

19. 3 + 5 + 6

20. 8 + 2 + 4

SHOW WHAT YOU KNOW

23

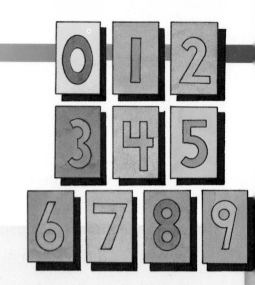

What's the Order?

Play the game What's the Order? You need to make numbers greater than or less than a given number by using digits drawn randomly. One player will make numbers less than 50. The other player will make numbers greater than 50.

Working together

Play the game What's the Order? with a partner.

Materials: 10 index cards with the digits 0 to 9 written on them, a game sheet

A. Make one game sheet. Write the number 50 halfway down a column on the sheet. Turn the digit cards face down.

B. Player 1 draws a card and records the digit under the heading Digits Drawn. The card is returned. Player 1 repeats this step until 3 digits are drawn and recorded.

C. Player 1 makes a two-digit number less than 50 by using 2 of the 3 digits drawn and writes it above the number 50 on the game sheet.

D. Player 2 draws 3 digits but makes a number greater than 50. That number is written below the 50.

E. Player 1 takes a second turn and must make a number less than the number made before.

F. Player 2, who makes numbers greater than 50, must make each number greater than the number made before.

G. The players take turns until one player has made 4 numbers.

H. A player may pass after looking at the numbers drawn. A player may be forced to pass when a number cannot be made that follows the rules.

Game Sheet	
Digits Drawn	**Number**
	___
	___
	___
	50
	___
	___
	___

Sharing Your Ideas

1. What hints would you give a player about playing this game?

Extending Your Thinking

2. Play the Three-Digit Game. Follow these directions.

a. All rules are the same as those for What's the Order? This time, write 500 halfway down your game sheet.

b. Players then follow the rules to make 8 three-digit numbers that are less than or greater than 500. All 3 digits must be used to make a number.

3. Play Place Them Anywhere. Follow these directions.

a. Each player makes a game sheet on a piece of paper as shown on page 24, but without numbers.

b. One player draws a card, calls out the digit, and puts the card back. The first player does this four times. All players record the 4 digits and then write a three-digit number in any space on their game sheets.

c. As players fill in their game sheets, they should remember that when their sheet is filled in each number must be greater than the one before it.

d. The first person to fill in the 8 spaces on the game sheet wins the game.

e. A player may pass and not write a number. This may be necessary if there are only one or two blank spaces left and if you cannot make a number you need.

Show What You Know

4. Which game did you find most challenging? Explain.

Name some numbers between 500 and 600. Are the numbers closer to 500 or 600?

Rounding to the Nearest Ten and Nearest Hundred

Astronauts Neil Armstrong and Edwin Aldrin collected about 20 kilograms of rocks when they landed on the moon.

The number 20 is a rounded number. Rounded numbers tell **about** how many.

Round 23 to the nearest ten.

23 is between 20 and 30.

23 is closer to 20.

23 rounded to the nearest ten is 20.

What is 26 rounded to the nearest 10?

Round 750 to the nearest hundred.

750 is halfway between 700 and 800.

When a number is halfway, round it to the greater number.

750 rounded to the nearest hundred is 800.

What is the greatest 3-digit number that will round to 800?

Check Your Understanding

Round each number to the nearest ten. Then round each number to the nearest hundred.

1. 167   **2.** 253   **3.** 406   **4.** 325   **5.** 842   **6.** 591

Share Your Ideas Discuss what is the least and greatest number of kilograms of rocks that Neil Armstrong and Edwin Aldrin could have collected.

Round to the nearest ten.

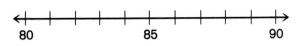

7. 84	**8.** 87	**9.** 81
13. 85	**14.** 89	**15.** 82

10. 281	**11.** 287	**12.** 286
16. 283	**17.** 285	**18.** 289

Round to the nearest hundred.

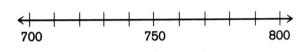

19. 730	**20.** 745	**21.** 795
25. 749	**26.** 753	**27.** 771

22. 225	**23.** 289	**24.** 278
28. 241	**29.** 250	**30.** 219

Round each number to the nearest ten. Then round each number to the nearest hundred.

31. 528	**32.** 654	**33.** 713	**34.** 366	**35.** 407
36. 9,859	**37.** 5,423	**38.** 3,264	**39.** 7,145	**40.** 5,099

Think and Apply

41. Rounded to the nearest ten, the mystery number is 50. What is the greatest whole number the mystery number could be?

42. Rounded to the nearest hundred, the mystery number is 700. What is the least whole number the mystery number could be?

43. What is the greatest two-digit whole number that rounded to the nearest ten, rounds to a two-digit number?

Draw a number line to show the greatest and least three-digit numbers that round to 600.

SHOW WHAT YOU KNOW

Rounding to the Nearest Thousand

The distance around Earth at the equator is 24,902 miles. To the nearest thousand, about how many miles is the distance around Earth?

▶ To round a number, follow these steps.

Step 1 > Find the rounding place.	24,902
Step 2 > Look at the digit to its right.	24,902
If the digit is less than 5, round down.	
If the digit is 5 or more, round up.	9 > 5 round up
Step 3 > Change each digit to the right of the rounding place to 0.	25,000

The distance around Earth is about 25,000 miles.

▶ Round money using the same steps.

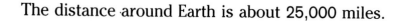

$1,530   to the nearest hundred dollars → $1,500

$1,530   to the nearest thousand dollars → $2,000

Which of these rounded amounts is more useful if you want to know about how much an item costs?

Check Your Understanding

Round each number to the nearest thousand.

1. 6,495   **2.** 5,618   **3.** 32,784   **4.** $7,500   **5.** $19,268   **6.** 14,499

Share Your Ideas   Use the steps above to explain how to round 963 to the nearest thousand.

Round each number to the nearest thousand.

7. 1,625   **8.** 4,397   **9.** 16,837   **10.** 675   **11.** 77,189

12. 8,040   **13.** 29,500   **14.** 3,248   **15.** 25,456   **16.** 134,610

Round each number to the nearest hundred dollars.

17. $2,679   **18.** $3,811   **19.** $403   **20.** $14,333   **21.** $9,999

Round each number to the nearest thousand dollars.

22. $1,567   **23.** $8,289   **24.** $6,435   **25.** $52,729   **26.** $49,501

Use the digits 4, 5, and 8.

27. Write 3 numbers that round to 500.

28. Write 3 numbers that round to 1,000.

Think and Apply

The table shows distances around the equators of five planets.

29. Rounded to the nearest thousand, which planet's distance around the equator is about 24,000 miles?

30. Rounded to the nearest thousand, which planet's distance around the equator is about 12,000 miles less than the Earth's?

31. Rounded to the nearest thousand, which planet's distance around the equator is about 6,000 miles more than Pluto's?

Planet	Distance Around the Equator in Miles
Mercury	9,734
Venus	23,770
Mars	13,188
Pluto	4,286
Earth	24,902

JOURNAL WRITING Explain why rounded numbers are used to tell how far planets are from the sun.

SHOW WHAT YOU KNOW

Math Around The World

ANCIENT EGYPTIAN NUMBERS

The Egyptians represented the numbers 1 through 9 with a form of tally marks.

| 1 | 2 | 3 | 4 | 5 | 6 | 7 | 8 | 9 |

Here is how they represented other numbers.

| 10 | 100 | 1,000 | 10,000 | 100,000 | 1,000,000 |

When the Egyptians wrote large numbers, symbols were written next to each other in a row. For example:

218 could be written like this.   60,060 could be written like this.

WORKING TOGETHER

1. Use Egyptian symbols to write these numbers.

   a. 431   **b.** 1,374   **c.** 62,589   **d.** 204,710

2. Compare your Egyptian numbers with those of a partner. How are they the same or different?

3. Now write Egyptian symbols for any three-digit number. Then challenge a partner to

   a. round the number to the nearest hundred.

   b. write the rounded number, using only one type of Egyptian symbol.

CHAPTER REVIEW/TEST

Add or subtract.

1. 7	2. 9	3. 8	4. 5
+5	−9	+7	−0

5. 12	6. 11	7. 16	8. 12
− 5	− 6	− 7	− 8

9. 9 + 4 + 1 = ☐   **10.** 7 + 6 + 3 = ☐

Write the related facts for each.

11. 6, 8, 14   **12.** 7, 9, 16   **13.** 9, 4, 13

Write the value of the underlined digit. Then write each number in expanded form.

14. 12<u>8</u>,265   **15.** 2,<u>6</u>40,400   **16.** 2<u>7</u>,540,501

Compare. Use >, <, or = for ●.

17. 7,169 ● 7,179   **18.** 36,802 ● 3,682   **19.** 27,891 ● 27,891

Round each number to the underlined place.

20. 1,8<u>2</u>5   **21.** 11,<u>2</u>61   **22.** 4<u>1</u>,489   **23.** 2,<u>3</u>68

Solve.

24. How many jet planes and helicopters are there in all?

25. How many more jet planes than rocket ships are there?

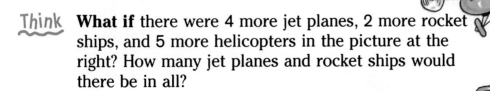

Think   **What if** there were 4 more jet planes, 2 more rocket ships, and 5 more helicopters in the picture at the right? How many jet planes and rocket ships would there be in all?

Braille Numbers

Blind people use the Braille alphabet to read and write. Raised dots stand for letters and numbers. People read by moving their fingers along the dots. They write with a typewriter that punches dots.

Look at these addition and subtraction facts in Braille. Write the correct numbers for each fact. Use the chart to help you. Then complete the chart.

1. • • + • • = 8

2. • – • = • •

3. • + • • = •

4. • – • = 7

5. • • – • = 2

6. • + • = • •

7. • • – • = • •

8. • • + • • = •

Braille Numbers	
0	
1	
2	
3	• •
4	
5	• .
6	
7	
8	
9	

Solve these problems using the chart.

9. • . – • = ☐

10. • + • • = ☐

11. Make your own addition and subtraction problems in Braille. Cut out dots from a piece of felt. Glue the dots onto a piece of paper. Give your problems to a friend to solve.

MAINTAINING SKILLS

Choose the correct answer. Write A, B, C, or D.

1. $7 + 5 = \square$

  A 11   **C** 14

  B 12   **D** not given

2. $7 + 6 + 3 = \square$

  A 16   **C** 17

  B 13   **D** not given

3.
$$\begin{array}{r} 12 \\ -\ 4 \\ \hline \end{array}$$

  A 10   **C** 8

  B 6   **D** not given

4. Which is a related fact to $8 + 7 = 15$?

  A $15 - 7 = 8$ **C** $16 - 7 = 9$

  B $7 + 7 = 14$ **D** not given

5. What is the value of 7 in 7,063?

  A 70   **C** 7,000

  B 700   **D** not given

6. Write eight thousand, fourteen.

  A 8,140   **C** 8,014

  B 814   **D** not given

7. Write $20,000 + 2,000 + 600 + 4$ in standard form.

  A 22,604   **C** 20,264

  B 22,640   **D** not given

8. What is the value of the digit 4 in 4,205,986?

  A hundred thousands   **C** ten millions

  B millions   **D** not given

9. Compare. 23,462   234,602

  A $<$ **C** $=$

  B $>$ **D** not given

10. Round 16,810 to the nearest thousand.

  A 17,000   **C** 16,000

  B 16,800   **D** not given

Use the picture to solve 11–12.

11. How many people are there in all?

  A 6   **C** 8

  B 5   **D** not given

12. How many more girls are there than boys?

  A 2   **C** 1

  B 3   **D** not given

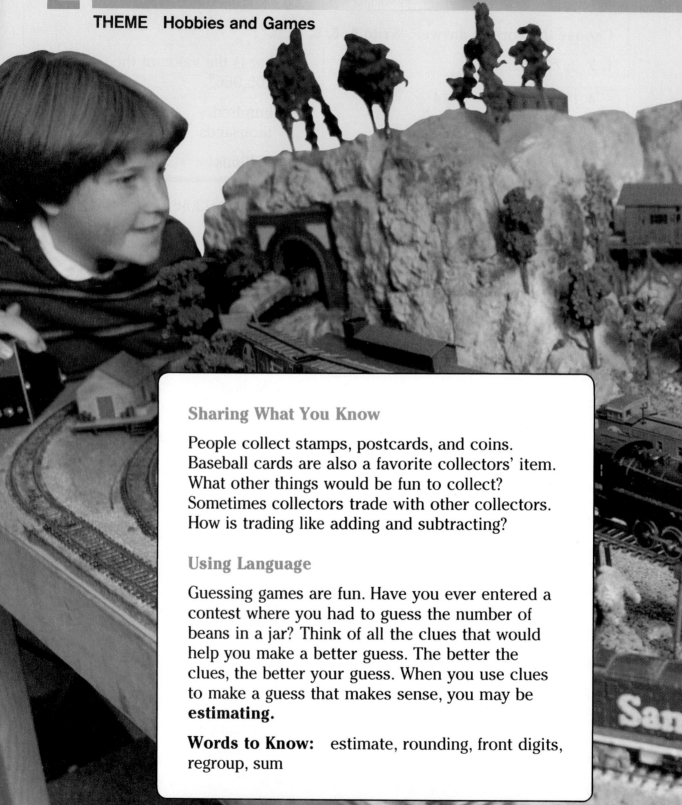

2 Using Addition and Subtraction

THEME Hobbies and Games

Sharing What You Know

People collect stamps, postcards, and coins. Baseball cards are also a favorite collectors' item. What other things would be fun to collect? Sometimes collectors trade with other collectors. How is trading like adding and subtracting?

Using Language

Guessing games are fun. Have you ever entered a contest where you had to guess the number of beans in a jar? Think of all the clues that would help you make a better guess. The better the clues, the better your guess. When you use clues to make a guess that makes sense, you may be **estimating.**

Words to Know: estimate, rounding, front digits, regroup, sum

Be a Problem Solver

Michael is entering a contest for *Puzzlers Magazine*. His number puzzle is "Take a number, add 5, subtract 3, add 7, subtract 6, add 2, subtract 5." Test Michael's puzzle. What number did you get? Try again. Notice anything?

Create a game of your own. Share the game with a partner.

ACTIVITY

Investigating Estimation

When you do not need an exact answer, you can estimate.

▶ An **estimate** tells **about** how many or how much.

Materials: Workmat 2, calculator

A. Make a chart like the one shown below or use Workmat 2.

B. Use the information from the sign. Find two different puzzles whose estimated total cost matches an amount in the chart.

C. Continue finding pairs of puzzles until you have completed the chart.

Puzzle	Price
Clown	$8.25
Lion	$8.50
Rocket	$4.05
Train	$5.75
Whale	$2.19
Xylophone	$1.49

Estimated Total Cost	First Puzzle	Second Puzzle
$8.00		
$9.00		
$10.00		
$11.00		

Sharing Your Results

1. How did you estimate the cost of each pair of puzzles?

2. Find a different pair of puzzles for the $10.00 estimated total cost.

3. Use your calculator. Find the exact total cost for each pair of puzzles in your chart. Compare the exact total cost with the estimated total cost.

Extending the Activity

Work with a partner.
Materials: Workmat 3, calculator

4. Cut out 5 toy advertisements from a newspaper.

5. Estimate how many of each item you could buy for $10.00 and for $25.00. Record your estimates in a chart like the one shown below or on Workmat 3.

6. Use your calculator. Find and record the exact total cost in your chart. Compare the exact total costs with your estimates.

Item	Estimated Number of Items for $10	Exact Cost	Estimated Number of Items for $25	Exact Cost

Show What You Know

7. For which items was the exact total more than the estimate? less than the estimate?

8. What should you do when estimating prices to be sure that you have enough money to buy the items?

9. Explain when you might need to use estimation as you are
- planning a party.
- furnishing a room.
- going on a trip.

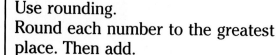
Round each number to its greatest place.
23   49   285   709   650

Estimating Sums

Anita in Miami is playing chess with Jeff in London by FAX machine. So far, Anita has made 27 moves, and Jeff has made 26 moves. About how many moves have been made in all?

You can estimate the sum in two ways.

Use rounding. Round each number to the greatest place. Then add.	Use front-end estimation. Add the tens. Then look at the ones and adjust.
27 rounds to 30 $+26 \longrightarrow +30$ $\quad\; 60$	$\begin{array}{r} 27 \\ +\ 26 \\ \hline 40 + 10 = 50 \end{array}$ $\quad$ 20 + 20 is 40. Since 7 + 6 is about 10, adjust to 40 + 10, or 50.

60 and 50 are both good estimates for the number of moves.

Another Example   Estimate $3.82 + $1.65.

Rounding

$3.82 rounds to $4.00
$+\ 1.65$ rounds to $+\ 2.00$
$\quad\; \$6.00$

Front-end

$3.82
$+\ 1.65$
$\$4.00 + \$1.00 = \$5.00$

$.82 + $.65 is about $1. Adjust to $5.

The sum is between $5.00 and $6.00.

Check Your Understanding

Estimate each sum two ways.

1. 83 + 49 = ☐   **2.** 304 + 59 = ☐   **3.** $5.25 + $.80 = ☐

Share Your Ideas   Look back at **3**. Describe how you estimated using front-end estimation.

Estimate each sum two ways.

4. 56
   +56

5. 94
   +23

6. 42
   + 9

7. 316
   +410

8. 538
   +600

Estimate each sum.

9. 285
   +195

10. 162
    + 67

11. 407
    +594

12. $5.20
    + 9.70

13. $9.40
    + .45

14. 84
    38
    +61

15. 724
    311
    +888

16. 34
    41
    +86

17. $1.01
    .13
    + .90

18. $4.44
    5.55
    + 6.66

19. 66 + 97 = ☐

20. 46 + 35 = ☐

21. 58 + 22 = ☐

22. 129 + 348 = ☐

23. 463 + 250 = ☐

24. $483 + $92 = ☐

25. Use your calculator. Find each exact sum in **4** through **8**. Then decide which of the two estimated sums is closer to the exact sum.

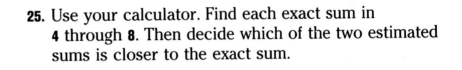

Think and Apply

26. Anita and Jeff played chess for 74 minutes before the break and 68 minutes after the break. About how many minutes did they play?

27. The longest chess game on record took $24\frac{1}{2}$ hours. One player made 97 moves and the other player made 96 moves. About how many moves were made in all?

28. Make up an addition example in which the rounded estimate and the front-end estimate are the same.

Which method of estimating is easier, rounding or using front-end estimation? Explain why.

Is 29 + 75 greater than or less than 100?

Adding Two-Digit Numbers

Mr. O'Day's class had a contest naming cities.
Team A named 36 cities, and Team B named
29 cities. How many cities did they name in all?

36 + 29 = □

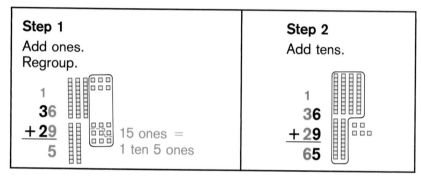

Step 1	Step 2	Check by adding up.
Add ones. Regroup.	Add tens.	
1 36 +29 5 15 ones = 1 ten 5 ones	1 36 +29 65	1 36 +29 65

The teams named 65 cities.

Another Example   69 + 54 = □

Add ones. Regroup.

1
69
+54   13 ones =
3   1 ten 3 ones

Add tens. Regroup.

1
69
+54   12 tens =
123   1 hundred 2 tens

Check by estimating.

69 rounds to → 70
+54 rounds to → +50
                120

Does your answer make sense?

Check Your Understanding

Add. Check by adding up or estimating.

1. 59
   +12

2. 48
   +44

3. 23
   +57

4. 42
   +73

5. 39
   +45

6. 61
   +47

Share Your Ideas   How can you tell by looking at
an exercise that you will have to regroup both ones
and tens?

Add. Check by adding up or estimating.

7.	8.	9.	10.	11.	12.
51 + 9	8 +34	19 +69	95 +13	72 +58	64 +87

13.	14.	15.	16.	17.	18.
23 +19	91 +22	86 +58	37 +47	45 +89	89 +58

19.	20.	21.	22.	23.	24.
46 +25	89 +23	67 +96	42 +99	97 +68	75 +88

Follow the rule to find each output.

Rule: Add 19.

	Input	Output
25.	13	
26.	76	
27.	87	

Rule: Add 36.

	Input	Output
28.	30	
29.	65	
30.	79	

Rule: Add 27

	Input	Output
31.	42	
32.	62	
33.	94	

Find the missing digit.

34.	35.	36.	37.	38.
12 +1☐ 27	☐5 +67 102	4☐ +28 76	☐☐ +78 ☐39	64 +☐☐ ☐23

Think and Apply

39. Susan named 17 cities in North America and 13 cities in South America. How many cities did she name in all?

40. Eric named a total of 41 cities. Todd named 26 cities in the United States and 14 cities in Europe. Who named more cities? How many more?

Common Error

41. Caution! What is wrong with this addition? How can estimation help you find the error? Find the correct sum.

27
+39
56 ← incorrect

Describe how you found the missing digit in **36**.

SHOW WHAT YOU KNOW

Mental Math: Column Addition

Bob and Tami built a house of cards. They used 36 cards for the first floor, 22 cards for the second floor, and 3 cards for a chimney. How many cards did they use in all?

36 + 22 + 3 = ☐

Step 1	Step 2
Add ones. Regroup.	Add tens.
$\begin{array}{r} 1 \\ 36 \\ 22 \\ +\ 3 \\ \hline 1 \end{array}$	$\begin{array}{r} 1 \\ 36 \\ 22 \\ +\ 3 \\ \hline 61 \end{array}$

Check by adding up.

$\begin{array}{r} 1 \\ 36 \\ 22 \\ +\ 3 \\ \hline 61 \end{array}$

They used a total of 61 cards.

You can use mental math to find the same sum.

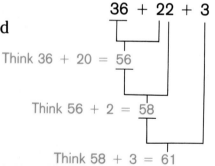

36 + 22 + 3

Think 36 + 20 = 56

Think 56 + 2 = 58

Think 58 + 3 = 61

Check Your Understanding

Add. Use mental math or paper and pencil.

1. 15 + 20 + 3 = ☐

2. 28 + 29 + 41 = ☐

3. 42 + 33 + 4 + 10 = ☐

4. 3 + 17 + 17 + 23 = ☐

Share Your Ideas Explain how to use mental math to find the sum in **3**.

Add. Use mental math or paper and pencil.

CHOICES

5.	6.	7.	8.	9.	10.
13	39	72	81	44	48
55	7	22	26	10	28
+31	+95	+ 2	+38	+14	+ 7

11.	12.	13.	14.	15.	16.
81	93	77	32	65	94
40	21	53	63	4	12
65	85	2	3	18	21
+34	+74	+38	13	2	45
			+25	+35	+13

17. $25 + 40 + 7 = \square$

18. $80 + 52 + 6 = \square$

19. $39 + 61 + 10 + 8 = \square$

20. $75 + 5 + 65 + 15 = \square$

21. This is a magic square. The sum must be the same in each row, each column, and each diagonal. Copy and complete the square.

14		
13	15	
18		

Think and Apply

22. How many cards were used to build the following castle?
First floor: 64 cards
Second floor: 56 cards
Third floor: 28 cards
Fourth floor: 20 cards

23. Eighty-six cards were used to build each of the four buildings in the fortress. Estimate how many cards were used to build the fortress. Then find the exact sum.

Look back at **5** through **10**. Which exercises were easier to solve using mental math than paper and pencil?

SHOW WHAT YOU KNOW

Adding Three-Digit Numbers

The Girl Scouts are playing a compass game. At the cabin, Pat found this card. How many meters is it to the next card?

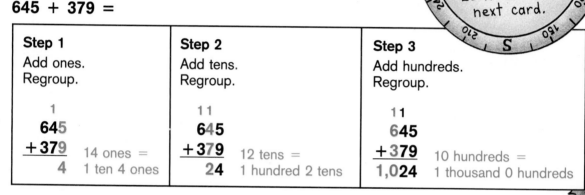

Leave the cabin.
Face east.
Walk 645 meters.
Turn north.
Walk 379 meters.
Look for the next card.

645 + 379 =

Step 1 Add ones. Regroup.	Step 2 Add tens. Regroup.	Step 3 Add hundreds. Regroup.
$\begin{array}{r} 1 \\ 645 \\ +379 \\ \hline 4 \end{array}$ 14 ones = 1 ten 4 ones	$\begin{array}{r} 11 \\ 645 \\ +379 \\ \hline 24 \end{array}$ 12 tens = 1 hundred 2 tens	$\begin{array}{r} 11 \\ 645 \\ +379 \\ \hline 1,024 \end{array}$ 10 hundreds = 1 thousand 0 hundreds

It is 1,024 meters to the next card.

Another Example $8.17 + $9.53 = \square$

Align decimal points.	Add as with whole numbers.	Place the decimal point and the dollar sign.
$\begin{array}{r} \$8.17 \\ +\ 9.53 \end{array}$	$\begin{array}{r} 1 \\ \$8.17 \\ +\ 9.53 \\ \hline 17\ 70 \end{array}$	$\begin{array}{r} 1 \\ \$8.17 \\ +\ 9.53 \\ \hline \$17.70 \end{array}$

Check Your Understanding

Add. Check by estimating or adding up.

1. $\begin{array}{r} 329 \\ +\ 47 \end{array}$
2. $\begin{array}{r} 614 \\ +288 \end{array}$
3. $\begin{array}{r} 506 \\ +547 \end{array}$
4. $\begin{array}{r} \$7.83 \\ +\ 6.60 \end{array}$
5. $\begin{array}{r} \$9.42 \\ +\ 9.78 \end{array}$

Share Your Ideas   Use 2, 3, 4, 5, 6, and 7. Put one number in each box, so that when you add, you must regroup ones and tens.

$\begin{array}{r} \square\square\square \\ +\square\square\square \end{array}$

Add. Check by estimating or adding up.

6. $\begin{array}{r} 106 \\ +\ \ 9 \\ \hline \end{array}$ 7. $\begin{array}{r} 542 \\ +349 \\ \hline \end{array}$ 8. $\begin{array}{r} 259 \\ +278 \\ \hline \end{array}$ 9. $\begin{array}{r} 635 \\ +\ 86 \\ \hline \end{array}$ 10. $\begin{array}{r} \$9.76 \\ +\ .74 \\ \hline \end{array}$

11. $\begin{array}{r} 867 \\ +\ 60 \\ \hline \end{array}$ 12. $\begin{array}{r} 439 \\ +196 \\ \hline \end{array}$ 13. $\begin{array}{r} 372 \\ +728 \\ \hline \end{array}$ 14. $\begin{array}{r} \$7.68 \\ +\ 4.98 \\ \hline \end{array}$ 15. $\begin{array}{r} \$6.88 \\ +\ 3.43 \\ \hline \end{array}$

16. $\begin{array}{r} 238 \\ +475 \\ \hline \end{array}$ 17. $\begin{array}{r} 492 \\ +364 \\ \hline \end{array}$ 18. $\begin{array}{r} 538 \\ +763 \\ \hline \end{array}$ 19. $\begin{array}{r} 977 \\ +346 \\ \hline \end{array}$ 20. $\begin{array}{r} 473 \\ +289 \\ \hline \end{array}$

21. $\begin{array}{r} \$5.91 \\ .19 \\ +\ .45 \\ \hline \end{array}$ 22. $\begin{array}{r} 686 \\ 36 \\ +\ 6 \\ \hline \end{array}$ 23. $\begin{array}{r} 943 \\ 254 \\ +362 \\ \hline \end{array}$ 24. $\begin{array}{r} \$7.25 \\ 4.97 \\ +8.86 \\ \hline \end{array}$ 25. $\begin{array}{r} \$5.94 \\ 6.05 \\ +7.16 \\ \hline \end{array}$

26. $123 + 976 = \square$ 27. $805 + 99 = \square$ 28. $666 + 334 = \square$

29. $\$7.57 + \$8.85 = \square$ 30. $\$5.96 + \$.04 = \square$ 31. $\$4.74 + \$.99 = \square$

Think and Apply

Find the total number of meters.

32. Walk 462 meters west.
    Turn south.
    Walk 559 meters.

33. Walk 196 meters south.
    Turn east.
    Walk 56 meters.
    Turn north.
    Walk 48 meters.

Logical Thinking

Leave the tent.
Walk 250 meters north.
Turn west and walk 160 meters.
Turn south and walk 150 meters.
Turn east and walk 160 meters.

34. Are you north, south, east, or west of the tent? How many meters?

Work with a partner. Make and exchange compass cards. Check each other's answers.

SHOW WHAT YOU KNOW

45

Round each number to the nearest thousand.
6,249   7,500   9,499   15,140   64,987

Adding Greater Numbers

Robert Trucot made the largest crossword puzzle on record. It had 12,489 *across* clues and 13,125 *down* clues! What is the total number of clues?

12,489 + 13,125 = ☐

You can add with paper and pencil.

Step 1	Step 2	Step 3	Step 4
Add ones. Regroup.	Add tens. Regroup.	Add hundreds. Regroup.	Add thousands and ten thousands.
1 **12,489** **+13,125** 4	11 **12,489** **+13,125** 14	11 **12,489** **+13,125** 614	11 **12,489** **+13,125** 25,614

You can also add with a calculator.
- Estimate first.   12,489 + 13,125 → 10,000 + 10,000 = 20,000
- Enter the numbers and operations.

- Read the display.   `25614.`

There are a total of 25,614 clues.

Check Your Understanding

Estimate. Then add. Use paper and pencil or a calculator.

1. 5,230
   + 970

2. $41.67
   + 58.35

3. 8,295
   +3,416

4. 16,507 + 76,097 = ☐   **5.** $217.48 + $64.93 = ☐

Share Your Ideas Describe the steps you followed in **3.**

Estimate. Then add. Use pencil and paper or a calculator.

6. 4,012
+ 6,846

7. 3,576
+ 3,137

8. $798.30
+   1.95

9. 6,268
+ 8,054

10. 57,519
+ 36,297

11. $238.74
+ 788.10

12. 96,784
10,673
+ 8,400

13. 28,835
43,926
+ 25,013

14. $149.62
69.73
+   99.57

15. $4.19 + $68.62 = ☐   **16.** 18,327 + 5,674 = ☐

17. $179.53 + $4.56 = ☐   **18.** 5,888 + 39,568 = ☐

Compare. Use >, <, or = for ⬭.

19. 2,384 + 926 ⬭ 4,310

20. 1,296 + 2,322 ⬭ 2,322 + 1,297

21. 1,468 + 2,890 ⬭ 2,199 + 2,039

22. 35,267 + 47,908 ⬭ 41,293 + 41,882

Think and Apply

Use each number from the box once to complete this story.

240	5,224
3,044	2,180

23. The large crossword puzzle in a magazine has more across clues than down clues. There are _____ (a) across clues and _____ (b) down clues. Altogether there are _____ (c) clues. On the average, it takes _____ (d) minutes to complete the puzzle.

Explain how you decided where to place the numbers in **23**.

1. 10 − 6

2. 6 + 9

3. 18 − 0

4. 14 − 7

5. 19 − 19

6. 6 + 7

7. 9 + ☐ = 10

8. 7 + ☐ = 16

9. ☐ + 4 = 13

10. ☐ − 2 = 9

11. 10 − ☐ = 5

12. ☐ − 7 = 7

13. ☐ − 10 = 8

Compare.
Use >, <, or = for ⬭.

14. 72 ⬭ 27

15. 41 ⬭ 413

16. 3,090 ⬭ 3,009

17. 2,080 ⬭ 2,008

18. 5,083 ⬭ 8,534

SHOW WHAT YOU KNOW

CHECKPOINT

Estimate each sum two ways. pages 36–39

1.	2.	3.	4.	5.
85 +14	506 +685	842 +728	$2.02 .25 + .80	57 19 + 6

Add. Check by adding up or estimating. pages 40–47

6.	7.	8.	9.	10.
55 +78	68 +99	46 +19	246 +374	595 +747

11.	12.	13.	14.	15.
246 +337	839 +187	$7.54 + 3.68	4,236 + 249	$83.57 + 12.64

16.	17.	18.	19.	20.
46 24 +39	38 75 +64	346 285 +394	$6.34 5.96 + 7.77	7,694 8,764 +9,300

21. 35 + 30 + 8 = ☐   22. 71 + 60 + 36 = ☐ 23. 234 + 865 = ☐

24. 383 + 224 + 99 = ☐ 25. 7,418 + 4,765 = ☐ 26. 5,999 + 48,659 = ☐

Choose the correct word to complete each sentence.

27. An _____ tells about how many or how much.

28. When you add two or more numbers, you find the _____.

29. You can estimate a sum by using _____ or_____.

Words to Know
estimate   front digits   rounding   sum

Solve.

30. During the basketball tournament, Rhonda scored 27 points, Pam scored 11 points, Su Li scored 36 points, Cara scored 18 points, and Peggy scored 7 points. What was the total of all their scores?

31. The fourth-grade class sold checkers and chess sets to sponsor their class trip. The girls earned $489.35. The boys earned $475.80. What were the total earnings for the class?

INVESTIGATING
PROBLEM SOLVING

THINK
EXPLORE
SOLVE
LOOK BACK

What Fits the Collection?

Sarah has $15 to spend on model cars. She collects only cars that were built in the United States before 1960.

Thinking Critically

Which cars might she buy? When you do problem solving lessons like this, work in a small group. Keep a written record of your work so you can share your thinking.

CATALOG FOR MODEL CARS				
Model	**Year**	**Country**	**Manufacturer**	**Cost**
Chevrolet	1957	United States	Make-Right	$5.25
Corvette	1963	United States	Build-It	6.25
Rolls Royce	1929	England	Designs	8.50
Thunderbird	1958	United States	Make-Right	4.75
Citroën	1965	France	Designs	2.50
Model-T Ford	1927	United States	Designs	4.75
Mercedes	1955	West Germany	Build-It	4.50
Buick	1956	United States	Build-It	3.75

Analyzing and Making Decisions

1. What information does the catalog contain?

2. What information is important to Sarah?

3. Which models will fit Sarah's collection?

4. Which models can she buy for $15? Show different groups of models that she might buy. Find the total cost of each group to test your groupings.

Look Back   What if she collected cars made only in the United States and England? How would that change what she could buy with $15?

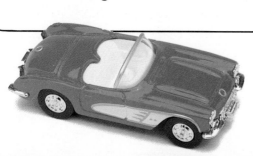

49

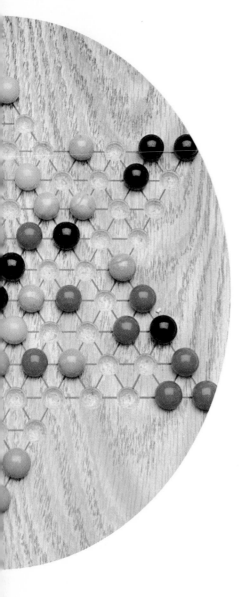

What's Extra?

Tom, Sally, and Carl collect marbles. Tom has 6 big marbles. That is 8 less than Sally has. Tom has 2 more marbles than Joe. Carl has the same number of marbles as Sally. How many marbles does Carl have?

Sometimes there is more information than you need to solve a problem. You must decide which information is important.

Solving the Problem

Think What are you asked to find out?

Explore Explain whether you need to know:
- **a.** How many marbles Sally has?
- **b.** How many marbles Tom has?
- **c.** How many marbles Carl has?

Who has the same number of marbles as Carl? How can you find out how many marbles this person has?

Solve How many marbles does Carl have?

Look Back Read the problem again. Put in the answer. Does your answer make sense?

Share Your Ideas

1. Rewrite this problem so there is no extra information.

2. How can you tell if you are given too much information?

CHOICES

Solve. Use a calculator where appropriate.

3. Rosa is playing a board game. She moves 5 spaces and scores 7 points. She then moves 7 spaces and scores 3 points. How many points did she score altogether?

4. Julian collects tropical fish. He keeps them in a 20 gallon tank. He has 7 guppies, 6 neons, and 3 catfish. How many fish does he have in all?

5. Ned's music book contains 15 songs. He knows 5 of the songs. Ned must practice each song he knows once. How many songs must he practice?

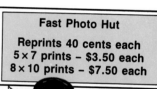

Fast Photo Hut

Reprints 40 cents each
5 × 7 prints – $3.50 each
8 × 10 prints – $7.50 each

6. Anita spent $44 for 10 rolls of slide film. She also spent $32 for 8 rolls of color print film. How many rolls of film did she buy?

Mixed Strategy Review

7. Ms. Parker goes to the Fast Photo Hut to order 2 reprints and one 5 x 7 picture. How much will her order cost?

8. Robin ordered one 8 x 10 print. Nora ordered two 5 x 7 prints and one reprint. Whose order cost more? Explain?

9. Tom ordered four reprints, six 5 x 7 prints, and four 8 x 10 prints. How many pictures in all did he order?

CREATE YOUR OWN

Write a problem with too much information. Have a partner solve it and tell what information is not needed.

THINK AND SHARE

What if you go to the store with $5.00 and buy something for $1.89? How can you find about how much change you will receive?

Estimating Differences

"*Ukulele* means 'jumping fleas,'" said Jake. He and Helen were reading about word origins in Arthur Steckler's books. Jake read 188 word histories. Helen read 97 word histories. About how many more did Jake read than Helen?

▶ You can estimate the difference by rounding.

Round each number to its greatest place. Then subtract.

$$188 \xrightarrow{\text{rounds to}} 200$$
$$-\ 97 \xrightarrow{\hspace{1cm}} -100$$
$$100$$

Jake read about 100 more word histories than Helen.

More Examples

a.
$$\$6.50 \xrightarrow{\text{rounds to}} \$7.00$$
$$-\ 4.39 \xrightarrow{\hspace{1cm}} -\ 4.00$$
$$\$3.00$$

b.
$$288 \xrightarrow{\text{rounds to}} 300$$
$$-\ 64 \xrightarrow{\hspace{1cm}} -\ 60$$
$$240$$

Check Your Understanding

Estimate each difference using rounding.

1. 62
  −43

2. 96
  −85

3. 290
  −149

4. $8.08
  − 3.99

5. $7.30
  − .50

Share Your Ideas Estimate 290 − 151 = □, using rounding. Now **look back** at 3. Why are the estimates different?

Estimate each difference, using rounding.

6.	7.	8.	9.	10.
74 − 38	89 − 81	63 − 16	55 − 8	$.92 − .61

11.	12.	13.	14.	15.
250 − 105	405 − 166	617 − 324	851 − 750	$7.63 − 6.82

16.	17.	18.	19.	20.
532 − 444	867 − 96	300 − 75	$679 − 94	$9.81 − 9.50

Estimate.

21. 89 − 7 = □
    a. 300   b. 100   c. 80

22. 404 − 78 = □
    a. 420   b. 320   c. 220

23. 165 + 85 = □
    a. 290   b. 310   c. 110

24. 299 + 214 = □
    a. 500   b. 300   c. 400

Estimate to compare. Use > or < for ⬤.

25. 48 + 24 ⬤ 87 − 36

26. 85 − 28 ⬤ 79 − 39

27. 839 − 147 ⬤ 610 + 251

28. 286 + 89 + 110 ⬤ 970 − 413

Think and Apply

29. Greg has read 25 word histories. Pat has read 38 word histories. About how many more word histories has Pat read?

30. Frank bought a book for $12.85 and a poster for $3.98. About how much change did he get back from a $20 bill?

31. Make up three subtraction examples for each estimate.

    a. 70 − 20 = 50   b. 400 − 100 = 300   c. 600 − 500 = 100

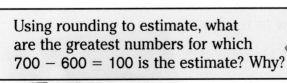

Using rounding to estimate, what are the greatest numbers for which 700 − 600 = 100 is the estimate? Why?

SHOW WHAT YOU KNOW

THINK AND SHARE

Find each missing number.
4 tens 3 ones = ☐ tens 13 ones
8 tens 8 ones = 7 tens ☐ ones

Subtracting Two-Digit Numbers

There are many different domino sets. A Double Eight set has 45 dominoes. A Double Six set has 28 dominoes. How many more dominoes are in a Double Eight set?

Subtract to find how many more.

45 − 28 = ☐

Step 1	Step 2	Step 3
Not enough ones. Regroup 1 ten.	Subtract ones.	Subtract tens.
3 15 4̸5̸ −2 8 4 tens 5 ones = 3 tens 15 ones	3 15 4̸5̸ −2 8 7	3 15 4̸5̸ −2 8 1 7

There are 17 more dominoes in a Double Eight set.

You can use mental math to subtract.

43   **Think**   What do you have   Add 3 to each number.
−17   to add to 17   43 + 3 ⟶   46
                  to reach 20?   17 + 3 ⟶ − 20
                                                       26

Check Your Understanding

Subtract. Use paper and pencil or mental math.

1. 51 − 9	2. 34 − 18	3. 62 −55	4. 98 −69	5. 75 −36	6. 43 − 9

Share Your Ideas   Explain how to use mental math to solve **2**.

Subtract. Use paper and pencil or mental math.

CHOICES

7. 32
  − 23

8. 54
  − 17

9. 27
  − 9

10. 45
  − 38

11. 71
  − 46

12. 86
  − 28

13. 61
  − 12

14. 93
  − 58

15. 48
  − 26

16. 60
  − 33

17. 24
  − 9

18. 52
  − 38

19. 82
  − 34

20. 31
  − 5

21. 53
  − 29

22. 75
  − 56

23. 96
  − 89

24. 78
  − 14

25. 81 − 24 = ☐

26. 74 − 35 = ☐

27. 56 − 38 = ☐

28. 45 − 39 = ☐

29. 92 − 47 = ☐

30. 61 − 13 = ☐

Find each missing digit.

31. 93
  − ☐4
   59

32. 62
  − 3☐
   26

33. ☐☐
  − 16
   68

34. 7☐
  − ☐7
   24

Think and Apply

35. There are 55 dominoes in a Double Nine set. There are 19 fewer dominoes in a Double Seven set. How many dominoes are in a Double Seven set?

36. Maria and Hilda played a total of 35 games of dominoes. Maria won 17 games. Who won more games? How many more?

Visual Thinking

The dots on a domino are called **pips.** These are the dominoes in a Double Three set. Look at the pattern.

37. How many dominoes will be in a Double Four set? Make a drawing to help you.

Look back at **25.** Why did you have to regroup? Explain how you regrouped.

SHOW WHAT YOU KNOW

Subtracting Three-Digit Numbers

Coin	Country	Number
Peso	Mexico	248
Shilling	England	190
Lira	Italy	85
Ruble	Russia	56
Mark	Germany	?

Anne collects coins from different countries. How many more pesos does she have than rubles?

248 − 56 = □

Step 1 Subtract ones.	Step 2 Not enough tens. Regroup 1 hundred.	Step 3 Subtract tens.	Step 4 Subtract hundreds.
248 − 56 ‾‾2	1 14 2̸4̸8 − 56 2 hundreds 4 tens = ‾‾‾2 1 hundred 14 tens	1 14 2̸4̸8 − 56 ‾‾92	1 14 2̸4̸8 − 56 ‾‾192

Anne has 192 more pesos than rubles.

Another Example $3.62 − $1.79.

Subtract money the same way you subtract other numbers.

Step 1	Step 2	Step 3		Check by adding.
5 12 $3.6̸2̸ − 1.79 ‾‾‾3	15 2 6̸ 12 $3.6̸2̸ − 1.79 ‾‾83	15 2 6̸ 12 $3.6̸2̸ − 1.79 $1.83	Place the dollar sign and decimal point.	$1.83 + 1.79 $3.62

Check Your Understanding

Subtract. Check by adding.

1. 461
   − 22

2. 523
   −370

3. 712
   −684

4. $1.54
   − .49

5. $6.95
   − 1.98

Share Your Ideas How can you tell just by looking at an exercise that you must regroup twice?

56

Subtract. Check by adding.

6. $\begin{array}{r} 115 \\ -\ \ 60 \\ \hline \end{array}$

7. $\begin{array}{r} 761 \\ -549 \\ \hline \end{array}$

8. $\begin{array}{r} 274 \\ -234 \\ \hline \end{array}$

9. $\begin{array}{r} \$4.92 \\ -\ 1.88 \\ \hline \end{array}$

10. $\begin{array}{r} \$8.36 \\ -\ 3.69 \\ \hline \end{array}$

11. $\begin{array}{r} 634 \\ -386 \\ \hline \end{array}$

12. $\begin{array}{r} 923 \\ -164 \\ \hline \end{array}$

13. $\begin{array}{r} 382 \\ -\ \ 46 \\ \hline \end{array}$

14. $\begin{array}{r} \$2.47 \\ -\ 1.89 \\ \hline \end{array}$

15. $\begin{array}{r} \$5.51 \\ -\ 2.53 \\ \hline \end{array}$

16. $\begin{array}{r} 589 \\ -436 \\ \hline \end{array}$

17. $\begin{array}{r} 211 \\ -\ \ 12 \\ \hline \end{array}$

18. $\begin{array}{r} 747 \\ -327 \\ \hline \end{array}$

19. $\begin{array}{r} \$6.32 \\ -\ 4.53 \\ \hline \end{array}$

20. $\begin{array}{r} \$9.25 \\ -\ 1.75 \\ \hline \end{array}$

21. $253 - 36 = \square$

22. $486 - 378 = \square$

23. $\$9.17 - \$.08 = \square$

24. $953 - 678 = \square$

25. $111 - 7 = \square$

26. $\$3.24 - \$2.57 = \square$

Follow the rule. Find each missing number.

Rule: Subtract 349.

	Input	Output
27.	468	
28.	511	
29.	833	

Rule: Subtract 72.

	Input	Output
30.		32
31.		194
32.		268

Think and Apply

Use the data from Anne's chart on page 56.

33. How many more pesos than shillings does Anne have?

34. Anne has 93 more pesos than German marks. How many German marks does she have?

DATA
35. Take a survey of your classmates. Ask them to name a favorite hobby or game. Decide how to record your results. Which hobby or game is most popular?

JOURNAL WRITING Write 2 subtraction story problems, using the data in the chart. Switch problems with a friend. Then solve.

SHOW WHAT YOU KNOW

> Find each missing number.
> 260 = 1 hundred 16 tens ☐ ones
> 508 = 4 hundreds ☐ tens 8 ones

Subtracting Across Zeros

Gina and Ramón each threw a flying disc five
times. Gina threw her disc for a total of 304 feet.
Ramón threw his disc for a total of 275 feet.
How much farther did Gina throw her disc?

304 − 275 = ☐

Step 1	Step 2	Step 3	Step 4
Not enough ones. There are no tens. Regroup 1 hundred.	Regroup 1 ten. Subtract ones.	Subtract tens.	Subtract hundreds.
2 10 $\cancel{3}\cancel{0}4$ −2 7 5	9 2 10 14 $\cancel{3}\cancel{0}\cancel{4}$ −2 7 5 9	9 2 10 14 $\cancel{3}\cancel{0}\cancel{4}$ −2 7 5 2 9	9 2 10 14 $\cancel{3}\cancel{0}\cancel{4}$ −2 7 5 2 9

Gina's disc traveled 29 feet farther than Ramón's.

Another Example   Find 700 − 369.

Step 1	Step 2	Step 3	Step 4
6 10 $\cancel{7}\cancel{0}0$ −3 6 9	9 6 10 10 $\cancel{7}\cancel{0}\cancel{0}$ −3 6 9 1	9 6 10 10 $\cancel{7}\cancel{0}\cancel{0}$ −3 6 9 3 1	9 6 10 10 $\cancel{7}\cancel{0}\cancel{0}$ −3 6 9 3 3 1

Check Your Understanding

Subtract. Check by adding.

1. 900 −671	**2.** $5.08 − .60	**3.** 604 −529	**4.** 300 −158

Share Your Ideas Look back at **4.** Explain why
you must regroup hundreds first.

58

Subtract. Check by adding.

5. 108
  − 29

6. 500
  −481

7. $3.10
  − .43

8. 602
  −176

9. 907
  −359

10. $6.04
  − 2.58

11. 730
  −109

12. 400
  −323

13. $8.07
  − 6.48

14. 200
  − 15

15. 306
  −298

16. $9.02
  − 7.65

17. 705
  −339

18. 804
  − 7

19. 560
  −162

Put one digit in each ☐ to make the example true.

20. Use the digits
    0, 1, 3, 5.

    7☐☐
    −☐☐4
    5 4 9

21. Use the digits
    0, 0, 4, 7.

    8☐☐
    −☐☐6
    3 2 4

Think and Apply

Use the information below to choose the correct number sentence. Then solve.

- Juan's flying disc traveled 196 feet farther than Maria's flying disc.
- Maria's flying disc traveled 178 feet.
- Dana's flying disc traveled 300 feet.

22. How much farther did Dana's flying disc travel than Maria's?
    a. 300 − 196 = ☐
    b. 196 + 178 = ☐
    c. 300 + 178 = ☐
    d. 300 − 178 = ☐

23. How many feet did Juan's flying disc travel?
    a. 300 + 196 = ☐
    b. 196 − 178 = ☐
    c. 300 − 196 = ☐
    d. 196 + 178 = ☐

Explain why the subtraction steps are different in these two examples.
500 − 199 = ☐   509 − 199 = ☐

SHOW WHAT YOU KNOW

What if you spent $13.25 for food? How much change should you get from a $20.00 bill?

Subtracting Greater Numbers

Mark has collected 3,250 bottle caps. His goal is to have 5,200 caps by June. How many more caps does Mark have to collect to reach his goal?

5,200 − 3,250 = ☐

Step 1	Step 2	Step 3	Step 4
Subtract ones.	Not enough tens. Regroup. Subtract tens.	Not enough hundreds. Regroup. Subtract hundreds.	Subtract thousands.
5,200 −3,250 —— 0	1 10 5,2̸0̸0 −3,2 5 0 —— 5 0	11 4 1̸10 5̸,2̸0̸0 −3,2 5 0 —— 9 5 0	11 4 1̸10 5̸,2̸0̸0 −3,2 5 0 —— 1,9 5 0

You can also use a calculator for large numbers.

- Estimate first.   5,200 − 3,250 → 5,000 − 3,000 = 2,000

- Enter the numbers and operations.

  5 2 0 0 − 3 2 5 0 =

- Read the display.   1950,

- Check the calculator difference with the estimate.

Mark has to collect 1,950 more bottle caps.

Check Your Understanding

Subtract. Choose paper and pencil or a calculator.

CHOICES

1. 5,263
   −3,139

2. 3,479
   − 656

3. 8,014
   −4,075

4. $296.50
   − 218.52

5. 72,001
   −14,610

Share Your Ideas Why is it important to estimate when you are using a calculator?

Subtract. Choose paper and pencil or a calculator.

CHOICES

6. 5,608
  − 4,195

7. 8,004
  − 6,872

8. $281.93
  − 178.21

9. 95,400
  − 51,793

10. 63,007
  − 57,548

11. 47,411
  − 12,445

12. 76,409
  − 43,742

13. 29,633
  − 12,719

14. 40,091
  − 30,131

15. 82,176
  − 34,279

16. 115,258
  − 64,769

17. 119,751
  − 99,981

Find the missing number.

18. 3,064 − ☐ = 1,371

19. ☐ − 72,256 = 25,744

Think and Apply

The table shows the number of bottle caps in Ken's collection.

Food Caps	14,640
Drink Caps	4,475
Detergent Caps	1,355

20. How many more food caps than drink caps does he have?

21. Ken has 238 salad dressing caps. How many of the food caps are not from salad dressing bottles?

22. One of the largest collections of bottle caps on record is a collection of 44,217 caps. About how many more caps does Ken need to have the same number of caps? Exactly how many more does he need?

Explain how you found the answers in **22**.

1. 7
  + 6

2. 13
  − 5

3. 9
  + 7

4. 15
  − 6

5. 6
  + 7

6. 11
  − 3

7. 8
  + 5

8. 18
  − 9

9. 9
  + 4

10. 12
  − 6

11. 7
  + 2

12. 12
  − 7

13. 8
  + 6

14. 13
  − 8

Compare.
Use >, <, or = for ⬤.

15. 46 ⬤ 64

16. 17 ⬤ 175

17. 760 ⬤ 706

18. 1,008 ⬤ 1,080

Round to the nearest ten.

19. 55

20. 36

21. 49

22. 64

23. 13

24. 18

SHOW WHAT YOU KNOW

61

What's the Score?

The Jackson family was playing Target-Ball at the local fair. The poster shows the prizes that they could win. The chart shows how many tickets a player can win for each score.

In Target-Ball points are scored in groups of 10. A person can play five games and then use the winning tickets to buy a prize.

PRIZES	COST
Small plastic dinosaur	5 tickets
Spider on a string	12 tickets
Small stuffed snake	16 tickets
Cat	27 tickets
Huge bear	43 tickets

Score	Number of Tickets
0–200	0
210–250	1
260–300	3
310–350	5
360–400	7
410–500	9

Use the information in the poster and chart above to solve. You may wish to use a calculator.

CHOICES

A. Mr. Jackson played Target-Ball 5 times. How many tickets might he have won in all?

B. Shelly Jackson played 5 games and won 20 tickets. Find 3 totals that she might have made to win 20 tickets.

C. Mrs. Jackson scored a total of 1,650 points in 5 games. Could she have won the cat if she always scored 210 or more? Explain.

D. Sam Jackson scored 200, 320, 420, 370, and 240 points. What prizes can he win?

Sharing Your Ideas

1. How did you choose the numbers when you tried to solve these problems?

Extending Your Thinking

The Jacksons also played Hit the Target.

2. Sam threw 5 balls and scored 250 points. All the balls hit the board. Find 3 ways he could have made that score.

3. Shelly has thrown 4 balls. They all hit the board. She has scored 200 so far. Have any of the balls hit the same section? Explain.

4. Mr. Jackson said that if Shelly could score between 350 and 450 points, he would mow the yard for her. Find 3 ways that she can score between 350 and 450 points on 5 throws or less.

Show What You Know

5. Look back at 2. How did you try to find the three different ways that Sam scored his points?

6. Look back at 4. **What if** you were Shelly trying to score between 350 and 450 points? Where would you aim first? Explain.

125
100
75
50
25

> Imagine that you have pennies, nickels, dimes, and quarters. Describe some groups of coins that have a value of 36¢.

Using Money

A model ship kit costs 91¢.
Count the money.

$.50 or 50¢ $.25 or 25¢ $.10 or 10¢ $.05 or 5¢ $.01 or 1¢

A book about sailboats costs $15.31.
Count the money.

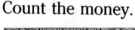

How did you count the money?
Did you start with the bill or coin
of greatest or least value?
Does it make a difference?

Check Your Understanding

Write the value of each group of bills and coins.

1.

2.

Share Your Ideas Describe how you found the
total value of the money in **2**.

Write the value.

3.

4.

5.

6. 4 one-dollar bills, 1 quarter, 2 nickels, 8 pennies

7. 3 ten-dollar bills, 1 half dollar, 1 quarter, 1 penny

8. 2 twenty-dollar bills, 4 quarters, 7 dimes, 2 nickels

Compare. Use >, <, or = for ⬤.

9. $4.85 ⬤ $4.58

10. $.38 ⬤ $.83

11. 2 quarters, 4 dimes ⬤ $1.00

12. $.89 ⬤ 1 half dollar, 3 dimes

13. $10.15 ⬤ 2 five-dollar bills, 2 dimes, 1 nickel

14. 4 dollars, 2 quarters, 1 dime ⬤ 3 dollars, 6 quarters, 2 nickels

Think and Apply

15. Kevin has 2 quarters, 3 dimes, and 4 pennies. Does he have more or less than $.90?

16. What are the fewest number of coins you need to have exactly 47¢? What are the coins?

Logical Thinking

17. Which coins would you have to move from **A** to **B** to have the same amount of money in each bank?

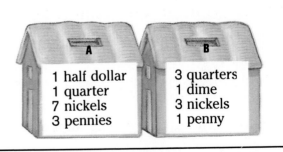

A
1 half dollar
1 quarter
7 nickels
3 pennies

B
3 quarters
1 dime
3 nickels
1 penny

Explain how you found the answer for **16**.

SHOW WHAT YOU KNOW

Investigating Counting Change

Pretend you are a clerk in a game store. A customer buys a racing car and pays with a $10 bill. Find out how much change to give.

Working together

Materials: play money

PRICES	
Stuffed Animal	$12.95
Racing Car	$ 7.29
Jump Rope	$ 2.49
Checkers	$ 4.15

A. There are different ways to count change.

- One way to find the change is to subtract.

    $10.00 − $7.29 = □

- Another way is to use mental math and count up.

    - Start with the cost.
    - Count the change until you reach the amount used to pay for the item.

$7.29 $7.30 $7.40 $7.50 $8.00 $9.00 $10.00

What is the total amount of change?
How does this answer compare to the subtraction answer?

B. Take turns being the clerk and the customer. Buy different games using different amounts of money.

Sharing Your Results

Solve. Use the prices on the sign above.

1. **What if** you bought checkers and paid with a $10 bill? How much change would you receive?

2. **What if** you bought a stuffed animal and paid with a $20 bill? How much change would you receive?

Extending the Activity

Play Buy a Game with a partner.

Materials: index cards, play money

3. List 12 names of board games.
   Price each game under $10.00.
   Write the name of each game and its price
   on a card.
   Shuffle the cards and place them face down.

4. To play:
   - Take turns "buying a game" by picking a game card.
   - Find the change from $10.00.
   - Record the game, cost, and change each time on a piece of paper.
   - After all the game cards have been used, add the numbers in the change column.
   - The player with the higher total is the winner.

5. Play the game again. This time buy two games on each turn. Find the change from $20.00.

Show What You Know

6. Which method did you use most often to find the change in Buy a Game? Is one method easier than the other? Explain.

7. **What if** you were a clerk in a store and your cash register did not automatically display the change? Which method for finding change would you use? Explain.

8. **Look back** at the chart on page **66**. If you got $8.56 change from $20.00, which two items did you buy?

ACHI
AN AFRICAN GAME

WORKING TOGETHER

Work in pairs. Draw a large Achi gameboard. Play four rounds of Achi. Follow the directions below.

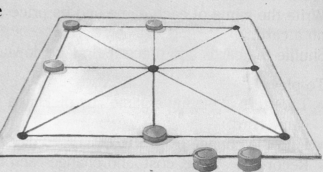

1. Take turns placing one counter at a time on an empty point on the game board.

2. When all eight counters are on the board, take turns moving one of your counters along a line to an empty point. The goal of the game is to get three counters in a row. The first player to do this is the winner. The winner scores 250 points. The other player scores 175 points.

3. After each round, record the scores. After playing the four rounds, answer these questions.

   • What is each person's total score?

   • Who has the most points? the fewest points?

   • What is the difference between the scores?

4. Discuss the game of Achi with your partner.

   • What strategies did you use to get your counters in a row?

   • Is it an advantage to place the first counter on the board? Why or why not?

CHAPTER REVIEW/TEST

Estimate each sum two ways.

1. 32	2. 548	3. 537	4. $55.32	5. 3,328
+49	+544	+ 48	+ 41.20	+4,965

Add. Check by adding up or estimating.

6. 85	7. 705	8. $4.36	9. 1,679	10. 79,298
+67	+499	+ 9.87	+2,478	+47,651

Estimate each difference using rounding.

11. 28	12. 606	13. $3.11	14. 2,410	15. $12.44
−16	−521	− .52	−1,322	− 7.50

Subtract. Check by adding.

16. 66	17. $5.02	18. 417	19. $4,007	20. 80,623
−59	− 2.45	− 28	− 474	−71,196

21. 585 − 224 = ☐   22. 7,380 − 5,187 = ☐   23. 59,277 − 2,355 = ☐

Solve. Tell whether any information is not needed.

24. There are 794 runners from 12 grade schools entered in the city track meet. There are 158 runners from 4 high schools. How many runners are there in all?

25. The rubles in Mario's coin collection are worth $97.63. His pesos are worth $236.90. How much more are his pesos worth than his rubles?

Think Amy sold her ski boots for $88 and her skis for $125. Then she bought a new tennis racket for $79 and tennis shoes for $49. How much money does she have left?

COMPUTER

Polygons

A closed plane figure with three or more sides is a *polygon.*

You can use the **Polygon Marker** in MathProcessor™ to make polygons.

- Click points to make the outline of the polygon.
- Then click back on the first point to close the figure.

MathProcessor™ Tools:

 Geometry Tools

 Number Space

 Writing Space

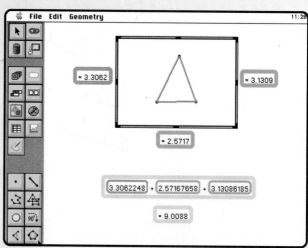

Doing the Computer Investigation

A. The distance around a polygon is the *perimeter.* Use the **Polygon Marker** to make a polygon. Then estimate its perimeter in centimeters. Open a **Writing Space**. Record your estimate and explain how you made it.

INVESTIGATION

B. To find the exact perimeter of your polygon, **link** each line segment to a **Number Space** to measure it. Then find the sum of all the line segments using a new **Number Space**. How close was your estimate to the exact answer?

C. Make a polygon that you think has a perimeter of 12 centimeters. **Link** each line segment to a **Number Space**. Then find the sum of all the line segments. What is the exact perimeter of your polygon? Was it close to 12 centimeters?

Sharing Your Results

1. Work with a partner. Take turns making polygons. Make as many different polygons as you can that have a perimeter of 23 centimeters.

2. Share your polygons with the class.

Extending the Computer Investigation

3. Make as many different polygons as you can that have a perimeter of 18 centimeters. Can you make a 3-sided figure? a 4-sided figure? a 5-sided figure? a 6-sided figure?

4. In the **Writing Space**, discuss your polygons. What happens to the length of the line segments as the number of sides increases?

Palindromes

How is the word *noon* like 12321?
They are both palindromes.

A **palindrome** is a word or number that reads the same forward and backward.

Name four other words that are palindromes.
Name four other numbers that are palindromes.

You can create a palindrome by using addition with a two-digit number.

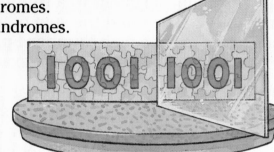

Follow the steps below.

- Start with a number that is not a palindrome.

      39

- Reverse the digits and add.

    + 93

- Is the sum a palindrome? No.

     132

- Reverse the digits of the sum and add.

    +231

- Is the new sum a palindrome?

     363

Reverse the digits and add until the sum is a palindrome.

1. 29   **2.** 36   **3.** 82   **4.** 95   **5.** 87

6. Start with your own two-digit number. Follow the steps to get a palindrome.

7. Make up a starting number that will require several additions to get a palindrome. Exchange starting numbers with a classmate and find the palindromes.

MAINTAINING SKILLS

Choose the correct answer. Write A, B, C, or D.

1. $8 + 9 = \square$

  A 16   **C** 19

  B 17   **D** not given

2. $\begin{array}{r} 15 \\ -\ 8 \\ \hline \end{array}$

  A 7   **C** 8

  B 9   **D** not given

3. Write $200 + 40 + 3$ in standard form.

  A 243   **C** 2,043

  B 234   **D** not given

4. What is the value of the digit 3 in 13,048,926?

  A ten millions   **C** millions

  B hundred thousands   **D** not given

5. Compare.   413,011 ⬛ 413,110

  A $<$ **C** $=$

  B $>$ **D** not given

6. Round 30,746 to the nearest thousand.

  A 30,000   **C** 30,700

  B 31,700   **D** not given

7. Estimate $572 + 215$.

  A 600   **C** 8,000

  B 800   **D** 1,000

8. $65 + 42 + 18 = \square$

  A 124   **C** 115

  B 125   **D** not given

9. $1{,}826 + 4{,}263 = \square$

  A 6,089   **C** 5,089

  B 6,189   **D** not given

10. Estimate $\$7.21 - \$3.68$.

  A $3.00   **C** $.30

  B $11.00   **D** $6.00

11. $615 - 168 = \square$

  A 547   **C** 447

  B 553   **D** not given

Use the picture to solve 12–13.

12. How many stars and rocket ships are there in all?

  A 6   **C** 8

  B 7   **D** not given

13. How many more stars are there than rocket ships?

  A 3   **C** 5

  B 4   **D** not given

Time · Data and Graphs

Sharing What You Know

Time out . . . On time . . . Find the time . . .
People have always needed to know the time. Four
thousand years ago people used a sundial to tell
time. Luckily inventors have made telling time
easier. Discuss some modern inventions that tell
time.

Using Language

What do you think we mean when we say that a
picture is worth a thousand words? A special
picture that shows information is called a **graph.**
Why do you think people use **graphs** to show
information? What kinds of graphs have you seen?
How do you think these graphs got their names?

Words to Know: graph, pictograph, bar graph,
line graph, tally mark, table

Be a Problem Solver

What if a clock shows 3:00? How many times will the hands of the clock cross in 24 hours?

Think about different ways to tell time. Look around your classroom and think about your home. List all the ways you can think of to tell time.

Telling Time

One of the earliest alarm clocks was made by Samuel Watson around 1715. **What if** you could set the alarm for 7:00 A.M.? Would it ring in the morning or at night?

▶ A.M. is used to show the time from midnight to noon.

▶ P.M. is used to show the time between noon and midnight.

It would ring in the morning.

▶ Time is measured in different units.

60 seconds (s) = 1 minute
60 minutes (min) = 1 hour
24 hours (h) = 1 day (d)

- read   eight-thirty or half past eight

- write   8:30

8:30 A.M. is eight-thirty in the morning.

- read   one forty-five or quarter to two

- write   1:45

1:45 P.M. is one forty-five in the afternoon.

Check Your Understanding

Read each time. Write the time, using numbers.

1.

2.

3.

4.

Share Your Ideas   Look back at **3**. How many minutes is it before eleven o'clock? Explain how you found your answer.

Read each time. Write the time, using numbers.

5.

6.

7.

8.

9.

10.

11.

12.

13. half past 2

14. quarter to 4

15. 17 min after 10

16. quarter past 11

Write the time, using A.M. or P.M.

17. The race started at nine o'clock in the morning.

18. Dan finished baseball practice at quarter to five.

19. Sarah ate lunch at twelve fifteen.

20. Cinderella's coach changed into a pumpkin at midnight.

Think and Apply

Write these times in order from earliest to latest.

21. 6:47 P.M.   6:47 A.M.   4:12 P.M.

22. noon   11:01 A.M.   2:03 P.M.

Write seconds, minutes, hours, or days for each.

23. Driving from California to Maine takes about 6 _____.

24. Watching a movie takes about 2 _____.

25. Weighing yourself takes about 10 _____.

26. Eating a meal takes about 20 _____.

> **L**ogical Thinking
>
> **27.** What is the time on a digital clock when the sum of the digits is the greatest?

Name six activities you will do tomorrow. Write the time you plan to do each activity, using A.M. or P.M.

SHOW WHAT YOU KNOW

At what time did you go to sleep last night?
At what time did you wake up this morning?
About how many hours did you sleep?

Elapsed Time

In 1903, Orville Wright flew the first successful
airplane. The flight lasted 12 seconds. Today
an airplane flight from Newark, New Jersey,
to Orlando, Florida can take 2 hours and
30 minutes. If a plane leaves Newark at
10:20 A.M., when is it due to land in Orlando?

Count 10:20 + 2 h to 12:20.
Then count 30 minutes.
The time will be 12:50.

The plane is due to land at 12:50 P.M.

Use the clocks below to estimate the elapsed time.

start   end

8:05 is close to 8:00.
9:20 is close to 9:30.
8:00 to 9:30 is one and
one-half hours.
So, 8:05 to 9:20 is about one
and one-half hours.

Check Your Understanding

Find each time.

1. 10 min after

2. 3 h and 35 min after

3. 1 h and 15 min before

Share Your Ideas A movie starts at 7:35 P.M. and
ends at 9:50 P.M. Explain how you can estimate
how long the movie lasts.

Find each time.

4. 3 h after

5. 30 min after

6. 10 min before

7. 20 min after
6:45 A.M.

8. 25 min before
12:35 P.M.

9. 4 h and 5 min after
7:35 A.M.

Estimate how much time has passed.

10.   start   end

11.   start   end

12. start   4:30 P.M.
     end   11:15 P.M.

13. start   10:10 A.M.
     end   1:32 P.M.

Think and Apply

14. A flight from Boston, Massachusetts, to Cleveland, Ohio, takes 1 hour and 35 minutes. If the plane leaves at 6:15 P.M., when is it due to land?

15. A plane leaves Kansas City, Missouri, at 7:17 P.M. and arrives in Dallas, Texas, at 8:45 P.M. About how long is the flight?

16. Mr. Taylor's flight leaves at 6:20 P.M. It takes him 20 minutes to get to the airport. He was told to check in at the airport at least 30 minutes before takeoff. When should he leave for the airport?

How much time do you spend in school each day?

SHOW WHAT YOU KNOW

ACTIVITY

Investigating Schedules

In 1804, Richard Trevithick built one of the first successful railroads. Today, travelers use schedules to find out when trains leave a city and when they arrive at other cities along the route.

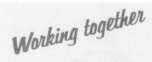

Materials: Workmat 4

A. Copy the train schedule shown below or use Workmat 4.

B. Use the travel facts to complete the train schedule.

TRAVEL FACTS

- Travel time is the same for each train.
- Chicago to Hammond takes 25 min.
- Hammond to Niles takes 2 h 12 min.
- Niles to Kalamazoo takes 51 min.
- Kalamazoo to Battle Creek takes 32 min.

TRAIN SCHEDULE

Train Number	Leaves Chicago	Arrives Hammond	Arrives Niles	Arrives Kalamazoo	Arrives Battle Creek
350	7:30 A.M.				
364	8:35 A.M.				
383	2:35 P.M.				
395	5:50 P.M.				

Sharing Your Results

1. Which train arrives in Battle Creek at 6:35 P.M.?

2. Which train arrives in Kalamazoo closest to noon?

3. How many minutes is the train ride from Hammond to Niles?

Extending the Activity

Work with a partner.
Materials: Workmat 5

4. Copy the train schedule shown below or use Workmat 5. Use the information given to complete the schedule. All the trains take the same amount of time to travel to each city.

TRAIN SCHEDULE

Train Number	Leaves Seattle	Arrives Tacoma	Arrives Olympia	Arrives Centralia	Arrives Portland
11	6:00 A.M.				
26	10:35 A.M.				
797	5:30 P.M.	6:24 P.M.	7:10 P.M.	7:30 P.M.	9:30 P.M.
1010	8:35 P.M.				

5. How many minutes is the ride from Tacoma to Centralia?

6. How many minutes is the ride from Olympia to Portland?

Show What You Know

7. Which train arrives in Portland closest to midnight?

8. Which train did Ms. Perry take and at which station did she get off?

- She left Seattle before 7:00 P.M.

- She got off the train between 11:00 A.M. and 3:00 P.M.

- She rode the train for more than 80 min but less than 2 h.

TREVITHICKS,
PORTABLE STEAM ENGINE.

Catch me who can.

Mechanical Power Subduing
Animal Speed.

Name the days of the week. Name the months of the year.

Using a Calendar

Each year, Silver Burdett & Ginn holds an Invention Convention for students in Grades 1 through 9. Student inventions are judged by inventors, scientists, and teachers. **What if** it was August and the convention was four months away? In which month would the convention be held?

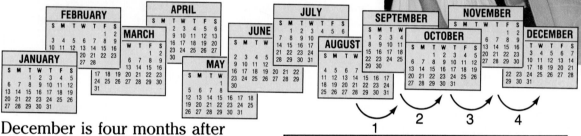

December is four months after August. The convention would be in December.

12 months = 1 year
7 days = 1 week
365 days = 1 year
366 days = leap year

Look at the calendar above. February has 28 days. In leap year it has 29 days.

Which months have 30 days? 31 days?

Check Your Understanding

Use the calendar above to answer these questions.

1. Which month is three months before December?

2. What is the date of the third Monday in June?

Share Your Ideas The first Friday in May is May 3. Without looking at the calendar, how can you tell the date of the second Friday in May? the third Friday?

Give the month that is 5 months after each month.

3. January   **4.** May   **5.** August   **6.** April

7. September   **8.** March   **9.** June   **10.** November

Give the month that is 4 months before each month.

11. July   **12.** May   **13.** October   **14.** March

15. December   **16.** April   **17.** February   **18.** August

What day and date is it? Use the calendar on page 82.

19. 4 days before April 10   **20.** 6 days after February 20.

21. 9 days before March 22   **22.** 8 days after June 12

23. 5 days before July 4   **24.** 3 days after December 30

Think and Apply

25. Jan started working on her invention August 20. She finished 3 weeks and 5 days later. What is the date she finished?

26. Steve finished his invention on March 12. He started working on it 3 months before. In which month did he start working on his invention?

27. Lisa had a meeting on the third Tuesday in April. She typed her report for the meeting 3 days before that. What day and date was that?

28. Jim went on a trip to New Orleans, Louisiana, on September 29. He returned 4 days later. What was the day and date of his return?

29. Tony writes the date April 21, 1991, using this form: 4/21/91. Write today's date in this way. Write your birthdate in this way.

What is the date 7 days after January 14, 1991? 21 days after? one year after?

SHOW WHAT YOU KNOW

> How can you estimate how many telephones are in the homes of all the students in your class?

Understanding Graphs: Pictographs and Bar Graphs

Alexander Graham Bell invented the telephone in 1876. Today most homes in the United States have at least one telephone.

The **pictograph** below shows the number of telephones in homes for each of five cities.

CITY	NUMBER OF TELEPHONES IN HOMES
Vernon	☎
Peabody	☎
Centerville	☎ ☎ ☎ ☎
Mayette	☎ ☎ ☎ ☎ ☎
Cummings	☎ ☎ ☎

Each ☎ stands for 2,000 telephones.

What do you think ☎ stands for?

How many telephones are there in homes in Cummings?

Check Your Understanding

Use the pictograph to answer each question.

1. In which city is there the greatest number of telephones in homes?

2. In which cities are there less than 8,000 home telephones?

3. How many more home telephones are in Centerville than in Vernon?

4. How many pictograph symbols would you need to draw to show 13,000 phones?

Share Your Ideas   Explain two ways to use the pictograph to find the answer to **3**.

The **bar graph** at the right shows the number of special telephones sold by the Telesound Company in one month.

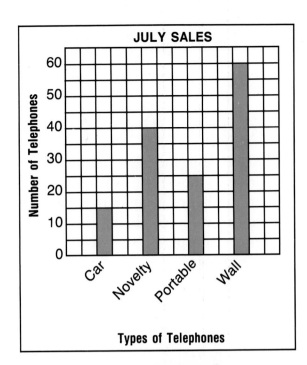

JULY SALES

Number of Telephones

Types of Telephones

5. How many portable phones did the company sell?

6. How many more wall phones than novelty phones did the company sell?

7. What is the total number of phones that were sold in July?

8. The total number of which two types of phones equals the number of novelty phones?

9. Of the total number of novelty phones, 13 looked like tennis rackets and 9 looked like dogs. The others looked like cats. How many phones were sold that looked like cats?

Think and Apply

The table at the right shows the number of phone calls made by the Lee family in one week.

10. Use the facts in the table to make a bar graph.

11. Write two word problems that can be solved using your graph. Give the problems to a classmate to solve.

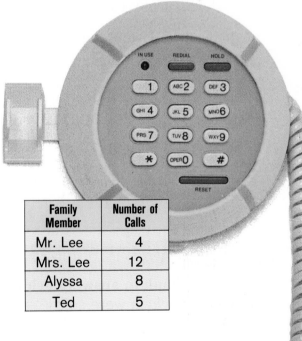

Family Member	Number of Calls
Mr. Lee	4
Mrs. Lee	12
Alyssa	8
Ted	5

JOURNAL WRITING Can you tell how many people live in Vernon by looking at the graph on page 84? Why or why not?

SHOW WHAT YOU KNOW

> How many movies do you see in one month? Do you see them on television? in a movie theater? in a drive-in movie theater?

Understanding Line Graphs

Richard Hollingshead, Jr. invented the drive-in movie. He set up a screen in his driveway and put a projector on top of his car. In 1933, Hollingshead opened the world's first drive-in movie.

A **line graph** shows changes over time. The line graph at the right shows the number of tickets sold by the Center Drive-In Movie Theater in different years from 1935 to 1985.

How many tickets were sold in 1955?

- Find the year 1955 on the graph.

- Look at the point on the graph above 1955.

- Look over to the number of tickets.

70,000 tickets were sold in 1955.

TICKETS SOLD

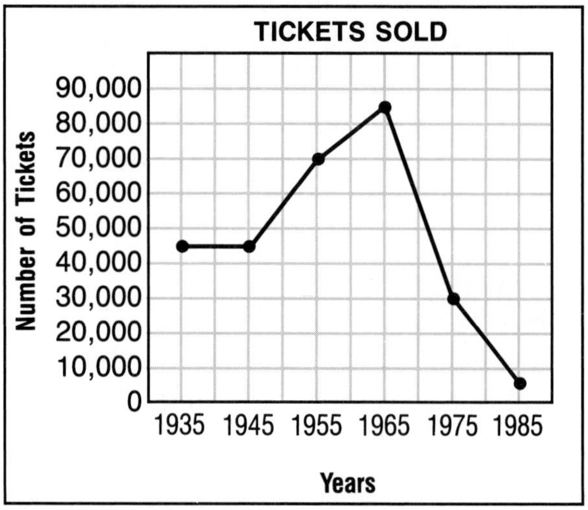

Check Your Understanding

Use the line graph to answer each question.

1. How many tickets were sold in 1945?

2. In what year were the most tickets sold?

3. In what year were the fewest tickets sold?

4. Between 1965 and 1975, did the number of tickets sold increase or decrease?

Share Your Ideas   Do you think that ticket sales will increase or decrease from 1985 to 1995? Explain.

Use the line graph to answer each question.

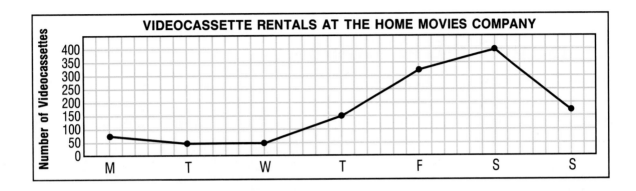

VIDEOCASSETTE RENTALS AT THE HOME MOVIES COMPANY

Number of Videocassettes: 0, 50, 100, 150, 200, 250, 300, 350, 400

Days: M T W T F S S

5. On which day were the most videocassettes rented?

6. On which days were the fewest videocassettes rented?

7. How many videocassettes were rented on Friday?

8. Between which two days was there no increase or decrease in the number of videocassettes rented?

9. How many more videocassettes were rented on Saturday than on Sunday?

Think and Apply

10. What was the total number of videocassettes rented in the week?

11. Between which two days was there the greatest increase in rentals?

12. On which three days did the company rent the most videocassettes? Why do you think this happened?

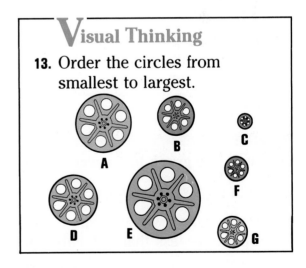

Visual Thinking

13. Order the circles from smallest to largest.

A B C D E F G

If you saw a graph of the number of rentals from last week, would it look like the graph above? Explain.

SHOW WHAT YOU KNOW

Would you make a pictograph or a line graph to show the temperature of your city over a one-week period? Explain.

Constructing Line Graphs

Thermometers measure temperature. The high temperatures in Salem, Oregon, for a one-week period are shown in the table.

Follow the steps below to make a line graph. Part of the finished graph is shown below.

- Draw a horizontal line (→) on grid paper. Write the days of the week under the line. Label the line *Days*.

- Draw a vertical line (↑) on the left. Let each box stand for 5 degrees. Start numbering as shown in the graph. Label the line *Degrees Fahrenheit*.

- Above each day, make a dot to show the number of degrees.

- Connect the points in order, beginning with the dot for Monday. Give the graph a title.

HIGH TEMPERATURES	
Day	Temperature in Degrees Fahrenheit
Monday	30°
Tuesday	35°
Wednesday	45°
Thursday	60°
Friday	50°
Saturday	55°
Sunday	50°

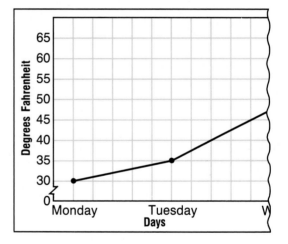

Check Your Understanding

Use your line graph to answer each question.

1. Which day was the warmest?

2. On which days was the high temperature less than 50° Fahrenheit?

Share Your Ideas How can you tell from the line graph that the temperature is getting cooler? getting warmer?

Use your line graph to answer each question.

3. From Thursday to Friday, did the high temperature increase or decrease?

4. How did the high temperature change from Wednesday to Sunday?

5. On what day was the high temperature in Salem 20 degrees warmer than the high temperature on Tuesday?

6. On what day was the high temperature 15 degrees cooler than the high temperature on Thursday?

7. When the temperature is 55° Fahrenheit or less, Mrs. Lahey turns on the furnace in her house. Which days during the week did Mrs. Lahey definitely have her furnace running?

Think and Apply

8. Look back at your line graph. Which day of the week do you think had the lowest temperature? Can you tell for certain? Why or why not?

 Work together with a partner.

9. Make a table to show the high temperatures in your city for one week.

10. Use the data in the table to make a line graph. Be sure to label the horizontal and vertical lines. Give the graph a title.

 Write three questions using the data in your graph. Then have a classmate answer the questions.

Mixed Review

1. 2
    3
    8
  $+5$

2. 25
  $+63$

3. 41
  -17

4. $5.86
  $+ 4.77$

5. 504 − 73

6. (5 + 8) + 6

7. 8 + (4 + 7)

8. 43 − 36

9. 308 − 99

Give the value of the digit 5.

10. 285

11. 5,239

12. 952

13. 538

Round to the nearest hundred.

14. 154

15. 826

16. 262

17. 3,861

SHOW WHAT YOU KNOW

CHECKPOINT

Write the time, using numbers. pages 76–81

1.

2.

3.

4.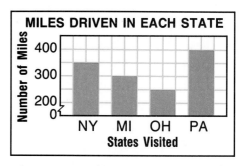

5. half past 2 in the morning

6. quarter to 10 in the evening

7. twenty past 4 in the afternoon

8. 45 min after 4:20 A.M.

9. 30 min before 2:45 P.M.

10. 2 h and 10 min before 4:20 A.M.

Use the graphs to answer the questions. pages 84–85

GARCIA'S VACATION EXPENSES	
	Dollars Spent
Gas for Car	$ $ $ $ $ $ $
Lodging	$ $ $ $ $ $ $ $ $
Food	$ $ $ $ $ $ $ $
Souvenirs	$ $ $ $
Entertainment	$ $ $

Each $ stands for $10.

MILES DRIVEN IN EACH STATE

Number of Miles — States Visited (NY, MI, OH, PA)

11. On what item did the Garcias spend the most money? How much did they spend?

12. In which states did the Garcias drive more than 300 miles? less than 300 miles?

Choose the correct word to complete each sentence.

13. A _____ uses picture symbols.

14. A _____ uses bars of different lengths.

15. A _____ shows change over time.

Words to Know

line graph
pictograph
bar graph

Make a line graph. pages 86–89

16. Use this information to show how many miles the Garcias drove each day: Monday, 240; Tuesday, 170; Wednesday, 140; Thursday, 180; Friday, 290.

INVESTIGATING
PROBLEM SOLVING

THINK
EXPLORE
SOLVE
LOOK BACK

Where Does the Water Cooler Go?

The scientists at Experimental Laboratories have requested a water cooler. They can have one but they must decide where to put it.

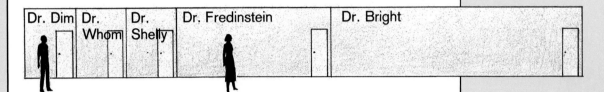

Dr. Dim | Dr. Whom | Dr. Shelly | Dr. Fredinstein | Dr. Bright

Thinking Critically

Look at the map of the offices. Help the scientists decide where the best place is to put the water cooler.

Work in a small group. You may wish to make drawings of the floor plan to help you.

Analyzing and Making Decisions

1. How many offices are there?

2. Which offices are close together? Which are far apart? Which offices are in the middle? Which are at each end of the laboratory?

3. Try putting the water cooler in several places. Test to see whether or not they are good places for the water cooler. Explain how you made your tests.

4. Where is the best place to put the water cooler? Explain.

Look Back   What if you could add two water coolers instead of one? Where would you put them?

Making and Using Tables

The museum is having a special fossil sale for its members. For $5 you can buy 1 unusual, 2 special, and 4 common fossils. Each time you spend $5 more, you receive twice as many fossils. For $10 you can buy 2 unusual, 4 special, and 8 common fossils. The museum limits sales to no more than $20 per person. How many fossils of each kind can you buy for $20?

Sometimes there are many facts given in a problem. Using a table is one way to organize these facts. A table can make facts easier to examine, and it can also show answers.

Solving the Problem

Think   What is the question? How many kinds of fossils are on sale?

Explore   What happens for each $5 you spend? Make a table that shows what you can buy.

Money	Unusual	Special	Common
$ 5	1	2	4
$10	2	4	8
$15	4		
$20			

Solve   How many fossils of each kind can you buy for $20?

Look Back   Does using the table help you solve the problem? Explain.

Share Your Ideas

1. What other questions could this table help you answer?

CHOICES **Solve. Use a calculator where appropriate.**

Teresa was doing a science experiment with plants. The table shows her record.

2. Which plant grew the most in one week? How much did it grow?

3. Which plant grew the most during the experiment? How much did it grow?

HEIGHT OF PLANTS			
Week	1	2	3
Plant A	1 in.	1 in.	4 in.
Plant B	2 in.	4 in.	6 in.
Plant C	2 in.	3 in.	4 in.

Tom and Sarah are making oatmeal.

4. Tom is using 3 cups of water. How much oatmeal should he use?

5. Sarah wants to make oatmeal for 9 people. How much oatmeal should she use?

Servings	Oat-Meal	Water or milk
3	1 cup	3 cups
6	2 cups	6 cups

Mixed Strategy Review

Use the information in the price list.

6. Bill wants to buy 1 Type A record, 1 Type B record, and 1 Type C record. How much money will he need?

7. Jane wants to buy 2 Type A records, 2 Type B records, and 2 Type C records. How much money will she need?

Record Prices
Type A $3.00
Type B $5.00
Type C $7.00
Type D $9.00

Megan kept a record of how far she drove.

8. On Monday she drove 175 miles. On Tuesday she drove 235 miles. On Wednesday she forgot to reset her trip counter. For both Tuesday and Wednesday she drove 382 miles. How far did she drive on Wednesday? Explain.

JOURNAL WRITING

CREATE YOUR OWN

Write a new problem using the information in the table about plant heights.

ACTIVITY

Investigating Collecting and Organizing Data

Words have different numbers of letters. What word length do you think occurs most often in books?

Working together

Materials: a book

A. Choose one page in the book that does not have any pictures on it.

B. Make a chart like the one shown.

C. Count the numbers of letters in each word on the page. Only include words with 1 to 10 letters. Make a **tally mark** for each word next to the correct number of letters.

D. Count the tally marks. Record the numbers in your chart. For example, in the chart shown, there are 6 words with 3 letters, and 2 words with 4 letters.

Word Lengths		Total Number of Words
1		
2		
3	ⲧⲏⲧ I	6
4	II	2
5		
6		
7		
8		
9		
10		

Sharing Your Results

Use your chart to answer each question.

1. How many 3-letter words did you find?

2. How many words have more than 5 letters?

3. Words with how many letters occur most often?

4. Words with how many letters occur least often?

94

Extending the Activity

Work with a partner.

Materials: a story you have written, your science book

5. Make two charts like the ones shown at the right.

6. Use the first chart. Count the words in each sentence of your story. Make a tally mark beside the correct number of words after counting each sentence.

7. Use the second chart. Count the words in the sentences from two pages of your science book. Make a tally mark beside the correct number of words after counting each sentence.

8. Count the tally marks and write the totals.

Show What You Know

Use your charts to answer each question.

9. What was the least number of words in a sentence in your story? in your science book?

10. What was the greatest number of words in a sentence in your story? in your science book?

11. What number of words occurred most often in sentences in your story? in your science book?

12. Do you think the results would be the same if you used a sixth-grade science book? a third-grade science book? Explain.

MY STORY	
Sentence Lengths	Total Number of Sentences
1 word	
2 words	
3 words	
4 words	
5 words	
6 words	
7 words	
8 words	
9 words	

MY SCIENCE BOOK	
Sentence Lengths	Total Number of Sentences
1 word	
2 words	
3 words	
4 words	
5 words	
6 words	
7 words	
8 words	
9 words	

The more the better.

95

ACTIVITY

Investigating Making Graphs

In 1873, a boy named Chester Greenwood was skating on a frozen pond in Maine. He had a wonderful idea about how to keep his ears warm—earmuffs! He decided to go into business making and selling earmuffs.

This pictograph shows the number of earmuffs sold from his factory in different years.

Working together

A. Copy this pictograph.

B. Fill in the pictograph symbols for the following data.

- In 1918, there were 200,000 earmuffs sold.
- In 1936, there were 400,000 earmuffs sold.

	NUMBER OF EARMUFFS SOLD
1883	☞
1918	
1935	🎧🎧🎧☞
1936	

Each 🎧 Stands for 100,000 earmuffs.
Each ☞ Stands for 50,000 earmuffs.

Sharing Your Results

Use the pictograph to answer each question.

1. In what year did the factory sell the most earmuffs? the least?

2. How many earmuffs were sold in 1935?

3. How many more earmuffs were sold in 1935 than in 1883?

Extending the Activity

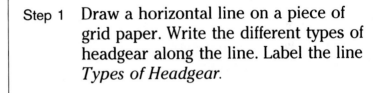

Hats	Caps	Earmuffs	Scarves

Work with a partner.

4. Take a survey of the students in your class to see what type of headgear they wear in cold weather.

5. Record your data in a table.

6. Construct a bar graph to show your data.

Step 1	Draw a horizontal line on a piece of grid paper. Write the different types of headgear along the line. Label the line *Types of Headgear.*
Step 2	Draw a vertical line on the left. Write a number beside each box. Label the line *Number of Students.*
Step 3	Draw bars to show the number of students who wear each type of headgear. Give the graph a title.

Use your bar graph to answer each question.

7. Which type of headgear is worn by the greatest number of students? the least?

8. Find the total number of students who wear the two least common types of headgear. How does this total compare with the number of students who wear the most common type?

Show What You Know

9. Write three story problems that can be solved by using your bar graph. Give them to a classmate to solve.

THINK AND SHARE

> Discuss what kind of graph you would use to show how many classmates have first names beginning with the same letter.

Comparing Graphs

Miki wants to make a graph to show the changes in her height each year from birth to 9 years. Which type of graph should she make?

▶ Use a line graph when you want to show how things change over time.

▶ Use a bar graph or a pictograph when you want to compare two or more things.

▶ Use a pictograph when a symbol can represent a large number.

Explain why Miki should make a line graph.

What kind of information would you show using a bar graph? pictograph?

Check Your Understanding

Would you use a pictograph, a bar graph, or a line graph to show the following? Explain.

1. the changes in a person's weight over a period of 10 years

2. to compare the heights of 5 people

3. to compare the number of oranges sold each week during February

4. the daily changes in the amount of water in the reservoir during June

Share Your Ideas Which type of graph did you choose in *Think and Share?* Would you choose a different type of graph now? Explain why or why not.

Decide which type of graph you would use

5. to compare the amounts of potatoes produced last year in three different states.

6. to show changes in the price of a movie ticket over 30 years.

7. to compare the numbers of students in four classes.

8. to compare the number of records sold each month of the year.

9. to show changes in the number of hours of homework over one week.

10. to compare bicycle sales for six stores.

Think and Apply

MATHPROCESSOR **Work with a partner. Use a Spreadsheet and Graphs.**

11. Conduct a survey. Pick a category such as colors or sports. List four or five choices. Ask 20 people each to pick a favorite. Record your data in the spreadsheet.

12. Display your data using three different graphs. Link your spreadsheet to each graph.

13. Compare the graphs. Which type of graph is best for your data? Explain why.

Write three questions that can be answered using your graph. Give the questions to a classmate to solve.

1. 543
    -365

2. 641
    $+782$

3. 8
    $+94$

4. 605
    -435

5. 700
    -547

6. $45.06 - 2.98$

7. $25 + 8,176$

8. $36 + 8 + 41$

Write each number in standard form.

9. 1 hundred 33

10. eighty-seven

11. five hundred ten

12. six hundred seventy-four

Compare. Use >, <, or = for ●.

13. 3,467 ● 3,647

14. 2,014 ● 2,009

15. 98 ● 96 + 2

16. 37 + 24 ● 70

SHOW WHAT YOU KNOW

99

Interview: Calculators and a Chemist

Carol Richards is a chemist for a food company. She invented a new type of carrot soup. She makes large batches of the soup for canning. "I use a calculator to figure out how many cups of ingredients are in one batch."

A. What if the circle graph shows the number of cups of each ingredient that is in one batch of carrot soup?

Almost half of the ingredients is carrots, so almost half of the graph is used to show this.
The second greatest amount is chicken broth. What is next in order? Give two ways you can tell.

B. How can you find out how many cups of ingredients are used for one batch? How many cups of ingredients are there?

BATCH OF CARROT SOUP

A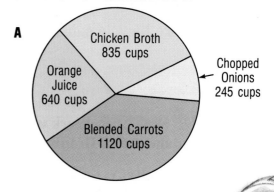

Chicken Broth 835 cups

Chopped Onions 245 cups

Orange Juice 640 cups

Blended Carrots 1120 cups

Sharing Your Ideas

Find the information in the circle graph above. Use a calculator to solve.

1. How many more cups of chicken broth are there than chopped onions?

2. How many cups of orange juice and chicken broth are used in all?

3. How many more cups of carrots are used than chopped onions?

4. How many cups of ingredients in the soup are not onions?

Extending Your Thinking

Find the information in the circle graphs. Use a calculator to solve.

5. Look at graph **B.** How many cups of tomatoes and peppers does the graph show for the batch of vegetable soup?

6. How many cups of ingredients are in the batch?

7. How many cups in the batch are not beef broth?

8. If you were making two batches of soup, how many cups of each ingredient would you need?

9. Look at graph **C. What if** the graph shows where Carol Richards spends her time each day at work? Where does Carol spend the least amount of time each day?

10. If you went to look for her, where would Carol most likely be?

11. What if the numbers below are the number of minutes Carol spends in each location? Match the numbers with the locations.

a. 105 minutes   **b.** 30 minutes
c. 90 minutes   **d.** 210 minutes

Show What You Know

Circle graph **D** stands for the 12 hours from 7 A.M. to 7 P.M. Each section stands for 1 hour.

12. Trace the circle. Label each section to show your activities in one day. Color each activity a different color.

13. Which activity do you do for the least amount of time? How could you see this?

BATCH OF VEGETABLE SOUP

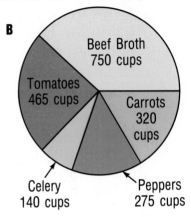

B

Beef Broth 750 cups

Tomatoes 465 cups

Carrots 320 cups

Celery 140 cups

Peppers 275 cups

**AT WORK
LOCATIONS OF ACTIVITIES**

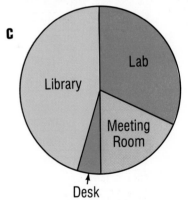

C

Library

Lab

Meeting Room

Desk

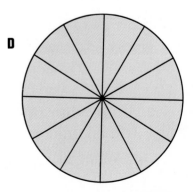

D

Math Around The World

THE CALENDAR ISLAMIC STYLE

WORKING TOGETHER

1. Work in small groups. Investigate the Islamic calendar. Find out what the Islamic calendar is based on, what year it dates from, and why their festivals move "backwards" through the seasons.

2. Use the chart below to answer these questions
How many months are there in a year?
How many days are there in a year?
What are the shortest months?

ISLAMIC CALENDAR	
Months of the Year	Number of Days in the Month
Muharram	30
Safar	29
Rabi I	30
Rabi II	29
Jumada I	30
Jumada II	29
Rajab	30
Shaban	29
Ramadan	30
Shawwal	29
Zulkadah	30
Zulhijjah	29

3. Share your findings with the class. Then compare the Islamic calendar with the calendar we use.

• What are the similarities and differences?

CHAPTER REVIEW/TEST

Use the clock face at the right to answer.

1. What time does the clock show?

2. What time will it be in 3 h and 20 min?

3. What time was it 25 min before the time shown?

4. How much time has passed since 12:10?

Use the graphs to answer the questions.

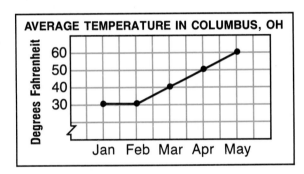

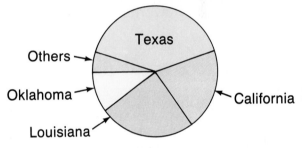

TOP OIL-PRODUCING STATES

5. In which two months did the average temperature remain the same?

6. How much did the temperature go up between April and May?

7. Which state produces the most oil?

8. Does Louisiana produce more or less oil than California?

Solve.

9. Greg began practicing piano at 4:30 P.M. He finished at 5:15 P.M. How long did he practice?

10. It costs $2 to buy 3 raffle tickets. Make a table. How much will 15 tickets cost?

Think The bus trip into the city takes 45 minutes. It takes 10 minutes to walk from the bus station to the museum. If Karen's bus leaves at 11:15 A.M., when can she be at the museum?

COMPUTER

Graphs

MathProcessor™ lets you make graphs easily. First, use the **Spreadsheet** to create a table of data. Then link the data in the **Spreadsheet** to **Graphs**.

The **Spreadsheet** and **Graphs** show the results of a survey of favorite yogurt flavors.

MathProcessor™ Tools:

📊 Graphs

⊞ Spreadsheet

✎ Writing Space

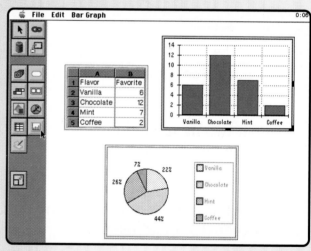

Doing the Computer Investigation

A. The table on the next page shows the types of music on radio station RTU. It also shows the number of hours each type of music is played each day.

Enter the data into a **Spreadsheet** and **link** it to a **Bar Graph**.

B. **Link** the spreadsheet to a **Circle Graph**. Use a **Writing Space**. Compare the **Circle Graph** to the **Bar Graph** that you made in **A**.

RADIO STATION RTU	
Type of Music	Hours Each Day
Jazz	6
Rap	4
Classical	2
Country	2
Rock	5
Blues	5

Sharing Your Results

1. Plan a day's programming for your own radio station. Decide what type of programs you will have. Plan the number of hours that each type of program will broadcast. Enter your data in a **Spreadsheet**. **Link** the **Spreadsheet** to a **Bar Graph** and to a **Circle Graph**.

2. Share your graphs with other classmates. How are your programming days alike? How are they different?

Extending the Computer Investigation

What do you do on Saturdays? Keep track of your activities for 24 hours next Saturday.

3. List your activities. Use categories such as playing, eating, sleeping, and so on. Enter your data in a **Spreadsheet**. **Link** your **Spreadsheet** to a **Graph**.

4. Open a **Writing Space**. Explain why you used the type of graph you did. Describe how different your graph might look if you kept track of your activities for a weekday.

Time Zones

There are four time zones in the continental United States. There is a one-hour time difference from one zone to the next.

When it is 4 P.M. in the Eastern Time Zone, it is
3 P.M. in the Central Time Zone.
2 P.M. in the Mountain Time Zone.
1 P.M. in the Pacific Time Zone.

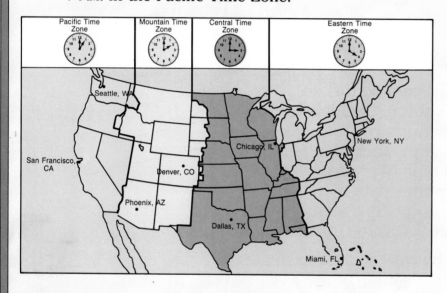

Use the map above and reference books to help you answer these questions.

1. When it is 7 P.M. in New York, what time is it in San Francisco?

2. When it is 10:30 A.M. in Denver, what time is it in Miami?

3. **What if** you leave Seattle at 11 A.M. Seattle time and fly for 6 hours to Washington, D.C.? What is the time in Washington, D.C. when you arrive?

4. Find out what time it is in Juneau, Alaska, and Honolulu, Hawaii, when it is 6 P.M. in San Francisco.

5. Draw a picture of what you might be doing at 8 A.M. Then draw a picture of what a fourth grader might be doing in the other 3 time zones when it is 8 A.M. in your time zone.

HOME CONNECTION

In Chapters **1–3** your child has been studying place value, addition, subtraction, time, and graphs. You can help your child use those skills in this project.

Watching the Sunset

Together keep a record of the time the sun sets.

Materials: one sheet of grid paper, a clock, pencil, paper

1. Find a place where you can watch for the sun to set each day. Choose a window or a place outdoors.

2. Make a table. Record the date and the time the sun sets each day for four weeks.

3. After four weeks use the data to make a line graph.

4. What trend do you see? What do you think causes this? Together try to find the answer.

SUNSETS		
Day	**Date**	**Time**
Monday		
Tuesday		
Wednesday		
Thursday		

CUMULATIVE REVIEW

Choose the correct answer. Write A, B, C, or D.

1. 4
    +9

  A 14   **C** 13

  B 12   **D** not given

2. 5 + 3 + 7 + 3 = □

  A 18   **C** 16

  B 13   **D** not given

3. 14 − □ = 8

  A 6   **C** 8

  B 7   **D** not given

4. What is the value of the digit 5 in 3,458?

  A hundreds   **C** tens

  B ones   **D** not given

5. Write four hundred twenty-one thousand twelve in standard form.

  A 42,112   **C** 421,120

  B 421,012   **D** not given

6. Compare. 589,463 ⬤ 499,892

  A <   **C** =

  B >   **D** not given

7. Round 41,626 to the nearest thousand.

  A 40,000   **C** 50,000

  B 41,000   **D** not given

8. Estimate $6.85 + $2.10.

  A $5.00   **C** $12.00

  B $9.00   **D** $7.00

9. 27 + 48 + 49 = □

  A 124   **C** 115

  B 104   **D** not given

10. 14,011
     +82,362

  A 68,351   **C** 95,373

  B 96,363   **D** not given

11. Estimate 688 − 318.

  A 1,000   **C** 500

  B 400   **D** 200

12. 68
     − 23

  A 55   **C** 45

  B 44   **D** not given

13. 800 − 456 = □

  A 344   **C** 354

  B 546   **D** not given

14. 62,400 − 3,635 = □

  A 58,835   **C** 58,765

  B 58,775   **D** not given

Choose the correct answer. Write A, B, C, or D.

15. Write the time for 10 minutes after 4.

  A 3:50   **C** 10:04

  B 4:15   **D** not given

16. What time will it be in 20 minutes?

  A 3:27   **C** 3:20

  B 3:17   **D** not given

17. How many children are in Grade 3?

CHILDREN	
Grade 1	🧍 🧍 🧍 🧍 🧍 🧍
Grade 2	🧍 🧍 🧍 🧍 🧍 🧍
Grade 3	🧍 🧍 🧍 🧍 🧍 🧍 🧍
Grade 4	🧍 🧍 🧍 🧍 🧍 🧍 🧍

Each 🧍 stands for 4 children.

  A 16   **C** 26

  B 14   **D** not given

18. What was the high temperature on Tuesday?

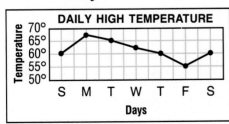

  A 62°   **C** 65°

  B 66°   **D** not given

Use the picture to solve 19–20.

Supplies	Price
Notebooks	3 for $1.50
Rulers	$ .20
Pencils	$ .05
Pens	$ .15

19. How much would 9 notebooks cost?

  A $1.00   **C** $2.00

  B $4.00   **D** not given

20. How much more is the cost of 3 notebooks than the cost of 1 pen?

  A $.20   **C** $1.35

  B $.25   **D** not given

Answer each question.

There were 15 fourth graders playing a game of soccer during lunch time. Six players were from Mr. Davis's class. Then 12 fifth graders joined in the game. How many students played in the game?

21. Which fact is not needed?

  A 15 fourth graders   **C** 6 from Mr. Davis's class

  B 12 fifth graders   **D** not given

22. How many students played in the soccer game?

  A 27   **C** 21

  B 33   **D** not given

4 Understanding Multiplication and Division

THEME Amazing Animals

Sharing What You Know

The words *school, swarm,* and *pride* all have something in common. They are all names of groups of animals. Naturalists are people who learn about wild animal populations. They track groups of animals. Knowing the number of animals in the group is important information. How do you think naturalists use mathematics?

Using Language

Look at the photographs on this page. Would these animals naturally be grouped together? The individual photographs were chosen to form a **composite picture.** In mathematics, a **composite number** is a number that has more than two factors. How is a composite number like a composite picture? How are they different?

Words to Know: factor, product, multiple, prime number, composite number, property, dividend, quotient

Be a Problem Solver

When giraffes walk, they pace. They first put their two left feet down, then their two right feet. A giraffe begins to pace. It moves its two left feet for the first step. Which feet does it move for the fifth step, the right feet or the left? How did you know? How would you know which feet the giraffe moved for any step?

Create a bulletin board of interesting facts about animals.

2 and 4 as Factors

This young centipede has 7 body segments.
There are 2 legs on each segment. How many
legs is this in all?

You can count by 2's.	You can add. Use doubles.	You can multiply.
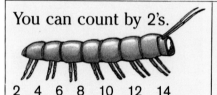 2 4 6 8 10 12 14	$7 + 7 = 14$	$7 \times 2 = 14$ $\begin{array}{r} 2 \leftarrow \text{factor} \\ \times 7 \leftarrow \text{factor} \\ \hline 14 \leftarrow \text{product} \end{array}$

This centipede has 14 legs.

This young millipede has 7 body segments.
There are 4 legs on each segment.
How many legs is this in all?

You can count by 4's.	You can use doubles. 4 is the double of 2.	You can multiply.
 4 8 12 16 20 24 28	$2 \times 7 = 14$ $4 \times 7 = 14 + 14$ $4 \times 7 = 28$	$7 \times 4 = 28$ $\begin{array}{r} 4 \\ \times 7 \\ \hline 28 \end{array}$

This millipede has 28 legs.

Check Your Understanding

Find each product.

1. $\begin{array}{r} 6 \\ \times 2 \end{array}$ $\begin{array}{r} 6 \\ \times 4 \end{array}$

2. $\begin{array}{r} 2 \\ \times 4 \end{array}$ $\begin{array}{r} 4 \\ \times 4 \end{array}$

3. $\begin{array}{r} 9 \\ \times 2 \end{array}$ $\begin{array}{r} 9 \\ \times 4 \end{array}$

4. $\begin{array}{r} 2 \\ \times 5 \end{array}$ $\begin{array}{r} 4 \\ \times 5 \end{array}$

5. $2 \times 7 = \square$ $4 \times 7 = \square$

6. $2 \times 10 = \square$ $4 \times 10 = \square$

Share Your Ideas Explain how knowing that
$2 \times 8 = 16$ can help you find the product of 4×8.

Find each product.

7. 2
× 3

8. 5
× 4

9. 2
× 2

10. 4
× 3

11. 7
× 4

12. 2
× 8

13. 1
× 4

14. 4
× 4

15. 4
× 6

16. 7
× 2

17. 2
× 1

18. 4
× 2

19. 2
× 9

20. 10
× 4

21. $2 \times 10 = \square$

22. $6 \times 2 = \square$

23. $2 \times 5 = \square$

24. $9 \times 4 = \square$

25. $5 \times 4 = \square$

26. $2 \times 4 = \square$

27. $9 \times 2 = \square$

28. $4 \times 8 = \square$

Compare. Use <, >, or = for ⬤.

29. $2 + 4$ ⬤ 4×2

30. 2×6 ⬤ $6 + 6$

31. 9×2 ⬤ 6×4

32. 1×2 ⬤ 2×0

33. 2×7 ⬤ 4×3

34. 4×4 ⬤ 8×2

Think and Apply

35. Insects have 6 legs. Ants and butterflies are insects. What is the total number of legs on 2 ants and 2 butterflies?

36. A crab has 5 pairs of legs. How many legs do 4 crabs have in all?

37. Carlos and Jan were catching lightning bugs. Jan caught 6 bugs. Carlos caught 8 bugs more than Jan. How many lightning bugs did they catch in all?

38. The science teacher has 18 pictures of insects to display on the bulletin board. She wants to arrange the pictures in groups of 4. How many pictures will not fit in the display?

39. If 2 is one of the factors in a multiplication problem, which numbers listed below could not be the product? Tell why.

6   11   18   24   32   37   40   41

Write a multiplication story problem with 2 as a factor and 10 as a product.

SHOW WHAT YOU KNOW

113

4 is the double of 2.   6 is the double of 3.
Name the doubles for 4, 5, 6, 7, 8, 9, and 10.

3 and 6 as Factors

A group of whales is called a pod of whales. In the Atlantic Ocean near Cape Cod, there were 7 pods of whales. There were 3 whales in each pod. How many whales were there in all?

You can count by 3's.	You can multiply.
● ● ● ● ● ● ● ● ● ● ● ● ● ● ● ● ● ● ● ● ● 3 6 9 12 15 18 21	$7 \times 3 = 21$ $\begin{array}{r} 3 \\ \times 7 \\ \hline 21 \end{array}$

There were 21 whales in all.

A group of chimpanzees is called a band. There were 6 bands of chimps in the forest. There were 7 chimps in each band. How many chimpanzees were there in all?

You can multiply.	You can use doubles. 6 is the double of 3.
$6 \times 7 = 42$ $\begin{array}{r} 7 \\ \times 6 \\ \hline 42 \end{array}$	$3 \times 7 = 21$ So: $6 \times 7 = 21 + 21$ $6 \times 7 = 42$

There were 42 chimpanzees in all.

Check Your Understanding

Find each product.

1. $\begin{array}{r} 6 \\ \times 3 \end{array}$
2. $\begin{array}{r} 6 \\ \times 1 \end{array}$
3. $\begin{array}{r} 4 \\ \times 3 \end{array}$
4. $\begin{array}{r} 6 \\ \times 9 \end{array}$
5. $\begin{array}{r} 3 \\ \times 8 \end{array}$
6. $\begin{array}{r} 6 \\ \times 6 \end{array}$
7. $\begin{array}{r} 10 \\ \times 3 \end{array}$

8. $6 \times 7 = \square$
9. $3 \times 2 = \square$
10. $5 \times 6 = \square$
11. $3 \times 9 = \square$

Share Your Ideas   Explain how knowing that $3 \times 9 = 27$ can help you find the product of 6×9.

Multiply.

| 12. 0
×3 | 13. 3
×6 | 14. 5
×6 | 15. 3
×1 | 16. 10
× 6 | 17. 9
×3 | 18. 3
×5 |

| 19. 2
×3 | 20. 8
×4 | 21. 1
×6 | 22. 4
×3 | 23. 9
×6 | 24. 2
×8 | 25. 6
×6 |

26. 6 × 2 = □   **27.** 6 × 8 = □   **28.** 3 × 3 = □   **29.** 3 × 8 = □

30. 3 × 7 = □   **31.** 4 × 6 = □   **32.** 3 × 10 = □   **33.** 7 × 6 = □

Follow the rule to find each output.

Rule: Multiply by 3.

	Input	Output
34.	2	
35.	8	
36.	6	
37.	5	

Rule: Multiply by 6.

	Input	Output
38.	2	
39.	8	
40.	6	
41.	5	

Think and Apply

42. There were 6 mobs of kangaroos with 4 kangaroos in each mob. How many kangaroos were there in all?

43. There were 3 braces of ducks with 2 ducks in each brace. There were 10 geese. How many ducks and geese were there altogether?

Visual Thinking

44. Draw the next picture. How many dots are in your picture? Describe the pattern.

Look back at **34** through **41**. Compare the outputs. Explain how they are related.

JOURNAL WRITING

SHOW WHAT YOU KNOW

What is the same about 2 × 4 and 4 × 2? What is different?

Multiplication Properties

Properties can help you remember multiplication facts.

Look at the examples below.

2 rings of 4

$$2 \times 4 = 8 \qquad \begin{array}{r} 4 \\ \times 2 \\ \hline 8 \end{array}$$

4 rings of 2

$$4 \times 2 = 8 \qquad \begin{array}{r} 2 \\ \times 4 \\ \hline 8 \end{array}$$

The order in which numbers are multiplied does not change the product.

What do you notice about the products?

Look at the examples below.

(3 × 2) × 4   3 × (2 × 4)
  6   × 4 = 24   3 ×   8   = 24

Do the work shown in parentheses first.

The way in which numbers are grouped does not change the product.

Use rings and dots to explore other properties.

Draw 6 rings with 1 dot in each.   Draw 6 rings with 0 dots in each.
Draw 9 rings with 1 dot in each.   Draw 9 rings with 0 dots in each.

What do you notice about the products?

| The product of any number and 1 is that number. | The product of any number and 0 is 0. |

Check Your Understanding

Use the properties. Find each product.

1. 0 × 0 = ☐   **2.** 1 × 9 = ☐   **3.** 0 × 7 = ☐   **4.** 8 × 1 = ☐

Share Your Ideas Which two properties explain why 10 × 0 = 0 if 0 × 10 = 0?

Use the multiplication properties to solve.

5. $3 \times 4 = 12$
$4 \times 3 = \square$

6. $9 \times 2 = 18$
$2 \times 9 = \square$

7. $3 \times 7 = 21$
$7 \times 3 = \square$

8. $5 \times 4 = 20$
$4 \times 5 = \square$

9. $6 \times 5 = 30$
$5 \times 6 = \square$

10. $4 \times 9 = 36$
$9 \times 4 = \square$

11. $8 \times 3 = 24$
$3 \times 8 = \square$

12. $7 \times 5 = 35$
$5 \times 7 = \square$

13. $\begin{array}{r} 5 \\ \times 0 \\ \hline \end{array}$

14. $\begin{array}{r} 3 \\ \times 1 \\ \hline \end{array}$

15. $\begin{array}{r} 1 \\ \times 7 \\ \hline \end{array}$

16. $\begin{array}{r} 2 \\ \times 1 \\ \hline \end{array}$

17. $\begin{array}{r} 0 \\ \times 9 \\ \hline \end{array}$

18. $\begin{array}{r} 1 \\ \times 0 \\ \hline \end{array}$

19. $\begin{array}{r} 8 \\ \times 1 \\ \hline \end{array}$

20. $\begin{array}{r} 0 \\ \times 2 \\ \hline \end{array}$

21. $\begin{array}{r} 1 \\ \times 1 \\ \hline \end{array}$

22. $\begin{array}{r} 10 \\ \times 0 \\ \hline \end{array}$

23. $\begin{array}{r} 8 \\ \times 0 \\ \hline \end{array}$

24. $\begin{array}{r} 10 \\ \times 1 \\ \hline \end{array}$

25. $\begin{array}{r} 0 \\ \times 6 \\ \hline \end{array}$

26. $\begin{array}{r} 1 \\ \times 5 \\ \hline \end{array}$

27. $3 \times (3 \times 3) = \square$

28. $(4 \times 2) \times 3 = \square$

29. $(1 \times 6) \times 4 = \square$

30. $(2 \times 3) \times 6 = \square$

31. $6 \times (3 \times 3) = \square$

32. $(2 \times 4) \times 4 = \square$

33. $(0 \times 3) \times 6 = \square$

34. $(2 \times 2) \times 2 = \square$

35. $2 \times (3 \times 2) = \square$

36. $0 \times 26 = \square$

37. $536 \times 0 = \square$

38. $1 \times 695 = \square$

Think and Apply

39. It costs $9 to buy a child's ticket for the circus. It costs twice as much to buy an adult's ticket. How much would it cost for 1 adult and 2 children to attend the circus?

40. Senior citizens' tickets cost $10 less than adult tickets. How much will it cost for 4 senior citizens to attend the circus?

41. The product of two numbers is 0. One of the factors is 0. Explain why you cannot tell what the other factor is.

The product of two numbers is 15. Could one of the factors be 1? 0? Explain.

SHOW WHAT YOU KNOW

117

Count by 10's to 100. Write the numbers as you say them. What is the same about every number you wrote?

5 and 10 as Factors

Every day Jack takes 7 groups of dogs for walks in the park. There are 5 dogs in each group. How many dogs does he walk in all?

You can count by 5's.	You can multiply.
5 10 15 _____	$7 \times 5 = 35$ $\begin{array}{r} 5 \\ \times 7 \\ \hline 35 \end{array}$

Jack walks 35 dogs.

What if Jack has 10 dogs in each group? How many dogs would he walk in all?

You can count by 10's.	You can multiply.
10 20 30 _____	$7 \times 10 = 70$ $\begin{array}{r} 10 \\ \times 7 \\ \hline 70 \end{array}$

Jack would walk 70 dogs.

Look at the two examples: $7 \times 5 = 35$ and $7 \times 10 = 70$
How do the factors compare?
How do the products compare?

Check Your Understanding

Multiply.

1. $\begin{array}{r} 8 \\ \times 5 \\ \hline \end{array}$
2. $\begin{array}{r} 10 \\ \times 4 \\ \hline \end{array}$
3. $\begin{array}{r} 5 \\ \times 4 \\ \hline \end{array}$
4. $\begin{array}{r} 10 \\ \times 9 \\ \hline \end{array}$
5. $\begin{array}{r} 5 \\ \times 6 \\ \hline \end{array}$
6. $\begin{array}{r} 10 \\ \times 6 \\ \hline \end{array}$
7. $\begin{array}{r} 7 \\ \times 5 \\ \hline \end{array}$

Share Your Ideas   Look at the pattern below. What are the next three facts?

$9 \times 10 = 90$ $10 \times 10 = 100$ $11 \times 10 = 110$
$12 \times 10 = \square$ $\square \times 10 = \square$ $\square \times 10 = \square$

118

Multiply.

8. $\begin{array}{r} 10 \\ \times\ 5 \\ \hline \end{array}$ **9.** $\begin{array}{r} 1 \\ \times 5 \\ \hline \end{array}$ **10.** $\begin{array}{r} 10 \\ \times\ 4 \\ \hline \end{array}$ **11.** $\begin{array}{r} 10 \\ \times\ 0 \\ \hline \end{array}$ **12.** $\begin{array}{r} 5 \\ \times\ 4 \\ \hline \end{array}$

13. $\begin{array}{r} 6 \\ \times 5 \\ \hline \end{array}$ **14.** $\begin{array}{r} 10 \\ \times\ 9 \\ \hline \end{array}$ **15.** $\begin{array}{r} 5 \\ \times 8 \\ \hline \end{array}$ **16.** $\begin{array}{r} 10 \\ \times\ 7 \\ \hline \end{array}$ **17.** $\begin{array}{r} 5 \\ \times 5 \\ \hline \end{array}$

18. $\begin{array}{r} 0 \\ \times 5 \\ \hline \end{array}$ **19.** $\begin{array}{r} 5 \\ \times 3 \\ \hline \end{array}$ **20.** $\begin{array}{r} 9 \\ \times 5 \\ \hline \end{array}$ **21.** $\begin{array}{r} 10 \\ \times\ 3 \\ \hline \end{array}$ **22.** $\begin{array}{r} 10 \\ \times\ 2 \\ \hline \end{array}$

23. $10 \times 8 = \square$ **24.** $7 \times 5 = \square$

25. $6 \times 10 = \square$ **26.** $(1 \times 10) \times 5 = \square$

Continue each pattern.

27. 75, 80, 85, 90, 95, —, —, —, —, —, —

28. 100, 110, 120, 130, 140, —, —, —, —, —, —

29. 100, 105, 110, 115, 120, —, —, —, —, —, —

Think and Apply

30. Paula walks 10 groups of dogs each day. There are 6 dogs in each group. How many dogs does she walk in all?

31. Each Saturday, Peter takes 8 dogs for a walk in the park. How many legs are there in all that can get tangled in the leashes?

32. Fred walked 6 groups of dogs with 4 dogs in each group. Marge walked 5 groups of dogs with 5 dogs in each group. Who walked more dogs? How many more?

Explain how knowing that $12 \times 10 = 120$ can help you find the product of 12×5.

SHOW WHAT YOU KNOW

7, 8, and 9 as Factors

There were 7 dogsled teams competing in one race. **What if** each sled was pulled by 7 dogs. How many dogs were in the race?

You can multiply. $7 \times 7 = 49$

$$\begin{array}{r} 7 \\ \times 7 \\ \hline 49 \end{array}$$

You can use multiplication facts you already know.

You know that $6 \times 7 = 42$.
7×7 is one more 7.
$7 \times 7 = 42 + 7$
$7 \times 7 = 49$

There were 49 dogs in the race.

More Examples

a. $8 \times 9 = 72$
$$\begin{array}{r} 9 \\ \times 8 \\ \hline 72 \end{array}$$

b. $9 \times 9 = 81$
$$\begin{array}{r} 9 \\ \times 9 \\ \hline 81 \end{array}$$
How can you find the product of 9×9 if you know that $8 \times 9 = 72$?

Check Your Understanding

Find each product.

1. $\begin{array}{r} 9 \\ \times 3 \\ \hline \end{array}$
2. $\begin{array}{r} 7 \\ \times 9 \\ \hline \end{array}$
3. $\begin{array}{r} 8 \\ \times 8 \\ \hline \end{array}$
4. $\begin{array}{r} 6 \\ \times 7 \\ \hline \end{array}$
5. $\begin{array}{r} 8 \\ \times 9 \\ \hline \end{array}$
6. $\begin{array}{r} 9 \\ \times 9 \\ \hline \end{array}$
7. $\begin{array}{r} 7 \\ \times 7 \\ \hline \end{array}$

8. $7 \times 8 = \square$ **9.** $9 \times 5 = \square$ **10.** $4 \times 8 = \square$ **11.** $4 \times 9 = \square$

Share Your Ideas   Explain how knowing that $6 \times 9 = 54$ can help you find the product of 7×9.

Multiply.

12. 3 $\times 8$	**13.** 1 $\times 7$	**14.** 7 $\times 7$	**15.** 9 $\times 5$	**16.** 8 $\times 6$	**17.** 10 $\times 7$	**18.** 9 $\times 3$
19. 5 $\times 8$	**20.** 8 $\times 2$	**21.** 9 $\times 7$	**22.** 10 $\times 8$	**23.** 2 $\times 9$	**24.** 7 $\times 5$	**25.** 4 $\times 9$
26. 4 $\times 7$	**27.** 9 $\times 6$	**28.** 8 $\times 7$	**29.** 7 $\times 6$	**30.** 9 $\times 9$	**31.** 7 $\times 3$	**32.** 8 $\times 9$

33. $2 \times 7 = \square$ **34.** $10 \times 9 = \square$ **35.** $8 \times 4 = \square$ **36.** $8 \times 8 = \square$

37. $(8 \times 1) \times 9 = \square$ **38.** $(2 \times 0) \times 8 = \square$ **39.** $7 \times (2 \times 4) = \square$

Compare. Use $<$, $>$, or $=$ for ●.

40. 5×7 ● 6×6 **41.** $72 + 9$ ● 9×9

42. 9×6 ● 8×7 **43.** 8×9 ● $(8 \times 8) + 8$

Think and Apply

44. A dogsled race had 6 teams with 7 dogs each and 8 teams with 9 dogs each. How many teams raced? How many dogs raced?

45. The product of two numbers is 35. Their sum is 12. What are the numbers?

Mathematics and History

Greek mathematicians found a way to add odd numbers beginning with 1.

To add the first <u>2</u> odd numbers: $1 + 3 = \underline{2} \times \underline{2}$, or 4
To add the first <u>3</u> odd numbers: $1 + 3 + 5 = \underline{3} \times \underline{3}$, or 9
To add the first <u>4</u> odd numbers: $1 + 3 + 5 + 7 = \underline{4} \times \underline{4}$, or 16

Use this method to find each sum.

46. $1 + 3 + 5 + 7 + 9$
47. $1 + 3 + 5 + 7 + 9 + 11 + 13 + 15$
48. $1 + 3 + 5 + 7 + 9 + 11 + 13 + 15 + 17$

Write a multiplication fact with 9 as a factor. Tell how you can use it to find another multiplication fact.

SHOW WHAT YOU KNOW

Patterns on the Multiplication Table

0, 4, 8, 12, 16, 20, . . . are multiples of 4.

▶ A **multiple** of 4 is any product that has 4 as a factor.

Look at the row showing multiples of 4 and the row showing multiples of 2. Describe the relationship between the columns.

×	0	1	2	3	4	5	6	7	8	9	10
0	0	0	0	0	0	0	0	0	0	0	0
1	0	1	2	3	4	5	6	7	8	9	10
2	0	2	4	6	8	10	12	14	16	18	20
3	0	3	6	9	12	15	18	21	24	27	30
4	0	4	8	12	16	20	24	28	32	36	40
5	0	5	10	15	20	25	30	35	40	45	50
6	0	6	12	18	24	30	36	42	48	54	60
7	0	7	14	21	28	35	42	49	56	63	70
8	0	8	16	24	32	40	48	56	64	72	80
9	0	9	18	27	36	45	54	63	72	81	90
10	0	10	20	30	40	50	60	70	80	90	100

4 × 8

To find 4 × 8 on the table, follow the row marked 4 and the column marked 8. They meet at 32. This is the product of 4 × 8.

Find the same product in another box on the table. Compare the factors.

Check Your Understanding

Use the multiplication table to find each number.

1. first multiple of 3

2. fifth multiple of 9

3. second multiple of 8

4. third multiple of 10

5. 2 × 8 = ☐   6. 5 × 7 = ☐   7. 6 × 4 = ☐

Share Your Ideas   Describe the relationship between the multiples of 3 and the multiples of 6. What other numbers on the multiplication table have the same relationship? Explain.

Use the multiplication table to find each number.

8. sixth multiple of 4

9. eighth multiple of 2

10. tenth multiple of 8

11. fourth multiple of 7

12. $8 \times 3 = \square$

13. $4 \times 3 = \square$

14. $6 \times 9 = \square$

15. $9 \times 9 = \square$

16. $7 \times 6 = \square$

17. $5 \times 8 = \square$

Write the number of times the product for each is on the multiplication table. Explain.

18. 5×0

19. 9×9

20. 0×0

21. 2×1

22. 10×10

23. 6×4

Name the factors for each product.

24. 36

25. 1

26. 81

27. 8

28. 12

29. 24

30. 100

31. 48

32. 25

33. 72

Think and Apply

34. Make a list of the multiples of 9 from 9 to 90. Add the digits of each multiple. Describe the pattern.

35. **Look back** at the pattern you found in **34.** How can it help you check your answer when you multiply by 9?

36. Find the multiples of 5 on the table. Look at the ones digit of the multiples. Use the pattern to find the ones digit in the product of 14×5.

Explain why you can find products on one side of the diagonal that match products on the other side of the diagonal.

SHOW WHAT YOU KNOW

CHECKPOINT

Find each product. pages 112–115, 118–123

1.	3 ×2	2.	4 ×3	3.	10 × 2	4.	10 × 4	5.	9 ×4	6.	7 ×2	7.	6 ×4

8.	7 ×7	9.	3 ×6	10.	5 ×6	11.	5 ×3	12.	10 × 6	13.	8 ×3	14.	9 ×6

15.	3 ×5	16.	8 ×5	17.	8 ×8	18.	7 ×8	19.	9 ×5	20.	7 ×6	21.	9 ×9

Use the properties. Find each product. pages 116–117

22. $8 \times 4 = 32$ 23. $9 \times 2 = 18$ 24. $7 \times 3 = 21$ 25. $5 \times 6 = 30$

$4 \times 8 = \square$ $2 \times 9 = \square$ $3 \times 7 = \square$ $6 \times 5 = \square$

26. $7 \times 0 = \square$ 27. $6 \times 1 = \square$ 28. $26 \times 1 = \square$ 29. $325 \times 0 = \square$

30. $(1 \times 2) \times 5 = \square$ 31. $(2 \times 2) \times 6 = \square$ 32. $4 \times (0 \times 2) = \square$

Choose the correct word to complete each sentence.

33. The numbers that are multiplied to get a product are the _____.

34. The answer in multiplication is the _____.

35. Knowing that any number multiplied by 0 is 0 is knowing a multiplication _____.

Words to Know
product factors property

Solve.

36. A stone fly has 2 pairs of wings. How many wings are there on 8 stone flies?

37. In the dog show, there are 8 breeds with 8 dogs each and 9 breeds with 10 dogs each. How many breeds are there in all? How many dogs?

How Much Time?

Mr. Sesky's class is going to spend a day at Sea Land park. At the park the students will form small groups and try to see as many different events as possible. They must be back at the bus entrance fifteen minutes before the bus leaves for home. Exhibits that are open all day usually take a half hour to see.

Thinking Critically

Plan a day at Sea Land.

Analyzing and Making Decisions

1. What can be seen at any time? What can be seen only at special times?

2. How much time should you plan for moving from one exhibit to the next? What else do you need to plan for?

3. Which events that can only be seen at special times do you want to see? Which of the other events do you want to see?

SEA LAND	
Park Hours: 9:00 A.M.–8:00 P.M.	
TODAY'S EVENTS	
DOLPHIN SHOW	10:00–10:45
	2:00–2:45
FLAMINGOS	ALL DAY
KILLER WHALE SHOW	10:00–10:30
MINIBUS TOUR	10:00–11:00
	2:00–3:00
PEARL DIVING SHOW	7:00–7:30
PENGUINS	ALL DAY
TROPICAL FISH	ALL DAY
WATER AND LIGHT SHOW	4:00–4:15

4. Plan your day. Are you able to plan all of your time? What don't you know? How does that affect your plans?

Look Back   If you were at the park from 10:00 A.M. to 3:00 P.M., how would you plan your day? If you arrived at 9:00 A.M., how would that change your plan?

Too Much or Too Little Information

Use a calculator where appropriate.

At the Wild Animal Kingdom, Joan and John want to know if their class can ride on the monorail. There are 4 cars on the monorail and each car has the same number of seats. There are 32 students in the class. Can they all ride the monorail at the same time?

Sometimes you do not have all the information you need to solve a problem.

Solving the Problem

Think   What do you need to find out? How many students are in John and Joan's class?

Explore   How many cars are there? How many seats are in each car? Do you have all the information you need to find out if all the students can ride the monorail?

Solve   Can they all ride the monorail at the same time? How many seats does each car need so the whole class could ride?

Look Back   What information do you need to solve the problem?

Share Your Ideas

1. You did not have all the information you needed to solve this problem or the one on page 125. What information did you have that would help you solve each problem?

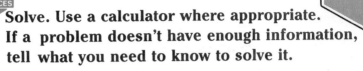

THINK
EXPLORE
SOLVE
LOOK BACK

CHOICES

Solve. Use a calculator where appropriate. If a problem doesn't have enough information, tell what you need to know to solve it.

The Montenaro family is having lunch at the picnic area in Animal Kingdom Park.

2. They need 2 tables to seat everyone. How many people are in the Montenaro family?

3. They rent a stroller for 4 hours. The rental rate is $2 per hour. How much does it cost to rent the stroller?

4. At Roland's table there were 3 more people than at Michael's table. How many people were at Roland's table?

5. The toll for the Keystone Bridge is $1.50. The toll for the Matthew Bridge is twice as much. How much is the toll for the Matthew Bridge?

Mixed Strategy Review

6. Jason bought 6 apples, 12 oranges and 5 cans of soup. How many pieces of fruit did he buy?

Use this information to solve 7 and 8.

KENESHA'S BASKETBALL RECORDS			
	Field Goals	Free Throws	Rebounds
Game 1	12	7	13
Game 2	10	10	17
Game 3	8	9	11

7. Each field goal is worth two points. Each free throw is worth one point. In which of the three games did Kenesha score the most points?

8. How many rebounds did Kenesha make during the three games?

CREATE YOUR OWN

Write a problem that has missing information. Ask a partner to tell you what information is missing.

JOURNAL WRITING

127

ACTIVITY

Investigating Factor Pairs

How many different rectangles can you draw using exactly 12 squares?

Working together

Materials: Workmat 1, ruler

A. Draw as many different rectangles as you can that contain exactly 12 squares.

B. Label each rectangle as shown below.
- Show the number of rows.
- Show the number of small squares in each row.

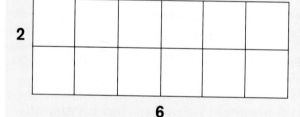

C. Record the numbers in a table like the one below.

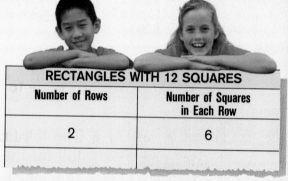

RECTANGLES WITH 12 SQUARES	
Number of Rows	Number of Squares in Each Row
2	6

D. Repeat Steps **A** through **C** using the following numbers: 7, 8, 24.

Sharing Your Results

Look back at the numbers you recorded.

1. For each rectangle with 12 squares, what is the product of the number of rows and the number of squares in a row?
Answer the same question for rectangles with 7, 8, and 24 squares.

2. Which of the numbers 7, 8, 12, or 24 has the greatest number of rectangles?

3. Which of the numbers 7, 8, 12, or 24 has the fewest number of rectangles?

Extending the Activity

The two numbers you recorded for each rectangle form a **factor pair.**

> 2, 6 is a factor pair of 12.
> 1, 8 is a factor pair of 8.

Work on your own.

4. Copy the table at the right.

5. Find all of the factor pairs for the numbers in the table. Make drawings of rectangles to help you.

Number	Factor Pairs
1	
2	
7	
8	
9	
11	
12	1, 12 2, 6 3, 4
18	
20	
24	
36	

Use the information in your table to answer these questions.

6. Which of the numbers have exactly one factor pair?

7. Which of the numbers have more than one factor pair?

Show What You Know

8. There are three numbers between 12 and 20 that each have exactly one factor pair. What are the numbers? Guess first. Then draw rectangles to check your guess.

9. 3, 3 is a factor pair for 9. Which other numbers in the table have factor pairs like this?

10. When both factors of a factor pair are the same, what is the shape of the rectangle?

129

ACTIVITY

Investigating Prime and Composite Numbers

Do the activity below to find which of the numbers from 1 through 20 have exactly two factors?

Working together

Materials: scrap paper, Workmat 1, ruler, completed table from page 129

A. Make a chart like the one shown for the numbers 1 through 20.

B. List the factor pairs for each number on a piece of scrap paper. Use your list of factor pairs from page 129 to get started. Draw rectangles when needed.

C. Look at your list of factor pairs and record each factor only once in the table. The factors for 8 are shown.

Number	Factors
1	
2	
3	
4	
5	
6	
7	
8	1, 2, 4, 8
9	
10	

Sharing Your Results

1. Which of the numbers in the table has exactly one factor?

2. Which of the numbers have exactly two factors?

3. Which of the numbers have more than two factors?

4. What number is a factor of every number?

Extending the Activity

▶ A number with exactly two factors is a **prime number.**

▶ A number with more than two factors is a **composite number.**

> 3 is a prime number.
> Its factors are 1 and 3.

▶ The number 1 has only one factor. It is neither prime nor composite.

> 6 is a composite number.
> Its factors are 1, 2, 3, 6.

Work with a partner.

5. What numbers from 1 through 20 are prime numbers? composite numbers?

6. Find a composite number with exactly 5 factors.

7. List all the factors of each number. Then tell if the number is prime or composite.

   a. 21   **b.** 25   **c.** 23

Show What You Know

8. What is the only prime number that is an even number?

9. How are all prime numbers greater than 2 alike?

10. Are all odd numbers prime numbers?

11. Describe the two factors of every prime number.

Count by 2's to 18. How many numbers did you say? Count by 5's to 30. How many numbers did you say?

Missing Factors

Ed Harrison collects bird eggs from all over the world. He has more than 800,000 eggs on display in his museum.

What if there are 20 eggs in one display case? If there are 4 eggs of each type, how many different types of bird eggs are in the case?

Find what number multiplied by 4 equals 20.

$$\square \times 4 = 20$$

One way to find the missing factor is to count by 4's.

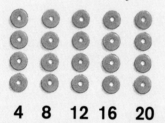

4   8   12   16   20

Another way is to list the multiples of 4.

$0 \times 4 = 0$
$1 \times 4 = 4$
$2 \times 4 = 8$
$3 \times 4 = 12$
$4 \times 4 = 16$
$\boxed{5 \times 4 = 20}$

5 is the missing factor.

There are 5 different types of bird eggs.

Check Your Understanding

Find each missing factor.

1. $\square \times 2 = 8$ **2.** $3 \times \square = 15$ **3.** $\square \times 5 = 45$ **4.** $7 \times \square = 42$

Share Your Ideas   Describe how to use multiples to find the missing factor for $\square \times 6 = 42$.

Find each missing factor.

5. $\square \times 4 = 0$ **6.** $3 \times \square = 27$ **7.** $6 \times \square = 12$ **8.** $\square \times 8 = 24$

9. $\square \times 10 = 10$ **10.** $8 \times \square = 40$ **11.** $\square \times 7 = 28$ **12.** $5 \times \square = 25$

13. $8 \times \square = 32$ **14.** $6 \times \square = 48$ **15.** $7 \times \square = 63$ **16.** $4 \times \square = 24$

17. $\square \times 4 = 6 \times 6$ **18.** $8 \times 2 = 4 \times \square$ **19.** $6 \times \square = 3 \times 10$

Choose the correct number sentence and solve.

20. What if there are 30 hummingbird eggs? If 10 eggs are in each display case, how many display cases of hummingbird eggs are there?

    a. $10 + 30 = \square$ **b.** $\square \times 10 = 30$

    c. $30 - \square = 10$ **d.** $10 \times 30 = \square$

21. Each ostrich egg weighs about 3 pounds. Together, the ostrich eggs weigh a total of 18 pounds. How many ostrich eggs are there?

    a. $18 \times \square = 3$ **b.** $3 + 18 = \square$

    c. $18 - 3 = \square$ **d.** $3 \times \square = 18$

Think and Apply

22. Eight hummingbird eggs together weigh the same as one penny. How many pennies are equal to the weight of 72 hummingbird eggs?

Use the same number for each $\square$. What different numbers will make each sentence true?

23. $49 = \square \times \square$ **24.** $60 - 51 = \square \times \square$

25. $\square \times \square + 2 < 4$ **26.** $\square + \square + \square = 3 \times \square$

Describe different ways you could use to solve $5 \times \square = 500$.

SHOW WHAT YOU KNOW

What if you and 3 friends want to share 40 counters equally? How can you decide how many counters to give each person?

2 and 4 as Divisors

The park ranger has 20 eaglets. She places 2 eaglets in each nest where eggs have not hatched. How many nests can she fill?

You can write a multiplication sentence and find the missing factor. Or you can divide.

Multiply.	Divide.
□ × 2 = 20 10 × 2 = 20	20 ÷ 2 = 10 ← quotient ↑ dividend ↑ divisor 10 ← quotient 2)‾2‾0‾ ↑ divisor ↑ dividend

10 × 2 = 20 and 20 ÷ 2 = 10 are related facts.

The ranger can fill 10 nests.

More Examples

a. 20 ÷ 4 = □
　Think □ × 4 = 20
　　　5 × 4 = 20
20 ÷ 4 = 5　　　4)‾2‾0‾ = 5

b. 16 ÷ 2 = □
　Think □ × 2 = 16
　　　8 × 2 = 16
16 ÷ 2 = 8　　　2)‾1‾6‾ = 8

▶ When you divide, think of the related multiplication fact.

Check Your Understanding

Find each quotient.

1. 2 ÷ 2 = □　　　　**2.** 12 ÷ 4 = □　　　　**3.** 8 ÷ 2 = □

4. 2)‾1‾0‾　　**5.** 4)‾1‾6‾　　**6.** 4)‾3‾6‾　　**7.** 2)‾1‾4‾　　**8.** 4)‾2‾4‾　　**9.** 2)‾1‾8‾

Share Your Ideas Explain how to use multiplication to find the quotient of 14 ÷ 2.

Find each quotient.

10. $10 \div 2 = \square$ **11.** $28 \div 4 = \square$

12. $8 \div 2 = \square$ **13.** $16 \div 2 = \square$

14. $12 \div 4 = \square$ **15.** $32 \div 4 = \square$

16. $28 \div 4 = \square$ **17.** $16 \div 2 = \square$

18. $2\overline{)6}$ **19.** $4\overline{)8}$ **20.** $4\overline{)20}$ **21.** $2\overline{)2}$

22. $4\overline{)4}$ **23.** $2\overline{)18}$ **24.** $4\overline{)32}$ **25.** $2\overline{)14}$

26. $4\overline{)40}$ **27.** $2\overline{)20}$ **28.** $4\overline{)16}$ **29.** $2\overline{)12}$

30. $4\overline{)36}$ **31.** $4\overline{)24}$ **32.** $2\overline{)4}$ **33.** $4\overline{)20}$

Compare. Use $>$, $<$, or $=$ for ⬤.

34. $10 \div 2$ ⬤ 2×9 **35.** $24 \div 4$ ⬤ 3×2

36. $20 \div 4$ ⬤ $16 \div 4$ **37.** $16 \div 2$ ⬤ $36 \div 4$

38. $20 \div 2$ ⬤ $40 \div 4$ **39.** $18 \div 2$ ⬤ $28 \div 4$

Think and Apply

40. Choose each fact related to $12 \div 4 = 3$.
a. $12 - 4 = 8$
b. $4 \times 3 = 12$
c. $12 \div 3 = 4$
d. $3 + 9 = 12$

41. Choose each fact related to $16 \div 8 = 2$.
a. $8 \times 2 = 16$
b. $8 + 2 = 10$
c. $16 \div 2 = 8$
d. $16 - 8 = 8$

Write two multiplication and two division sentences using the numbers 2, 4, and 8. How are the products and the dividends related?

SHOW WHAT YOU KNOW

Mixed Review

1. $35 + 8 + 27$

2. $46 + 23 + 32$

3. $14 + 37 + 8$

4. $249 - 183$

5. $\$4.58 + \$3.97$

6. $\$8.00 - \$4.73$

Round to the nearest hundred.

7. 385   **8.** 749

9. 2,620   **10.** 4,299

11. 7,450   **12.** 2,087

Find each time.

13. 3 hours after

14. 1 hour before

15. 1 hour and 15 minutes after 4:20

16. 35 minutes before 9:45

135

Write 4 related multiplication and division facts using the numbers 3, 6, and 18.

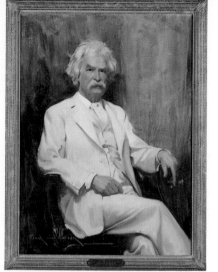

National Portrait Gallery, Smithsonian Institution; Gift of the artist

3 and 6 as Divisors

In 1865, Mark Twain wrote the story "The Celebrated Jumping Frog of Calaveras County." Since then, frog-jumping contests have been held every year in the United States.

There were 24 frogs in the first frog-jumping contest in Dayton. At the start of the contest, the frogs were placed in groups of 3. How many groups were there?

$24 \div 3 = \square$

You can write a multiplication sentence. Then find the missing factor.	You can divide.
Think $\square \times 3 = 24$ $8 \times 3 = 24$	$24 \div 3 = 8 \quad 3\overline{)24}^{\,8}$ How could you make a drawing to find the quotient?

There were 8 groups of frogs.

More Examples

a. $24 \div 6 = \square$
   Think $\square \times 6 = 24$
   $4 \times 6 = 24$
   $24 \div 6 = 4 \qquad 6\overline{)24}^{\,4}$

b. $48 \div 6 = \square$
   Think $\square \times 6 = 48$
   $8 \times 6 = 48$
   $48 \div 6 = 8 \qquad 6\overline{)48}^{\,8}$

Check Your Understanding

Find each quotient.

1. $9 \div 3 = \square$

2. $12 \div 6 = \square$

3. $21 \div 3 = \square$

4. $6\overline{)36}$

5. $3\overline{)12}$

6. $6\overline{)54}$

7. $3\overline{)15}$

8. $6\overline{)42}$

9. $3\overline{)27}$

Share Your Ideas Describe three different ways to find the quotient of $18 \div 3$.

Divide.

10. $36 \div 6 = \square$ **11.** $30 \div 3 = \square$ **12.** $48 \div 6 = \square$

13. $3\overline{)3}$ **14.** $6\overline{)18}$ **15.** $3\overline{)12}$ **16.** $3\overline{)6}$ **17.** $4\overline{)32}$ **18.** $1\overline{)6}$

19. $6\overline{)30}$ **20.** $3\overline{)27}$ **21.** $3\overline{)24}$ **22.** $3\overline{)18}$ **23.** $3\overline{)9}$ **24.** $6\overline{)54}$

25. $3\overline{)15}$ **26.** $6\overline{)42}$ **27.** $3\overline{)21}$ **28.** $6\overline{)24}$ **29.** $2\overline{)18}$ **30.** $6\overline{)12}$

Find the rule. Then complete each table.

31. Rule: ?

Input	Output
12	2
24	4
32. 6	
33. 36	
54	9

34. Rule: ?

	Input	Output
35.	6	
	12	4
	27	9
36.	24	
	15	5

37. Rule: ?

	Input	Output
	4	1
38.	36	
	16	4
	8	2
39.	24	

Think and Apply

40. In some contests, frogs are given 15 seconds to make 3 jumps. One frog jumped about 6 feet on each jump. About how many feet did it jump in all three jumps?

41. What if the frog that won the contest jumped a total of 21 feet in 3 jumps? Each jump was about the same length. About how many feet was each jump?

42. There are 40 frogs entered in a frog-jumping contest. Only 8 frogs can race at a time. How many races will there have to be to find a winner?

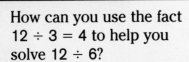

How can you use the fact $12 \div 3 = 4$ to help you solve $12 \div 6$?

SHOW WHAT YOU KNOW

Write the multiples of 5 up to 100. Write the multiples of 10 up to 100. Which numbers appear in both lists?

5 and 10 as Divisors

There are 30 students going on a trip to the zoo. Each van can carry 5 students. How many vans are needed for the trip?

$30 \div 5 = \square$

Think $\square \times 5 = 30$
$\quad\quad\quad 6 \times 5 = 30$

$30 \div 5 = 6$

$$5\overline{)30} = 6$$

Six vans are needed.

What if there were 29 students going? How many vans would be needed?

More Examples

a. $60 \div 10 = \square$

Think $\square \times 10 = 60$
$\quad\quad\quad 6 \times 10 = 60$

$60 \div 10 = 6$

$$10\overline{)60} = 6$$

b. $15 \div 5 = \square$

Think $\square \times 5 = 15$
$\quad\quad\quad 3 \times 5 = 15$

$15 \div 5 = 3$

$$5\overline{)15} = 3$$

Check Your Understanding

Divide.

1. $25 \div 5 = \square$

2. $40 \div 10 = \square$

3. $45 \div 5 = \square$

4. $100 \div 10 = \square$

5. $15 \div 5 = \square$

6. $90 \div 10 = \square$

7. $5\overline{)40}$

8. $5\overline{)35}$

9. $10\overline{)80}$

10. $5\overline{)20}$

11. $10\overline{)50}$

12. $10\overline{)70}$

Share Your Ideas   Make a list of the multiples of 10 from 10 to 100. Divide each number by 10. Describe how the quotient is like the dividend.

Find each quotient.

13. $10 \div 10 = \square$ **14.** $35 \div 5 = \square$ **15.** $40 \div 5 = \square$

16. $5\overline{)15}$ **17.** $10\overline{)20}$ **18.** $5\overline{)30}$ **19.** $10\overline{)80}$ **20.** $10\overline{)30}$ **21.** $5\overline{)20}$

22. $5\overline{)10}$ **23.** $5\overline{)45}$ **24.** $10\overline{)60}$ **25.** $10\overline{)90}$ **26.** $4\overline{)28}$ **27.** $10\overline{)40}$

28. $5\overline{)25}$ **29.** $6\overline{)42}$ **30.** $5\overline{)50}$ **31.** $10\overline{)70}$ **32.** $10\overline{)50}$ **33.** $5\overline{)5}$

Find each missing number.

34. $\square \times 5 = 45$ **35.** $6 \times \square = 60$ **36.** $\square \div 5 = 7$

Write +, −, ×, or ÷ in the ○ to make each sentence true.

37. $5 \div 5 = 10 \bigcirc 10$ **38.** $14 \div 2 = 3 \bigcirc 4$

39. $12 \div 2 < 3 \bigcirc 3$ **40.** $4 \times 2 > 28 \bigcirc 4$

Think and Apply

41. The king cobra is about 18 feet long. This is about 3 times the length of a common cobra. About how many feet long is a common cobra?

42. The shortest non-poisonous snake in the world is the thread snake. The length of 10 thread snakes is about 60 inches. About how long is one thread snake?

DATA
43. Conduct a survey. List 4 or 5 animals that are found at a zoo. Ask 20 people to pick their favorite animal. Make a bar graph to show your results.

Logical Thinking

- One zoo has 6 snakes in all.
- Their total length is 31 feet.
- There is at least one of each snake listed in the table.
- There are more cobras than water moccasins.

44. How many of each kind of snake are in the zoo?

Snakes	Length (in feet)
Cobra	6
Copperhead	2
Rattlesnake	7
Water Moccasin	4

Describe numbers that can be divided evenly by 10. Can they also be divided evenly by 5?

SHOW WHAT YOU KNOW

Which gives the greater quotient, dividing a number by 6 or by 7?

7, 8, and 9 as Divisors

Dairy cows are milked in milking parlors. There are 63 cows on Bucks Dairy Farm. If 7 cows can be milked in one shift, how many shifts will it take to milk all the cows?

$63 \div 7 = \square$

Think $\square \times 7 = 63$
$\quad\quad 9 \times 7 = 63$

$63 \div 7 = 9$ $\quad\quad 7\overline{)63}$ $\;^{9}$

It will take 9 shifts to milk all the cows.

What if there were 64 cows? How many shifts would it take?

More Examples

a. $56 \div 8 = \square$

Think $\square \times 8 = 56$
$\quad\quad 7 \times 8 = 56$

$56 \div 8 = 7$ $\quad\quad 8\overline{)56}$ $\;^{7}$

b. $72 \div 9 = \square$

Think $\square \times 9 = 72$
$\quad\quad 8 \times 9 = 72$

$72 \div 9 = 8$ $\quad\quad 9\overline{)72}$ $\;^{8}$

Check Your Understanding

Find each quotient.

1. $16 \div 8 = \square$ **2.** $9 \div 9 = \square$ **3.** $14 \div 7 = \square$

4. $8\overline{)32}$ **5.** $9\overline{)81}$ **6.** $8\overline{)24}$ **7.** $9\overline{)45}$ **8.** $8\overline{)56}$ **9.** $7\overline{)49}$

Share Your Ideas What if you forgot the division fact for $54 \div 9$? Discuss other ways you could find the quotient.

Divide.

10. $18 \div 9 = \square$ 11. $40 \div 8 = \square$ 12. $21 \div 7 = \square$

13. $90 \div 9 = \square$ 14. $28 \div 7 = \square$ 15. $70 \div 7 = \square$

16. $7\overline{)42}$ 17. $8\overline{)72}$ 18. $9\overline{)45}$ 19. $9\overline{)54}$ 20. $7\overline{)35}$ 21. $8\overline{)48}$

22. $9\overline{)81}$ 23. $8\overline{)56}$ 24. $8\overline{)32}$ 25. $9\overline{)63}$ 26. $9\overline{)36}$ 27. $8\overline{)80}$

28. $7\overline{)56}$ 29. $9\overline{)27}$ 30. $7\overline{)63}$ 31. $9\overline{)72}$ 32. $8\overline{)64}$ 33. $7\overline{)49}$

For each of the exercises below fill each $\square$ with the same number to make the sentence true.

34. $\square + \square + \square + \square = 36$ 35. $64 \div \square = \square$

36. $\square \times \square + 1 = 82$ 37. $80 \div \square + 2 = 10$

Think and Apply

38. The dairy farmer has a total of 72 bales of hay to place out in the field. He wants to put the same amount of hay in 8 different locations. How many bales should he place in each location?

39. **Look back** at the problem at the top of page 140. **What if** the owner of Bucks Dairy Farm purchased 35 more cows? How many shifts would it take to milk all the cows on the farm?

Name each mystery number.

40. If you divide the mystery number by 8, you get 2.

41. If you divide the mystery number by 7, you get 4.

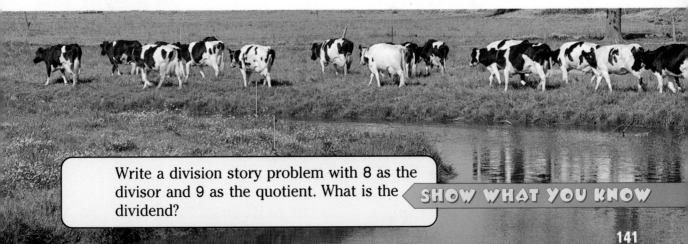

Write a division story problem with 8 as the divisor and 9 as the quotient. What is the dividend?

SHOW WHAT YOU KNOW

141

0 and 1 in Division

0 and 1 are special numbers.

▶ When you divide a number by 1, the quotient is that number.

$8 \div 1 = 8$ $1\overline{)8}^{\,8}$ Think $\square \times 1 = 8$
                                         $8 \times 1 = 8$

▶ When you divide any number by itself, the quotient is 1.

$5 \div 5 = 1$ $5\overline{)5}^{\,1}$ Think $\square \times 5 = 5$
                                         $1 \times 5 = 5$

▶ When you divide 0 by any number, except zero, the quotient is 0.

$0 \div 2 = 0$ $2\overline{)0}^{\,0}$ Think $\square \times 2 = 0$
                                         $0 \times 2 = 0$

▶ You cannot divide a number by 0.

$4 \div 0 = \square$ Think $\square \times 0 = 4$ There is no number that will make this sentence true.

$0 \div 0 = \square$ Think $\square \times 0 = 0$ There is no single number that will make this sentence true.

Check Your Understanding

Solve.

1. $0 \div 7 = \square$ **2.** $9 \div 1 = \square$ **3.** $10 \div 10 = \square$ **4.** $0 \div 9 = \square$

Share Your Ideas What numbers from 0 through 10 will make this sentence true: $\square \div \square = 1$? Use the same number in each $\square$.

Find each quotient. If you cannot divide, explain why.

5. $7 \div 0 = \square$

6. $63 \div 7 = \square$

7. $9 \div 1 = \square$

8. $81 \div 9 = \square$

9. $0 \div 0 = \square$

10. $7 \div 1 = \square$

11. $1\overline{)6}$

12. $3\overline{)0}$

13. $1\overline{)6}$

14. $8\overline{)8}$

15. $1\overline{)10}$

16. $3\overline{)15}$

17. $4\overline{)4}$

18. $1\overline{)4}$

19. $9\overline{)0}$

20. $8\overline{)24}$

21. $0\overline{)6}$

22. $2\overline{)20}$

Use patterns and mental math to find each quotient.

23. $15 \div 1 = \square$

24. $0 \div 36 = \square$

25. $48 \div 48 = \square$

26. $182 \div 182 = \square$

27. $500 \div 1 = \square$

28. $0 \div 999 = \square$

Think and Apply

Write the related multiplication and division facts for each.

29. 5, 6, 30

30. 6, 7, 42

31. 1, 9, 9

32. 0, 0, 4

33. 8, 4, 32

34. 10, 15, 150

Logical Thinking

Use each number once from the sign at the right to complete this story.

35. A prairie dog is a rodent that makes barking sounds like a dog. The tail of a prairie dog is about _____(a) inches long. The length of a prairie dog is about 4 times the length of its tail, or about _____(b) inches long. The prairie dog uses its feet to dig tunnels for shelter. Each of the prairie dog's _____(c) front feet has 4 toes. Each of its 2 back feet has _____(d) toes. Altogether, a prairie dog has _____(e) toes.

When will you have only one multiplication and one related division fact? Write the related facts for two examples.

SHOW WHAT YOU KNOW

Even and Odd Numbers

Can you predict whether the sum of two addends
will be even or odd? Experiment to find out.

Working together

A. Predict these results.
even + even = _____
even + odd = _____
odd + odd = _____

B. Test your predictions.
Make up some addition examples.
Record the examples in a table
like the one shown. Tell whether
each sum is even or odd.

C. Explore subtraction with even and
odd numbers. Make up some
examples and a subtraction table
to record the results.

D. Repeat step **C**, using multiplication
examples.

Example		Sum
	even + even	
	even + odd	
	odd + odd	

Sharing Your Ideas

Look back at your tables.

1. What do you know about the addends if the sum is
odd? if the sum is even?

2. What is the result of subtracting two even numbers?
two odd numbers? When is a difference odd?

3. What do you know about the factors if the
product is odd? if the product is even?

Extending Your Thinking

Work on your own. Use a calculator to explore operations with even and odd numbers. Do the patterns you discovered hold true for greater numbers?

Try these exercises.

4. 2,375 + 86,412

5. 46,238 − 21,375

6. 13,865 + 17,293

7. 2,864 × 1,394

8. 61,689 − 35,237

9. 3,895 × 2,438

10. Try some numbers on your own. Did you find any numbers that do not follow the patterns you discovered?

Show What You Know

11. Choose the example whose sum is odd. Explain how you know.

a. 12
  + 26

b. 45
  + 23

c. 38
  + 25

12. Choose the example whose product is even. Explain how you know.

a. 18
  × 3

b. 13
  × 9

c. 23
  × 3

13. Write a story about even and odd numbers.

THINK
EXPLORE
SOLVE
LOOK BACK

145

ACTIVITY

Investigating Inverse Operations

Mystery Number [?]

The result is [23].

The mystery number has been entered.
Our first contestant multiplied by 3.
Our second contestant added 5.
The result is 23.

It's your turn to solve the mystery.

Materials: calculator

A. Choose any number. Add 5. Then subtract 5. What is the result? Try it with other numbers. After adding, what can you do to get back to the original number?

B. Use your calculator. Choose any number. Multiply by 3. Divide by 3. What is the result? Try it with other numbers. After multiplying, what can you do to get back to the original number?

C. Look at the flowchart. Explain how you can work backward to find the mystery number.

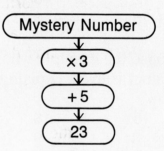

Sharing Your Results

1. Suppose you added 5 to a number. What can you do to get back to the original number?

2. Suppose you divided a number by 4. What can you do to get back to the original number?

Extending the Activity

Addition and subtraction are **inverse operations.**

Multiplication and division are **inverse operations.**

**Work on your own. Use your calculator and
inverse operations to find each mystery number.**

3.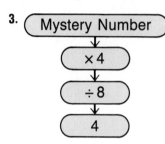

4.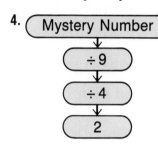

5.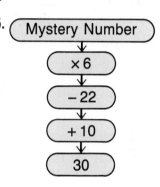

**Play the Mystery Number game with a partner.
Take turns. Use your calculator.**

6. Enter a number secretly in your calculator.

7. Enter a sequence of operations and numbers.
Have your partner record them.

8. When the result is displayed, give the calculator
to your partner to find the mystery number.

Show What You Know

9. Describe the method
you use to find a
mystery number.
Explain why the
method works.

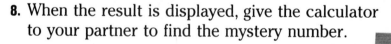
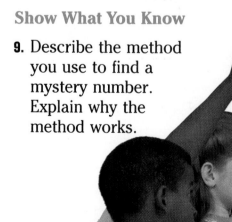

MEXICAN ENCHILADAS

WORKING TOGETHER

1. Work in small groups. Look in an encyclopedia or book about Mexico. Find three foods that are grown there. Make a list of the foods.

   • Are any of the foods grown where you live?

   • Are any sold in stores where you live?

   Compare your list with those of other groups.

2. The ingredients listed in the chart below show what to buy to make Mexican enchiladas for 4 people. How much of each ingredient would be needed to make enchiladas for 8 people? for 40 people?

MEXICAN ENCHILADAS			
Ingredients for Mexican Enchiladas	Number of Servings		
	4	8	40
tortillas	4 tortillas		
oil	3 tablespoons		
cheese	2 ounces		
hot peppers	1 tablespoon		
chili powder	1 tablespoon		
enchilada sauce	6 tablespoons		
tomatoes	2 medium		

3. Compare your chart with those of other groups. Discuss how you could calculate the amount of each ingredient needed for 80 people.

CHAPTER REVIEW/TEST

Multiply.

1. 3 ×2	**2.** 5 ×4	**3.** 9 ×6	**4.** 4 ×3
5. 8 ×5	**6.** 9 ×1	**7.** 6 ×0	**8.** 4 ×9
9. 7 ×8	**10.** 5 ×9	**11.** 8 ×6	**12.** 9 ×9

13. 6 × 7 = □   **14.** 5 × 0 = □   **15.** 8 × 10 = □

Find each missing factor.

16. 6 × □ = 54   **17.** □ × 8 = 64   **18.** 5 × □ = 5

19. □ × 5 = 45   **20.** 7 × □ = 63   **21.** □ × 9 = 72

Divide.

22. 5)25   **23.** 4)32   **24.** 1)9   **25.** 6)36

26. 27 ÷ 9 = □   **27.** 64 ÷ 8 = □   **28.** 49 ÷ 7 = □

29. 90 ÷ 10 = □   **30.** 0 ÷ 5 = □   **31.** 6 ÷ 6 = □

Solve. If there is not enough information, tell what is missing.

32. The trainer had 48 huskies. He needed the same number of dogs for each of 6 dog sled teams. How many dogs were on each team?

33. Each day, Nancy frames 6 pictures of animals. It takes about 10 minutes to frame each picture. How many days will it take her to frame all her pictures?

 Think The library has 45 books about animals. There are 6 each about cats, insects, birds, fish, whales, and monkeys. The rest of the books are about dogs. How many books about dogs does the library have?

EXTENSION

Factor Trees

The factors of 24 are 1, 2, 3, 4, 6, 8, 12, and 24.
The prime factors of 24 are 2 and 3.

▶A **prime factor** is a factor that is a prime number.

You can use a factor tree to find prime factors.
Here is how to make a factor tree for 24.

Write 24 at the top of the tree.

Find two factors that have a product of 24.

Find factors whose products are 4 and 6.

24
4 × 6

24
4 × 6
2 × 2 × 2 × 3

2 and 3 are
prime numbers.

24 can be written as 2 × 2 × 2 × 3.
The prime factors of 24 are 2 and 3.

Here is another factor tree for 24.
Notice that the prime factors of a number
are always the same.

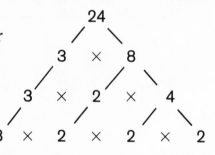

Complete these factor trees.

1.
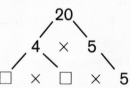

2.
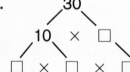

3.
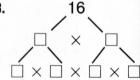

Draw a factor tree to find the prime factors of each number.

4. 8   5. 63   6. 50   7. 48

8. **Look back** at **1** through **3**. Then design your own factor tree.

150

MAINTAINING SKILLS

Choose the correct answer. Write A, B, C, or D.

1.
```
   826
 +379
```
A 1,195   C 1,105

B 1,205   D not given

2. $863.13 + $24.45 = □

A $888.56   C $838.68

B $887.58   D not given

3.
```
   90,038
 −24,634
```
A 65,404   C 74,635

B 66,404   D not given

4. What time is it?

A 1:50   C 12:10

B 12:50   D not given

5. About how many miles did Mr. Owen travel in 1990?

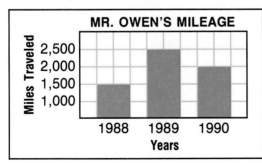

MR. OWEN'S MILEAGE

A 1,300   C 1,400

B 2,500   D not given

6. $(2 \times 4) \times 3 = □$

A 24   C 9

B 18   D not given

7. $9 \times □ = 63$

A 7   C 6

B 8   D not given

8. $60 \div 10 = □$

A 10   C 12

B 6   D not given

Use the table to solve 9–10.

FURNITURE DELIVERY RATES

Distance	Cost
0–10 miles	$25.00
11–50 miles	$35.00
51–100 miles	$50.00
more than 100	$60.00

9. How much more does it cost to deliver furniture 75 miles than to deliver it 15 miles?

A $60.00   C $10.00

B $25.00   D not given

10. How many families were moved a total of 8 miles each if the moving company collected a total of $75.00 from all the families?

A 2   C 4

B 3   D not given

5 Multiplying by One-Digit Numbers

Sharing What You Know

Traffic jams! Horns beeping! People late! Cars everywhere! Even small towns have traffic problems. What kinds of vehicles help to reduce traffic on our highways? Why do these vehicles help? If you were reporting on the traffic, how would you use mathematics in your work?

Using Language

Pollution! Fuel cost! Traffic! Today, people are worried about the large number of cars on the highways. Some people join car pools. In this way **multiple** groups of people can get to their jobs in fewer cars. When we use the word **multiple** in mathematics, we think of a number that is the product of two numbers. Can you think of some things that come in multiples of 2?

Words to Know: multiple, factor, product, estimate, regroup, decimal point, dollar sign

Be a Problem Solver

Your class is leaving on a field trip at 8 A.M. You need to decide how many vehicles you will use. If a car can carry 5 students and a van can carry 8 students, how many cars and vans would you plan to use? **What if** you wanted to use the fewest number of vehicles?

Write a short article explaining to drivers why car pools are important.

THINK AND SHARE > How are these sums alike? different?
$2 + 2 = \square$ $20 + 20 = \square$ $200 + 200 = \square$

Mental Math: Exploring Patterns

You can multiply numbers mentally! Use what you know about basic facts and follow the patterns below.

$3 \times 2 = 6$
$3 \times 20 = 3 \times 2 \times 10 = 60$
$3 \times 200 = 3 \times 2 \times 100 = 600$
$3 \times 2,000 = 3 \times 2 \times 1,000 = 6,000$

$4 \times 7 = 28$
$4 \times 70 = 280$
$4 \times 700 = 2,800$
$4 \times 7,000 = 28,000$

What patterns do you see?

Make up a rule to help you multiply mentally when one factor is a multiple of 10, 100, or 1,000.

Does your rule work for these products? Why or why not?

5	50	500	5,000
$\times 2$	$\times 2$	$\times 2$	$\times 2$
10	100	1,000	10,000

Check Your Understanding

Use your rule. Find these products mentally.

1. $2 \times 7 = \square$
   $2 \times 70 = \square$
   $2 \times 700 = \square$
   $2 \times 7,000 = \square$

2. $4 \times 6 = \square$
   $4 \times 60 = \square$
   $4 \times 600 = \square$
   $4 \times 6,000 = \square$

3. $9 \times 2 = \square$
   $9 \times 20 = \square$
   $9 \times 200 = \square$
   $9 \times 2,000 = \square$

4. 30
   $\times 9$

5. 400
   $\times 5$

6. 200
   $\times 8$

7. 2,000
   $\times 5$

8. 6,000
   $\times 8$

Share Your Ideas   How does knowing $9 \times 7 = 63$ help you find the product of $9 \times 70,000$?

Multiply mentally. Use patterns to help you.

9. $2 \times 3 = \square$
$2 \times 30 = \square$
$2 \times 300 = \square$
$2 \times 3,000 = \square$

10. $4 \times 4 = \square$
$4 \times 40 = \square$
$4 \times 400 = \square$
$4 \times 4,000 = \square$

11. $5 \times 6 = \square$
$5 \times 60 = \square$
$5 \times 600 = \square$
$5 \times 6,000 = \square$

12. $\begin{array}{r} 10 \\ \times\ 7 \\ \hline \end{array}$

13. $\begin{array}{r} 30 \\ \times\ 6 \\ \hline \end{array}$

14. $\begin{array}{r} 50 \\ \times\ 8 \\ \hline \end{array}$

15. $\begin{array}{r} 90 \\ \times\ 4 \\ \hline \end{array}$

16. $\begin{array}{r} 300 \\ \times\ 5 \\ \hline \end{array}$

17. $\begin{array}{r} 900 \\ \times\ 6 \\ \hline \end{array}$

18. $\begin{array}{r} 100 \\ \times\ 8 \\ \hline \end{array}$

19. $\begin{array}{r} 7,000 \\ \times\ 4 \\ \hline \end{array}$

20. $\begin{array}{r} 3,000 \\ \times\ 9 \\ \hline \end{array}$

21. $\begin{array}{r} 9,000 \\ \times\ 5 \\ \hline \end{array}$

Follow the rule to find each output.

Rule: Multiply by 8.

	Input	Output
22.	10	
23.	20	
24.	30	
25.	40	

Rule: Multiply by 200.

	Input	Output
26.	2	
27.	3	
28.	4	
29.	5	

Rule: Multiply by 4,000.

	Input	Output
30.	4	
31.	5	
32.	6	
33.	7	

Think and Apply

34. Bus tickets are sold in books of 20. How many tickets are there in 9 books? 90 books? 900 books?

35. Bridge tokens are sold in rolls of 8. How many tokens are there in 500 rolls?

36. When a mystery number is multiplied by 9, the product is 3,600. What is the number?

37. When a mystery number is multiplied by 7, the product is 56,000. What is the number?

Visual Thinking

38. Here are three views of a cube.

What is opposite the ★?

Explain how to find the product of $8 \times 70,000$.

SHOW WHAT YOU KNOW

Would you round each of these numbers to the same place or a different place?
64   79   150   324   7,392   8,601

Estimating Products

The Pony Express was started in 1860 to carry mail between Missouri and California. One day a rider used 5 different horses. He rode each horse 17 miles. Did he ride more than 100 miles in all?

Sometimes an estimate is all you need.

One way to estimate the product is to round. Then multiply the rounded factors.

$$\begin{array}{r} 17 \\ \times\ 5 \end{array} \xrightarrow{\text{rounds to}} \begin{array}{r} 20 \\ \times\ 5 \\ \hline 100 \end{array} \longleftarrow \text{estimated product}$$

Explain how you can use the estimate to tell that the rider traveled less than 100 miles.

Another Example

Estimate 4 × 321.

$$\begin{array}{r} 321 \\ \times\ 4 \end{array} \xrightarrow{\text{rounds to}} \begin{array}{r} 300 \\ \times\ 4 \\ \hline 1,200 \end{array} \longleftarrow \text{estimated product}$$

Predict whether the exact product will be greater or less than the estimate. Explain.

Check Your Understanding

Estimate each product. Predict whether the exact product will be greater or less than the estimate.

1.	2.	3.	4.	5.
27	51	139	372	260
× 2	× 4	× 3	× 2	× 5

Share Your Ideas Explain why rounding to estimate 3 × 15 gives a product greater than the exact product.

Estimate each product.

6. 35
   × 2

7. 29
   × 5

8. 52
   × 3

9. 87
   × 5

10. 74
    × 6

11. 408
    × 3

12. 267
    × 4

13. 392
    × 2

14. 123
    × 8

15. 758
    × 9

16. 214
    × 7

17. 150
    × 4

18. 950
    × 3

19. 628
    × 8

20. 564
    × 5

21. 4 × 329

22. 6 × 635

23. 5 × 199

24. 8 × 450

25. 2 × 3,615

26. 5 × 25,000

Choose the most reasonable estimate.

27. The time it takes to drive 100 miles in a car
    1 hour   2 hours   10 hours

28. The distance Kim walks to school each day
    1 mile   10 miles   100 miles

29. If Megan rides her bike about 14 miles a week, the number of miles she rides in a month
    25 miles   50 miles   90 miles

30. If Henry earns $35 each week, the amount of money he earns in 6 weeks
    $60 $100 $200

Think and Apply

31. A Pony Express rider worked 12 hours a day, every day of the week. Did a rider work more or less than 70 hours a week? Explain.

32. The trip from St. Joseph to Sacramento took 9 days. Riders traveled 204 miles each day. About how many miles was the trip in all?

Write one possible multiplication example for each.

33. One factor is 4.
    The estimated product is 160.

34. One factor is 79.
    The estimated product is 240.

JOURNAL WRITING
Does rounding to estimate 438 × 5 give a product greater than or less than the exact product? Explain.

SHOW WHAT YOU KNOW

Investigating Multiplication

Steve and Taka are playing Toss-Up to Win. They are each trying to write a multiplication example that has the greatest product. Steve tossed the digits 1, 3, and 5.

Steve wrote 3 × 51.

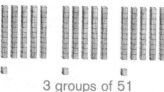

3 groups of 51

Taka wrote 5 × 31.

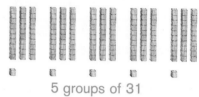

5 groups of 31

Whose product is greater? How do you know?

Working together

Play Toss-Up to Win until one player gets 10 points. Build the greatest product you can.

Materials: 3 number cubes, base-ten blocks

Game rules for each player

A. Roll 3 number cubes. Use the numbers to make a 1-digit factor and a 2-digit factor. Write the factors.

B. Estimate to predict whose product will be greater. Write the estimates.

C. Use base-ten blocks to show the multiplication. Compare. Whose product is greater?

D. Win 1 point for having the greater product. Win 1 point for predicting the greater product.

Sharing Your Results

1. Use base-ten blocks to show 6 × 15. Explain how you can use the fact that 15 = 10 + 5.

2. Explain how estimation can help you win the game.

Extending the Activity

Work in a small group.

3. Complete a chart like the one shown below to find each product. Use base-ten blocks to show the multiplication.

4. Show the product using the least number of blocks possible.

5. Roll 3 number cubes to make your own factors. Do three more examples.

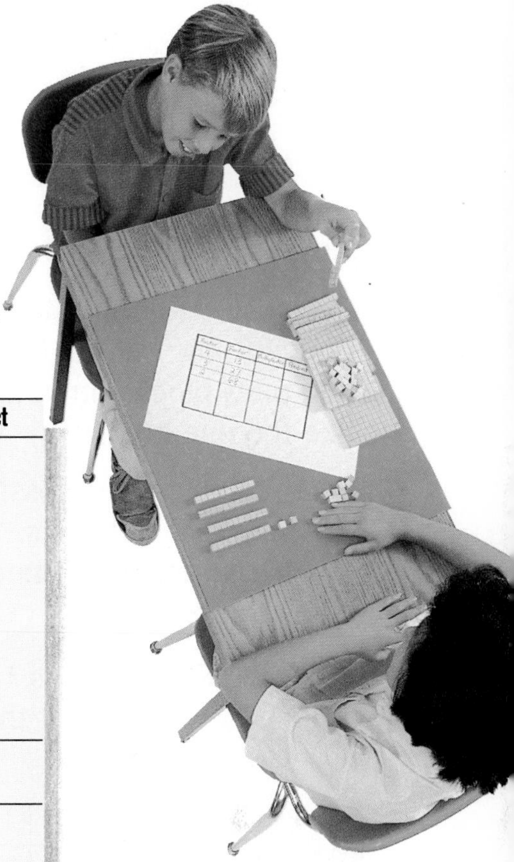

Factor	Factor	Multiplication	Product
4	13		52
3	27		
2	68		

Show What You Know

6. **Look back** at your chart. When did you need to regroup the blocks? How could you tell?

7. Write *true* or *false*. Discuss.
   a. When you multiply whole numbers, the product is always greater than the factors.

   b. Adding $12 + 12 + 12$ is the same as multiplying 3×12.

ACTIVITY

Understanding Multiplication

In multiplication, how is regrouping tens like regrouping ones?

Working together

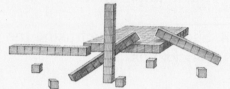

Materials: base-ten blocks, Workmat 6

A. Use base-ten blocks to show 2 groups of 54. Combine the blocks. Record the number of tens and ones blocks on your workmat or on a chart like the one below.

B. Regroup whenever possible so you are using the least number of blocks. Record the number of hundreds, tens, and ones after regrouping. Write the product.

C. Repeat steps **A** and **B** for 4 groups of 54. Then repeat the steps using numbers that you choose.

Number of Groups	Number in Each Group	Before Regrouping			After Regrouping			Product
		Total Number of Hundreds	Tens	Ones	Total Number of Hundreds	Tens	Ones	
2	54							
4	54							

Sharing Your Results

1. Look at the first line of the chart above. What digit is in the tens place after regrouping? Why?

2. Look at the second line of the chart. What digit is in the tens place after regrouping? Why?

3. How can you tell when you need to regroup ones for tens?

4. How can you tell when you need to regroup tens for hundreds?

Extending the Activity

Look at the multiplication examples below.
How are they the same? Describe how each
shows multiplication.

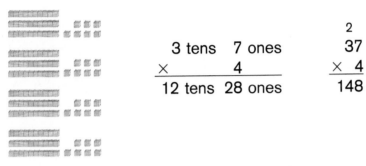

$$
\begin{array}{r}
3 \text{ tens} \quad 7 \text{ ones} \\
\times \qquad\qquad 4 \\
\hline
12 \text{ tens} \quad 28 \text{ ones}
\end{array}
$$

$$
\begin{array}{r}
2 \\
37 \\
\times \ 4 \\
\hline
148
\end{array}
$$

**Find the product. Choose one of the methods
above. Estimate to be sure your answer
makes sense.**

5. 4 groups of 16

6. 3 groups of 26

7. 7 groups of 14

8. 5 groups of 32

9. 2 groups of 63

10. 6 groups of 19

Show What You Know

11. Which method of multiplication did you
choose for **5** through **10**? Explain your choices.

12. What is the greatest number of groups of 27
that will have a total less than 100?

13. Describe how to use base-ten blocks to find
the product for 4 groups of 207. Explain how
you use regrouping.

Estimate each product.
3 × 16 = □   3 × 32 = □   3 × 45 = □

Multiplying Two-Digit Numbers

Before railroads, people often used covered wagons to move across the country. Some wagon trains were small. Others had almost 100 wagons. If each wagon was drawn by 6 horses, how many horses were needed for 13 wagons?

6 × 13 = □

Step 1 Multiply ones. Regroup.	**Step 2** Multiply tens. Add any extra tens.
1 **13** **× 6** 18 ones = **8** 1 ten 8 ones	1 **13** **× 6** 6 tens + 1 ten = **78** 7 tens

There were 78 horses needed in all.

Another Example

Multiply ones.
Regroup.

2
94
× 6
─────
4   24 ones =
     2 tens 4 ones

Multiply tens.
Add any extra tens.
Regroup if necessary.

2
94
× 6
─────
564   54 tens + 2 tens =
       56 tens, or
       5 hundreds 6 tens

Estimate to check.

94 $\xrightarrow{\text{rounds to}}$ 90
× 6   × 6
─────   ─────
                 540

Compare the product with the estimate. Does the product make sense?

Check Your Understanding

Multiply. Use base-ten blocks if needed. Estimate to check.

1. 21 × 4	**2.** 19 × 5	**3.** 25 × 3	**4.** 38 × 2	**5.** 71 × 4	**6.** 23 × 4

Share Your Ideas   In which of the above exercises did you regroup tens? How can you tell?

Multiply. Estimate to check.

7. 61
    × 5

8. 13
    × 7

9. 84
    × 8

10. 36
    × 2

11. 95
    × 7

12. 28
    × 3

13. 47
    × 2

14. 18
    × 4

15. 53
    × 4

16. 92
    × 3

17. 72
    × 6

18. 44
    × 7

19. 39
    × 3

20. 65
    × 4

21. 81
    × 7

22. 63
    × 6

23. $3 \times 43 = \square$

24. $2 \times 28 = \square$

25. $4 \times 59 = \square$

26. $9 \times 83 = \square$

27. $7 \times 56 = \square$

28. $2 \times 38 = \square$

Compare. Use >, <, or = for ⬤.

29. 4×50 ⬤ 5×41

30. 2×28 ⬤ 4×14

31. $(3 \times 24) + 24$ ⬤ (4×24)

Think and Apply

32. On a good day, a wagon train could travel 17 miles. At that speed, how many miles could it travel in 5 days?

33. Today a passenger train from New York to Boston can travel at 44 miles per hour. How many miles does it travel in 5 hours?

JOURNAL WRITING Write a multiplication example where it is necessary to regroup tens.

Mixed Review

1. 46
    + 25

2. $4.36
    + 2.85

3. $54 \div 9$

4. 406
    − 287

5. 7
    × 5

Write the related addition and subtraction for each.

6. 4, 5, 9

7. 8, 6, 14

8. 9, 8, 17

Give the value of the underlined digit.

9. 2,<u>6</u>43

10. <u>3</u>,279

11. 1,4<u>8</u>5

12. <u>2</u>1,298

Find each missing number.

13. $6 \times \square = 72$

14. $\square - 27 = 38$

15. $168 + \square = 324$

16. $81 \div \square = 9$

SHOW WHAT YOU KNOW

How could you use the product of 2 × 15 and 2 × 300 to find the product of 2 × 315?

Multiplying Three-Digit Numbers

Travel on the Erie Canal was popular in the 1800s. The trip by barge across New York from Troy to Rochester was 248 miles. How many miles long was a round trip?

I got a mule, her name is Sal,

Fif - teen miles on the E - rie Ca - nal!

2 × 248 = □

Estimate first.

2 × 248 —rounds to→ 2 × 200, or 400.

Then multiply.

Step 1 Multiply ones. Regroup if necessary.	**Step 2** Multiply tens. Add any extra tens.	**Step 3** Multiply hundreds.
$\begin{array}{r} 1 \\ 24\mathbf{8} \\ \times\quad 2 \\ \hline 6 \end{array}$ 16 ones = 1 ten 6 ones	$\begin{array}{r} 1 \\ 248 \\ \times\quad 2 \\ \hline 96 \end{array}$ 8 tens + 1 ten = 9 tens	$\begin{array}{r} 1 \\ 248 \\ \times\quad 2 \\ \hline 496 \end{array}$ 2 × 2 hundreds = 4 hundreds

Compare the product with your estimate.
A round trip was 496 miles.

More Examples

a.
$$\begin{array}{r} 411 \\ \times\quad 8 \\ \hline 3{,}288 \end{array}$$

b.
$$\begin{array}{r} 2 \\ 172 \\ \times\quad 4 \\ \hline 688 \end{array}$$

c.
$$\begin{array}{r} 2 \\ 205 \\ \times\quad 4 \\ \hline 820 \end{array}$$

Check Your Understanding

Estimate. Then find each product.

1.
$$\begin{array}{r} 130 \\ \times\quad 6 \end{array}$$

2.
$$\begin{array}{r} 811 \\ \times\quad 7 \end{array}$$

3.
$$\begin{array}{r} 328 \\ \times\quad 3 \end{array}$$

4.
$$\begin{array}{r} 494 \\ \times\quad 2 \end{array}$$

5.
$$\begin{array}{r} 109 \\ \times\quad 5 \end{array}$$

Share Your Ideas Explain the steps you followed to find the product in **5**.

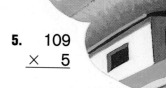

Estimate. Then find each product.

6.	600 × 8	**7.**	710 × 9	**8.**	164 × 2	**9.**	209 × 4	**10.**	325 × 3
11.	402 × 7	**12.**	218 × 4	**13.**	163 × 3	**14.**	272 × 2	**15.**	114 × 5
16.	103 × 9	**17.**	601 × 6	**18.**	291 × 2	**19.**	138 × 3	**20.**	354 × 2

21. $3 \times 243 = \square$ **22.** $5 \times 160 = \square$ **23.** $2 \times 347 = \square$

Multiply. Use mental math, paper and pencil, or a calculator. Explain your choices.

CHOICES

24. $(2 \times 3) \times 70 = \square$ **25.** $(4 \times 8) \times 100 = \square$

26. $104 \times (4 \times 2) = \square$ **27.** $(3 \times 3) \times 911 = \square$

Think and Apply

28. Mr. Ames drives 39 miles each day. How far does he drive in 5 days?

DATA

29. Use a road map of the United States. Find your state capital. Find the capital of a nearby state. What is the round trip highway distance between the capitals?

Common Error

30. Caution! What is wrong with this multiplication? Explain the error. Find the correct product.

$$
\begin{array}{r}
2 \\
408 \\
\times \quad 3 \\
\hline
1{,}264 \\
\end{array}
\longleftarrow \text{incorrect}
$$

Describe three ways to find the product of $2 \times 61 \times 3$.

SHOW WHAT YOU KNOW

Explain how to use the base-ten blocks to find the total number in 4 groups of 327.

Regrouping More Than Once

An iceboat moves on runners over icy waterways.
It can travel 145 miles per hour.
At that speed, how many miles can the
iceboat travel in 7 hours?

7 × 145 = □

Estimate first.

7 × 145   ⎯rounds to⟶   7 × 100, or 700.

Do you think the exact product will be greater
than or less than the estimate? Explain.

Then multiply.

Step 1 Multiply ones. Regroup if necessary.	**Step 2** Multiply tens. Add any extra tens. Regroup if necessary.	**Step 3** Multiply hundreds. Add any extra hundreds. Regroup if necessary.
3 **145** **× 7** **5** 35 ones = 3 tens 5 ones	3 3 **145** **× 7** **15** 28 tens + 3 tens = 31 tens, or 3 hundreds 1 ten	3 3 **145** **× 7** **1,015** 7 hundreds + 3 hundreds = 10 hundreds, or 1 thousand

The iceboat can travel 1,015 miles in 7 hours.

Check Your Understanding

Estimate. Then multiply.

1. 39
    × 4

2. 56
    × 2

3. 562
    × 5

4. 828
    × 3

5. 209
    × 6

 Share Your Ideas   Describe how you found the
product in **4**.

Estimate. Then multiply.

6. 87
    × 2

7. 56
    × 4

8. 23
    × 7

9. 92
    × 8

10. 45
    × 9

11. 651
    × 3

12. 994
    × 2

13. 576
    × 5

14. 436
    × 6

15. 708
    × 4

16. 382
    × 5

17. 842
    × 4

18. 617
    × 6

19. 520
    × 4

20. 297
    × 4

Use mental math or paper and pencil to find each product.

21. $3 \times 96 = \square$

22. $5 \times 48 = \square$

23. $3 \times 809 = \square$

24. $6 \times 273 = \square$

25. $6 \times 701 = \square$

26. $4 \times 239 = \square$

Compare. Use >, <, or = for ⬤.

27. 3×287 ⬤ $459 + 403$

28. 4×362 ⬤ 2×724

29. 6×273 ⬤ $508 + 850$

30. $1,620 - 528$ ⬤ 6×182

Think and Apply

Use the information in the table to solve each problem.

31. How many miles can the helicopter travel in 2 hours?

32. How many more miles can the iceboat travel than the hot-air balloon in 4 hours?

33. The jet plane can travel from Boston to San Francisco in 6 hours. What is the distance between the cities?

Vehicle	Speed in Miles Per Hour
Blimp	20
Helicopter	45
Hot-air balloon	9
Iceboat	145
Jet plane	450

Describe how you would find the product of $3 \times 456 \times 2$.

SHOW WHAT YOU KNOW

167

CHECKPOINT

Multiply mentally. pages 154-155

| 1. | 10
× 9 | 2. | 400
× 6 | 3. 8,000
× 5 | 4. | 300
× 8 | 5. 5,000
× 4 |

Choose the most reasonable estimate. pages 156-157

6. Ana usually swims 18 laps in a pool three times a week. About how many laps does she swim each week?

   a. 20   **b.** 60   **c.** 140

7. Jan earns $96 each month. About how much does she earn in 6 months?

   a. $200   **b.** $400   **c.** $600

Multiply. pages 158-167

| 8. | 26
× 3 | 9. | 51
× 9 | 10. | 48
× 3 | 11. | 27
× 5 | 12. | 79
× 8 |

| 13. | 217
× 4 | 14. | 251
× 3 | 15. | 609
× 4 | 16. | 638
× 5 | 17. | 437
× 6 |

Use a word to complete each sentence.

18. The answer in multiplication is called the _____.

19. One of the numbers that is multiplied is called a _____.

20. If you don't need an exact answer you can _____.

21. If you multiply and your answer is 12 tens you should _____.

Words to Know
factor
estimate
product
regroup

Solve. If a fact is missing, tell what it is.

22. You need 110 plastic forks for a picnic. There are 24 forks in a package. Will 5 packages of forks be enough?

23. There were 2 play performances every day. At each performance 375 people saw the play. How many people in all saw the play?

168

INVESTIGATING

PROBLEM SOLVING

THINK
EXPLORE
SOLVE
LOOK BACK

When Is the Best Time to Buy?

Whim's Poster Art Store has a special plan for setting prices. Every day that an item is not sold, its price is reduced by $2. The price drops until it reaches its lowest price. When an item is sold, a new and different item takes its place. The posters shown are going on sale today. You have $30.

Thinking Critically

You visit the store 4 days later. What would you buy?

Analyzing and Making Decisions

Use a calculator where appropriate.

1. How much does a price change each day?

2. Identify a reason that a price may not change.

3. What will the price for each poster be in 4 days?

4. What could happen to an item if you waited 4 days to buy it?

5. Decide what you would buy in 4 days. Are you sure you could buy those posters then? Why or why not?

Look Back   Look at your decision. **What if** you had $40? How would that change your decision? Why might a store have a pricing plan like this?

Starting Price: $32
Lowest Price: $16

Starting Price: $24
Lowest Price: $12

Starting Price: $20
Lowest Price: $10

Starting Price: $8
Lowest Price: $4

Starting Price: $12
Lowest Price: $6

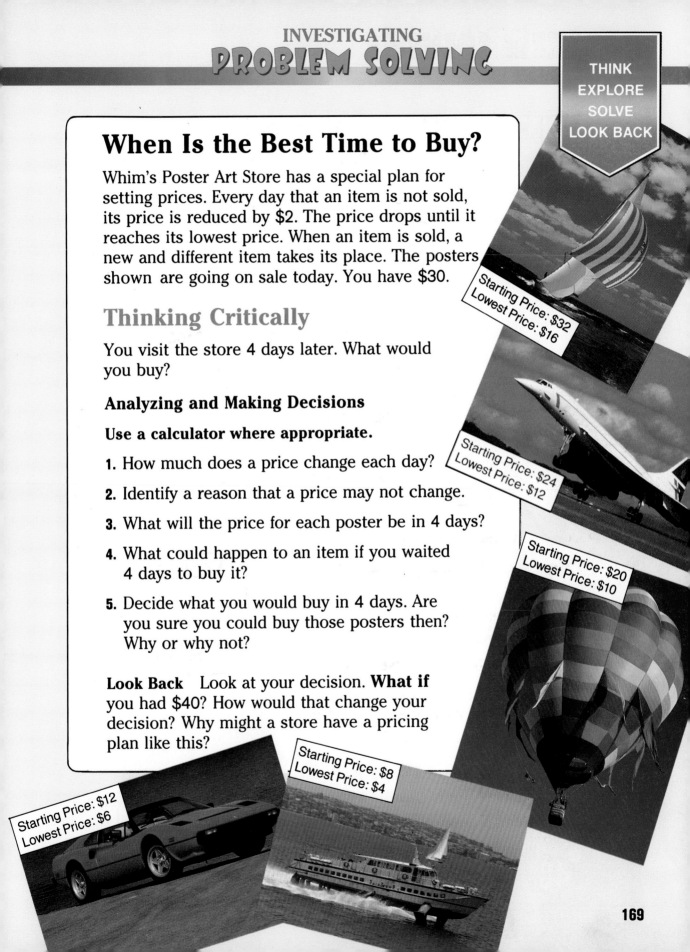

Week	Miles
1	21
2	23
3	26
4	30
5	
6	
7	
8	

Using Patterns

Elaine now rides her bike 20 miles a week. Her goal is to ride at least 50 miles a week to be ready for a bike race. She has 8 weeks to prepare. She plans to ride 21 miles this week, 23 the next, 26 the next, and 30 the next. If she continues this pattern, will she reach her goal?

Patterns occur in many problems. When they do, finding the pattern rule can help you solve the problem.

Solving the Problem

Think   What goal is Elaine trying to reach? The facts are shown in the table.

Explore   How far is she riding each of the first 4 weeks? How does the number of miles she rides change each week? Look at the changes. What is the pattern?

Solve   How many miles will she ride in each of the eight weeks? Will she reach her goal of 50 miles a week? Explain.

Look Back   Was finding the pattern important in solving the problem? Explain.

Share Your Ideas

1. Did the table help you find the pattern? Explain. In the poster problem on page 169 would a table have helped? Explain.

Extending Your Thinking

Solve. Use a calculator where appropriate.

Use the table to answer 2 and 3.

2. In the game Hare and Turtle you have to pay carrots to move spaces. The chart shows how many carrots you have to pay for each move.
   a. What is the pattern?
   b. How many carrots do you have to pay to move 5 spaces?

Spaces Moved	Carrots Paid
1	1
2	3
3	6
4	10

3. Peter has 25 carrots. What is the greatest number of spaces he can move next turn?

Use the bus schedule to answer 4 and 5.

4. "It's 4:10 P.M., when will the next bus come?" asked Erica. "I don't know. That part of my schedule is missing," said Donna. If the pattern continues when do you think it will arrive?

Bus Schedule
2:55 P.M.
3:10 P.M.
3:40 p.m.
3:55 P.M.

5. **What if** it were 2:30 P.M.? When would the next bus come?

Mixed Strategy Review

6. It takes Bryant 10 minutes to walk to school and twice as long to walk home.
   a. How long does it take him to walk to and from school?
   b. Why might it take him twice as long to walk home?

CREATE YOUR OWN

Pretend you are playing the game Hare and Turtle. You have 18 carrots. Write a problem using that information.

7. Stan paid 50 cents for a pack of 25 baseball cards and 25 cents for a pack of 10 cards. How many baseball cards did he buy?

8. **Look back** at 7. It contains extra information that is not needed to answer the question. Rewrite this problem without this extra information.

171

What if you multiply each of these numbers by 9? How many digits would there be in each product?   284   4,807   10,249

Multiplying Greater Numbers

The *Voyager's* first trip around the world took 9 days. The plane flew an average of 2,889 miles per day. How many miles was the trip?

9 × 2,889 = ☐

You can multiply with pencil and paper.

Step 1 Multiply ones. Regroup if necessary.	**Step 2** Multiply tens. Add extra tens. Regroup if necessary.	**Step 3** Multiply hundreds. Add extra hundreds. Regroup if necessary.	**Step 4** Multiply thousands. Add extra thousands. Regroup if necessary.
8 2,889 × 9 —— 1	88 2,889 × 9 —— 01	8 88 2,889 × 9 —— 001	8 88 2,889 × 9 —— 26,001

You can multiply with a calculator.

- Enter the numbers and commands.
- Read the display.
- Estimate to check.

2,889   _rounds to_ →   3,000.
9 × 3,000 = 27,000

The trip was 26,001 miles long.

Use mental math, pencil and paper, or a calculator to multiply.

1. 5,124 × 8	**2.** 6,739 × 5	**3.** 2,002 × 9	**4.** 8,092 × 6	**5.** 3,407 × 7

Share Your Ideas   Why should you estimate when you solve a problem with a calculator?

Use mental math, pencil and paper, or a calculator to multiply. Check each product with an estimate.

6. 6,027 × 9	**7.** 3,648 × 6	**8.** 1,509 × 4	**9.** 9,999 × 2	**10.** 1,115 × 9
11. 3,387 × 2	**12.** 1,202 × 4	**13.** 3,085 × 6	**14.** 4,201 × 3	**15.** 1,624 × 8
16. 4,285 × 5	**17.** 2,354 × 7	**18.** 1,894 × 4	**19.** 3,294 × 6	**20.** 2,485 × 8

Choose a number from each box to make the sentence true. Use each number only once.

    A   **B**

21. ☐ × ☐ = 3,156

22. ☐ × ☐ = 11,206

23. ☐ × ☐ = 8,701

A	B
4	1,243
2	789
7	5,603

Think and Apply

24. The fastest passenger plane is the Concorde. It can travel 1,450 miles per hour. At this speed, how far can it travel in 4 hours?

Logical Thinking

The cities on the signpost are represented by the circles on Highway 1. Decide which city is represented by each circle.

25. Where should the signpost be placed?
26. Write the name of the city for each circle.
27. Find the distance between each city.

Lynn   202 mi
Dudley 165 mi
Akron 113 mi
Denton 40 mi
Canton 52 mi

JOURNAL WRITING

Look back at **21** through **23**. Explain how you found the correct factors for each product.

SHOW WHAT YOU KNOW

Write these amounts of money, using the dollar sign and decimal point.

73¢   114¢   375¢   1426¢

Multiplying Money

What does it cost to rent a bicycle for 4 hours?

$4 \times \$9.75 = \square$

First estimate.

$\$9.75$ rounds to $\$10.00$.

$4 \times \$10.00 = \$40.00$

	Special Rides (Hourly Rates)
Airboat	$16.50
Bicycle	$9.75
Dune Buggy	$28.50
Helicopter	$93.50
Hot-Air Balloon	$105.50

Then multiply.

Step 1	Step 2	Step 3	
2	3 2	3 2	
$9.75	$9.75	$9.75	Write the dollar sign and decimal point in the product.
× 4	× 4	× 4	
0	00	$39.00	

Check the product with the estimate. Does the product make sense?

Renting the bicycle costs $39.00.

Check Your Understanding

Estimate. Then multiply. Check each product with the estimate.

1. $.73
    × 4

2. $2.99
    × 3

3. $8.45
    × 5

4. $10.03
    × 9

5. $15.62
    × 2

Share Your Ideas   When you multiply money, how do you know where to place the decimal point in the product?

Estimate. Then multiply. Check each product with the estimate.

6. $1.36
 × 8

7. $2.15
 × 7

8. $3.08
 × 4

9. $8.49
 × 2

10. $2.67
 × 5

11. $20.05
 × 3

12. $64.33
 × 2

13. $18.94
 × 4

14. $32.70
 × 9

15. $13.98
 × 6

16. 2 × $6.24 = □

17. 3 × $.62 = □

18. 5 × $1.58 = □

19. 4 × $12.46 = □

20. 6 × $3.54 = □

21. 7 × $4.23 = □

Find each missing factor.

22. □ × $3.50 = $14.00

23. □ × $1.25 = $10.00

24. □ × $6.89 = $20.67

25. □ × $12.99 = $38.97

Think and Apply

Use the information on the sign on page 174 to solve.

26. What is the charge for a 2-hour helicopter ride?

27. How much more is a 3-hour dune buggy ride than a 3-hour airboat ride?

28. How much change would you receive from $50 after paying for a 3-hour bicycle ride?

29. About how many hours could you ride the dune buggy for the cost of one hour in a hot-air balloon?

Make up a rule for estimating the cost of items so that the actual cost will never be more than your estimate.

Test Taker

Analogies are logic questions that sometimes appear on tests. Try the analogies below.

30. Addition is to subtraction as multiplication is to _____.

Think Subtraction "undoes" addition. What "undoes" multiplication?

31. Second is to minute as minute is to _____.

32. Factors are to product as addends are to _____.

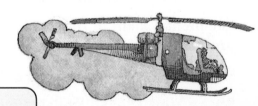

SHOW WHAT YOU KNOW

THINK AND SHARE

What if you had $15, and a game costs $4.99? How many games could you buy? How much money would you have left?

Mental Math: Strategies

Cathy Draker is buying 3 motorcycle posters. What is the total cost of the posters?

$$3 \times \$3.95 = \square$$

Cathy uses mental math.

She thinks $3.95 is 5¢ less than $4.00.
So $3 \times \$3.95 = 3 \times \$4.00 - \$.15$
$= \$12.00 - \$.15$ Why did she
$= \$11.85$ subtract 15¢?

Then she estimates to check. Does the product
$3 \times \$4.00 = \$12.00$ make sense?

The total cost of the posters is $11.85.

TRANSPORTATION MUSEUM GIFT SHOP

Motorcycle Poster	$ 3.95
Bicycle Book	$ 8.25
Sailboat Kit 100 pieces	$10.75
Jet Plane Model 88 pieces	$ 4.92
Train Set 103 pieces	$34.99

Another Example

$$6 \times \$1.04 = \square$$

Think $6 \times \$1.04 = (6 \times \$1.00) + (6 \times \$.04)$
$= \$6.00 + \$.24$
$= \$6.24$

Check Your Understanding

Use mental math to find each product. Check each product with an estimate.

1. $5 \times \$.99 = \square$

2. $4 \times \$1.02 = \square$

3. $7 \times \$5.90 = \square$

Share Your Ideas Explain how you found the product for **3**.

Use mental math to find each product. Check each product with an estimate.

4.	$3.01 × 6	**5.**	$4.50 × 2	**6.**	$7.20 × 2	**7.**	$9.11 × 4
8.	$1.97 × 2	**9.**	$2.98 × 5	**10.**	$4.05 × 8	**11.**	$6.98 × 3

Use mental math or paper and pencil to find each product.

12.	409 × 6	**13.**	205 × 4	**14.**	198 × 2
15.	$5.15 × 5	**16.**	$6.90 × 7	**17.**	$9.50 × 4
18.	9,999 × 3	**19.**	$81.95 × 2	**20.**	$30.02 × 3

Think and Apply

Use the information on the sign on page 176 and mental math to solve these problems.

21. What is the total cost of 2 train sets?

22. What is the total number of pieces in 4 train sets?

23. How much more do 3 bicycle books cost than one sailboat kit?

24. What is the total cost of 4 bicycle books and 1 jet plane model?

What if you gave the sales clerk $50 to buy 10 jet plane models? Explain how you could use mental math to figure out your change.

SHOW WHAT YOU KNOW

Which Trip Would You Choose?

Mr. Herbert's fourth-grade class is going on a field trip. There are 21 students plus 5 adults going on the trip. They have received a copy of the bus fares.

BUS FARES	
Location	**Cost per Person**
Zoo	$3
Aquarium	$4
Amusement park	$9
Space museum	$7
History museum	$5
The Capitol	$8

You may wish to use a calculator to help you find the cost of the trip.

CHOICES

A. How much will the bus cost to take one person to each location?

B. The class is allowed two field trips per year. They may not spend more than $400 on transportation. Find at least 5 different pairs of places that they could go.

Sharing Your Ideas

1. The class can go to both the zoo and the aquarium for the same fare as going to the space museum. What two other places cost the same as one place?

2. To which two places would you choose to go? Why?

3. Which two places will cost the class more than $400?

Extending Your Thinking

4. Mr. Herbert found that some of the field trip locations have these other expenses.

Other Expenses per Person	
Zoo	$2
Aquarium	$3
Amusement park	$8
Space museum	$4
History museum	Free
The Capitol	Free

What is the total cost of each trip? Which two trips can the class take when other expenses are included?

5. Each person (adults and students) has been asked to bring $5 to help to pay for the field trips. How much money will this add to the $400? What will the new total be? Now which two field trips can the students take?

Show What You Know

6. How were you able to find out the new expenses for the trips?

7. **Look back** at **5**. Each person brings $5. Now which two field trips would you pick? Did you change your mind? Why?

CALLING AROUND THE WORLD

WORKING TOGETHER

Would you enjoy a phone call with someone in a different country? What would you talk about?

1. Work in a group. Choose a country to call. Find out some things that make that country unique. For instance:

   • What is the weather like?

   • What languages are spoken?

   • What are some of the customs or traditions?

2. Use the information you find to write a script for a phone call between a group member and someone living in the country you chose. The call should last about 9 minutes.

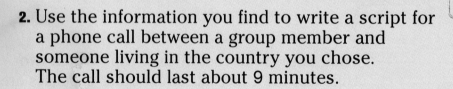

3. Have two group members role-play the call. Have a third member time the conversation.

4. Find the answers to these questions.

   • What is the rate for the first minute?

   • What is the rate for each additional minute?

   • What is the length of the call?

   • What is the total cost of the call?

5. Now have all the groups work together. Choose another country.

   • If you called someone there and spoke for 8 minutes, would the call cost more or less than each group's original call? Why?

CHAPTER REVIEW/TEST

Estimate first. Then multiply.

1. $\begin{array}{r} 43 \\ \times\ 5 \\ \hline \end{array}$

2. $\begin{array}{r} 93 \\ \times\ 2 \\ \hline \end{array}$

3. $\begin{array}{r} 40 \\ \times\ 8 \\ \hline \end{array}$

4. $\begin{array}{r} 176 \\ \times\ 3 \\ \hline \end{array}$

5. $\begin{array}{r} 501 \\ \times\ 9 \\ \hline \end{array}$

6. $\begin{array}{r} 4,000 \\ \times\ 7 \\ \hline \end{array}$

7. $\begin{array}{r} 2,009 \\ \times\ 4 \\ \hline \end{array}$

8. $\begin{array}{r} 3,868 \\ \times\ 5 \\ \hline \end{array}$

9. $4 \times 248 = \square$

10. $3 \times 526 = \square$

11. $6 \times 297 = \square$

Multiply.

12. $\begin{array}{r} 34 \\ \times\ 3 \\ \hline \end{array}$

13. $\begin{array}{r} 39 \\ \times\ 7 \\ \hline \end{array}$

14. $\begin{array}{r} \$.83 \\ \times\ 5 \\ \hline \end{array}$

15. $\begin{array}{r} 46 \\ \times\ 6 \\ \hline \end{array}$

16. $\begin{array}{r} 238 \\ \times\ 4 \\ \hline \end{array}$

17. $\begin{array}{r} \$8.41 \\ \times\ 3 \\ \hline \end{array}$

18. $\begin{array}{r} 150 \\ \times\ 6 \\ \hline \end{array}$

19. $\begin{array}{r} \$31.89 \\ \times\ 6 \\ \hline \end{array}$

20. $\begin{array}{r} 308 \\ \times\ 5 \\ \hline \end{array}$

21. $\begin{array}{r} \$7.10 \\ \times\ 4 \\ \hline \end{array}$

22. $\begin{array}{r} \$20.05 \\ \times\ 6 \\ \hline \end{array}$

23. $\begin{array}{r} 299 \\ \times\ 4 \\ \hline \end{array}$

Solve.

24. Beth took $12.00 to the air show. She wanted to get 3 souvenirs that cost $3.95 each. Did she have enough money? Explain.

25. Bill wrote the pattern 1, 4, 7, 10, ... What are the next three numbers in his pattern?

Think The Churchill School students sold books of play tickets. Mary sold 6 books. John sold twice as many books as Mary. Wey sold twice as many books as John. Linda sold 4 more books than John. If there are 8 play tickets in each book, how many tickets did the students sell in all?

COMPUTER

Multiplying with Frames

You can show multiplication with the
MathProcessor™.

- You can use **Frames** to model the multiplication.
- You can put items in the **Manipulative Workspace** to show multiplication.
- You can use a **Number Space** to find the product. The **Number Space** works like a calculator.

MathProcessor™ Tools:

 Frames

 Base-ten Blocks, Money

 Number Space

 Writing Space

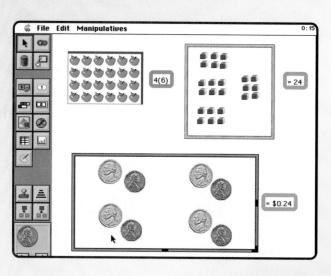

Doing the Computer Investigation

A. Find the total number of round balloons in three packages. Use **Base-ten Blocks. Link** the **Blocks** to a **Number Space** to find the total. Write the number sentence in a **Writing Space.**

24 Long Balloons 99¢

16 Round Balloons 50¢

8 Animal Balloons 35¢

INVESTIGATION

B. Find the total cost of five packages of animal balloons. Use **Money** in a **Manipulative Workspace** to model the problem. Write the number sentence in a **Writing Space**.

C. How many more balloons are there in 4 packages of long balloons than in 4 packages of animal balloons? Use **Frames**. Model the problem. Then try to model the problem another way. Describe your models in a **Writing Space**.

Sharing Your Results

1. How many different ways can you find to buy exactly 48 balloons? In a **Writing Space**, describe the strategies you used to find the different ways.

2. Share your results with your classmates.

Extending the Computer Investigation

What if you are in charge of decorating three classrooms for a holiday fair at your school? You want to put 35 balloons in each room. You want some of each type of balloon in each room. What packages of balloons will you buy? What will they cost? How many balloons will be left over?

3. Use the MathProcessor™ to help you explore your choices. Record your answers in a **Writing Space**. Explain why you made the choices you did.

Napier's Bones

John Napier was a Scottish mathematician who invented an unusual method of multiplying. He used a special set of sticks or "bones" with the multiples of the numbers 0 through 9 on them. Look at the 6 bone shown at the right. All of the bones, from 0 through 9, follow the same pattern.

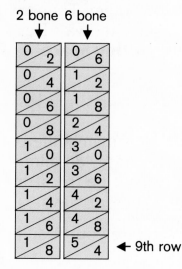

6 bone

← 1 × 6
← 4 × 6
← 7 × 6
← 9 × 6

Work in a small group.

Materials: construction paper or tongue depressors

1. Make a set of Napier's bones for the numbers 0 through 9. Label each bone.

2. Use your bones to find 9 × 26. Place the 2 bone and the 6 bone side-by-side. Look down to the 9th row.

3. Add the digits along each diagonal as shown below. Begin at the right. Regroup if necessary.

2 bone 6 bone

← 9th row

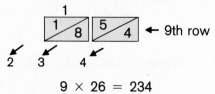

2 bone 6 bone

9 × 26 = 234

Use Napier's method. Find each product.

5 bone 9 bone
(2 × 5) (2 × 9)

4. 2 × 59 = □

5. 3 × 45 = □

4 bone 5 bone
(3 × 4) (3 × 5)

6. 5 × 32 = □   7. 3 × 64 = □   8. 8 × 89 = □   9. 7 × 48 = □

MAINTAINING SKILLS

Choose the correct answer. Write A, B, C, or D.

1. Write the time for quarter past five.

   A 4:45   **C** 5:30

   B 5:15   **D** not given

2. What time will it be 55 minutes after 1:15?

   A 2:10   **C** 2:05

   B 1:55   **D** not given

3. $0 \times 6 = \square$

   A 6   **C** 1

   B 0   **D** not given

4. $8 \times 5 = \square$

   A 13   **C** 40

   B 45   **D** not given

5. $\square \times 7 = 49$

   A 6   **C** 8

   B 7   **D** not given

6. $20 \div 5 = \square$

   A 6   **C** 4

   B 5   **D** not given

7. $0 \div 6 = \square$

   A 0   **C** 6

   B 1   **D** not given

8. $800 \times 4 = \square$

   A 3,200   **C** 2,400

   B 320   **D** not given

9. Estimate 91×3.

   A 3,000   **C** 270

   B 200   **D** not given

10.
$$\begin{array}{r} 824 \\ \times\ \ \ 4 \\ \hline \end{array}$$

   A 3,286   **C** 2,496

   B 3,296   **D** not given

11. $\$18.45 \times 5 = \square$

   A $91.20   **C** $90.25

   B $90.05   **D** not given

Tell what information is missing.

12. The sea-lion trainer feeds each sea-lion 5 buckets of fish a day. How many pounds of fish is this?

   A number of sea lions   **C** pounds in a bucket

   B number of fish   **D** not given

13. The water tank sprang a leak and lost 5,000 gallons of water. How much water is in the tank now?

   A amount of water before the leak   **C** amount of time since full

   B water lost   **D** not given

6 Multiplying by Two-Digit Numbers

Sharing What You Know

Addresses, birth dates, and zip codes—we all have them. Numbers give important information about each of us. Which numbers tell facts about you that you can change? Which numbers give facts that you cannot change? What kind of information can you communicate with numbers?

Using Language

Modern electronic equipment is an important factor in communicating news. What are some other factors that would affect what is in today's news program? Each **factor** influences the whole final product, the news program. In mathematics, two **factors** such as 2 and 8 are multiplied to give the product 16. How are the two meanings of **factor** related?

Words to Know: multiple, factors, product, partial product

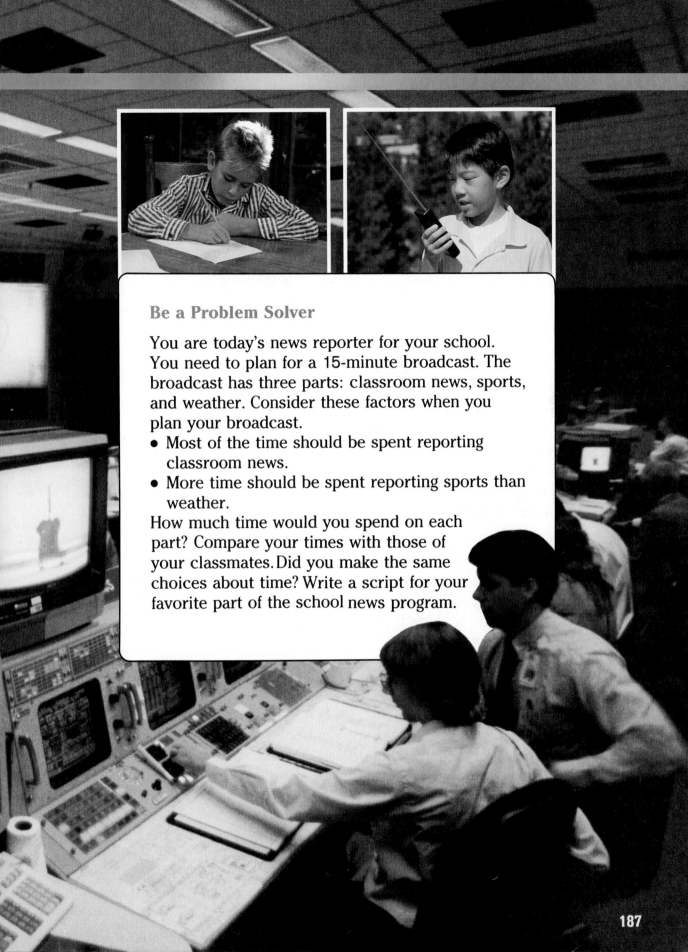

Be a Problem Solver

You are today's news reporter for your school. You need to plan for a 15-minute broadcast. The broadcast has three parts: classroom news, sports, and weather. Consider these factors when you plan your broadcast.

- Most of the time should be spent reporting classroom news.
- More time should be spent reporting sports than weather.

How much time would you spend on each part? Compare your times with those of your classmates. Did you make the same choices about time? Write a script for your favorite part of the school news program.

20 and 90 are multiples of 10. Name other multiples of 10. How are the multiples alike?

Mental Math: Exploring Patterns

Jack is an amateur radio operator. He can send and receive 12 words in Morse code each minute. At this speed, how many words can Jack send and receive in 20 minutes?

$20 \times 12 = n$ You can use n instead of □ to show a missing number.

Use what you know about multiplication and patterns with zeros to find the product.

$2 \times 12 = 24$
$2\underline{0} \times 12 = 24\underline{0}$

Jack can send and receive 240 words in 20 minutes.

Look for patterns in these examples.

17	17	60	60	500	500
$\times 1$	$\times 10$	$\times 7$	$\times 70$	$\times 4$	$\times 40$
17	170	420	4,200	2,000	20,000

Explain how the products in each pair are the same and how they are different.

Check Your Understanding

Find each product. Use patterns to help you.

1.
16	16
$\times 2$	$\times 20$

2.
42	42
$\times 1$	$\times 10$

3.
700	700
$\times 9$	$\times 90$

Share Your Ideas   How does knowing $5 \times 7 = 35$ help you find 50×70?

Find each product. Use patterns to help you.

4. $1 \times 10 = n$
$10 \times 10 = n$

5. $4 \times 22 = n$
$40 \times 22 = n$

6. $6 \times 50 = n$
$60 \times 50 = n$

7. $3 \times 200 = n$
$30 \times 200 = n$

8. $4 \times 610 = n$
$40 \times 610 = n$

9. $8 \times 800 = n$
$80 \times 800 = n$

10. $\begin{array}{r} 34 \\ \times 20 \\ \hline \end{array}$

11. $\begin{array}{r} 28 \\ \times 30 \\ \hline \end{array}$

12. $\begin{array}{r} 54 \\ \times 50 \\ \hline \end{array}$

13. $\begin{array}{r} 102 \\ \times \ 90 \\ \hline \end{array}$

14. $\begin{array}{r} 405 \\ \times \ 70 \\ \hline \end{array}$

15. $\begin{array}{r} 240 \\ \times \ 40 \\ \hline \end{array}$

Use mental math or estimation to match each number sentence with its product.

CHOICES

16. $50 \times 90 = n$
17. $50 \times 190 = n$
18. $500 \times 190 = n$
19. $500 \times 1,900 = n$

a. 95,000
b. 4,500
c. 9,500
d. 950,000

Find each missing number.

20. $n \times 40 = 20 \times 80$

21. $90 \times n = 50 \times 180$

22. $30 \times 100 = n \times 50$

23. $80 \times 70 = 70 \times n$

Think and Apply

24. To get a license as a ham radio operator, you must be able to send and receive 14 words in Morse code each minute. How many words is that in 10 minutes?

25. Nara can send and receive 15 words a minute. At that speed, how many words can she send and receive in a half hour?

JOURNAL WRITING

Write a rule for finding the product when multiplying by ten or a multiple of ten.

SHOW WHAT YOU KNOW

About how many pages are in a daily newspaper? About how much does a newspaper weigh?

Mental Math: Multiplying by Tens

The heaviest newspaper ever printed was the October 17, 1965 Sunday New York Times. It weighed $7\frac{1}{2}$ pounds and had 946 pages. **What if** you had to deliver 20 of these newspapers? How many pages would you deliver?

$20 \times 946 = n$

Step 1 Write 0 in the ones place. $\begin{array}{r} 946 \\ \times\ 20 \\ \hline 0 \end{array}$ ← 0×946	Step 2 Multiply by tens. $\overset{1}{}$ $\begin{array}{r} 946 \\ \times\ 20 \\ \hline 18{,}920 \end{array}$ ← 2 tens $\times$ 946

You would deliver 18,920 pages.

How many of these newspapers do you think you could carry at one time?

About how many separate trips would you need to make to deliver the newspapers?

Check Your Understanding

Find each product.

1. $\begin{array}{r} 31 \\ \times 60 \end{array}$ 2. $\begin{array}{r} 96 \\ \times 30 \end{array}$ 3. $\begin{array}{r} 234 \\ \times\ 50 \end{array}$ 4. $\begin{array}{r} 567 \\ \times\ 20 \end{array}$ 5. $\begin{array}{r} 308 \\ \times\ 90 \end{array}$ 6. $\begin{array}{r} 880 \\ \times\ 70 \end{array}$

Share Your Ideas What if the zero key on your calculator is broken? Explain how you can use your calculator and patterns to find the product of 40×720.

Find each product.

7. $\begin{array}{r} 18 \\ \times\, 40 \end{array}$ **8.** $\begin{array}{r} 22 \\ \times\, 50 \end{array}$ **9.** $\begin{array}{r} 85 \\ \times\, 20 \end{array}$ **10.** $\begin{array}{r} 34 \\ \times\, 90 \end{array}$ **11.** $\begin{array}{r} 60 \\ \times\, 10 \end{array}$ **12.** $\begin{array}{r} 93 \\ \times\, 30 \end{array}$

13. $\begin{array}{r} 55 \\ \times\, 50 \end{array}$ **14.** $\begin{array}{r} 72 \\ \times\, 60 \end{array}$ **15.** $\begin{array}{r} 44 \\ \times\, 10 \end{array}$ **16.** $\begin{array}{r} 188 \\ \times\, 80 \end{array}$ **17.** $\begin{array}{r} 239 \\ \times\, 70 \end{array}$ **18.** $\begin{array}{r} 440 \\ \times\, 20 \end{array}$

19. $60 \times 0 = n$ **20.** $50 \times 9 = n$ **21.** $40 \times 78 = n$

Follow the rule to find each output.

Rule: Multiply by 60.

	Input	Output
22.	35	
23.	175	
24.	300	

Rule: Multiply by 20.

	Input	Output
25.	20	
26.	140	
27.	400	

Find each missing number. Choose mental math, paper and pencil, or a calculator.

CHOICES

28. $(40 \times 70) + n = 3{,}000$

29. $26 \times 90 = n + 40$

30. $60 \times n = 3 \times 820$

31. $(50 \times 50) + 50 = n \times 50$

Think and Apply

32. The Sunday paper in 1965 sold for 50 cents. How much money in cents would you collect for 20 papers? How much is that in dollars?

33. Each paper weighed $7\frac{1}{2}$ pounds. Two papers weighed a total of 15 pounds. How many pounds did the 20 papers weigh in all?

Visual Thinking

34. Which two designs are exactly the same?

a. ●—○—●—●—○—●

b. ●—○—●—○—○—●

c. ●—○—○—●—○—●

d. ●—○—●—●—○—●

JOURNAL WRITING

Explain how you can find the product of 50×400 mentally.

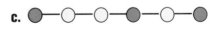

SHOW WHAT YOU KNOW

THINK AND SHARE — Think about 20 × 35 = 700. Name other multiplication examples that will give products close to 700.

Estimating Products

Janet and Luis wanted to find out how fast they can talk. Luis timed Janet while she read aloud for 1 minute. Then he counted that she had said 94 words. At that speed, about how many words could Janet say in 12 minutes?

$12 \times 94 = n$

Do Janet and Luis need an estimate or an exact answer? Explain.

One way to estimate is to round each factor to its greatest place. Then multiply.

$$94 \xrightarrow{\text{rounds to}} 90$$
$$\times 12 \longrightarrow \times 10$$
$$900 \leftarrow \text{estimated product}$$

Janet could say about 900 words in 12 minutes.

More Examples

$$826 \xrightarrow{\text{rounds to}} 800$$
$$\times\ 65 \longrightarrow \times\ 70$$
$$56,000$$

$$395 \xrightarrow{\text{rounds to}} 400$$
$$\times\ 13 \longrightarrow \times\ 10$$
$$4,000$$

Check Your Understanding

Estimate each product.

1.	37	2.	49	3.	82	4.	250	5.	917	6.	628
	× 26		× 41		× 74		× 55		× 30		× 89

Share Your Ideas Look back at **1** and **3**. Will the exact products be greater than or less than the estimates? Explain.

Estimate each product.

7. $\begin{array}{r} 28 \\ \times 58 \\ \hline \end{array}$ **8.** $\begin{array}{r} 61 \\ \times 44 \\ \hline \end{array}$ **9.** $\begin{array}{r} 79 \\ \times 33 \\ \hline \end{array}$ **10.** $\begin{array}{r} 45 \\ \times 25 \\ \hline \end{array}$

11. $\begin{array}{r} 154 \\ \times\ \ 29 \\ \hline \end{array}$ **12.** $\begin{array}{r} 239 \\ \times\ \ 63 \\ \hline \end{array}$ **13.** $\begin{array}{r} 846 \\ \times\ \ 35 \\ \hline \end{array}$ **14.** $\begin{array}{r} 499 \\ \times\ \ 77 \\ \hline \end{array}$

15. 15×81 **16.** 54×37

Estimate to choose the correct answer.

17. $\begin{array}{r} 52 \\ \times 64 \\ \hline \end{array}$ **a.** 328 **b.** 3,328 **c.** 8,328

18. $\begin{array}{r} 380 \\ \times\ \ 24 \\ \hline \end{array}$ **a.** 4,120 **b.** 6,120 **c.** 9,120

19. $\begin{array}{r} 278 \\ \times\ \ 46 \\ \hline \end{array}$ **a.** 12,788 **b.** 32,788 **c.** 150,000

Think and Apply

20. Work together with a partner. Time each other reading a page of a book aloud. How many words can you read in 1 minute? About how many words could you read in a half hour?

Use the information below to answer 21.

- In a speech in 1961, President Kennedy said 327 words in 1 minute.
- Karen's computer can print 720 characters in 1 minute.

21. Write a multiplication word problem in which an exact answer is needed and another in which an estimate is needed.

> **Look back** at the word problems you wrote for **21.** Explain why you can use an estimate for one and not the other.

Mixed Review

1. $\begin{array}{r} 408 \\ \times\ \ \ \ 3 \\ \hline \end{array}$

2. $\begin{array}{r} 692 \\ +346 \\ \hline \end{array}$

3. $\begin{array}{r} 725 \\ -234 \\ \hline \end{array}$

4. $\begin{array}{r} \$14.82 \\ +\ \ \ 3.46 \\ \hline \end{array}$

5. 529×6

6. $49 \div 7$

7. $22 + 89 + 36$

8. 9×8

9. $236 - 49$

Estimate.

10. 389×4

11. $238 - 102$

12. 275×6

13. $347 + 135$

Write the greatest and least number using each digit once.

14. 1, 2, 9, 5, 3

15. 0, 2, 4, 8, 7

SHOW WHAT YOU KNOW

ACTIVITY

Investigating Multiplication by Tens and Ones

Investigate how a drawing can help you find the product of 13 × 24.

Working together

Materials: Workmat 11, ruler

A. Draw a rectangle 24 units by 13 units.

Think 24 = 20 + 4
Mark 20 units and 4 units across the top.

Think 13 = 10 + 3
Mark 10 units and 3 units along the side.

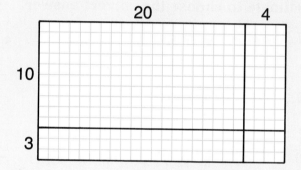

B. Use the marks you have made to draw these sections:
- 10 squares by 20 squares
- 10 squares by 4 squares
- 3 squares by 20 squares
- 3 squares by 4 squares

C. Find the number of small squares in each section. Find the number of squares in all. Record your work.

D. Take turns choosing any 2-digit factors you wish. Repeat the activity at least 3 times.

Sharing Your Results

Use the rectangle you drew for 13 × 24.

1. How did you find the number of small squares in each section?

2. What multiplication sentence could you use to find the number of squares in each section?

3. How could you use the drawing to find
3 × 24 = 72? 10 × 24 = 240?

Extending the Activity

The rectangle at the right shows
23 × 45.

► The number of squares in a section
or group of sections is called a
partial product. The sum of all the
partial products is the total product.

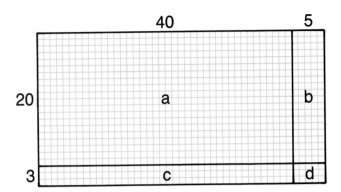

**Work with a partner. Compare the rectangle above
to this multiplication example.**

Multiply ones.

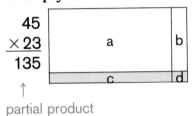

```
  45
× 23
 135
  ↑
partial product
```

Multiply tens.

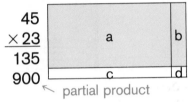

```
  45
× 23
 135
 900
```
↖ partial product

Add.

```
  45
× 23
 135
+900
1,035 ← product
```

**Draw a rectangle to show each multiplication
example. Find each product.**

4. 16
   × 19

5. 17
   × 21

6. 22
   × 25

7. 31
   × 49

Show What You Know

Look back at 7 to answer each of these questions.

8. Explain in your own words how a
   drawing helped you find the
   product of 49 × 31.

9. Draw a rectangle to show 31 × 49.
   Are the partial products the same
   as those for 49 × 31? Are the
   products the same? Explain.

Multiplying Two-Digit Numbers

Look at the bar graph. How many hours of news does WING-TV broadcast in 12 weeks?

$12 \times 16 = n$

Estimate first.

$$\begin{array}{r} 12 \\ \times 16 \end{array} \xrightarrow{\text{rounds to}} \begin{array}{r} 10 \\ \times 20 \\ \hline 200 \end{array}$$

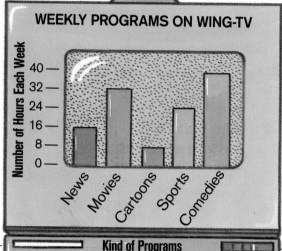

WEEKLY PROGRAMS ON WING-TV

Number of Hours Each Week: 40, 32, 24, 16, 8, 0

News Movies Cartoons Sports Comedies

Kind of Programs

Then multiply.

Step 1 Multiply by ones.	Step 2 Multiply by tens.	Step 3 Add.
$\begin{array}{r} 1 \\ 12 \\ \times 16 \\ \hline 72 \leftarrow 6 \times 12 \end{array}$	$\begin{array}{r} 1 \\ 12 \\ \times 16 \\ \hline 72 \\ 120 \leftarrow 10 \times 12 \end{array}$	$\begin{array}{r} 1 \\ 12 \\ \times 16 \\ \hline 72 \\ +120 \\ \hline 192 \end{array}$ Check the product with the estimate. Does it make sense?

WING-TV broadcasts 192 hours of news.

Check Your Understanding

Multiply. Estimate to check.

1. $\begin{array}{r} 16 \\ \times 16 \end{array}$
2. $\begin{array}{r} 22 \\ \times 14 \end{array}$
3. $\begin{array}{r} 17 \\ \times 32 \end{array}$
4. $\begin{array}{r} 40 \\ \times 91 \end{array}$
5. $\begin{array}{r} 92 \\ \times 23 \end{array}$
6. $\begin{array}{r} 80 \\ \times 42 \end{array}$

Share Your Ideas Which of the above exercises would be easier if you changed the order of the factors?

Multiply. Estimate to check.

7. $\begin{array}{r} 40 \\ \times\,24 \\ \hline \end{array}$

8. $\begin{array}{r} 73 \\ \times\,11 \\ \hline \end{array}$

9. $\begin{array}{r} 32 \\ \times\,23 \\ \hline \end{array}$

10. $\begin{array}{r} 59 \\ \times\,60 \\ \hline \end{array}$

11. $\begin{array}{r} 18 \\ \times\,51 \\ \hline \end{array}$

12. $\begin{array}{r} 29 \\ \times\,32 \\ \hline \end{array}$

13. $\begin{array}{r} 60 \\ \times\,39 \\ \hline \end{array}$

14. $\begin{array}{r} 91 \\ \times\,80 \\ \hline \end{array}$

15. $\begin{array}{r} 27 \\ \times\,33 \\ \hline \end{array}$

16. $\begin{array}{r} 16 \\ \times\,55 \\ \hline \end{array}$

17. $\begin{array}{r} 35 \\ \times\,20 \\ \hline \end{array}$

18. $\begin{array}{r} 70 \\ \times\,64 \\ \hline \end{array}$

19. $12 \times 14 = n$

20. $25 \times 32 = n$

21. $61 \times 90 = n$

Find each missing digit. Choose pencil and paper or a calculator.

CHOICES

22. $\begin{array}{r} 52 \\ \times\,3\square \\ \hline 52 \\ \square\,\square\,6\,\square \\ \hline \square,\square\square\square \end{array}$

23. $\begin{array}{r} 18 \\ \times\,\square\,4 \\ \hline \square\,\square \\ 540 \\ \hline \square\square\square \end{array}$

24. $\begin{array}{r} \square\square \\ \times\,92 \\ \hline 140 \\ 63\square\square \\ \hline \square,\square\square\square \end{array}$

Think and Apply

Use the graph on page 196 to solve.

25. How many hours of sports does WING-TV broadcast in 12 weeks?

26. How many hours of cartoons does WING-TV broadcast in 1 year?

27. How many hours of movies and comedies does WING-TV broadcast in 13 weeks?

28. How many more hours of sports than news are broadcast in 26 weeks?

Test Taker

Sometimes when you take a test you can save time by estimating.

Try using estimation to choose the correct answer for each exercise.

29. $44 \times 21 = n$
    a. 624   b. 924   c. 1,224

30. $17 \times 55 = n$
    a. 935   b. 1,235   c. 1,935

Look back at **28.** Describe two ways to solve it. Which way do you think is easier? Why?

SHOW WHAT YOU KNOW

Estimate. Will the actual products be greater than or less than the estimates?

$39 \times 7 = n$ $32 \times 24 = n$ $71 \times 54 = n$

Multiplying: More Regrouping

Elena works for a car rental company in Arizona. Todd works for the same company in Georgia. They send messages to each other through a computer network. Last year Elena and Todd sent 27 messages each week for 52 weeks. How many messages did they send in all?

$$52 \times 27 = n$$

First estimate.

$$
\begin{array}{r}
27 \\
\times 52
\end{array}
\xrightarrow{\text{rounds to}}
\begin{array}{r}
30 \\
\times 50 \\
\hline
1,500
\end{array}
$$

Then multiply.

Step 1 Multiply by ones.	Step 2 Multiply by tens.	Step 3 Add.
$\begin{array}{r} 1 \\ 27 \\ \times 52 \\ \hline 54 \end{array} \leftarrow 2 \times 27$	$\begin{array}{r} 3 \\ \cancel{1} \\ 27 \\ \times 52 \\ \hline 54 \\ 1350 \end{array} \leftarrow 50 \times 27$	$\begin{array}{r} 3 \\ \cancel{1} \\ 27 \\ \times 52 \\ \hline 54 \\ +1\,350 \\ \hline 1,404 \end{array}$ Check the product with the estimate. Does it make sense?

Elena and Todd sent 1,404 messages.

Check Your Understanding

Find each product. Estimate to check.

1.	2.	3.	4.	5.	6.
$\begin{array}{r} 37 \\ \times 42 \end{array}$	$\begin{array}{r} 46 \\ \times 13 \end{array}$	$\begin{array}{r} 25 \\ \times 26 \end{array}$	$\begin{array}{r} 69 \\ \times 57 \end{array}$	$\begin{array}{r} 53 \\ \times 39 \end{array}$	$\begin{array}{r} 78 \\ \times 67 \end{array}$

Share Your Ideas   Before multiplying, how can you tell which of the exercises above would have 4-digit products?

Find each product. Estimate to check.

7. 24
   ×35

8. 48
   ×18

9. 36
   ×94

10. 52
    ×76

11. 67
    ×43

12. 80
    ×55

13. 39
    ×87

14. 86
    ×25

15. 41
    ×69

16. 98
    ×33

17. 75
    ×68

18. 27
    ×59

19. 48
    ×57

20. 63
    ×28

21. 59
    ×32

22. 76
    ×41

23. 39
    ×22

24. 47
    ×53

25. $25 \times 57 = n$

26. $34 \times 49 = n$

27. $86 \times 68 = n$

28. $83 \times 64 = n$

29. $45 \times 66 = n$

30. $38 \times 29 = n$

Find each missing number.

31. $10 \times 40 = 320 + n$

32. $20 \times 46 = 950 - n$

33. $1{,}100 - n = 22 \times 49$

34. $43 \times 25 = 975 + n$

35. $47 \times 35 = (40 \times 35) + (n \times 35)$

36. $62 \times 95 = (n \times 95) + (2 \times 95)$

Think and Apply

37. One factor is 47 and the other factor is 85. What is the product?

38. The factors are 7, 9, and 75. What is the product?

39. Elena uses her computer to keep track of the automobiles she rents. She rented at least 36 cars each day during the month of July. What is the least number of cars she could have rented during July?

Arrange the digits 4, 5, 6, and 7 in the boxes to get the greatest product.

SHOW WHAT YOU KNOW

CHECKPOINT

Find each product. Use patterns to help you. pages 188–189

1. 19   19
    × 3   ×30

2. 57   57
    × 2   ×20

3. 700   700
    × 8   × 80

Find each product. pages 190–191

4. 59
    ×40

5. 625
    × 30

6. 239
    × 60

7. 500
    × 80

8. 299
    × 70

9. $64 \times 50 = n$

10. $83 \times 20 = n$

11. $40 \times 820 = n$

Estimate each product. pages 192–193

12. 37
     ×23

13. 781
     × 45

14. 436
     × 24

15. 176
     × 78

16. 279
     × 63

17. 42×384

18. 89×614

19. 23×290

Multiply. pages 194–199

20. 26
     ×27

21. 89
     ×54

22. 82
     ×19

23. 72
     ×61

24. 92
     ×28

25. 48
     ×19

26. 38
     ×43

27. 16
     ×22

28. 29
     ×64

29. 50
     ×73

30. $42 \times 38 = n$

31. $26 \times 32 = n$

32. $40 \times 82 = n$

33. $92 \times 24 = n$

34. $74 \times 45 = n$

35. $38 \times 16 = n$

Solve.

36. Jim spoke to his friend Bill on the phone for a half hour. If the phone company charges 12¢ a minute, how much will the call cost?

37. There are 300 students going on a school trip. Each bus holds 48 people. Do you need more than 6 buses? Explain.

THINK
EXPLORE
SOLVE
LOOK BACK

How Many Words?

A telegraph operator can send about 25 words per minute in Morse code.

Thinking Critically

Can 12 handwritten pages on $8\frac{1}{2}$-inch by 11-inch paper be sent in 1 hour? Work with a partner as you experiment to find out.

Analyzing and Making Decisions

1. About how many handwritten words are on a line about $8\frac{1}{2}$ inches long? Estimate. Then experiment to find out.

2. About how many lines are on a handwritten page that is 11 inches long? How many words in all would be on a page? Estimate.

3. About how many words can the telegraph operator send in 1 hour? Can 12 handwritten pages be sent in 1 hour by a telegraph operator? Explain.

4. Estimate how many words are carried in 1 hour when you talk on the telephone. If you find out how many words could be spoken in 1 minute or 2 minutes, would that help you to find out? Explain.

Look Back   What if you had to give a 10-minute speech? About how many pages of your handwriting would this 10-minute speech be? How would finding the number of words spoken in 1 minute help you?

Two-Step Problems

Peter talked long distance on the telephone for 15 minutes. The rate for the first minute was $.34. The rate for each additional minute was $.12. What was the total cost of the call?

Sometimes you need to find the answer to a hidden question before you can solve a problem. We call a problem like this a two-step problem.

Solving the Problem

Think   What is the question?

Explore   How long did Peter talk? How much does the first minute cost? How much does each additional minute cost? How much did all of the additional minutes cost?

Solve   What is the total cost of the call?

Look Back   What was the hidden question? What did you have to find out before you could tell how much the call cost?

Share Your Ideas

1. How would the answer to this problem be different if each additional minute cost $.15?

2. **What if** the telephone company charged the same price for all the minutes of your call? Would you need to use two steps to solve the problem? Explain.

Extending Your Thinking

Solve. Use a calculator where appropriate.

CHOICES

3. On Monday, 15 cartons of telephones were delivered to Marie's Shop. There were 12 telephones in each carton. On Tuesday, 12 cartons were delivered with 10 telephones in each carton. How many telephones in all were delivered?

4. Louis sold 15 cartons with 12 dial phones in each. He sold 8 cartons with 24 push-button phones in each. Did he sell more dial phones or push-button phones? Explain.

5. Leah mailed 5 postcards for $.15 each and 4 letters for $.25 each. How much did she pay in postage?

6. The Best Rating Company called 1,000 people to find out what T.V. show they were watching. The Game of the Night had 343 viewers. The Rerun Movie had 193 viewers, and the Variety Show had 253 viewers. Everyone else was either not home or not watching T.V. How many people were not home or not watching T.V.?

CREATE YOUR OWN

Create a two-step problem using the information for One Day Mail Service.

Mixed Strategy Review

Use the information on the poster to solve 7–9.

7. Andy sent 11 packages using Quick Service. How much did it cost to send them?

8. Michelle sent 7 packages and bought 3 boxes for $2 each. How much did she spend?

9. Andy sent 4 packages using Very Quick Service. How much did it cost to send them?

One-Day Mail Service
Very Quick Service: Arrives before 10:00 A.M.
Price $10.50
Quick Service: Arrives before 3:00 P.M.
Price $ 6.75

Estimate how many letters your family gets in one week. At that rate, about how many letters would your family get in one year?

Multiplying Three-Digit Numbers

Hank Aaron received so much mail in 1974 that he could have received 103 letters every hour of every day. How many letters a day is that?

$24 \times 103 = n$

Step 1 Multiply by ones.	Step 2 Multiply by tens.	Step 3 Add.
1 103 $\times24$ $412 \leftarrow 4 \times 103$	1 103 $\times24$ 412 $2060 \leftarrow 20 \times 103$	1 103 $\times24$ 412 $+2\,060$ $2,472$

That is 2,472 letters a day.

Another Example

	Multiply by ones.	Multiply by tens.	Add.
549 $\times35$	24 549 $\times35$ 2745	$1\,2$ $\not2\not4$ 549 $\times35$ 2745 16470	$1\,2$ $\not2\not4$ 549 $\times35$ $2\,745$ $+16\,470$ 19,215

Check Your Understanding

Multiply. Check your product with an estimate.

1. $67 \times 406 = n$
2. $12 \times 568 = n$
3. $25 \times 279 = n$

Share Your Ideas Look back at **3**. Explain how you found the product.

Multiply. Check your product with an estimate.

4. 132
    × 13

5. 404
    × 22

6. 390
    × 41

7. 561
    × 52

8. 870
    × 30

9. 215
    × 63

10. 608
    × 28

11. 922
    × 70

12. 716
    × 19

13. 483
    × 82

14. $11 \times 398 = n$

15. $35 \times 560 = n$

16. $91 \times 674 = n$

17. $80 \times 751 = n$

18. $44 \times 807 = n$

19. $56 \times 499 = n$

Follow the rule to find each output.

Rule: Multiply by 26.

	Input	Output
20.	46	
21.	309	
22.	470	
23.	895	

Rule: Multiply by 83.

	Input	Output
24.	54	
25.	600	
26.	830	
27.	926	

Think and Apply

28. There was enough mail one year for each person in the United States to have mailed 589 letters. **What if** each student in your class mailed that many letters? How many would that be?

29. If you mailed 7 letters each week for 5 years, how many letters would that be?

30. Hank Aaron's record number of home runs is 56 more than 3 times 233. What is his record?

Common Error

Cara estimated the product for 92×425. Then she multiplied.

    425
    × 92
    850
    3825
    4,675 ← Incorrect

31. How did Cara know that she had made an error? What is the correct product?

What is the least product you can get when you multiply a 3-digit number by a 2-digit number? the greatest?

SHOW WHAT YOU KNOW

THINK AND SHARE

> How could you write these amounts of money using dollar signs and decimal points?
> 90 cents   200 cents   1400 cents

Multiplying Money

A magazine costs $1.25 an issue.
What does it cost to buy 52 issues?

Estimate first.
52 × $1.25 ──rounds to──> 50 × $1.00 or $50.00

Then multiply.

Step 1 Multiply by ones.	**Step 2** Multiply by tens.	**Step 3** Add.
1 $1.25 × 52 250	2 1 ✗ $1.25 × 52 250 6250	2 1 ✗ $1.25 × 52 2 50 62 50 $65.00 Write the dollar sign and the decimal point in the product.

Check the product with the estimate. Does the product make sense?

It costs $65.00 to buy 52 issues.

Why are there two digits to the right of the decimal point when you write money amounts?

Check Your Understanding

Estimate. Then find each product.

1. $.50
    × 24

2. $.89
    × 30

3. $1.52
    ×   46

4. $9.02
    ×   17

5. $5.74
    ×   82

Share Your Ideas   Explain how you know where to put the decimal point in each product.

Estimate. Then find each product.

6. $.46
   × 13

7. $.99
   × 20

8. $1.56
   × 45

9. $3.98
   × 69

10. $7.09
    × 84

11. $6.40
    × 92

12. $2.57
    × 35

13. $5.84
    × 59

14. $9.70
    × 27

 Find the missing number. Use mental math or paper and pencil.

15. n × $.43 = $4.30

16. n × $.67 = $67.00

17. 10 × n = $320.00

18. 100 × n = $80.00

Think and Apply

Use the table to answer 19 through 21.

Magazine	Newsstand 1 Issue	Subscription 24 Issues
News	$ .89	$20.00
Space Age	$1.50	$32.30
Tel-Star	$2.05	$45.75
U-Know	$2.95	$62.80

19. What is the cost of 16 issues of *News* magazine at the newsstand price?

20. How much greater is the newsstand price for 24 issues of *Tel-Star* than the subscription price?

21. Is $20.00 enough to buy 11 issues of *Tel-Star* magazine at the newsstand price? Explain.

Make up a multiplication word problem using the information in the table.

Mixed Review

1. 48
   25
   +36

2. 48
   −39

3. 428
   × 3

4. 81 ÷ 9

5. 9 × 8

6. 63 ÷ 7

7. 24 × 7

8. 8 × 5

9. 36 ÷ 9

10. 95 × 4

Use mental math to solve.

11. 9 × 4,000

12. 3 × $3.95

13. 486 ÷ 486

14. 642 × 392 × 0

15. 98 ÷ 1

List these numbers in order from least to greatest.

16. 438   348   843

17. 304   3,400   340

18. 632   362   2,632

SHOW WHAT YOU KNOW

Multiplying Greater Numbers

Science-By-Mail™ is a program at the Museum of Science in Boston, Massachusetts. The museum mails science problems to students. The students mail their answers back to the museum. One year, the museum mailed 18 pages of problems to each of the 5,264 students in the program. How many pages of problems were mailed?

18 × 5,264 = n

You can find the product using paper and pencil.

Step 1 Multiply by ones.	Step 2 Multiply by tens.	Step 3 Add.
5,264 × 18 ‾‾‾‾‾‾‾ 42,112 ← 8 × 5,264	5,264 × 18 ‾‾‾‾‾‾‾ 42,112 52,640 ← 10 × 5,264	5,264 × 18 ‾‾‾‾‾‾‾ 42,112 52,640 ‾‾‾‾‾‾‾ 94,752

You can find the product using your calculator.

Press:    Display shows: 94752.

There were 94,752 pages of problems mailed.

Check Your Understanding

Estimate first. Then use mental math, paper and pencil, or a calculator to find each product.

1. 199	2. 207	3. 930	4. 4,080	5. 7,251
× 21	× 70	× 45	× 30	× 59

Share Your Ideas Which of the products above are easiest to solve using mental math? Explain.

Estimate first. Then use mental math, paper and pencil, or a calculator to find each product.

CHOICES

6. 324	7. 591	8. 850	9. 1,205	10. 8,758
× 20	× 47	× 60	× 35	× 19

11. 5,001	12. 2,683	13. 4,206	14. 3,340	15. 6,451
× 24	× 32	× 57	× 90	× 18

16. $4.59	17. $60.14	18. $98.03	19. $17.95	20. $52.34
× 73	× 55	× 28	× 40	× 99

21. 70 × 260 = n
22. 42 × 536 = n
23. 90 × 9,000 = n

24. 28 × 7,063 = n
25. 16 × 3,200 = n
26. 74 × 2,982 = n

27. 6 × 5 × 9,200 = n
28. 3 × 14 × 6,050 = n

**Use mental math or estimation. Write +, −, or ×
in each box. Check with your calculator.**

CHOICES

29. 69 □ 700 > 40,000

30. 25 □ 1,000 < 19 × 1,100

31. 82 × 4,000 < 250,000 □ 200,000

32. 56 □ 395 > 20,694 □ 5,123

Think and Apply

33. **What if** the museum sent newsletters about the science program to 892 schools. If each newsletter costs 21¢ to mail, what was the cost of mailing the newsletters?

34. **What if** the cost of joining Science-By-Mail is $40.00 for a group of up to 4 students? What would be the cost for all the students in your class to join the program?

35. **Look back** at **30**. Explain how you decided what operation sign to write in the box.

If the zero key on your calculator is broken, how can you find the product of 36 × 47,200?

SHOW WHAT YOU KNOW

Interview: Calculators and a School Chorus Tour

Tom and Jim Maloney of Rockville Centre, New York, sing in the school chorus. Next summer, the chorus is going to Europe.

Tom and Jim need to earn money for their trip. For both of them the trip will cost a total of $1,275.00. Tom said, "I used a calculator to figure out how much money we will earn." The table shows the amount of money Tom and Jim earn on each job.

How much money will they earn raking 15 yards?
15 × $7.50 = $112.50
Tom and Jim will earn $112.50.

Job	Money Earned
paper route	$32.75 per week
raking leaves	$7.50 per yard
walking dogs	$.65 per walk per dog
cleaning garages	$11.00 per garage
weeding	$9.85 per garden

Sharing Your Ideas

Find the information in the table above. You may wish to use your calculator to solve.

1. How much money will Tom and Jim earn weeding 10 gardens?

2. How much money will the boys earn cleaning 12 garages?

3. How much money will the boys earn for walking one dog 34 times?

4. How much money will the boys earn from their paper route in 25 weeks?

Extending Your Thinking

Use the information in the table on page 210. Use mental math or your calculator to solve.

CHOICES

5. On Saturday, the boys weeded 2 gardens and walked 1 dog. How much money did they earn that day?

6. **What if** Jim rakes 1 yard a day for 1 week? How much money will he earn?

7. Will the boys earn more money from cleaning 20 garages or from raking 20 yards? How much more?

8. **What if** Tom walks one dog each day during the month of October? How much money will he earn?

9. How much money will the boys earn weeding 19 gardens and raking 32 lawns?

Show What You Know

10. Estimate whether Tom and Jim can earn enough money from their paper route in a year to pay for the trip. Now solve the problem with your calculator.

11. List two jobs that you do (or would like to do) to earn money. Combine your list with those of your classmates. Which are the most common jobs? Put them in order, starting with the most common one.

LET'S CELEBRATE

WORKING TOGETHER

1. Work in groups. Choose an occasion that is special to your culture or another culture. Plan a celebration.

   • Decide what food and other items you need.

   • Decide how much of each item is needed for the entire class.

   • Write a list of things to buy for the celebration.

2. Go to three different stores to find the prices of the items on your shopping list. Record the prices for each store on a form.

NAME OF STORE:

Item	Number of People Item Serves	Quantitiy Needed for Class	Price per Item	Total

3. Compare the prices of the items from each store.

   • How much will it cost to buy the items at each store?

   • Which store is the best one to shop at? Why?

   • Will you have enough money to buy everything on your list if everyone in the class contributes $2? If not, what can you do?

4. Share the plans for your celebration with the class. Discuss each group's celebration. Consider the following.

   • Which celebration costs the most? the least?

   • Which celebration has the most variety of foods?

CHAPTER REVIEW/TEST

Find each product.

1. $\begin{array}{r} 92 \\ \times\,20 \\ \hline \end{array}$

2. $\begin{array}{r} 40 \\ \times\,60 \\ \hline \end{array}$

3. $\begin{array}{r} 135 \\ \times\ 30 \\ \hline \end{array}$

4. $\begin{array}{r} 469 \\ \times\ 50 \\ \hline \end{array}$

Estimate each product.

5. 82×98

6. 167×83

7. 502×45

Multiply.

8. $\begin{array}{r} 17 \\ \times\,27 \\ \hline \end{array}$

9. $\begin{array}{r} 32 \\ \times\,56 \\ \hline \end{array}$

10. $\begin{array}{r} 87 \\ \times\,39 \\ \hline \end{array}$

11. $\begin{array}{r} \$2.43 \\ \times\ \ \ 54 \\ \hline \end{array}$

12. $\begin{array}{r} 358 \\ \times\ 46 \\ \hline \end{array}$

13. $\begin{array}{r} 863 \\ \times\ 23 \\ \hline \end{array}$

14. $\begin{array}{r} \$7.83 \\ \times\ \ \ 72 \\ \hline \end{array}$

15. $\begin{array}{r} 348 \\ \times\ 64 \\ \hline \end{array}$

16. $\begin{array}{r} 1{,}185 \\ \times\ \ \ 27 \\ \hline \end{array}$

17. $\begin{array}{r} 5{,}118 \\ \times\ \ \ 43 \\ \hline \end{array}$

18. $\begin{array}{r} \$4{,}958 \\ \times\ \ \ \ \ 65 \\ \hline \end{array}$

19. $\begin{array}{r} 1{,}704 \\ \times\ \ \ 89 \\ \hline \end{array}$

20. $\begin{array}{r} \$2{,}695 \\ \times\ \ \ \ \ 57 \\ \hline \end{array}$

21. $\begin{array}{r} \$8.45 \\ \times\ \ \ 73 \\ \hline \end{array}$

22. $\begin{array}{r} \$15.40 \\ \times\ \ \ \ 67 \\ \hline \end{array}$

23. $\begin{array}{r} \$54.63 \\ \times\ \ \ \ \ 73 \\ \hline \end{array}$

Solve.

24. It cost $1.34 per minute for Peg to call her grandmother. How much will it cost for Peg to talk to her for 15 minutes?

25. Aaron can type 43 words a minute. His friend Sean can type 11 more words a minute than Aaron can. How many words can they type in 10 minutes?

Think The local weekly paper is printed in 3 sections. This week there are 46 pages in Section A, 33 pages in Section B, and 28 pages in Section C. How many pages are there in 24 copies of the newspaper? 240 copies?

The Multiplication Game

To play the multiplication game, you will need:
- number cards marked 0 through 9
- paper and pencil

Follow these steps to play the game. Any number of people can play.

1. Each player writes the following on a piece of paper.

2. Choose a leader who shuffles the number cards and then picks one and shows it to the players. Write the number in one of the boxes on your own paper.

3. Then the leader picks another number. Again, write the number in one of the remaining boxes on your own paper.

4. Play continues until the leader has picked 6 numbers. (Note: Each player needs to use only 5 numbers to complete the multiplication example. So each player chooses 1 number to discard.)

5. Solve your own multiplication example. The player with the greatest product wins. That player may pick the cards for the next game.

HOME CONNECTION

In Chapters **4-6** your child has been learning how to multiply by one- and two-digit numbers. He or she can now change this pizza recipe for one person into a recipe for your family. Have a pizza party and enjoy it!

A Pizza Party

Pizza for One Person

Ingredients:

4oz shredded mozzarella cheese

6oz spaghetti sauce

2 crescent rolls in refrigerated tube

3 slices of pepperoni

Steps:

- Break open tube of crescent rolls and separate triangles. Put two triangles side by side.
- Cover with spaghetti sauce, then with cheese.
- Put pepperoni slices on pizza.
- Bake using temperature and time shown on the crescent rolls tube.

1. Invite your family to a pizza party.

2. Multiply each ingredient by the number of people.

3. Gather all of the ingredients in one place.

4. Work together. Follow the steps on the recipe card to make the pizza.

CUMULATIVE REVIEW

Choose the correct answer. Write A, B, C, or D.

1. $4 \times 7 = \square$

   A 21   **C** 14

   B 28   **D** not given

2. $(3 \times 3) \times 4 = \square$

   A 36   **C** 13

   B 24   **D** not given

3.   10
     $\times\ 0$

   A 0   **C** 1

   B 10   **D** not given

4. $36 \div 4 = \square$

   A 8   **C** 9

   B 6   **D** not given

5. $6\overline{)36}$

   A 7   **C** 6

   B 5   **D** not given

6. $54 \div 6 = \square$

   A 8   **C** 7

   B 9   **D** not given

7. $8\overline{)72}$

   A 9   **C** 8

   B 7   **D** not given

8. $90 \times 5 = \square$

   A 560   **C** 45

   B 400   **D** not given

9.   67
     $\times\ 5$

   A 335   **C** 225

   B 305   **D** not given

10. $271 \times 8 = \square$

   A 1,668   **C** 2,148

   B 2,168   **D** not given

11.   265
     $\times\ 3$

   A 785   **C** 685

   B 795   **D** not given

12. $4,507 \times 8 = \square$

   A 32,006   **C** 36,056

   B 3,206   **D** not given

13. $6 \times \$1.42 = \square$

   A $8.42   **C** $8.52

   B $6.42   **D** not given

14. $6 \times \$54.38 = \square$

   A $326.28   **C** $326.26

   B $325.28   **D** not given

Choose the correct answer. Write A, B, C, or D.

15. $40 \times 50 = n$

  A 200   **C** 20,000

  B 2,000   **D** not given

16.
$$\begin{array}{r} 610 \\ \times\ 30 \\ \hline \end{array}$$

  A 183,000   **C** 1,830

  B 18,300   **D** not given

17. Estimate 86×51.

  A 500   **C** 400

  B 3,000   **D** 4,500

18. $43 \times 26 = n$

  A 344   **C** 1,118

  B 1,108   **D** not given

19.
$$\begin{array}{r} 29 \\ \times 84 \\ \hline \end{array}$$

  A 2,436   **C** 2,203

  B 348   **D** not given

20. $516 \times 48 = n$

  A 24,768   **C** 6,192

  B 24,582   **D** not given

21. $\$.85 \times 54 = n$

  A $7.65   **C** $45.90

  B $45.70   **D** not given

Use the table to solve 22–23.

BATTERY	LENGTH OF CHARGE
Brand A	5 hours
Brand B	4 hours
Brand C	6 hours

22. Each of the 3 batteries was used in a radio, one after another. They were only changed when the charge ran out. How long did the radio play?

  A 10 hours   **C** 15 hours

  B 14 hours   **D** not given

23. Battery A will last how much longer than battery B?

  A 1 hour   **C** 3 hours

  B 2 hours   **D** not given

Solve.

24. Raoul swims laps in a pool. The first week he swims 2 laps, the second week 4 laps, the third week 6 laps, and the fourth week 8 laps. How many laps will he swim the next week if he continues this pattern?

  A 7   **C** 8

  B 9   **D** not given

25. Which week will he swim 12 laps if he continues the pattern?

  A fifth   **C** seventh

  B sixth   **D** not given

7 Dividing

THEME   The World of Sports

Sharing What You Know

Sports can be enjoyed by everyone! Disabled athletes compete in such sports as swimming, diving, track and field, and skiing. They also take part in wheelchair events, including basketball. The winner of each event is the person who finishes the race in the fastest time, or the team that scores the most points. Choose one event. How might mathematics be used in that event?

Using Language

Athletes work hard to improve their averages. What does it mean that a basketball player has an average score of 15 points a game? Say a player scored 10, 17, and 18 points in 3 games. The average of 10, 17, and 18 is 15. In mathematics, an **average** is the sum of a group of numbers divided by how many numbers there are in the group. How are the meanings of **average** alike?

Words to Know: divisor, dividend, quotient, remainder, average

Be a Problem Solver

In the first 100-yard relay race there are 4 runners on each team. In the second 100-yard relay race there are 2 runners on each team. In which relay race does each runner run a longer distance?

Prepare questions that you would ask a famous athlete if you were doing an interview for your school newspaper.

Mental Math: Dividing

Each gymnastics team has 7 members. There are 23 gymnasts in the class. How many teams can be formed? How many gymnasts will not be on a team?

$23 \div 7 = n$

Think $7 \times n$ is close to 23.
Try $7 \times 2 = 14$
        $7 \times 3 = 21$
        $7 \times 4 = 28$ 28 is too great.
                             Try $n = 3$.

Divide.

quotient → **3 R2**
divisor → 7)23 ← dividend
        − 21
           2 ← remainder

Check by multiplying.

        3 ← quotient
      ×7 ← divisor
       21
      + 2 ← remainder
       23 ← dividend

Three teams can be formed. Two gymnasts will not be on a team.

Look at the example above. What does 21 stand for?

Check Your Understanding

Divide. Use mental math. Check by multiplying.

1. 3)14   **2.** 5)39   **3.** 9)44   **4.** 9)65

Share Your Ideas   Describe how to use multiplication to find the quotient and remainder for $50 \div 8$.

Divide. Use mental math. Check by multiplying.

5. $2\overline{)19}$ **6.** $6\overline{)11}$ **7.** $8\overline{)31}$ **8.** $3\overline{)28}$ **9.** $4\overline{)38}$

10. $8\overline{)70}$ **11.** $4\overline{)15}$ **12.** $9\overline{)81}$ **13.** $5\overline{)47}$ **14.** $7\overline{)27}$

15. $21 \div 6 = n$ **16.** $17 \div 2 = n$ **17.** $38 \div 9 = n$

18. $56 \div 8 = n$ **19.** $41 \div 5 = n$ **20.** $n \div 5 = 5\,R1$

When you divide by each number, what remainders are possible?

21. 5 **22.** 1 **23.** 7 **24.** 8 **25.** 9

Find each number.

26. The divisor is 2. The dividend is 13. The quotient is 6. What is the remainder?

27. The dividend is 44. The remainder is 4. The quotient is 5. What is the divisor?

Think and Apply

28. Of the 46 students in the gymnastics class, 38 are trying out for gymnastic teams. If there are 9 gymnasts on each team, how many teams can there be?

29. There are 7 gymnasts on Team A and 9 gymnasts on Team B. Each girl is given 2 minutes to perform her floor routine. Is $\frac{1}{2}$ hour enough time for all the gymnasts to perform? Explain.

30. When 10 and 22 are divided by 6, they have remainders of 4. Find three other numbers that have remainders of 4 when divided by 6.

Visual Thinking

31. Draw the square that completes the pattern.

 Explain why the remainder must be less than the divisor.

Mental Math: Patterns

The total playing time in an ice hockey game is 60 minutes. There are 3 playing periods. Each period is the same length. How long is each period?

$60 \div 3 = n$

Divide.   Check.

Think

$60 \div 3 = n$ ← $6 \div 3 = 2$ $20 \times 3 = 60$

$60 \div 3 = 20$

Each hockey period is 20 minutes long.

Look at these examples.

$8 \div 4 = 2$	$9 \div 3 = 3$	$24 \div 6 = 4$
$80 \div 4 = 20$	$90 \div 3 = 30$	$240 \div 6 = 40$
$800 \div 4 = 200$	$900 \div 3 = 300$	$2{,}400 \div 6 = 400$

Explain the pattern in the quotients.

Check Your Understanding

Divide. Use mental math. Check by multiplying.

1. $72 \div 8 = n$ **2.** $60 \div 6 = n$

   $720 \div 8 = n$ $600 \div 6 = n$

3. $42 \div 7 = n$ **4.** $27 \div 9 = n$

   $420 \div 7 = n$ $270 \div 9 = n$

Share Your Ideas Explain how to use a basic division fact and patterns with zeros to find each quotient.

$810 \div 9 = n$ $3{,}600 \div 6 = n$

Divide. Use mental math. Check by multiplying.

5. $35 \div 5 = n$
$350 \div 5 = n$

6. $36 \div 4 = n$
$360 \div 4 = n$

7. $54 \div 9 = n$
$540 \div 9 = n$

8. $100 \div 2 = n$

9. $480 \div 6 = n$

10. $39 \div 6 = n$

11. $2\overline{)180}$ **12.** $9\overline{)56}$ **13.** $7\overline{)560}$ **14.** $5\overline{)3,000}$ **15.** $3\overline{)270}$

16. $6\overline{)1,800}$ **17.** $7\overline{)630}$ **18.** $4\overline{)2,000}$ **19.** $8\overline{)6,400}$ **20.** $2\overline{)1,600}$

Find each missing number.

21. $n \div 4 = 40$

22. $n \div 2 = 2,000$

23. $n \div 3 = 500$

24. $n \div 6 = 500$

25. $400 \div n = 80$

26. $1,200 \div n = 400$

**Look for patterns to help you find each quotient.
Then write the next two examples for each pattern
and find their quotients.**

27. $4\overline{)40}$ $4\overline{)80}$ $4\overline{)120}$ $4\overline{)160}$ $4\overline{)200}$

28. $5\overline{)500}$ $5\overline{)1,000}$ $5\overline{)1,500}$ $5\overline{)2,000}$ $5\overline{)2,500}$

Think and Apply

29. Use mental math to find
$600 \div 3$, $90 \div 3$, and $3 \div 3$.
Add the quotients. Then use a
calculator to find $693 \div 3$. What
do you notice? Explain.

30. Use the method described in **29**
to find each of these quotients.
a. $482 \div 2 = n$
b. $488 \div 4 = n$
c. $660 \div 6 = n$

Create a rule about the number of zeros in
the quotient and the dividend. Compare your
rule with a friend's rule.

SHOW WHAT YOU KNOW

Investigating Division

You can use base-ten blocks
to play Divvy Up.

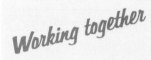

Materials: spinner, base-ten blocks, Workmat 7

A. Spin the spinner two times and
use the numbers to form a two-
digit number, for example, 26.

B. Model the number, using the
fewest possible base-ten blocks,
for example,

C. Spin again to find the number of
groups. Share the blocks equally,
using the number shown by the
spin, for example, 4. When
necessary, exchange tens blocks
for ones blocks.

D. Record your results on the
workmat or in a chart like
the one below. Repeat the
activity at least four times.

Starting Number		Number of Groups	Drawing to Show Equal Groups	Number in Each Group		Number Left Over
tens	ones			tens	ones	
2	6	4				

Sharing Your Results

1. Describe the steps you followed to share the
blocks. When did you have to exchange blocks?

2. Compare the number of blocks left over each
time with the number of groups. Are there more
groups or more blocks? Explain.

Extending the Activity

▶ When you share equally, you are dividing.

Work with a partner.

Materials: base-ten blocks, Workmat 8

3. Take turns thinking of a 3-digit number.

4. Show the number, using the fewest possible base-ten blocks.

5. Show how to divide the blocks into 2, 3, and 4 groups.

6. Record your results on the workmat or in a chart like the one shown below.

7. Repeat the activity 2 times.

Starting Number			Number of Groups	Drawing to Show Equal Groups	Number in Each Group			Number Left Over
h	t	o			h	t	o	

Show What You Know

8. How did you decide which blocks to divide first?

9. Use these words to describe the columns in your chart: *dividend, divisor, quotient, remainder.*

10. Sandy made these 7 groups from 23 counters. Did she divide? Explain your answer.

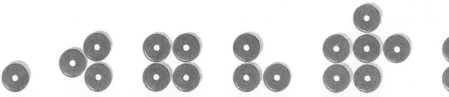

225

ACTIVITY

Understanding Division

Predicting the number of digits in the quotient
first can help you divide.

Working together

Materials: base-ten blocks, Workmat 9

A. Show 63 using the fewest possible
base-ten blocks.

B. Write the division example 5)63
on a chart like the one shown
below or use Workmat 9.
Predict the number of digits in
the quotient. Mark an x for
each digit.

C. Divide the blocks for 63 equally
into 5 groups. When necessary
exchange 1 tens block for
10 ones blocks.

D. Complete the chart. How many
digits are in the quotient?
Compare the quotient with
your prediction.

E. Repeat steps **A** through **D** using
the division example 6)49.

F. Take turns making your own
division examples with 2-digit
dividends. Repeat the activity
at least 4 times.

Example	Dividend	Divisor	Prediction	Quotient	Remainder
5)63	63	5	xx 5)63	12	3
6)49					

Sharing Your Results

1. How did you know when to put the x in the
tens place in the quotient?

2. How did you know when to put the x in the
ones place in the quotient?

Extending the Activity

Follow these steps using base-ten blocks to divide 3)71.

3. Predict the number of digits in the quotient.

4. Divide 7 tens into 3 groups. Each group gets 2 tens. How many tens are left?

5. Divide 11 ones into 3 groups. Each group gets 3 ones. How many ones are left?

6. Does the number of digits in the quotient match the prediction?

Work with a partner. Take turns predicting the number of digits in the quotient. Record each quotient and remainder. Use base-ten blocks if you wish.

7. 2)28   **8.** 3)40   **9.** 5)75

10. 4)99   **11.** 3)60   **12.** 2)83

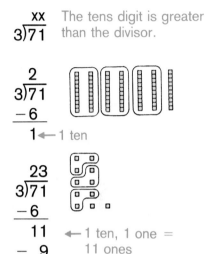

$$\overset{\text{xx}}{3)\overline{71}}$$ The tens digit is greater than the divisor.

$$\begin{array}{r} 2 \\ 3)\overline{71} \\ -6 \\ \hline 1 \end{array}$$ ←1 ten

$$\begin{array}{r} 23 \\ 3)\overline{71} \\ -6 \\ \hline 11 \\ -9 \\ \hline 2 \end{array}$$ ←1 ten, 1 one = 11 ones

Show What You Know

13. What is the greatest number the remainder can be when you divide by 2? by 3? by 4? by 5? Explain.

14. How many digits would be in the quotient of 432 ÷ 5? Explain.

Which of the numbers below are multiples of 6? multiples of 8?

160 300 120 240 4,800 7,200

Estimating Quotients

Keith is putting 265 baseball cards into a photo album. He can put 9 cards on each page. About how many pages will he fill?

Estimate 265 ÷ 9.

One way to estimate is to change the dividend to a number that can be divided easily by 9.

$$9\overline{)265} \rightarrow 9\overline{)270} \rightarrow \overset{30}{9\overline{)270}}$$

Think 9)27
27 is close to 26, and can be divided equally by 9.

Keith will fill about 30 pages.

TOM SEAVER

More Examples

$$4\overline{)87} \rightarrow \overset{20}{4\overline{)80}} \qquad\qquad 9\overline{)869} \rightarrow \overset{100}{9\overline{)900}}$$

Think 4)8   **Think** 9)9

Check Your Understanding

Choose the division problem that gives the closest estimate. Then find the estimate.

1. 2)52   **a.** 2)20   **b.** 2)40   **c.** 2)60

2. 3)159   **a.** 3)150   **b.** 3)180   **c.** 3)210

3. 5)920   **a.** 5)500   **b.** 5)1,000   **c.** 5)1,500

Share Your Ideas Explain how you decided which division problem to use to estimate the quotient in **3**.

Choose the division problem that gives the closest estimate. Then find the estimate.

4. $4\overline{)56}$ a. $4\overline{)40}$ b. $4\overline{)80}$ c. $4\overline{)120}$

5. $3\overline{)93}$ a. $3\overline{)60}$ b. $3\overline{)90}$ c. $3\overline{)120}$

6. $2\overline{)786}$ a. $2\overline{)400}$ b. $2\overline{)600}$ c. $2\overline{)800}$

7. $9\overline{)378}$ a. $9\overline{)270}$ b. $9\overline{)360}$ c. $9\overline{)450}$

Write a division problem that gives a close estimate. Then find the estimate.

8. $2\overline{)88}$ 9. $3\overline{)57}$ 10. $9\overline{)97}$ 11. $3\overline{)882}$ 12. $2\overline{)990}$

13. $6\overline{)386}$ 14. $8\overline{)910}$ 15. $4\overline{)170}$ 16. $5\overline{)420}$ 17. $7\overline{)224}$

18. $4\overline{)336}$ 19. $2\overline{)665}$ 20. $6\overline{)552}$ 21. $5\overline{)5,136}$ 22. $9\overline{)2,000}$

Think and Apply

Use the table to solve.

23. **What if** there are 8 baseball cards in each package? About how many packages of baseball cards are there?

24. **What if** there are 6 football cards in each package? If a customer just bought 5 packages, about how many packages of football cards are left?

25. **What if** the hockey and soccer cards are packaged together and there are 7 cards in each package? About how many packages of these cards are there?

SPORTS CARDS	
Type	Number of Cards
Baseball	584
Basketball	650
Football	354
Hockey	183
Soccer	289

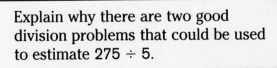

JOURNAL WRITING

Explain why there are two good division problems that could be used to estimate $275 \div 5$.

SHOW WHAT YOU KNOW

> How many digits can be in the quotient if you divide a two-digit number by a one-digit number. Explain your answer.

Dividing Two-Digit Numbers

A tennis can holds 3 balls. If there are 88 tennis balls, how many full cans will there be? How many balls will be left over?

$88 \div 3 = n$

Step 1 Decide where to place the first digit in the quotient. $3\overline{)88}$ **Think** There are enough tens to divide.	**Step 2** Divide. Then multiply. $\begin{array}{r} 2 \\ 3\overline{)88} \\ 6 \end{array}$ **Think** $3\overline{)8}$ $6 \leftarrow 2 \times 3$	**Step 3** Subtract and compare. $\begin{array}{r} 2 \\ 3\overline{)88} \\ -6 \\ \hline 2 \end{array}$ $2 < 3$
Step 4 Bring down ones. Divide. Then multiply. $\begin{array}{r} 29 \\ 3\overline{)88} \\ -6\downarrow \\ \hline 28 \\ 27 \end{array}$ **Think** 2 tens 8 ones = 28 ones $3\overline{)28}$	**Step 5** Subtract and compare. $\begin{array}{r} 29\,R1 \\ 3\overline{)88} \\ -6\downarrow \\ \hline 28 \\ -27 \\ \hline 1 \end{array}$ $1 < 3$ Write the remainder in the quotient.	Check by estimating. $3\overline{)88} \rightarrow \begin{array}{r} 30 \\ 3\overline{)90} \end{array}$

There will be 29 full cans. One ball will be left over.

Check Your Understanding

Divide. Check by estimating.

1. $3\overline{)38}$ 2. $2\overline{)77}$ 3. $5\overline{)70}$ 4. $4\overline{)87}$ 5. $7\overline{)92}$

Share Your Ideas Sometimes division steps are repeated. How do you know when you have finished dividing?

Divide. Check by estimating.

6. $2\overline{)27}$ 7. $8\overline{)68}$ 8. $4\overline{)83}$

9. $6\overline{)84}$ 10. $3\overline{)57}$ 11. $2\overline{)63}$

12. $9\overline{)55}$ 13. $8\overline{)98}$ 14. $3\overline{)64}$

15. $6\overline{)86}$ 16. $7\overline{)78}$ 17. $5\overline{)49}$

18. $5\overline{)93}$ 19. $4\overline{)37}$ 20. $9\overline{)53}$

21. $2\overline{)45}$ 22. $6\overline{)29}$ 23. $3\overline{)68}$

24. $7\overline{)94}$ 25. $5\overline{)78}$ 26. $8\overline{)34}$

27. $63 \div 4 = n$ 28. $67 \div 8 = n$

29. $89 \div 3 = n$ 30. $38 \div 5 = n$

31. $76 \div 6 = n$ 32. $93 \div 8 = n$

33. $89 \div 9 = n$ 34. $41 \div 3 = n$

Think and Apply

35. If Patty gives 6 tennis lessons a day, how many days will it take her to give 98 lessons?

36. A tennis ball measures about 3 inches across. About how many balls placed side by side will form a line 6 feet long? (There are 12 inches in a foot.)

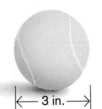

|← 3 in. →|

37. Use each of the digits 2, 3, and 6. Put one digit into each box to give the greatest possible quotient. $\square\overline{)\square\square}$ Then find the least possible quotient.

> **Look back** at **37**. Explain how you decided where to place the digits to make the greatest and least quotients.

Tell if each quotient will be greater than or less than 99. Explain how you know.

$327 \div 9 = n$ $958 \div 6 = n$ $600 \div 7 = n$

Dividing Three-Digit Numbers

There are 118 children signed up for swimming lessons. The swim coach plans to put 6 children in each group. How many groups will there be?

$118 \div 6 = n$

Step 1 Decide where to place the first digit in the quotient. $6\overline{)118}$ **Think** Not enough hundreds. There are enough tens to divide.	**Step 2** Divide. Then multiply. $\begin{array}{r} 1 \\ 6\overline{)118} \\ 6 \end{array}$ **Think** $6\overline{)11}$	**Step 3** Subtract and compare. $\begin{array}{r} 1 \\ 6\overline{)118} \\ -6 \\ \hline 5 \end{array}$ $5 < 6$
Step 4 Bring down ones. Divide. Then multiply. $\begin{array}{r} 19 \\ 6\overline{)118} \\ -6\downarrow \\ \hline 58 \\ 54 \end{array}$ **Think** 5 tens 8 ones = 58 ones $6\overline{)58}$	**Step 5** Subtract and compare. $\begin{array}{r} 19 \\ 6\overline{)118} \\ -6\downarrow \\ \hline 58 \\ -54 \\ \hline 4 \end{array}$ $4 < 6$ Write the remainder in the quotient. Since there are 4 children left, there will have to be another group.	Check by multiplying. $\begin{array}{r} 19 \leftarrow \text{quotient} \\ \times\ 6 \leftarrow \text{divisor} \\ \hline 114 \\ +\ 4 \leftarrow \text{remainder} \\ \hline 118 \leftarrow \text{dividend} \end{array}$

There will be 20 groups.

Check Your Understanding

Find each quotient. Check by multiplying.

1. $2\overline{)246}$ **2.** $8\overline{)894}$ **3.** $4\overline{)357}$ **4.** $3\overline{)473}$ **5.** $6\overline{)298}$

Share Your Ideas When you are dividing, why should you compare after you subtract?

Find each quotient. Check by multiplying.

6. $4\overline{)348}$ 7. $2\overline{)130}$ 8. $8\overline{)729}$ 9. $5\overline{)419}$ 10. $6\overline{)737}$

11. $3\overline{)254}$ 12. $7\overline{)987}$ 13. $6\overline{)600}$ 14. $9\overline{)852}$ 15. $4\overline{)532}$

16. $3\overline{)693}$ 17. $6\overline{)82}$ 18. $9\overline{)500}$ 19. $5\overline{)785}$ 20. $8\overline{)240}$

21. $4\overline{)226}$ 22. $6\overline{)366}$ 23. $2\overline{)147}$ 24. $7\overline{)499}$ 25. $6\overline{)562}$

26. $5\overline{)172}$ 27. $3\overline{)635}$ 28. $8\overline{)95}$ 29. $9\overline{)558}$ 30. $4\overline{)173}$

31. $2\overline{)967}$ 32. $4\overline{)724}$ 33. $7\overline{)400}$ 34. $6\overline{)292}$ 35. $9\overline{)351}$

36. $93 \div 5 = n$ 37. $144 \div 3 = n$ 38. $809 \div 6 = n$

39. $400 \div 4 = n$ 40. $333 \div 2 = n$ 41. $645 \div 9 = n$

Use $+$, $-$, $\times$, or $\div$ for ●.

42. $170 \div 5 > 93 \,●\, 3$

43. $64 \,●\, 6 > 2{,}100 \div 7$

44. $573 \,●\, 3 = 456 - 265$

45. $900 \,●\, 9 + 50 = 50 \,●\, 3$

Think and Apply

46. A lap in swimming is the distance from one end of a pool to the other end. Barry swam 4 laps in an indoor pool for a total of 300 feet. How long is the pool?

47. The students sold 615 tickets to the swim meet. They sold twice as many adult tickets as student tickets. How many adult tickets did they sell?

Logical Thinking

48. What is the mystery number? It is a two-digit number less than 30. When you divide the number by 2, 3, 4, or 6, you always get a remainder of 1. When you divide the number by 5, you get a remainder of 0.

What is the greatest three-digit number that gives a two-digit quotient and a remainder of 0 when divided by 2?

SHOW WHAT YOU KNOW

CHECKPOINT

Divide. Use mental math. pages 220–223

1. $6\overline{)50}$ **2.** $8\overline{)57}$ **3.** $9\overline{)540}$ **4.** $3\overline{)90}$ **5.** $6\overline{)39}$

6. $38 \div 4 = n$ **7.** $800 \div 2 = n$ **8.** $490 \div 7 = n$

Write a division problem that gives a close estimate. Then find the estimate. pages 228–229

9. $8\overline{)91}$ **10.** $6\overline{)43}$ **11.** $5\overline{)138}$ **12.** $4\overline{)296}$ **13.** $7\overline{)374}$

Divide. Check by estimating. pages 224–231

14. $8\overline{)99}$ **15.** $7\overline{)91}$ **16.** $4\overline{)89}$ **17.** $6\overline{)74}$ **18.** $9\overline{)32}$

19. $6\overline{)59}$ **20.** $4\overline{)67}$ **21.** $7\overline{)83}$ **22.** $5\overline{)78}$ **23.** $3\overline{)59}$

24. $61 \div 5 = n$ **25.** $83 \div 3 = n$ **26.** $49 \div 6 = n$

Find each quotient. Check by multiplying. pages 232–233

27. $5\overline{)183}$ **28.** $9\overline{)785}$ **29.** $8\overline{)965}$ **30.** $3\overline{)988}$ **31.** $4\overline{)607}$

32. $9\overline{)236}$ **33.** $3\overline{)493}$ **34.** $4\overline{)782}$ **35.** $7\overline{)385}$ **36.** $5\overline{)629}$

37. $679 \div 6 = n$ **38.** $138 \div 4 = n$ **39.** $263 \div 3 = n$

Look at $76 \div 8 = 9$ R4. Choose a vocabulary word to name each number.

40. 76   **41.** 8

42. 9   **43.** 4

Words to Know
divisor
dividend
remainder
quotient

Solve.

44. There are 333 seats in the stadium. If there are 9 rows, how many seats are in each row?

45. A hockey puck weighs 6 ounces. How many hockey pucks are in a carton that weighs 3 pounds? (A pound is equal to 16 ounces.)

INVESTIGATING
PROBLEM SOLVING

THINK
EXPLORE
SOLVE
LOOK BACK

How Many Players on a Team?

Sixty-seven students are forming teams for a table-tennis league. The team organizers want some students to be substitutes.

Thinking Critically

How many students might be on each team? How many teams might there be?

Work with a partner and make different plans. Be sure there are an equal number of members on each team.

Analyzing and Making Decisions

1. What are some reasons for having teams?

2. If you had 3 people on a team, you could have 22 teams and 1 substitute or 21 teams and 4 substitutes. Which plan would you choose? Explain.

3. **What if** you had 4 people on a team? How many teams would you have? How many substitutes would you have?

4. Make teams that have 5 or more members each. How many substitutes would you have?

5. How many students would *you* put on a team? How many teams would you have? How many substitutes would you have? Explain why you chose these numbers.

Look Back   Look at **5.** How many games would you have each of your teams play? Explain.

What's the Operation?

Karen, Marta, Chariza, and Beth are in the 20-km cross-country ski relay. In this relay each member skis the same distance. How far must each person ski?

In order to solve a problem, you usually must decide whether to add, subtract, divide, or multiply. Choosing the correct number operation is an important problem solving skill.

Solving the Problem

Think   What is the question?

Explore   How many cross-country skiers are there? How long is the race? Do they each go the same distance? Will a number operation help you solve the problem? Explain.

Solve   How far must each person ski?

Look Back   Does your answer make sense? How can you check your answer?

Share Your Ideas

1. What number operation did you use to solve the problem? Why? What operation did you use to check your work? Why did you select this operation for checking?

2. Could you have used a different number operation to solve the problem? Explain.

Extending Your Thinking

Solve. Use a calculator where appropriate.

CHOICES

3. Nan runs a newsstand. She makes 18 cents on each issue of *The Sports Page* that she sells. How much money did she make on the 21 issues that she sold last Tuesday?

4. Len paid a $3 deposit on a shirt that has a total cost of $19.50. How much more does Len owe on the shirt?

Use this information for 5 and 6.

Louisa entered a swim meet to raise money for charity. She made $35 in the freestyle competition, $25 in the butterfly competition, and $15 in the breast-stroke event.

5. How much money in all did she raise for charity?

6. How much more money did she raise in the freestyle event than in the breast-stroke competition?

Mixed Strategy Review

Use this information for 7 and 8.

A fourth-grade class put on a play to raise money for softball team uniforms. On Friday evening, 70 adults and 25 children attended the play. On Saturday evening, 90 adults and 28 children attended the play. During the Sunday matinee, 122 adults and 65 children attended the play.

7. How many people in all attended the play?

8. How many more adults than children attended the play?

CREATE YOUR OWN

Write a problem that uses a number operation. Have a partner solve it and tell you what operation was used to solve it.

ACTIVITY

Investigating Averages

This chart shows the number of games won by the members of the bowling team.

Member	Games Won
Pang	6
Tom	5
Karen	4
Joe	8
Sally	7

Working together

Materials: paper, 40 counters

A. Write the names from the chart above on a piece of paper as shown. Let one counter stand for one game. Place the correct number of counters above each name.

B. Move some of the counters so that each name has the same number of counters above it. How many counters are above each name? That number is called the **average.** Each player won an average of how many games?

C. What if Sally had won 9 games? How would that change the average? Explain why you could say that the average is between 6 and 7.

D. Repeat the activity. Use the numbers 9, 8, 6, 5, 6, and 8. What is the average of the new numbers?

Pang   Tom   Karen   Joe

Sharing Your Results

1. Describe in your own words what average means.

2. Is the average of a group of numbers always one of the numbers? Explain.

Extending the Activity

▶Another way to find the average is to use division. First add the numbers. Then divide by the number of addends. The quotient is the average.

$$6 + 4 + 5 + 8 + 7 = 30$$
$$30 \div 5 = 6$$
↑
average

Work with a partner. Find each average. Use the division method described above. Check each answer by using counters or drawing a picture.

3. 12, 18, 9

4. 6, 4, 9, 13, 8

5. 6, 9, 5, 7, 11

6. 9, 10, 15, 12

7. 8, 12, 4, 10, 16

8. 7, 6, 19, 10, 3

Work on your own. Use counters, pencil and paper, or a calculator to find each average.

9. 14, 18, 11

10. 6, 12, 5, 13, 19

11. 2, 6, 2, 2

12. 48, 30, 43, 27

13. 5, 8, 5

14. 37, 38, 43, 43, 39

Show What You Know

15. Look back at **13.** Find three other numbers that have the same average.

16. The average of five numbers is 20. Four of the numbers are 17, 18, 12, and 10. What is the fifth number? Explain how you know.

17. Conduct a survey. Ask 5 students how many inches tall they are. Record the data in a table.
a. Find the average height.
b. What will the average be if you add in your height?

Find each product mentally. Then, write a related division example for each.

$2 \times 304 = n$ $301 \times 3 = n$ $2 \times 202 = n$

Zeros in the Quotient

In a relay race 4 runners ran a total of 420 yards. Each person ran the same number of yards. How many yards did each person run?

$420 \div 4 = n$

Step 1 Decide where to place the first digit in the quotient.	Step 2 Divide the hundreds. Then multiply.	Step 3 Subtract and compare.
$4\overline{)420}$ **Think** There are enough hundreds to divide.	$\begin{array}{r} 1 \\ 4\overline{)420} \\ 4 \end{array}$ **Think** $4\overline{)4}$	$\begin{array}{r} 1 \\ 4\overline{)420} \\ -4 \\ \hline 0 \end{array}$ $0 < 4$
Step 4 Bring down tens. Divide.	Step 5 Bring down ones. Divide. Then multiply.	Step 6 Subtract and compare.
$\begin{array}{r} 10 \\ 4\overline{)420} \\ 4\downarrow \\ \hline 02 \end{array}$ **Think** $4\overline{)2}$ Not enough tens to divide. Write 0 in the quotient.	$\begin{array}{r} 105 \\ 4\overline{)420} \\ -4\downarrow\downarrow \\ \hline 020 \\ 20 \end{array}$ **Think** 2 tens 0 ones = 20 ones $4\overline{)20}$	$\begin{array}{r} 105 \\ 4\overline{)420} \\ -4 \\ \hline 020 \\ -20 \\ \hline 0 \end{array}$ $0 < 4$

Each person ran 105 yards.

Check Your Understanding

Divide. Estimate to check.

1. $2\overline{)406}$ 2. $6\overline{)542}$ 3. $4\overline{)920}$ 4. $3\overline{)911}$

Share Your Ideas Explain why there is a zero in the tens place of the quotient in **4**.

Divide. Estimate to check.

5. $2\overline{)101}$ 6. $6\overline{)725}$ 7. $4\overline{)73}$ 8. $7\overline{)210}$ 9. $3\overline{)301}$

10. $9\overline{)498}$ 11. $3\overline{)619}$ 12. $2\overline{)440}$ 13. $5\overline{)100}$ 14. $8\overline{)815}$

15. $4\overline{)160}$ 16. $7\overline{)938}$ 17. $5\overline{)547}$ 18. $2\overline{)700}$ 19. $6\overline{)482}$

20. $3\overline{)626}$ 21. $4\overline{)363}$ 22. $4\overline{)762}$ 23. $2\overline{)614}$ 24. $6\overline{)543}$

25. $206 \div 3 = n$ 26. $399 \div 2 = n$ 27. $910 \div 9 = n$

Find each missing digit.

28.
```
      □□ R□
   3)7□
    -6
     □6
    -□□
      □
```

29.
```
      1□□ R□
   5)5□□
    -□
     039
    -35
      □
```

30.
```
      2□□ R□
   4)□6□
    -□
     1□
    -□6
      □1
     -□
      □
```

Think and Apply

Choose the correct number sentence. Then solve. Use mental math or paper and pencil.

CHOICES

31. Dan ran around the track 2 times for a total run of 880 yards. How many yards is the distance around the track?

   a. $880 + 2 = n$ **b.** $2 \times 880 = n$

   c. $880 \div 2 = n$ **d.** $880 - 2 = n$

32. Jodie ran 15 miles. It took her about 8 minutes to run each mile. How many hours did Jodie run?

   a. $8 \times 15 = n$ **b.** $15 \div 8 = n$

   c. $8 \times 15 \times 60 = n$ **d.** $8 \times 15 \div 60 = n$

Common Error

33. Use estimation to explain why the quotient is incorrect. Then find the correct quotient.

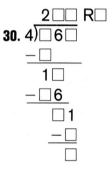

```
       29  ← incorrect
   3)627
    -6
    027
    -27
      0
```

What if the number zero disappeared? Write a short story to describe life without zero.

SHOW WHAT YOU KNOW

Three students shared 249 pennies. Write each student's share, using a dollar sign and a decimal point.

Dividing Money

Rita bought 8 Ping-Pong balls for $4.96. What was the cost of each ball?

$4.96 ÷ 8 = n

Divide money the same way you divide other numbers.

```
    $ .62              Check
8)$4.96                  1
  -4 8↓    Remember    $ .62
    16     to write the × 8
           dollar sign  $4.96
  -16      and the
    0      decimal
           point in the
           quotient.
```

Each Ping-Pong ball cost $.62.

More Examples

```
   $ 7.05              $4.99
8)$56.40             2)$9.98
  -56 ↓↓               -8 ↓
   0 40                 1 9
  -40                 -1 8↓
    0                    18
                       -18
                         0
```

Divide. Check by multiplying.

1. 3)$.87   **2.** 5)$7.00   **3.** 6)$3.72   **4.** 7)$14.35

Share Your Ideas   Explain how to use estimation to tell if the decimal point is in the right place in the quotient in **2**.

Divide. Check by multiplying.

5. $2\overline{)\$.98}$ **6.** $6\overline{)\$.72}$ **7.** $3\overline{)\$4.05}$ **8.** $5\overline{)\$2.00}$

9. $4\overline{)\$8.36}$ **10.** $7\overline{)\$5.25}$ **11.** $6\overline{)\$8.52}$ **12.** $8\overline{)\$9.28}$

13. $5\overline{)\$9.05}$ **14.** $3\overline{)\$2.22}$ **15.** $5\overline{)\$4.60}$ **16.** $4\overline{)\$3.88}$

17. $\$.90 \div 3 = n$ **18.** $\$7.30 \div 2 = n$ **19.** $\$6.00 \div 4 = n$

20. $\$5.94 \div 9 = n$ **21.** $\$4.96 \div 8 = n$ **22.** $\$8.50 \div 5 = n$

Compare. Use >, <, or = for ●.

23. $\$8.94 \div 2$ ● $\$9.69 \div 3$ **24.** $\$6.75 \div 5$ ● $\$5.48 \div 4$

25. $\$7.64 \div 4 + \$7.08$ ● $2 \times \$4.50$

Choose the correct number sentence and solve.

26. A package of 6 arrows costs $8.82. What is the cost of 1 arrow?

   a. $6 \times \$8.82 = n$
   b. $\$8.82 \div 6 = n$
   c. $\$8.82 - 6 = n$
   d. $\$8.82 + 6 = n$

27. A horseshoe costs $2.94. What is the cost of 3 horseshoes?

   a. $\$2.94 \div 3 = n$
   b. $\$2.94 + \$3.00 = n$
   c. $3 \times \$2.94 = n$
   d. $3 \times n = \$2.94$

Think and Apply

28. What is the cost of 1 badminton racket?

29. What is the cost of a net and 2 poles?

30. How many birdies can you buy for $11.00?

31. The badminton team bought 8 rackets and 12 birdies. There are 4 people on the team. What is the average cost per person?

BADMINTON SUPPLIES	
Rackets	2 for $9.98
Birdies	6 for $5.22
Net	$12.49
Poles	2 for $6.50

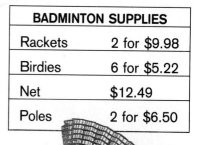

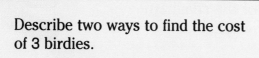 Describe two ways to find the cost of 3 birdies.

SHOW WHAT YOU KNOW

What Is the Unit Cost?

The basketball team is having its end-of-the-year banquet. Several parents and players are buying the supplies.

Three boxes of Brand A spaghetti noodles cost $1.89. Two boxes of Brand B cost $1.38. The boxes hold the same amount. Which brand of spaghetti costs less?

A. How can you find out which brand costs less? How can you find out how much one box of each brand of spaghetti costs? Find out which brand of spaghetti costs less.

B. Which costs less per can, 3 cans of spaghetti sauce for $2.79 or 6 cans of spaghetti sauce for $5.16?

Sharing Your Ideas

1. How were you able to compare the cost of the two brands of spaghetti?

2. Was it important that the boxes held the same amount? Explain.

3. How did you compare the cost of the spaghetti sauce? Could you do it another way?

Extending Your Thinking

The parents decided to compare the prices of food at two stores. They could then tell which store had the better buys.

	Save-A-Lot Store	Spend-Less Store
Hot dogs	Pack of 8 $1.84	Pack of 4 $.96
Rolls	Pack of 8 $1.12	Pack of 10 $1.30
Hamburger	5 lb/$7.95	3 lb/$4.47
Potato salad	3 lb/$4.23	4 lb/$6.20
Tomatoes	6 for $1.14	5 for $.95
Baked beans	9 cans/$3.51	7 cans/$2.87
Carrots	1 lb/$.49	3 lb/$1.50
Juice	3 cartons/$5.43	2 cartons/$4.10

4. Compare the prices. The cost of one pound or one can of any item is called the unit price. Find the unit price for each item.

5. Which store has the better price for each of the different items?

6. At which store would you suggest the parents shop?

7. What would the parents pay if they bought 2 cartons of juice at the Save-A-Lot Store?

Show What You Know

8. How would you decide where they should shop?

9. Is it always best to buy the item that costs less? Explain.

10. How did you find out how much 2 cartons of juice would cost from Save-A-Lot?

Investigating Dividing by Tens

Study these examples. Look for patterns as you play the game below.

$$\frac{2}{4\overline{)8}} \qquad \frac{20}{4\overline{)80}} \qquad \frac{200}{4\overline{)800}} \qquad \frac{2{,}000}{4\overline{)8{,}000}}$$

Working together

Materials: index cards, calculator

A. Copy each number below on a separate index card.

120	180	240
1,200	1,800	2,400
12,000	18,000	24,000

These are Dividend Cards that will be used by both players. Shuffle and place them face down on a desk.

B. Copy each number below on a separate index card.

2   3   6   20   30   60

These are Divisor Cards. Each person should have a complete set.

C. Choose a player to go first. This player turns over a Dividend Card and chooses a Divisor Card. The player then divides and records the quotient on a piece of paper. Both cards are then placed in a discard pile.

D. Take turns. The game is over when all the Dividend Cards are used. Use a calculator to find the sum of your quotients. The player with the greater sum wins.

Sharing Your Results

1. Which pairs of dividends and divisors in the game have quotients of 4?

2. If your Dividend Card was 1,800, which Divisor Card would give the greatest quotient?

3. What is the greatest quotient that can be formed in the game?

Extending the Activity

Work on your own.
Divide. Use mental math. Check by multiplying.

4. $63 \div 7 = n$
$630 \div 70 = n$

5. $48 \div 8 = n$
$480 \div 80 = n$

6. $72 \div 8 = n$
$7{,}200 \div 80 = n$

7. $540 \div 9 = n$
$5{,}400 \div 90 = n$

8. $400 \div 5 = n$
$4{,}000 \div 50 = n$

9. $120 \div 3 = n$
$1{,}200 \div 30 = n$

10. $30\overline{)180}$

11. $50\overline{)3{,}500}$

12. $20\overline{)160}$

13. $80\overline{)6{,}400}$

14. $60\overline{)3{,}600}$

15. $70\overline{)280}$

16. $40\overline{)160}$

17. $90\overline{)4{,}500}$

Find each missing number.

18. $360 \div n = 40$

19. $4{,}900 \div n = 70$

20. $n \div 20 = 90$

21. $63{,}000 \div n = 90$

Show What You Know

22. Explain a good strategy for winning the game on page 246.

23. Describe the pattern in the quotients. Explain.

a. $20\overline{)8{,}000}^{\,400}$ $\qquad$ $20\overline{)800}^{\,40}$ $\qquad$ $20\overline{)80}^{\,4}$

b. $2\overline{)24{,}000}^{\,12{,}000}$ $\quad$ $20\overline{)24{,}000}^{\,1{,}200}$ $\quad$ $200\overline{)24{,}000}^{\,120}$ $\quad$ $2{,}000\overline{)24{,}000}^{\,12}$

c. $7\overline{)42}^{\,6}$ $\qquad$ $70\overline{)420}^{\,6}$ $\qquad$ $700\overline{)4{,}200}^{\,6}$ $\qquad$ $7{,}000\overline{)42{,}000}^{\,6}$

THINK AND SHARE

Which problems have remainders of 0?

$20\overline{)1,200}$ $30\overline{)451}$ $8\overline{)720}$ $60\overline{)814}$

How can you tell?

Dividing by Multiples of Ten

Mr. Johnson sells baseball buttons at the stadium.
He has 94 Houston Astros buttons. He puts 30
buttons on each board. How many full boards
does he have? How many buttons are left over?

$94 \div 30 = n$

Step 1	Step 2	Step 3	Check
Decide where to place the first digit in the quotient.	Divide. Then multiply.	Subtract and compare.	
$30\overline{)94}$ Think Not enough tens. Divide ones.	$\begin{array}{r} 3 \\ 30\overline{)94} \\ 90 \end{array}$ Think $3\overline{)9}$	$\begin{array}{r} 3\,R4 \\ 30\overline{)94} \\ -90 \\ \hline 4 \end{array}$ $4 < 30$ Write the remainder in the quotient.	$\begin{array}{r} 30 \\ \times\ 3 \\ \hline 90 \\ +\ 4 \\ \hline 94 \end{array}$

He has 3 full boards. There are 4 buttons left over.

More Examples

$$\begin{array}{r} 2\,R5 \\ 40\overline{)85} \\ -80 \\ \hline 5 \end{array} \qquad \begin{array}{r} 4\,R14 \\ 90\overline{)374} \\ -360 \\ \hline 14 \end{array} \qquad \begin{array}{r} 3\,R29 \\ 70\overline{)239} \\ -210 \\ \hline 29 \end{array}$$

Check Your Understanding

Divide. Check by multiplying.

1. $30\overline{)76}$ **2.** $40\overline{)125}$ **3.** $20\overline{)176}$ **4.** $50\overline{)482}$ **5.** $70\overline{)292}$

Share Your Ideas Explain why you would want to
know the number of digits in the quotient before
you divide.

248

Divide. Check by multiplying.

6. $20\overline{)52}$ 7. $40\overline{)75}$ 8. $20\overline{)89}$

9. $70\overline{)490}$ 10. $80\overline{)200}$ 11. $30\overline{)101}$

12. $60\overline{)545}$ 13. $90\overline{)630}$ 14. $20\overline{)132}$

15. $90\overline{)559}$ 16. $80\overline{)708}$ 17. $30\overline{)197}$

18. $183 \div 20 = n$ 19. $348 \div 50 = n$

20. $888 \div 90 = n$ 21. $236 \div 60 = n$

Find the rule. Then complete each table.

22. Rule:

Input	Output
40	2
23. 80	
120	6
24. 180	
25. 200	

26. Rule:

Input	Output
42	1 R2
27. 81	
28. 135	
210	5 R10
29. 387	

Think and Apply

Find each missing digit.

30. $\square0\overline{)305}$ 6 R$\square$

31. $30\overline{)\square27}$ 7 R$\square$

32. There are 184 people going to the stadium by bus. Each bus holds 40 people. How many buses are needed? Explain.

Look back at **32**. Write a division word problem in which you must treat the remainder the same way. Give your problem to a friend to solve.

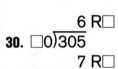

SHOW WHAT YOU KNOW

249

LET THE GAMES BEGIN

WORKING TOGETHER

1. Work in groups. Choose three games or sports, each from a different culture or part of the world.

2. Research the game or sport to find the following.

   • Where was it first played?

   • How is it played?

   • How many players are needed for a team?

3. Find out how many fourth grade students attend your school.

4. Use division to form teams so that everyone in the fourth grade can play. Record your findings in a chart.

Game or Sport	Country Where First Played	Number of Fourth-Graders in School	Players Needed per Team	Number of Possible Teams

5. Share and compare your games and sports with the class. Talk about the following.

   • Which game or sport needed the most people to make one team? the fewest people?

   • For which could the most teams be made?

   • What connection can you make between these two facts?

   • Which game or sport could best be played with the number of fourth graders at your school? Why?

CHAPTER REVIEW/TEST

Divide. Use mental math.

1. 5)300   **2.** 9)810   **3.** 4)38   **4.** 7)29

Write a division problem that gives a close estimate. Then find the estimate.

5. 4)76   **6.** 6)114   **7.** 7)357   **8.** 8)549

Divide. Check by multiplying or estimating.

9. 3)56   **10.** 8)97   **11.** 3)63   **12.** 4)54

13. 8)584   **14.** 5)487   **15.** 4)371   **16.** 6)678

17. 9)817   **18.** 6)639   **19.** 2)901   **20.** 7)774

21. 6)$4.98   **22.** 9)$5.76   **23.** 3)$.96   **24.** 8)$8.24

Find each average.

25. 12, 6, 9   **26.** 4, 7, 8, 13   **27.** 4, 12, 2, 8, 9

Divide. Check by multiplying.

28. 20)94   **29.** 30)162   **30.** 70)646   **31.** 60)328

Solve.

32. Sue bought 3 tennis shirts. Each shirt was the same price. If she paid $55.26 in all, how much did she pay for each shirt?

33. In the first 3 quarters of a basketball game, one team scored 16 points, 22 points, and 24 points. How would you find the total points scored?

Think

Mr. Lopez sells football pennants in 6 locations in the football stadium. He wants to have the same number of pennants in each location. He has 4 boxes of pennants. There are 144 pennants in each box. How many pennants should he place in each location?

Divisibility

A number is **divisible** by another number when the remainder is 0.

Use these rules to test whether one number is divisible by another.

A number is divisible by 2 if its last digit is 0, 2, 4, 6, or 8.

A number is divisible by 5 if its last digit is 0 or 5.

A number is divisible by 10 if its last digit is 0.

A number is divisible by 3 if the sum of its digits is divisible by 3.
729 is divisible by 3.

$729 \rightarrow 7 + 2 + 9 = 18$
18 is divisible by 3, so 729 is divisible by 3.

Use the rules to play this game with a friend.

Materials: 2 number cubes, one numbered 1 through 6, the other numbered 0 through 5

Follow these steps.

1. Player 1 tosses the number cubes and forms a two-digit number. Player 2 uses the same digits to form a different two-digit number if possible.

2. Test your numbers. You score one point every time your number is divisible by either 2, 3, 5, or 10.

3. Take turns tossing the number cubes. The player with the greater total number of points after three turns wins.

MAINTAINING SKILLS

Choose the correct answer. Write A, B, C, or D.

1. Estimate 38 × 5.

   A 20   **C** 2,000

   B 200   **D** 15

2.   406
     ×   3

   A 138   **C** 1,212

   B 1,218   **D** not given

3. 3,562 × 5 = □

   A 17,810   **C** 17,510

   B 17,800   **D** not given

4. $4.68
     ×   4

   A $16.42   **C** $18.72

   B $10.72   **D** not given

5. 60 × 40 = n

   A 24,000   **C** 2,400

   B 240   **D** not given

6.   85
    ×42

   A 3,570   **C** 2,370

   B 510   **D** not given

7. 386 × 24 = n

   A 2,316   **C** 9,262

   B 9,244   **D** not given

8. 62 × $4.53 = n

   A $36.24   **C** $280.86

   B $249.86   **D** not given

9. 4)‾18‾

   A 4 R1   **C** 4 R3

   B 3 R3   **D** not given

10. 85 ÷ 6 = n

   A 14 R1   **C** 14 R3

   B 12 R2   **D** not given

11. Find the average.   15, 19, 26

   A 60   **C** 21

   B 20   **D** not given

Solve.

12. Tracey has 12 telephone service calls to make today. Each service call takes an average of 35 minutes. How many minutes of service will this be?

   A 420 minutes   **C** 120 minutes

   B 47 minutes   **D** not given

13. Mr. Cramer receives 2 newspapers each weekday, 1 on Saturday, and 3 on Sunday. How many newspapers does he receive each week?

   A 6   **C** 14

   B 9   **D** not given

Sharing What You Know

Did you ever hear the famous saying "Remember the Alamo?" The Alamo is a fort where a famous battle took place in 1836. Today the Alamo is a monument to freedom. It stands in the middle of the city of San Antonio, Texas. Look at the photo of San Antonio. Why do you think people say that the city grew up around the Alamo? What do you notice about the way the streets are laid out?

Using Language

On what street do you live? Does your street cross another street? When two streets cross, they **intersect**. Talk about streets that intersect near your home. In mathematics, **intersecting lines** are lines that cross at one point. How are the streets near your house like intersecting lines? How are they different?

Words to Know: polygon, vertex, angle, parallel lines, intersecting lines, perpendicular lines, congruent, similar, symmetrical

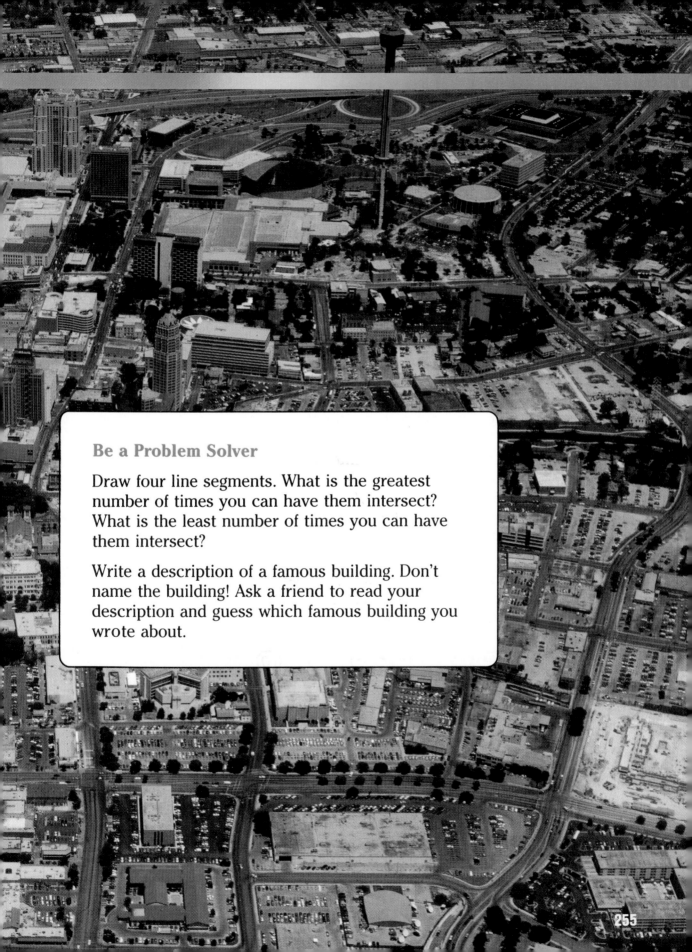

Be a Problem Solver

Draw four line segments. What is the greatest number of times you can have them intersect? What is the least number of times you can have them intersect?

Write a description of a famous building. Don't name the building! Ask a friend to read your description and guess which famous building you wrote about.

How are these shapes the same? How are they different?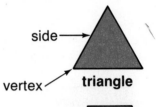

Identifying Polygons

Triangles, squares, and rectangles are examples of **plane figures.**

A closed plane figure with 3 or more straight sides is a **polygon.** Two sides meet to form a **vertex.**

side →
vertex — **triangle**

side →
vertex — **square**

side →
vertex — **rectangle**

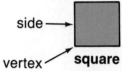
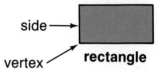

▶ A triangle has 3 sides and 3 vertices.
▶ A square has 4 equal sides and 4 vertices.
▶ A rectangle has 4 sides and 4 vertices.
  Opposite sides of a rectangle are equal.

Polygons are named by the number of sides.

quadrilateral	**pentagon**	**hexagon**	**octagon**
4 sides	5 sides	6 sides	8 sides
4 vertices	5 vertices	6 vertices	8 vertices

What kinds of polygons are rectangles and squares?

Check Your Understanding

Name each polygon. Write the number of sides and vertices.

1.    2.   3.   4.

Share Your Ideas Can a polygon have only 2 vertices? Explain.

Name each polygon. Write the number of sides and vertices.

5.

6.

7.

8.

9.

10.

11.

12.

13.

14.

15.

16.

17. **Look back** at **5** through **16**. Which quadrilaterals have special names? Write the number of the exercise and the name.

Think and Apply

18. Are all squares rectangles? Explain.

19. Are all rectangles squares? Explain.

20. Are all rectangles quadrilaterals? Why or why not?

21. Are all quadrilaterals rectangles? Why or why not?

22. Draw a quadrilateral that is not a square and not a rectangle.

23. What do you think is the greatest number of sides a polygon can have?

Mathematics and History

The Ancient Greeks named the polygons.

Poly means many.
Gon means angles.
Septa means seven.
Nona means nine.

24. Draw a septagon and a nonagon. How many sides does each have? how many vertices?

JOURNAL WRITING

Is a circle a polygon? Why or why not?

SHOW WHAT YOU KNOW

Look around your classroom. Draw the outlines of some of the objects you see. Name the polygons in your drawing.

Lines, Line Segments, and Rays

Ellen Fitz is an architect. This is her drawing of the front of a new bank. You can find one door by finding **points** *A*, *B*, *C*, and *D*. The bottom of the door is shown with a line segment. It has **endpoints** *A* and *D*.

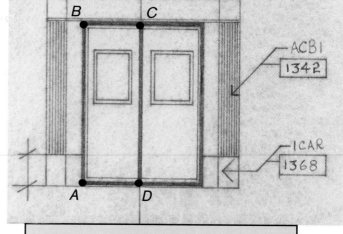

Write as $\overline{AD}$ or $\overline{DA}$.
Read as line segment *AD* or line segment *DA*.

▶ A **line segment** is straight. It has 2 endpoints.

Name all the line segments that form the door.

▶ A **line** is also straight. It has no endpoints. A line goes on and on in both directions.

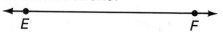

Write as $\overleftrightarrow{EF}$ or $\overleftrightarrow{FE}$.
Read as line *EF* or line *FE*.

▶ A **ray** is part of a line with one endpoint. It goes on and on in one direction.

Write as $\overrightarrow{AB}$.
Read as ray *AB*.

Check Your Understanding

Name each figure.

1.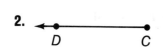

2.

3.

4.

Share Your Ideas Fold a piece of paper in half. Open it up and look at the fold. Is it a line or a line segment? Explain.

Name each figure.

5.
A
B

6.
C
D

7.
M   N

8.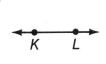
F
E

9.
K   L

10.
P
O

Use the figure at the right.

11. Name the line segments that have *D* as an endpoint.

12. Which point is an endpoint of four line segments? Name the segments.

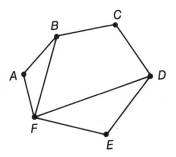
B   C
A
F
E   D

13. How many line segments are in the figure?

Think and Apply

Use the figure at the right.

H   J   K   L

14. Name the line segments.

15. Name the rays.

16. **What if** you placed point *I* between point *H* and point *J*? Name all the line segments. Name all the rays.

How are lines, line segments, and rays alike? How are they different?

Mixed Review

1. 247
   +385

2. 3,864
   − 827

3. 24
   × 6

4. $.64
   + .82

5. 4,532
   ×   6

6. 6,930 − 472

7. 3,042 ÷ 4

8. $3.92 − $.53

9. 6,145 ÷ 6

10. 216 ÷ 8

11. (9 × 1) × 8

12. $16.40 ÷ 4

13. 4,284 ÷ 3

14. 6,240 + 207

15. 8 × 432

16. 23 × 32

17. 235 + 146

SHOW WHAT YOU KNOW

THINK AND SHARE

Name the line segments that have W as an endpoint. Do the same for X, Y, and Z.
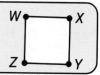

Identifying Angles

The San Francisco Bay Bridge is shown at the right. Parts of the bridge form different geometric shapes.

Two rays with the same endpoint form an **angle.**

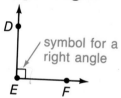

vertex

Write as ∠BAC or ∠CAB. Read as angle BAC or angle CAB.

The endpoint of the two rays is the **vertex.** The vertex of ∠BAC is point A.

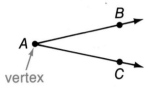

An angle that forms a square corner is a **right angle.**

symbol for a right angle

An angle less than a right angle is an **acute angle.**

An angle greater than a right angle is an **obtuse angle.**

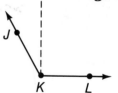

Find all 3 kinds of angles in the bridge above.

Check Your Understanding

Identify each angle. Write *acute, right,* or *obtuse.*

1.

2. N   O

M

3.

L

K   J

4.

H

G   I

Share Your Ideas Draw and label some angles. Have a friend name the angles and identify them as acute, right, or obtuse.

Identify each angle. Write *acute, right,* or *obtuse.*

5.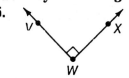

6.

7.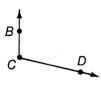

8.

9.

10.

11.

12.

Use the figure at the right.

13. Name two right angles.

14. Name six acute angles.

15. Name two obtuse angles.

16. If ∠*MHL* and ∠*LHK* are put together, what type of angle is formed?

17. If ∠*MHK* and ∠*KHI* are put together, what type of angle is formed?

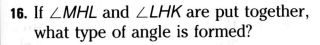

Think and Apply

18. Draw right angle *RPQ*. Draw $\overrightarrow{PS}$ between $\overrightarrow{PR}$ and $\overrightarrow{PQ}$.

19. Use your drawing. Name all the angles. Tell if they are acute, right, or obtuse.

20. Draw a square, a rectangle, and an acute triangle. How many angles did you draw? How many right angles did you draw?

Logical Thinking

21. The faces of this cube are numbered. If the numbers are in order, what is the sum of the numbers on all the faces?

Draw acute angles *ABC* and *BAC*. Do they have the same vertex? Explain.

SHOW WHAT YOU KNOW

THINK AND SHARE

Name 2 streets in your town that never cross each other. Name 2 streets that do cross each other.

Pairs of Lines

The longest roller coaster, "The Beast," is near Cincinnati, Ohio. The cars run on parallel rails that are 7,400 feet long.

Lines that never cross are called **parallel lines.**

$\overleftrightarrow{AB}$ is parallel to $\overleftrightarrow{CD}$.

Lines that cross are called **intersecting lines.**

$\overleftrightarrow{EF}$ intersects $\overleftrightarrow{GH}$ at point J.

Lines that intersect at right angles are called **perpendicular lines.**

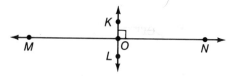

$\overleftrightarrow{KL}$ intersects $\overleftrightarrow{MN}$ at point O.

There are 4 right angles. Name them.

Check Your Understanding

Write *parallel* or *intersecting* for each pair of lines. If the lines are also perpendicular, write *perpendicular*.

1.

2.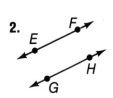

3.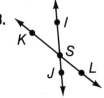

4.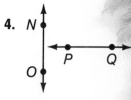

Share Your Ideas Look back at **4.** Explain your answer.

Write *parallel* or *intersecting* for each pair of lines.
If the lines are also perpendicular, write *perpendicular*.

5.

6.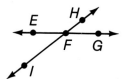

7.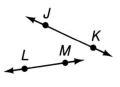

8.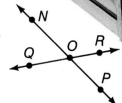

9.

10.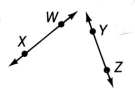

11.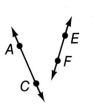

12.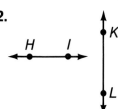

Use the figure to complete each sentence.

13. $\overleftrightarrow{AB}$ is perpendicular to _____ and _____.

14. $\overleftrightarrow{CD}$ intersects _____, _____, and _____.

15. $\overleftrightarrow{GJ}$ is not parallel to _____ and _____.

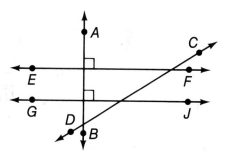

Draw each of the following. Give examples of each in your classroom.

16. intersecting lines

17. parallel lines

18. perpendicular lines

Think and Apply

Some objects have parallel or perpendicular parts.
Write *parallel* or *perpendicular* for each object.

19. rungs of a ladder

20. hands of a clock at 3:00

21. line segments that form the letter T

22. legs of a chair

23. Draw a polygon with 3 sets of parallel line segments. What type of polygon did you draw?

Explain the difference between parallel, intersecting, and perpendicular lines.

SHOW WHAT YOU KNOW

Why is a circle not a polygon? What other shapes can you think of that are not polygons?

Circles

The first Ferris wheel was built by George Ferris in Chicago in 1893. The outline of the Ferris wheel forms a circle.

▶ A **circle** is named by its center. All points on a circle are the same distance from the center.

Point *N* is the center of circle *N*. *A*, *B*, and *C* are points on the circle.

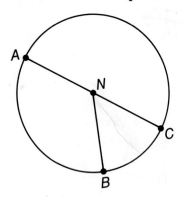

▶ A **radius** is a line segment from the center to any point on the circle.

$\overline{NA}$ is a radius.
Name two more radii.

▶ A **diameter** is a line segment with both endpoints on the circle. A diameter always passes through the center of the circle.

$\overline{AC}$ is a diameter.

Check Your Understanding

Use the figure at the right.

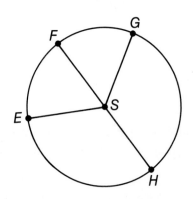

1. Name the center of the circle.

2. Name four radii.

3. Name a diameter.

Share Your Ideas   Are all the radii in circle *S* the same length? Explain why or why not.

Use the figure at the right.

4. Name the center.

5. Name five radii.

6. Name two diameters.

7. Is $\overline{JN}$ a radius? Why or why not?

8. Are all diameters the same length? Explain.

9. How does the length of a diameter compare with the length of a radius?

Use the figure at the right.

10. Name the diameter.

11. Name two triangles.

12. Name four right angles.

Think and Apply

13. The first Ferris wheel had a diameter of 250 feet. What was the radius of the wheel?

14. **MATHPROCESSOR** Use the circle tool in a Geometry Workspace to draw a large circle. Then use the polyline tool or line segments to make a design inside the circle. Use the circle tool to make other circles.

DATA
15. Are the diameters of all bicycle wheels the same? Measure the wheels of at least 5 bicycles. Record your data in a table.

Draw a circle with diameter $\overline{AB}$ and radius $\overline{CD}$. Name the center and another radius.

SHOW WHAT YOU KNOW

CHECKPOINT

Name each figure. pages 256–259

1.

2.

3.

4.

5.

6.

7.

8.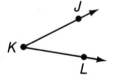

Identify each angle. Write *acute*, *right*, or *obtuse*. pages 260–261

9.

10.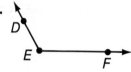

11.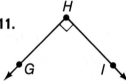

12.

Use the circle to answer 13–16. pages 264–265

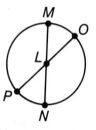

13. Name 4 radii.

14. Name the center.

15. Name 2 diameters.

16. Name the circle.

Match each word with its definition.

17. lines that never cross

18. lines that cross

19. the point where two sides of a polygon meet

20. a closed plane figure with 3 or more straight sides

21. lines that intersect at right angles

22. two rays with the same endpoint

Words to Know
perpendicular
polygon
vertex
intersecting
angle
parallel

Solve.

23. Jim drew a picture of a rectangle. How many right angles does it have?

24. Eva drew a picture of 3 triangles, 4 squares, and 2 circles. How many polygons did she draw?

PROBLEM SOLVING

What Is the Shortest Path?

Mr. Steiner plans to visit three shops that open onto a parking lot. He will need to return to his car with packages after visiting each shop.

Thinking Critically

Where should Mr. Steiner park his car so that he will walk the shortest distance?

Use Workmat 10 and a centimeter ruler. Work in a group as you try to find the best place to park.

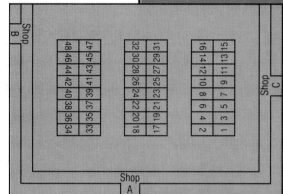

Analyzing and Making Decisions

1. Choose some spaces in the parking lot as Mr. Steiner's parking place. Draw lines from each space to the three shops. Measure and keep a record of the total walking distance from each parking space you choose.

2. **What if** he parked in front of one of the shops? Which shop would be the best choice? Why?

3. Could he walk less steps by parking farther out in the lot? Experiment to find out.

4. Where is the best place for Mr. Steiner to park his car?

Look Back   What if Mr. Steiner did not want to return to his car after visiting each store? He can only walk in the parking lot when he leaves his car and returns to his car. Now where is the best place for him to park? Which shop should he visit first?

Making and Using Drawings

The Empire State Building is south of the New York Public Library. Kim and his family left the north entrance of the library to walk to the Empire State Building. They got lost. This is where they walked: 3 blocks east, 5 blocks south, 3 blocks west, 2 blocks north, 4 blocks east; then 6 blocks south, and 4 blocks west. Where were they?

Sometimes a drawing helps you see what is happening in a problem. The drawing helps you decide what to do.

Solving the Problem

Think   What is the question?

> **Explore**   How will a drawing help you answer the questions? Use grid paper and copy the map on this page. Follow the route Kim and his family followed.

> **Solve**   Where were the family when they stopped walking?

> **Look Back**   Write directions that direct someone from the library to the Empire State Building.

> **Share Your Ideas**

> **1.** How did a drawing help you solve both this problem and the one on page 267? Could you have done these problems without one? Explain.

The grid map shows:

	X Start		
	Library		
Empire State Building			
	▫ Entrance		

Compass: N, W, E, S

Extending Your Thinking

Solve. Use a calculator where appropriate.

CHOICES

2. You are at Building B. You walk 1 block east, 2 blocks south, 2 blocks east, and 1 block north. What buildings do you pass?

3. From Building C, how can you pass Buildings A, B, and D and return to Building C?

4. What is the least number of blocks you would need to walk in order to see every building? Start at building A.

5. You are at Building E and are meeting people from Buildings B and F. Where should you meet so that the three of you will walk the fewest total blocks?

Mixed Strategy Review

6. An electrician is checking the elevator in an office building. The elevator rises at the rate of one floor every 2 seconds. At this rate, how many floors will the elevator rise in 20 seconds if it does not stop anywhere?

7. Look at **6.** The elevator starts at Floor 1. Where will the elevator be in 20 seconds?

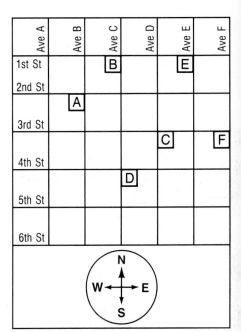

	Ave A	Ave B	Ave C	Ave D	Ave E	Ave F
1st St			B		E	
2nd St						
	A					
3rd St						
					C	F
4th St						
				D		
5th St						
6th St						

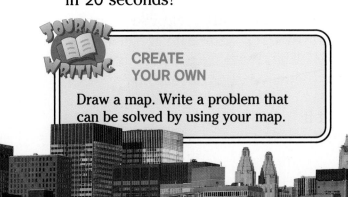

CREATE YOUR OWN

Draw a map. Write a problem that can be solved by using your map.

Are all the windows in your classroom the same length and width? How could you find out?

Congruent Figures

The two towers of the World Trade Center in New York City are called the twin towers. Look at the rectangular faces of the buildings. They are the same size and shape.

Congruent figures have exactly the same size and shape.

Congruent line segments have the same length.

A   B   C   D

Are triangles *DEF* and *GHI* congruent? Follow these steps to find out.
- Trace one of the triangles.
- Place the tracing on top of the other triangle.

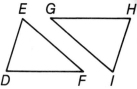

Congruent figures match exactly.

When figures are congruent, their matching sides and angles are congruent.

$\overline{EF}$ is congruent to $\overline{IG}$.
Which side is congruent to $\overline{DE}$?

$\angle EFD$ is congruent to $\angle IGH$.
Which angle is congruent to $\angle DEF$?

Check Your Understanding

Are the figures congruent? Write *yes* or *no*.

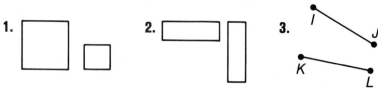

1.

2.

3.

Share Your Ideas How can you find out if two squares are congruent without tracing one of them?

Are the figures congruent? Write _yes_ or _no_.

4.

5.
•K

I——•J

•L

6.

7.

8.

9.

Use the figures at the right.
Pentagon _ABCDE_ is congruent to pentagon _PQRST_.

10. Which side is congruent to $\overline{EA}$?

11. Which side is congruent to $\overline{CD}$?

12. Which side is congruent to $\overline{DE}$?

13. Which angle is congruent to $\angle ABC$?

14. Which angle is congruent to $\angle BCD$?

15. Which angle is congruent to $\angle DEA$?

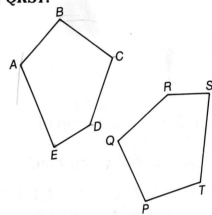

[**Think and Apply**]

What if you did not want to trace and match figures to see if they were congruent? What could you measure to be sure each pair of figures below is congruent?

16. 2 triangles

17. 2 squares

18. 2 circles

Visual Thinking

19. Remove 2 toothpicks to leave 7 congruent squares.

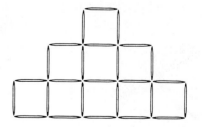

Find pairs of congruent figures in your classroom. Tell why they are congruent.

SHOW WHAT YOU KNOW

Investigating Similar Figures

Can you make a figure larger
or smaller without changing its shape?

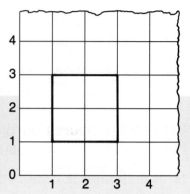

Working together

Materials: Workmats 1 and 11

A. Use Workmats 1 and 11. Number the lines as
shown above.

B. Draw a triangle on Workmat 11. Label the
triangle, using letters of the alphabet. Exchange
drawings with your partner.

C. Make your partner's triangle larger by using
Workmat 1. Copy the triangle using the numbers
as a guide. Label the large triangle with the
same letters as the small triangle.

D. Draw another triangle using Workmat 1.
Exchange drawings. Make your partner's
triangle smaller by using Workmat 11. Label
each pair of triangles with the same letters.

Sharing Your Results

Use your triangles to answer these questions.

1. How are all triangles the same? different?

2. Do all triangles have the same shape? Explain.

3. **Look back** at each pair of triangles. How are
they the same? How are they different?

Extending the Activity

Figures are **similar** if they have the same shape. They do not have to be the same size.

Work on your own.
Materials: Workmats 1 and 11

4. Draw a rectangle, a square, and another quadrilateral on Workmat 1.

5. Copy the figures on Workmat 11.

6. Are the matching quadrilaterals similar? Why or why not?

Look at the polygons below. Write the letters of the polygons that are similar to the first polygon.

7. 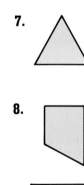   a. 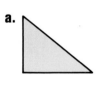   b. 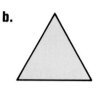   c.   d.

8.   a.    b.   c.   d.

9.    a.   b.    c.   d.

Show What You Know

Write *true* or *false*. Explain each answer.

10. All rectangles are similar.

11. All squares are similar.

12. All polygons that are congruent are similar.

13. All polygons that are similar are congruent.

> Fold a piece of paper in half. Cut a design around the fold. Do not cut the fold. Open the paper. How do the two sides compare?

Symmetry

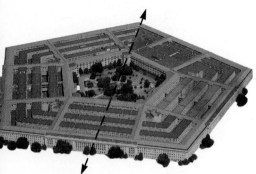

The Pentagon near Washington, D.C., is the largest office building in the world. One half of the building is congruent to the other half. The building is symmetrical.

The dotted line shown at the left is a **line of symmetry.** It divides the building into two congruent parts.

Some shapes have exactly one line of symmetry.

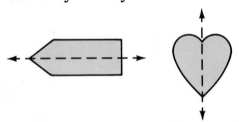

Some shapes have more than one line of symmetry.

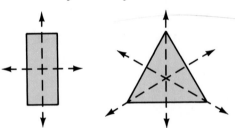

To test for symmetry, trace a figure. Then fold it in half. If the halves are congruent, the figure is symmetric.

Is the figure at the right symmetric? Explain.

Check Your Understanding

Is the dotted line a line of symmetry? Write *yes* or *no*.

1.

2.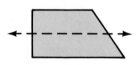

3.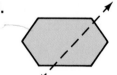

4.

Share Your Ideas Look back at **4.** How many lines of symmetry does a circle have? Explain.

Is the dotted line a line of symmetry?
Write *yes* or *no*.

5.

6.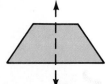

7.

Write the number of lines of symmetry for each figure. Trace the figure. Then fold it to help find the answer.

8.

9.

10.

11.

12.

13.

Think and Apply

14. Fold a piece of paper in half. Cut a design around the fold. Do not cut the fold.

  a. Predict the number of lines of symmetry the figure will have.

  b. Open the paper. Draw in all the lines of symmetry. Was your prediction correct?

  c. Have a friend check your work.

15. Which of the letters below are symmetrical?

A B C D E F G H

Find examples of symmetric figures in your classroom. Sketch them. Then draw the lines of symmetry.

SHOW WHAT YOU KNOW

Investigating Geometry in Motion

Look at yourself in a mirror. Blink your right eye. Which eye is your reflection blinking? Now, try other mirror images!

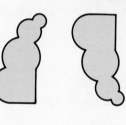

Working together

Materials: hand-held mirror

Look at the figures below. Experiment placing a mirror outside the first figure to get a reflection that looks like the second figure.

A.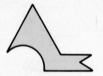

B.

C.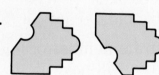

D.

Sharing Your Results

1. Where did you place your mirror for each pair of figures?

   a. Figure *A* **b.** Figure *B* **c.** Figure *C* **d.** Figure *D*

2. Look at the triangle at the right. Place a mirror above, below, and on both sides of it. Draw the reflections.

Extending the Activity

Work with a partner.

Materials: Workmat 12, a hand-held mirror

Either use a mirror or move the cards, cut from Workmat 12, to get from *A* to *B*. Record what you do for each.

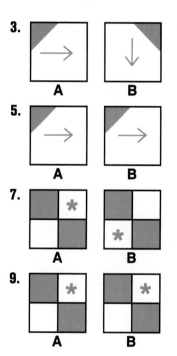

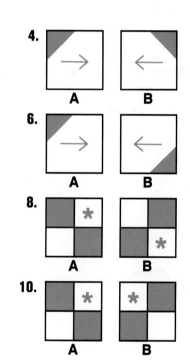

3. A B **4.** A B

5. A B **6.** A B

7. A B **8.** A B

9. A B **10.** A B

Show What You Know

11. In which exercises did you use a mirror to get *B*?

12. In which exercises did you move *A* to get *B*? Describe the motion.

13. Design a card so that no matter how you move the card or use a mirror on the card, the design will look exactly the same.

Exploring Flips, Slides, and Turns

You can move geometric figures to new positions in many different ways.

Materials: scrap paper, scissors, Workmat 1

A. Cut out a quadrilateral like the one shown below. Trace it on Workmat 1. **Flip** the figure over a line as shown. Trace it again. Discuss how the figure changed.

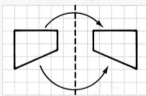

B. Use the same quadrilateral and Workmat 1. **Slide** the figure to the right and down as shown. Discuss how the figure changed.

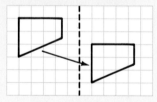

C. Use the same quadrilateral and Workmat 1. This time **turn** the figure around a point as shown. Discuss how the figure changed.

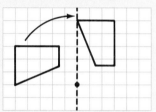

D. Take turns moving the quadrilateral. Have one person move the figure. Have the other person name the move as either a flip, slide, or turn.

Sharing Your Results

Look back at A, B, and C above.

1. How did the figure change when you flipped it? slid it? turned it?

2. Explain how a flip is different from a turn.

Extending the Activity

Work on your own.
Materials: Workmats 1 and 13

3. Use Workmat 1 and the figures cut
from Workmat 13. Look at **a**
through **d** below. Decide which
motion was used to get from the
first figure to the second. Use the
same motion to help you draw the
final figure.

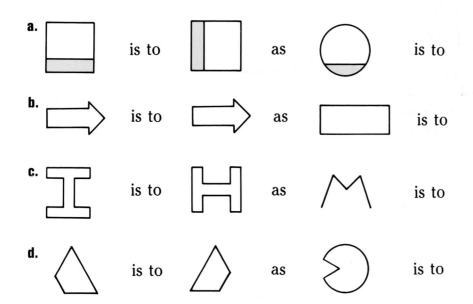

a. ☐ is to ☐ as ◯ is to

b. ⇨ is to ⇨ as ▭ is to

c. I is to H as ⋀ is to

d. △ is to △ as ◖ is to

Show What You Know

4. Look back at **3.** Tell whether each move was a
flip, slide, or turn.

Making New Shapes

You can make discoveries about shapes by using a geoboard.

Working together

Materials: geoboard, rubber bands, Workmat 14

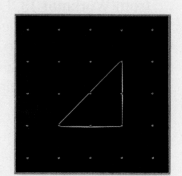

A. Make a triangle with one rubber band on your geoboard. Your rubber band should touch 6 pegs. Record your work on the workmat.

B. Try to make these changes by moving the rubber band as little as possible.

Record your work on the workmat paper.

1. Change the triangle to a square.

2. Change the square to a rectangle that is not a square.

3. Change the rectangle to a pentagon (5-sided figure).

4. Change the pentagon to a hexagon (6-sided figure).

Sharing Your Ideas

1. Which change caused you to move the rubber band the most?

2. Which figure took up the most space?

Extending Your Thinking

What new shapes can you make with these shapes? You may use two or more rubber bands. Record all your work on Workmat 14 paper. What can you make:

3. with any two triangles that are the same size?

4. with a triangle and a rectangle?

5. with any number of triangles and rectangles?

6. with any number of triangles?

Show What You Know

7. What different shapes were you able to make?

8. Were you able to make some shapes in different ways? If so, give an example of one.

AFRICAN PATTERNS

Math Around The World

WORKING TOGETHER

1. Work in small groups to investigate African patterns. Look in magazines or books about Africa to find objects that have patterns on them. Talk about the shapes and colors in the patterns. Try to find a picture of an African tunic called a *dashiki*.

2. Create a pattern for an African dashiki. With the group, make the following decisions.

   • What geometric figures will we use?

   • Should all of our figures be the same size?

   • What colors will we use?

   • How often will we repeat shapes, sizes, and colors?

   • Will we use flips, slides, or turns?

3. Follow these directions to make your pattern.

   • Place the shapes you have chosen in a pattern on a piece of grid paper.

   • Trace each shape and then color it.

   • Repeat the pattern two more times.

4. Share your designs with the class. Challenge classmates to figure out the pattern.

CHAPTER REVIEW/TEST

Name each figure.

1.

2.

3.

4.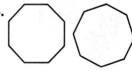

5.

6.

7.

8.

9.

10.

Are the figures congruent? Write *yes* or *no*.

11.

12.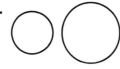

13.

14.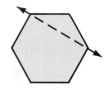

Is the dotted line a line of symmetry? Write *yes* or *no*.

15.

16.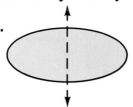

17.

18.

Solve.

19. Triangles *ABC* and *DEF* are congruent. Each of the sides of triangle *ABC* is 4 inches long. What is the sum of the lengths of the sides of triangle *DEF*?

20. $\overleftrightarrow{EF}$ is perpendicular to $\overleftrightarrow{AB}$. $\overleftrightarrow{AB}$ is parallel to $\overleftrightarrow{CD}$. Does $\overleftrightarrow{EF}$ intersect $\overleftrightarrow{CD}$? Make a drawing to decide.

Think The total distance around a quadrilateral is 20 inches. If the quadrilateral is a square what is the length of each side? **What if** the quadrilateral is a rectangle? What are some possible lengths for each side? Draw different rectangles to help you decide.

COMPUTER

Flips and Congruent Figures

The polygons at the right are congruent.

You can use MathProcessor™ to test for congruent and symmetric figures.

First, draw Polygon *A*. Use a **Square Grid** to help you. Then draw a congruent figure, Polygon *B*. **Select** and move Polygon *B* onto Polygon *A*. If the two polygons match exactly, they are congruent. If they are not congruent, adjust Polygon *B* and test again.

MathProcessor™ Tools:

 Geometry Tools

 Writing Space

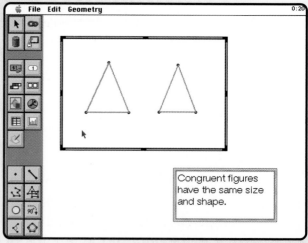

Congruent figures have the same size and shape.

Doing the Computer Investigation

A. Use a **Square Grid** background. Use the **Polygon Marker** to draw a polygon. Then draw another one that is the same. Select and move one figure on top of the other. If the two polygons match exactly, they are congruent.

INVESTIGATION

B. Use the **Polygon Marker**. Draw a polygon with one line of symmetry. Draw a congruent figure. Select and flip the second figure. Move it onto the first one to test for symmetry. If the two figures match exactly, they are symmetric.

Sharing Your Results

1. Draw a polygon that has two lines of symmetry. Draw a congruent polygon. Flip one of the polygons on top of the other. Are they symmetric?

2. Share your results with your classmates.

Extending the Computer Investigation

3. Explore 4-sided polygons. Can you draw a 4-sided polygon with no line of symmetry? with one line of symmetry? with two lines of symmetry? with four lines of symmetry?

4. Share your results with your classmates. What do you notice about the types of 4-sided figures that have no line of symmetry? two lines of symmetry? four lines of symmetry?

Hidden Figures

How many rectangles can you find in this figure?
If you said four, look again!

One way to find all the rectangles
is to make a list.
- Label each region.
- List rectangles that contain one region,
  two regions, three regions, and so on.

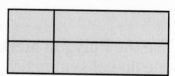

There are 4 one-region rectangles. **a, b, c, d**
There are 4 two-region rectangles. **ab, cd, ac, bd**
List any three-region rectangles you find.
List any four-region rectangles you find.

a	b
c	d

Did you find a total of 9 rectangles?

**Copy the polygons. Label the regions. Make a list
to help you answer the questions.**

1. How many rectangles are in the
   figure? (Remember, all squares
   are rectangles.)

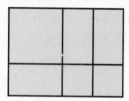

2. How many triangles are in the
   figure?

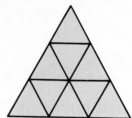

3. How much are these figures worth?
   Score 3 points for each triangle.
   Score 4 points for each quadrilateral.

   a.

   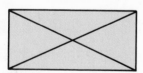

   b.

   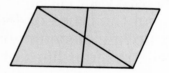

4. Design your own figure using triangles and
   quadrilaterals. Have a classmate decide how
   much it is worth.

MAINTAINING SKILLS

Choose the correct answer. Write A, B, C, or D.

1. $20 \times 410 = n$

   A 82,000   **C** 820

   B 8,200   **D** not given

2. Estimate 49×28.

   A 150   **C** 100

   B 8,000   **D** 1,500

3. 549
   $\times\ 38$

   A 20,862   **C** 20,852

   B 6,039   **D** not given

4. $48 \times \$5.16 = n$

   A \$247.68   **C** \$247.52

   B \$61.92   **D** not given

5. $7\overline{)490}$

   A 700   **C** 7

   B 70   **D** not given

6. $97 \div 4 = n$

   A 24 R3   **C** 24 R2

   B 27 R1   **D** not given

7. $3\overline{)1,208}$

   A 42 R2   **C** 402 R2

   B 402 R3   **D** not given

8. $513 \div 70 = n$

   A 8 R23   **C** 7 R23

   B 7 R33   **D** not given

9. Name the shape.

   A rectangle   **C** triangle

   B pentagon   **D** not given

10. What point is the center?

   A P **C** O

   B Q **D** not given

Choose the correct number operation to solve each problem.

11. Amy scored 15 points in her last basketball game. Her team's final score was 38. How many points did the rest of the team score?

   A multiply   **C** subtract

   B add   **D** not given

12. Tickets to the tennis match cost \$4.75 each. The Bates family had 5 tickets to the match. How much did the tickets cost them?

   A add   **C** divide

   B subtract   **D** not given

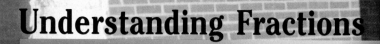

Understanding Fractions

THEME Artists and Their Work

Sharing What You Know

Not all artists work with a paintbrush. Sculptors often work with a chisel and mallet. At other times, they work with their hands. Many sculptors make figures of animals—birds, cats, dogs, and lots more. What do you think Bernard Langlais called his alligator sculpture?

Using Language

Look at the sculpture "Three Alligators." Each alligator is 1 of 3 alligators in the sculpture. In mathematics, the **fraction** $\frac{1}{3}$ means 1 of 3 equal parts. Are the 3 alligators all the same size? Could you say that each alligator is exactly $\frac{1}{3}$ of the total sculpture? Why or why not?

Words to Know: fraction, numerator, denominator, group, equivalent fractions, mixed numbers

Be a Problem Solver

A sculptor has only $\frac{1}{2}$ of her tools in her studio. She gets $\frac{1}{2}$ of her remaining tools from her car. Does she now have all her tools in her studio? Explain.

List the materials that artists use in their work. Compare your list with those of other students. Did any materials appear on more than $\frac{1}{2}$ of the lists?

Identifying Fractional Parts of a Region

Tara's painting has 3 equal parts. There is 1 red part.

▶ A **fraction** may name part of a region.

1 red part → **1** ← numerator
3 parts in all → **3** ← denominator

Read $\frac{1}{3}$ as one third.

The fraction $\frac{1}{3}$ tells what part of the painting is red.

What fraction tells what part of the painting is not red?

More Examples

a.

$\frac{3}{5}$, or three fifths, is blue.

b.

$\frac{1}{6}$, or one sixth, is *not* blue.

c.

$\frac{4}{4}$, or four fourths, is blue.

$\frac{4}{4} = 1$, or one whole

Check Your Understanding

Write the fraction that tells what part is blue.

1.

2.

3.

4.

Share Your Ideas How many thirds equal one whole region? How many fourths? fifths?

Write the fraction that tells what part is blue.

5.

6.

7.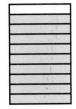

8.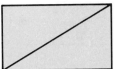

9.

10.

Write a fraction for each.

11. one half   **12.** two fifths   **13.** three eighths

14. seven tenths   **15.** five sixths   **16.** one third

Think and Apply

Write a fraction for each answer.

17.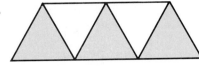

_____ is blue.
_____ is not blue.

18.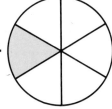

_____ is blue.
_____ is not blue.

What is wrong with this story?

19. Chuck and Frank ordered a pizza. The waiter asked them, "Do you want the pizza sliced into 6 or 8 pieces?" "Well," said Chuck, "I don't think we can eat 8 pieces. You better slice it into only 6 pieces."

Mixed Review

1.
$$\begin{array}{r} 36 \\ \times 12 \end{array}$$

2.
$$\begin{array}{r} 236 \\ - \ 43 \end{array}$$

3. $5\overline{)93}$

4.
$$\begin{array}{r} 34 \\ 28 \\ +47 \end{array}$$

5. 4,236 + 2,432

6. (3 × 2) × 6

7. $6.43 × 32

8. 9 × (3 × 3)

Round to the nearest ten.

9. 46

10. 395

11. 1,279

12. 4,999

Find each time.

13. 30 min after 9:35

14. 2 h and 10 min before 1:45

15. 3 h and 25 min after 3:20

16. 1 h and 40 min after 11:05 P.M.

How much of the region is green? green or red? not red?

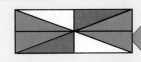

SHOW WHAT YOU KNOW

Draw a polygon. Shade $\frac{5}{6}$ of the region. Explain the steps you followed.

Parts of a Group

Collages are pictures made of different materials glued together. There are 9 shapes in this collage. What fraction of the group of shapes is rectangular?

▶A fraction may be used to name part of a group.

$\frac{3}{9}$ ← 3 rectangular shapes
　 ← 9 shapes in all

$\frac{3}{9}$ of the shapes are rectangular.

What fraction of the group of shapes is not rectangular?

$\frac{6}{9}$ ← 6 shapes are not rectangular
　 ← 9 shapes in all

$\frac{6}{9}$ of the shapes are not rectangular.

Check Your Understanding

Write the fraction that tells what part is blue.

1.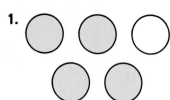

2.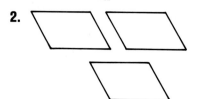

3.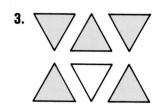

Share Your Ideas Explain the meaning of the numerator and denominator in your answer for **2**.

Write the fraction that tells what part is blue.

4.

5.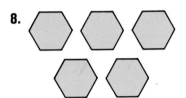

6.

7.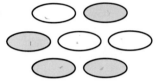

8.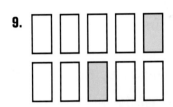

9.

Use the collage at the right. Write the fraction that tells what part of the group of shapes are

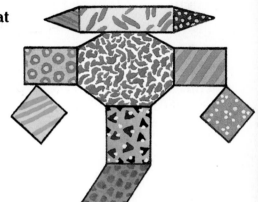

10. squares.

11. triangles.

12. quadrilaterals.

13. rectangles.

14. polygons.

15. not polygons.

Think and Apply

16. There are 3 girls and 4 boys who are making collages in art class. What part of the group is boys?

17. The art teacher chose 7 out of 10 collages to display in an art show. What part of the group was not chosen?

Use the collage above. Write the fraction that tells what part of the group of shapes

18. are triangles or squares.

19. have four right angles.

20. have two pairs of parallel sides.

How is finding a fraction for a part of a group like finding a fraction for part of a region?

SHOW WHAT YOU KNOW

Finding Parts of a Group

There is red paint in $\frac{1}{6}$ of the tubes. How many tubes of red paint are there?

Find $\frac{1}{6}$ of 12.

Think   12 tubes, 6 equal groups
Divide by 6. $12 \div 6 = 2$

$\frac{1}{6}$ **of 12 = 2**

There are 2 tubes of red paint.

Another Example

Find $\frac{2}{3}$ of 12.

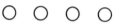

Step 1

Think   12 circles, 3 equal groups
Divide by 3. $12 \div 3 = 4$
There are 4 circles in each group.

$\frac{2}{3}$ of 12 = 8

Step 2

Think   2 groups are blue.
Multiply by 2. $2 \times 4 = 8$

groups   number in each group

Check Your Understanding

Find the part of each group.

1.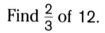

    $\frac{1}{3}$ of 6

2.

    $\frac{3}{4}$ of 8

3.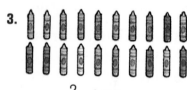

    $\frac{2}{5}$ of 20

Share Your Ideas   Look back at 1. How can you use your answer to find $\frac{2}{3}$ of 6?

294

Find the part of each group.

4.

$\frac{1}{3}$ of 12

5.

$\frac{7}{10}$ of 10

6.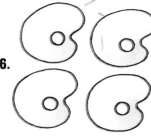

$\frac{2}{2}$ of 4

7.

$\frac{1}{5}$ of 10

8.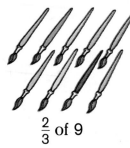

$\frac{2}{3}$ of 9

9.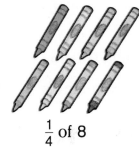

$\frac{1}{4}$ of 8

10. $\frac{1}{3}$ of 15

11. $\frac{5}{6}$ of 12

12. $\frac{1}{2}$ of 20

13. $\frac{3}{4}$ of 40

14. $\frac{1}{4}$ of 16

15. $\frac{1}{4}$ of 100

Find each missing number.

16. $\frac{1}{2}$ of $\square$ = 2

17. $\frac{1}{4}$ of $\square$ = 3

18. $\frac{1}{10}$ of $\square$ = 8

Think and Apply

19. The tip of a nose is about halfway between the chin and eyebrows. If the tip of Kevin's nose is 3 inches from his eyebrows, about how many inches would his nose be from his chin?

20. John has 12 colored pencils. What if $\frac{1}{4}$ of them are broken? How many pencils are broken?

Logical Thinking

21. Ruth painted some pictures. She sold half the pictures at an art sale. She gave half of those that were left to her mother. She kept the remaining 4 pictures for herself. How many pictures did Ruth paint?

Find $\frac{3}{5}$ of 40. Explain how you can use that answer to find $\frac{2}{5}$ of 40.

SHOW WHAT YOU KNOW

CHECKPOINT

Write the fraction that tells what part is blue. pages 290–293

1.

2.

3.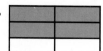

4.

5.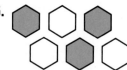

6.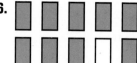

7.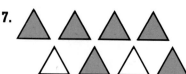

Write a fraction for each. pages 290–291

8. seven tenths

9. two thirds

10. four sixths

Find the part of each group. pages 294–295

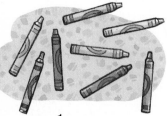

11. $\frac{1}{2}$ of 8

12. $\frac{1}{3}$ of 9

13. $\frac{1}{6}$ of 12

14. $\frac{3}{4}$ of 8

15. $\frac{2}{3}$ of 9

16. $\frac{3}{4}$ of 12

Choose the correct word to complete each sentence.

17. A _____ can name part of a region.

18. A fraction can name part of a _____.

19. The number below a fraction bar is the _____.

20. The number above a fraction bar is the _____.

Words to Know
numerator
fraction
denominator
group

Solve.

21. Jack has 10 jars of paint. Four of them are yellow. What fraction of the jars are yellow?

22. Ann had 8 crayons. She lost 3 of them. What fraction of the crayons are lost?

THINK
EXPLORE
SOLVE
LOOK BACK

How Much Red, Yellow, and Blue?

Look at the painting *Position in Grey, Red, Yellow, and Blue* I by Piet Mondrian.

Thinking Critically

About what fraction of this painting is made up of a combination of the primary colors red, blue, and yellow? Use Workmat 15 to help you.

Analyzing and Making Decisions

1. Look at the painting quickly. What fraction is made up of primary colors?

2. **What if** you had a tracing of the painting? How could you cut up parts of the tracing to help you estimate?

3. **What if** you cut out large squares from grid paper or used blocks? How could that help you find out?

4. Can you think of another way to estimate the area? Explain.

5. What fraction of the painting is made up of the primary colors?

Look Back   Which method of estimating do you think was the best? Explain. What part of the painting is red? Why do you think looking at the painting quickly and using methods of estimation might provide different answers?

Experimentation

Mr. Linden is making a design on a counter with tiles. The design is in the shape of a rectangle 12 inches by 17 inches. He is using square tiles that are 1 inch by 1 inch. The outer border is made up of a row of blue tiles. The second ring is a row of yellow tiles. The third ring is a row of orange. The remaining tiles are green. How many tiles of each color will he need?

Sometimes the best way to solve a problem is to do an experiment. You can carry out the action of the problem by using grid paper.

Solving the Problem

Think   What is the question? What are the facts?

Explore   Draw an outline of the design on a sheet of grid paper. How many squares did you show for the length? for the width? Continue to experiment by counting and then coloring the correct number of tiles.

Solve   How many tiles of each color are needed?

Look Back   Why was it important to outline the correct number of grid squares?

Share Your Ideas

1. **What if** the rectangle were 24 inches by 24 inches? What would you do differently to solve the problem?

2. What could you have used instead of grid paper to do the experiment?

Extending Your Thinking

Solve. Use a calculator where appropriate.

Use this information to solve 3–4.

Jan is using green, yellow, red, and brown paint to make posters.

3. She can use only three different colors on each poster. How many different color combinations can she use?

4. What if she can use only two colors? How many different color combinations can she use?

Denise was looking at four paintings. Three of them had blue in them. Four of them had red in them. Two of them had yellow in them. The paintings had no other colors in them.

5. What is the greatest number of paintings that could have all three colors?

6. What if two paintings had only blue and red? What colors would be in each of the other two paintings?

Mixed Strategy Review

Use this information to solve 7–8.

The museum sold copies of the paintings. A small print was $2.50. A medium size one was $5.00, and the large one was $7.95.

7. Maria bought two large prints and one small print. How much did they cost?

8. How much change did she receive?

THINK
EXPLORE
SOLVE
LOOK BACK

CREATE YOUR OWN

Write a problem for which someone must experiment to solve it.

ACTIVITY

Investigating Equivalent Fractions

Equivalent fractions name the same amount. Folding pieces of paper can help you see how.

Working together

Materials: 7 congruent strips of paper

A. Make fraction strips as described below.

Strip 1: Label the strip 1.

Strip 2: Fold the strip in half. Label each part $\frac{1}{2}$.

Strip 3: Fold the strip in half twice. Label each part $\frac{1}{4}$.

Strip 4: Fold the strip in half three times. Label each part $\frac{1}{8}$.

Strip 5: Fold the strip into three equal parts. Label each part $\frac{1}{3}$.

Strip 6: Fold the strip into three equal parts and then fold it in half. Label each part $\frac{1}{6}$.

Strip 7: Fold the strip into three equal parts and then fold it in half twice. Label each part $\frac{1}{12}$.

B. Place the strips on a desk in the order that you made them. Find as many different parts that match as you can.

Sharing Your Results

Use your fraction strips to answer each question.

1. How many fourths will cover $\frac{1}{2}$ exactly? how many sixths? how many eighths?

2. How many tenths do you think it would take to cover $\frac{1}{2}$ exactly? Explain.

Extending the Activity

$\frac{2}{4}$ covers $\frac{1}{2}$ exactly.

So $\frac{2}{4}$ and $\frac{1}{2}$ are equivalent fractions.

$\frac{1}{2}$	

$\frac{1}{4}$	$\frac{1}{4}$	$\frac{1}{4}$	$\frac{1}{4}$

Use your fraction strips to find these equivalent fractions.

3. $\frac{1}{2} = \frac{\square}{8}$

4. $\frac{1}{2} = \frac{\square}{12}$

5. $\frac{1}{4} = \frac{\square}{8}$

6. $\frac{1}{3} = \frac{\square}{6}$

7. $\frac{4}{4} = \frac{\square}{6}$

8. $\frac{3}{12} = \frac{\square}{4}$

9. $\frac{6}{8} = \frac{\square}{4}$

10. $\frac{12}{12} = \frac{\square}{8}$

▶ Another way to find an equivalent fraction is to multiply the numerator and the denominator by the same number.

$$\frac{1}{2} = \frac{1 \times 2}{2 \times 2} = \frac{2}{4} \qquad\qquad \frac{1}{2} = \frac{1 \times 3}{2 \times 3} = \frac{3}{6}$$

Look for a pattern in the equivalent fractions below. Describe each pattern. Write three more equivalent fractions for each.

11. $\frac{1}{2} = \frac{2}{4} = \frac{3}{6} = \frac{4}{8} = \frac{5}{10} =$ _____ = _____ = _____

12. $\frac{1}{3} = \frac{2}{6} = \frac{3}{9} = \frac{4}{12} = \frac{5}{15} =$ _____ = _____ = _____

13. $\frac{1}{4} = \frac{2}{8} = \frac{3}{12} = \frac{4}{16} = \frac{5}{20} =$ _____ = _____ = _____

Show What You Know

14. Use your fraction strips. Name 6 fractions equivalent to 1.

15. Describe how to find a fraction equivalent to $\frac{1}{4}$ by using fraction strips and by multiplying.

> Shade all of one rectangular region. Shade half of the other region. How many halves are shaded in all?

Mixed Numbers

Sherri designs and makes quilts. She cuts circular pieces of material into fifths to make her pattern.

Make circle models to show fifths.

Seven fifths is the same as one and two fifths. $\frac{7}{5} = 1\frac{2}{5}$ ← mixed number

▶A **mixed number** is made up of a whole number and a fraction.

Twelve sixths is the same as two. $\frac{12}{6} = 2$

$\llcorner$ whole number

Check Your Understanding

Write a mixed number or a whole number that tells what part is blue. Use fraction pieces or paper models to help you.

1.   **2.**   **3.**

Share Your Ideas   Draw a picture to show that $\frac{6}{2}$ is another name for 3.

302

Write a mixed number or a whole number that tells what part is blue.

4.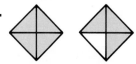

5.

6.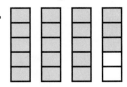

7.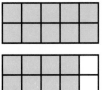

8.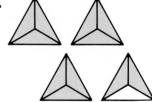

9.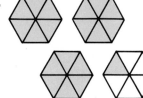

Is the fraction greater than 1? Write *yes* or *no*. If yes, write the fraction as a mixed number or a whole number. Make a drawing to help you.

10. $\frac{11}{10}$ **11.** $\frac{9}{10}$ **12.** $\frac{6}{3}$ **13.** $\frac{8}{5}$

Think and Apply

14. Sherri needs $\frac{1}{3}$ of a circle to make a flower for her quilt. How many flowers can she make with 4 circles?

15. Look back at **14**. Are 2 circles enough to make 5 flowers? Explain.

16. Name three fractions that may be written as whole numbers. For each fraction, how is the numerator related to the denominator?

JOURNAL WRITING

Name 3 fractions you can write as mixed numbers. How do numerators compare to denominators?

Mixed Review

1.   385
      × 46

2. $8.07
      × 24

3.   324
      +583

4.   4,864
      − 239

Name each figure.

5.   A — B

6.   M   N   O

7.   Q   R

8.   X   Y

9.

10.

11.

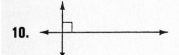

Is There a Bigger Half?

Several people are painting backgrounds for an art show. Each painter has painted $\frac{1}{2}$ of the background. Did they paint the same amount of space, or did one person paint more?

Working together

Materials: Workmat 16 and counters

A. Which is smaller, $\frac{1}{4}$ of circle **A** or $\frac{1}{4}$ of circle **B**, or are they the same? Check by cutting them out and comparing.

B. Which is larger, $\frac{1}{3}$ of rectangle **C** or $\frac{1}{3}$ of rectangle **D**, or are they the same size? Check by cutting them out and comparing them.

C. Which is smaller, $\frac{1}{3}$ of circle **A** or $\frac{1}{3}$ of circle **B**? Which is larger, $\frac{1}{4}$ of rectangle **C** or $\frac{1}{4}$ of rectangle **D**? Check by shading.

A. B.
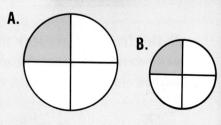

C.
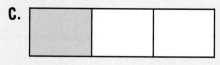

D.
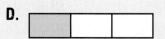

Sharing Your Ideas

1. Is $\frac{1}{2}$ of an object always equal to $\frac{1}{2}$ of another object? Explain.

2. If you are very hungry, is it sometimes better to have $\frac{1}{3}$ of a pizza instead of $\frac{1}{2}$ of a pizza? Explain.

Extending Your Thinking

Use counters to help you solve these problems.

3. There are 20 people in the full violin section of the orchestra. Today, $\frac{1}{2}$ of them are present.

    There are 10 people in the full trumpet section. Today one half of them are present. Which section has more people present, or do they have the same number present?

4. There are 12 people in the viola section, but only $\frac{1}{3}$ of them are present. There are 24 singers, but only $\frac{1}{3}$ of them are present. Which section has more people present, or do they have the same number present?

5. Look at **4. What if** only $\frac{1}{4}$ of each group were present? How would you answer the question now?

6. On Saturday, I spent $\frac{1}{2}$ of my free time painting and $\frac{1}{2}$ of my free time drawing. Did I spend more time painting or drawing, or did I spend the same amount of time doing both?

7. I played $\frac{1}{2}$ of Moonlight Sonata, and then I played $\frac{1}{2}$ of The Blue Danube Waltz. Which song took longer, or did they take the same amount of time?

Show What You Know

8. Look at **6** and **7**. Which question could you answer? Explain. Which question could you not answer? Explain.

RAP, RHYTHM, AND FRACTIONS

WORKING TOGETHER

Did you know that rhythm and math have a lot in common? One especially rhythmic kind of music is rap.

Work in small groups to investigate how the beat and rhythm of music is written. This illustration uses $\frac{4}{4}$ time to show how whole, half, quarter, and eighth notes are related.

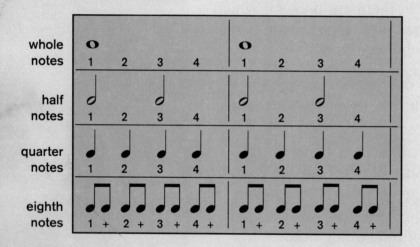

1. Choose a form of body percussion to perform this rhythm.

2. Work together to alter the rhythm. Replace notes with notes of equal value. Try out the new rhythm.

3. Write a rap by making up words that go along with your new rhythm. Then perform your rap for the class.

CHAPTER REVIEW/TEST

Write a fraction for the part that is blue.

1.

2.

3.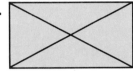

4.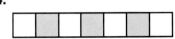

5.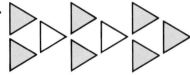

6.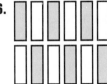

7.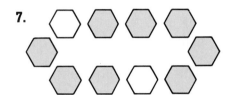

Find the part of each group.

8. $\frac{1}{2}$ of 6

9. $\frac{2}{3}$ of 12

10. $\frac{1}{4}$ of 20

11. $\frac{2}{5}$ of 20

12. $\frac{3}{4}$ of 12

13. $\frac{1}{5}$ of 15

14. $\frac{3}{8}$ of 16

15. $\frac{5}{9}$ of 18

Write a mixed number or a whole number that tells what part is blue.

16.

17.

18.

Solve.

19. Peter has 8 pencils. Six of them are yellow. What fraction of his pencils are yellow?

20. Measure the width of your desk. What can you find in the classroom that is $\frac{1}{2}$ the width of your desk?

Think Beth's painting has 18 flowers in it. Of the 18, $\frac{1}{2}$ are yellow and $\frac{1}{3}$ are pink. The rest of the flowers are red. How many red flowers are in the painting?

Fractions and Music

A **time signature** is at the beginning of a piece of music. It looks like a fraction. It shows how beats are grouped in a measure.

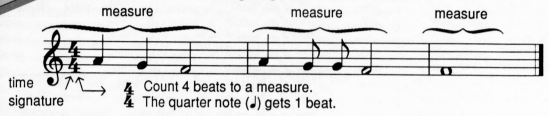

measure   measure   measure

time signature ⟶ $\frac{4}{4}$ Count 4 beats to a measure.
$\frac{4}{4}$ The quarter note (♩) gets 1 beat.

The chart below shows how many beats to a note when the time signature is $\frac{4}{4}$ or $\frac{3}{4}$.

Note	Name	Number of Beats Note is Held
𝅝	whole note	4 beats
𝅗𝅥	half note	2 beats
♩	quarter note	1 beat
♪	eighth note	$\frac{1}{2}$ beat

1. If the time signature is $\frac{4}{4}$, how many quarter notes can be in a measure? how many half notes?

2. If the time signature is $\frac{3}{4}$, how many quarter notes can be in a measure? how many eighth notes?

3. Write a rhythm pattern in $\frac{4}{4}$ time, like the example below. Use eighth, quarter, half, or whole notes. Then add words to your rhythm pattern.

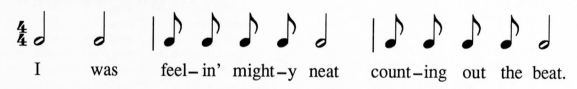

$\frac{4}{4}$ I   was   feel—in' might—y neat   count—ing out the beat.

4. Tap out the pattern you wrote. Have a partner count the steady beat (one, two, three, four) while you perform.

MAINTAINING SKILLS

Choose the correct answer. Write A, B, C, or D.

1. $8\overline{)69}$

  A 8 R7   **C** 7 R1

  B 8 R5   **D** not given

2. Estimate $506 \div 7$.

  A 700   **C** 70

  B 40   **D** 400

3. $5\overline{)496}$

  A 88 R1   **C** 87 R1

  B 99 R1   **D** not given

4. $\$2.22 \div 3 = n$

  A $.74   **C** $7.40

  B $.84   **D** not given

5. Name the shape.

  A rectangle   **C** parallelogram

  B square   **D** not given

6. Name the figure.

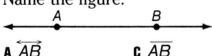

  A $\overleftrightarrow{AB}$ **C** $\overline{AB}$

  B $\overrightarrow{AB}$ **D** not given

7. Name the angle.

  A acute   **C** right

  B obtuse   **D** not given

8. What fractional part is shaded?

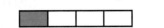

  A $\frac{1}{2}$ **C** $\frac{1}{4}$

  B $\frac{3}{4}$ **D** not given

9. What fractional part is shaded?

  A $\frac{2}{5}$ **C** $\frac{2}{3}$

  B $\frac{3}{5}$ **D** not given

10.

$$\frac{1}{4} = \frac{\square}{8}$$

  A 2   **C** 4

  B 1   **D** not given

Use the picture to solve 11–12.

11. How much more does the large bike cost than the small bike?

  A $20.70   **C** $29.30

  B $59.30   **D** not given

12. Al's father bought bicycles for Al and his sister. If he bought 2 large bikes, what was the total cost?

  A $168.40   **C** $178.50

  B $139.90   **D** not given

Sharing What You Know

In the United States you buy vegetables by the pound. You pay for them with dollars and cents. In Italy you would buy *vegetali* (veg-eh-taah-lee) by the kilogram. You would pay for them with lire. How might mathematics help people who travel around the world?

Using Language

Most countries use the metric system of measurement. Your mathematics book weighs about 1 **kilogram**. **Kilo-** means *thousand* in Greek, so a kilogram is 1,000 grams. What do you think the words **kilometer** and **kiloliter** mean? What are some other metric units? Where have you seen measurements using metric units?

Words to Know: liter, kiloliter, meter, kilometer, gram, kilogram, degree Celsius

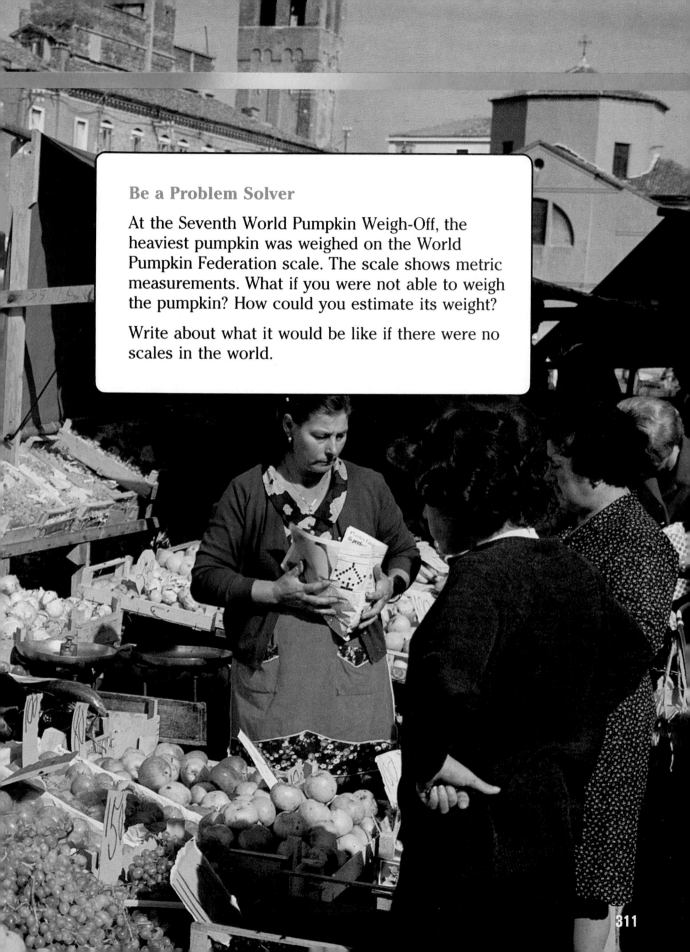

Be a Problem Solver

At the Seventh World Pumpkin Weigh-Off, the heaviest pumpkin was weighed on the World Pumpkin Federation scale. The scale shows metric measurements. What if you were not able to weigh the pumpkin? How could you estimate its weight?

Write about what it would be like if there were no scales in the world.

ACTIVITY

Investigating Decimals

What if you were in Mexico and wanted to spend only part of a dollar to buy a souvenir?

Working together

Materials: Workmat 11, scissors, colored pencils

A. Make a list of 8 items that you can buy for less than 1 dollar. List the items and the cost.

B. Cut out eight 10-by-10 pieces of grid paper. How many small squares are there on each piece? Let each piece stand for a one-dollar bill, since 1 dollar has the value of 100 cents.

C. Write the names of the items from your list on the back of the pieces of grid paper. Shade the front of each to show what part of a dollar you need to pay for the item.

D. Exchange your pieces of grid paper with another pair of students. Make a list of each item you receive. Use a dollar sign and a decimal point to record how much each item costs.

Sharing Your Results

1. Show the list you wrote in Step **D** to the students whose grid paper pieces you have. Check that your prices match their prices.

2. How many small squares would you shade to show $.94? $.38?

3. **Look back** at **2**. What part of a hundred is each amount? Write your answers as fractions.

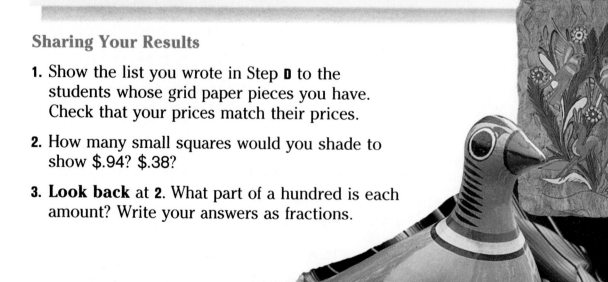

Extending the Activity

Work on your own.

Materials: Workmats 11 and 17, scissors, colored pencils

A

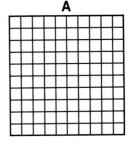

4. Use Workmat 11 to make figures like the ones shown at the right, or use Workmat 17.

5. How many small squares are there in Figure A? Shade enough of Figure A to show $.60. How many small squares did you shade?

6. How many strips are there in Figure B? Shade enough of Figure B to show $.60. How many strips did you shade?

B

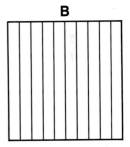

7. Did you shade the same amount of Figures A and B? Explain.

How much would you shade to show each amount? Use grid paper to help you if you wish.

8. Show $.80.

9. Show $.20.

How many small squares? strips?   How many small squares? strips?

Show What You Know

10. **Look back** at **8** and **9**. Write fractions to show how much of each figure you shaded.

11. How many strips equal 90 small squares?

12. How many squares equal 10 strips?

13. Could you shade strips to show 75 squares? Explain your answer.

> Draw 10 circles. Shade 5 of them red, 3 yellow, and 2 green. What part of the group of circles is red? yellow? green?

Relating Fractions and Decimals

People in Portugal often use mosaic tiles for decorating the floors and walls of their homes.

There are 10 strips in the tile below. Six tenths of the strips are blue.

We can write six tenths two ways.

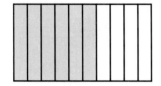

ones	tenths
0 .	6

↑
decimal point

fraction → $\frac{6}{10}$ = **0.6** ← decimal

There are 100 small squares in the tile below. Six hundredths of the squares are blue.

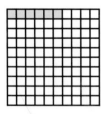

ones	tenths	hundredths
0 .	0	6

$\frac{6}{100}$ = **0.06**

Check Your Understanding

Write a decimal for each fraction.

1. $\frac{3}{10}$　　　　**2.** $\frac{17}{100}$　　　　**3.** $\frac{9}{10}$　　　　**4.** $\frac{8}{100}$　　　　**5.** $\frac{54}{100}$

Share Your Ideas Explain the difference between 0.9 and 0.09. Use grid paper to help you.

314

Write a decimal for each fraction.

6. $\frac{7}{10}$ **7.** $\frac{2}{100}$ **8.** $\frac{68}{100}$

9. $\frac{15}{100}$ **10.** $\frac{5}{10}$ **11.** $\frac{50}{100}$

12. $\frac{9}{10}$ **13.** $\frac{40}{100}$ **14.** $\frac{8}{10}$

Write a fraction for each decimal.

15. 0.5   **16.** 0.18   **17.** 0.9

18. 0.2   **19.** 0.43   **20.** 0.85

21. 0.03   **22.** 0.01   **23.** 0.71

Compare. Use >, <, or = for ⬤.

24. 0.4 ⬤ $\frac{2}{10}$ **25.** $\frac{50}{100}$ ⬤ 0.50

26. $\frac{65}{100}$ ⬤ 0.61   **27.** 0.3 ⬤ $\frac{7}{10}$

28. 0.08 ⬤ $\frac{80}{100}$ **29.** 0.59 ⬤ 0.6

Think and Apply

Write each number as a decimal and as a fraction.

30. Barbara rode her bicycle eight tenths of a mile to school.

31. The winner of the race was twenty-four hundredths of a second faster than the person who finished next.

Explain how to change $\frac{3}{10}$ and $\frac{3}{100}$ to decimals.

Mixed Review

1.   51
     × 9

2.   87
     × 6

3.   250
     × 8

4.   409
     × 7

5. $2.74
     × 5

6. $6.39
     × 8

7.   4,836
     + 957

8.   9,003
     − 589

9.   2 × 74

10.   3 × 63

11.   8 × 92

12.   6 × 135

13.   7 × 108

14.   4 × $1.98

15.   5 × $3.20

SHOW WHAT YOU KNOW

315

Write these fractions as decimals.

$$\frac{4}{10} \qquad \frac{35}{100} \qquad \frac{78}{100} \qquad \frac{7}{10}$$

Relating Mixed Numbers and Decimals

Julie took a gondola tour of Venice. The tour was 2.75 kilometers long.

ones	tenths	hundredths
2 .	7	5

$$2\frac{75}{100} \qquad = \qquad 2.75$$

Read as two *and* seventy-five hundredths.

More Examples

ones	tenths
1 .	4

$$1\frac{4}{10} = 1.4$$

Read as one and four tenths.

ones	tenths	hundredths
1 .	0	4

$$1\frac{4}{100} = 1.04$$

Read as one and four hundredths.

Check Your Understanding

Write the letter for the correct decimal.

1. six and six tenths   **a.** 6.0   **b.** 6.6   **c.** 0.06   **d.** 0.006

2. one and five tenths   **a.** 1.05   **b.** 15.0   **c.** 1.5   **d.** 0.15

3. thirty-two hundredths   **a.** 0.32   **b.** 3.20   **c.** 0.032   **d.** 320.0

4. six and one hundredth   **a.** 610   **b.** 61.0   **c.** 6.10   **d.** 6.01

Share Your Ideas Explain the difference between 2.0, 0.2, and 0.02.

Write a decimal for each.

5.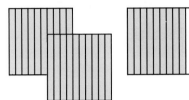

6.

7.

8.

Write a decimal for each.

9. $4\frac{6}{10}$　　　　**10.** $\frac{55}{100}$　　　　**11.** $7\frac{7}{10}$　　　　**12.** $9\frac{3}{100}$

13. three tenths　　　　　　**14.** two and five tenths

15. twelve hundredths　　　　**16.** eighty-six hundredths

17. one and ten hundredths　　**18.** seven and four hundredths

Write in words.

19. 8.1　　　**20.** 0.08　　　**21.** 0.7　　　**22.** 4.99　　　**23.** 20.02

Think and Apply

Write the decimal for each number.

24. The water taxi traveled one and four tenths kilometers from St. Mark's Square to the glass factory.

25. Venice is famous for its glass blowers. One glass blower made a pitcher in the shape of a swan. The pitcher holds one and seventy-five hundredths liters of water.

Common Error

26. Caution! What is wrong with this decimal? Explain. Give the correct decimal.

Word name: seven hundredths

Decimal: 0.7 ← incorrect

Use grid paper to show why 0.3 is equal to 0.30.

SHOW WHAT YOU KNOW

Comparing and Ordering Decimals

What if the tour of Windsor Castle takes 3.2 hours and the Tower of London tour takes 3.25 hours? Which tour takes more time?

Shade grid paper to show each decimal.
Compare the shaded parts.

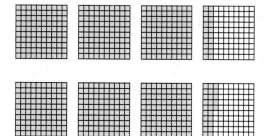

ones	tenths	hundredths
3 .	2	0
3 .	2	5

← Write a 0 to help line up the digits.

same   **0.20 < 0.25**
So 3.20 < 3.25

The Tower of London tour takes more time.

List 1.7, 1.17, and 1.71 in order from greatest to least.

Step 1 Use grid paper or a place value chart.	**Step 2** Compare the decimals two at a time.	**Step 3** Find the next greatest decimal.
<table><tr><td>1.</td><td>7</td><td>0</td></tr><tr><td>1.</td><td>1</td><td>7</td></tr><tr><td>1.</td><td>7</td><td>1</td></tr></table>	**1.70 > 1.17** **1.70 < 1.71** 1.71 is the greatest.	**1.71 > 1.70 > 1.17**

Check Your Understanding

Use grid paper to show each decimal. Then compare. Use >, <, or =.

1. 1.67 ⬤ 1.69   **2.** 0.5 ⬤ 0.05   **3.** 5.9 ⬤ 5.90

Write in order from greatest to least.

4. 2.81   2.09   2.79   **5.** 4.3   4.05   4.35   **6.** 5.1   5.16   5.14

Share Your Ideas   Explain how you ordered the decimals in **6**.

Compare. Use >, <, or = for ●.

7. 0.9 ● 0.10

8. 8.4 ● 8.5

9. 7.09 ● 7.90

10. 2.93 ● 29.3

11. 0.30 ● 0.3

12. 1.0 ● 0.89

13. 4.63 ● 4.61

14. 3.01 ● 3.0

15. 0.58 ● 0.6

16. 0.2 ● 0.02

17. 19.5 ● 195

18. 5.8 ● 5.80

List these decimals in order from greatest to least.

19. 2.4   1.6   3.8

20. 0.4   1.02   0.71

21. 10.5   11.56   1.5   1.6

22. 8.8   8.08   0.88   80.8

List these decimals in order from least to greatest.

23. 6.25   6.31   6.3

24. 13.9   3.91   1.93

25. 5.4   5.04   5.54   5.45

26. 0.1   0.01   1.01   1.0

Fill in the □ to make each statement true.

27. 9.1 > 9.□

28. 7.□3 < 7.13

29. 2.89 < 2.□0

30. 4.6□ > 4.68

31. □.98 > 8.99

32. 6.□□ < 6.01

Think and Apply

33. Cam walked 4.3 blocks to see Big Ben. Joan walked 4.8 blocks to see Hyde Park. Who walked farther?

34. Use all the digits 0, 1, 2, and 3. Put one digit in each box to make the least decimal number. Explain your thinking.

☐☐ . ☐

Name all the decimals in hundredths that are between 5.01 and 5.1.

SHOW WHAT YOU KNOW

ACTIVITY

Investigating Adding and Subtracting Decimals

Use grids to play this decimal game.

1.00

0.54   0.46

Working together

Materials: seven 10-by-10 grids cut from Workmat 11

A. Label one grid *1.00.* Cut each of the other grids into two pieces. Cut only on grid lines. Make each piece a different number of small squares. Label each piece in decimals to hundredths.

B. Shuffle the grid pieces. Place them face down on the table. Take turns with your partner. Choose two pieces.
- If the pieces together cover 1.00 exactly, score 0 points.
- If the pieces cover less than 1.00, score 1 point.
- If the pieces cover more than 1.00, score 2 points.

When all the pieces have been used, the player with the lower total score wins.

Sharing Your Results

1. Find all pairs that together make 1.00. Record the decimal numbers for the pairs.

2. Name two pieces that together are greater than 1.00. What mixed number tells how much the two pieces are together?

3. Name two pieces that together cover less than 1.00. Write the sum of the two pieces. What decimal tells how much more is needed to exactly cover the whole?

Extending the Activity

Work with a partner.

Materials: grid pieces from page 320, chart like the one shown below

4. Mix the grid pieces and place them in a stack. Take turns with a partner.

- Pick two pieces. Call the pieces A and B. Record the decimal names of the pieces on the chart.

- Find the total number of small squares in the two pieces. Record this sum as a decimal.

- Find how many more small squares one piece has than the other. Record this difference as a decimal.

Turn	Piece A	Piece B	Sum	Difference
Jim				
Mary				
Jim				

Try these examples. Shade grids to help you if you wish.

5. $0.4 + 0.3$

6. $0.35 + 0.74$

7. $0.75 - 0.26$

8. $0.98 - 0.8$

Show What You Know

Look back at your completed chart.

9. Which two pieces have the greatest sum? What is their difference?

10. Which two pieces have the least difference? What is their sum?

11. Explain how you know when the sum of two decimals will be less than one, or equal to or greater than one.

321

Find each sum or difference.

$623 + 49 = n$ $206 - 187 = n$

$590 + 853 = n$ $439 - 264 = n$

Adding and Subtracting Tenths

Mr. Chan rode his bicycle 2.7 kilometers to the park. Then he rode 1.6 kilometers to the library. How many kilometers did he ride altogether?

$2.7 + 1.6 = n$

Step 1 Line up the decimal points.	Step 2 Add tenths. Regroup.	Step 3 Add ones.	Step 4 Place the decimal point.
$\downarrow$ $\begin{array}{r} 2.7 \\ +1.6 \end{array}$	$\begin{array}{r} 1 \\ 2.7 \\ +1.6 \\ \hline 3 \end{array}$ 13 tenths = 1 one 3 tenths	$\begin{array}{r} 1 \\ 2.7 \\ +1.6 \\ \hline 4 \quad 3 \end{array}$	$\begin{array}{r} 2.7 \\ +1.6 \\ \hline 4.3 \end{array}$

Mr. Chan rode 4.3 kilometers.

Another example   Find $25.3 - 8.6$.

Step 1 Line up the decimal points.	Step 2 Not enough tenths. Regroup ones. Subtract tenths.	Step 3 Continue to subtract and regroup. Place the decimal point.
$\downarrow$ $\begin{array}{r} 25.3 \\ -\ 8.6 \end{array}$	$\begin{array}{r} 4\ 13 \\ 2\cancel{5}.\cancel{3} \\ -\ 8.6 \\ \hline 7 \end{array}$ 5 ones 3 tenths = 4 ones 13 tenths	$\begin{array}{r} 1\ 14 \\ \cancel{4}\ \ 13 \\ 2\cancel{5}.\cancel{3} \\ -\ 8.6 \\ \hline 16.7 \end{array}$ 2 tens 4 ones = 1 ten 14 ones

Add or subtract.

1. $8.4 - 0.9$ **2.** $42.2 + 7.8$ **3.** $10.9 + 7.5$

4. $14.9 - 2.3$ **5.** $36.5 - 35.6$ **6.** $507.1 - 124.3$

Share Your Ideas   Explain why it is important to line up decimal points when you are adding or subtracting decimals.

Add or subtract.

7. $\begin{array}{r} 5.4 \\ +0.9 \\ \hline \end{array}$

8. $\begin{array}{r} 0.8 \\ +0.6 \\ \hline \end{array}$

9. $\begin{array}{r} 3.2 \\ -2.7 \\ \hline \end{array}$

10. $\begin{array}{r} 47.1 \\ -\ 6.5 \\ \hline \end{array}$

11. $\begin{array}{r} 29.5 \\ +\ 1.4 \\ \hline \end{array}$

12. $\begin{array}{r} 40.5 \\ -30.7 \\ \hline \end{array}$

13. $\begin{array}{r} 85.2 \\ +83.4 \\ \hline \end{array}$

14. $\begin{array}{r} 51.9 \\ -12.9 \\ \hline \end{array}$

15. $\begin{array}{r} 236.8 \\ +364.3 \\ \hline \end{array}$

16. $\begin{array}{r} 600.2 \\ -\ 43.2 \\ \hline \end{array}$

17. $\begin{array}{r} 1.3 \\ +9.9 \\ \hline \end{array}$

18. $\begin{array}{r} 34.7 \\ -\ 5.2 \\ \hline \end{array}$

19. $\begin{array}{r} 350.5 \\ +361.6 \\ \hline \end{array}$

20. $\begin{array}{r} 125.4 \\ -\ 72.8 \\ \hline \end{array}$

21. $\begin{array}{r} 706.0 \\ +248.1 \\ \hline \end{array}$

22. $6.7 + 0.8$

23. $8.4 - 0.6$

24. $43.8 - 25.9$

25. $110.0 - 20.1$

26. $14.3 + 94.9$

27. $276.1 + 5.8$

Find each missing digit.

28. $\begin{array}{r} 0.7 \\ +0.\square \\ \hline \square.1 \end{array}$

29. $\begin{array}{r} 51.\square \\ -\ 0.4 \\ \hline 5\square.7 \end{array}$

30. $\begin{array}{r} 1\square\square.6 \\ +\ 86.\square \\ \hline \square 08.5 \end{array}$

31. $\begin{array}{r} \square\square\square.\square \\ -\ 43.5 \\ \hline 88.5 \end{array}$

Follow the rule. Give the output for each input.

Rule: Add 1.7.

	Input	Output
32.	3.9	
33.	28.6	
34.	104.3	

Rule: Subtract 0.9.

	Input	Output
35.	6.2	
36.	14.3	
37.	501.1	

Think and Apply

38. The largest palace in the world is the Old Palace Museum in Beijing, China. The palace covers a rectangular area. It is 959.7 meters long and 749.5 meters wide. How much greater is the length than the width? What is the perimeter of the palace?

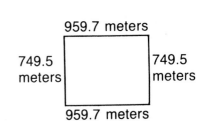

959.7 meters

749.5 meters

749.5 meters

959.7 meters

Explain how adding and subtracting decimals is like adding and subtracting whole numbers. Explain how it is different.

SHOW WHAT YOU KNOW

How many tenths are there in one? How many hundredths are there in 1 tenth?

Adding and Subtracting Hundredths

In the Japanese puppet show the horse is 1.4 meters tall. The donkey is 1.25 meters tall. How much taller is the horse than the donkey?

1.4 − 1.25 = n

Step 1 Line up the decimal points. Write zeros where needed.	Step 2 Not enough hundredths. Regroup tenths. Subtract hundredths.	Step 3 Subtract tenths.	Step 4 Subtract ones. Place the decimal point.
$\begin{array}{r} 1.40 \\ -1.25 \\ \hline \end{array}$	$\begin{array}{r} {}^{3\,10} \\ 1.4\llap{/}0 \\ -1.25 \\ \hline 5 \end{array}$ 4 tenths 0 hundredths = 3 tenths 10 hundredths	$\begin{array}{r} {}^{3\,10} \\ 1.4\llap{/}0 \\ -1.25 \\ \hline 15 \end{array}$	$\begin{array}{r} {}^{3\,10} \\ 1.4\llap{/}0 \\ -1.25 \\ \hline 0.15 \end{array}$

The horse is 0.15 meter taller than the donkey.

Find 2.4 + 4.87.

Step 1	Step 2	Check.
$\begin{array}{r} 2.40 \\ +4.87 \\ \hline \end{array}$ Line up the decimal points.	$\begin{array}{r} {}^{1} \\ 2.40 \\ +4.87 \\ \hline 7.27 \end{array}$ Regroup as necessary. Place the decimal point.	$\begin{array}{r} 2.40 \\ +4.87 \\ \hline 7.27 \end{array}$ ↑ Check by adding up.

Check Your Understanding

Add or subtract. Write zeros where needed.

1. $\begin{array}{r} 4.67 \\ +0.46 \\ \hline \end{array}$

2. $\begin{array}{r} 5.19 \\ -2.83 \\ \hline \end{array}$

3. $\begin{array}{r} 18.25 \\ +\ 2.9 \\ \hline \end{array}$

4. $\begin{array}{r} 20.1 \\ -10.64 \\ \hline \end{array}$

5. $\begin{array}{r} 8.92 \\ -2.47 \\ \hline \end{array}$

Share Your Ideas Explain why you write zeros at the end of some decimals before adding and subtracting.

Add or subtract. Write zeros where needed.

6. $\begin{array}{r} 2.45 \\ +\,0.82 \\ \hline \end{array}$
7. $\begin{array}{r} 4.80 \\ -\,3.56 \\ \hline \end{array}$
8. $\begin{array}{r} 16.07 \\ +\ \ 2.03 \\ \hline \end{array}$
9. $\begin{array}{r} 44.3 \\ -\,21.28 \\ \hline \end{array}$
10. $\begin{array}{r} 38.25 \\ +\,23.4\ \ \\ \hline \end{array}$

11. $\begin{array}{r} 70.10 \\ -\,28.09 \\ \hline \end{array}$
12. $\begin{array}{r} 53.69 \\ +\ \ 4.18 \\ \hline \end{array}$
13. $\begin{array}{r} 13.02 \\ -\ \ 8.75 \\ \hline \end{array}$
14. $\begin{array}{r} 8 \\ +\,4.26 \\ \hline \end{array}$
15. $\begin{array}{r} 0.18 \\ -\,0.04 \\ \hline \end{array}$

16. $\begin{array}{r} 69.80 \\ +\,56.43 \\ \hline \end{array}$
17. $\begin{array}{r} 31.5 \\ +\ \ 6.84 \\ \hline \end{array}$
18. $\begin{array}{r} 29.4 \\ -\,12.32 \\ \hline \end{array}$
19. $\begin{array}{r} 98.4 \\ -\,24.14 \\ \hline \end{array}$
20. $\begin{array}{r} 6 \\ -\,4.37 \\ \hline \end{array}$

21. $8.07 - 0.51$
22. $1.43 + 9.57$
23. $2.39 + 1.47$

24. $2.4 - 1.36$
25. $21.66 + 2.6$
26. $82.15 - 3.9$

Place decimal points in the addends to get the sum. Use estimation to help you.

27. $21 + 35 = 5.6$
28. $46 + 205 = 25.1$

29. $123 + 47 = 127.7$
30. $38 + 142 = 18.0$

31. $906 + 138 = 22.86$
32. $26 + 371 + 5 = 44.7$

Think and Apply

33. The horse puppet is 0.38 meter taller than the lion puppet. The lion puppet is 1.12 meters tall. How tall is the horse puppet?

34. The grandmother puppet is 0.45 meter shorter than the father puppet. The father puppet is 1.3 meters tall. How tall is the grandmother puppet?

35. The dragon puppet is 0.18 meter taller than the swan. The swan is 0.5 meter taller than the mouse. The mouse puppet is 0.42 meter tall. How much taller is the dragon than the mouse?

JOURNAL WRITING

Look back at **30**. Explain how you decided where to place the decimal points.

SHOW WHAT YOU KNOW

325

CHECKPOINT

Complete. pages 312–317

	Decimal	Fraction or Mixed Number	Words
1.	10.7		
2.		$\frac{53}{100}$	
3.			six and two tenths
4.	0.35		

Compare. Use >, <, or = for ⬤. pages 318–319

5. 0.4 ⬤ 0.37   **6.** 0.6 ⬤ 0.60   **7.** 436 ⬤ 43.6

8. 0.15 ⬤ 0.19   **9.** 20.07 ⬤ 20.70   **10.** 9.3 ⬤ 0.93

List these numbers in order from least to greatest. pages 318–319

11. 7.45 7 7.39   **12.** 7.76 7.6 7.07

13. 0.3 3.0 0.03   **14.** 7.04 7.40 7.07

Add or subtract. Write zeros where needed. pages 320–325

15. 5.3
  $+8.2$

16. 13.7
  $-\ 1.4$

17. 7.3
  -1.6

18. 4.52
  $+0.76$

19. 15.37
  $-\ 4.15$

20. 14.84
  $+75.37$

21. 4.7
  $+5.36$

22. 6.84
  -3.95

23. 0.58
  $+5.8$

24. 8.7
  -0.62

25. 15.8 + 11.21   **26.** 3.4 − 2.9   **27.** 3 + 6.7

Solve.

28. There is a walking tour of the gardens at an English castle. It takes 2.7 hours. The guided tour of the castle museum takes 3.25 hours. What is the total time for both tours?

29. Look back at **28.** How much longer is the museum tour than the garden tour?

INVESTIGATING
PROBLEM SOLVING

**THINK
EXPLORE
SOLVE
LOOK BACK**

How Fast Do Cities Grow?

The populations of many United States cities have changed greatly since 1950. Study the estimated populations of the cities given below.

Thinking Critically

Which cities are gaining population? Which cities are losing population? Study the population numbers to answer the questions.

City	1950	1960	1970	1980
New York	7,890,000	7,780,000	7,900,000	7,070,000
Chicago	3,620,000	3,550,000	3,370,000	3,010,000
Los Angeles	1,970,000	2,480,000	2,810,000	2,970,000
Philadelphia	2,070,000	2,000,000	1,950,000	1,690,000
Houston	600,000	940,000	1,230,000	1,600,000
Phoenix	110,000	440,000	580,000	790,000

Analyzing and Making Decisions

1. Which cities increased in population between 1950 and 1980? Do they have anything in common? Explain.

2. Which cities decreased in population? What do they have in common?

3. Which cities gained the most people between 1950 and 1980? Which city lost the most people in this period?

4. Identify the city that is described by each statement.
   a. This city of more than 1 million people grew rapidly all the time from 1950 to 1980.
   b. This city stayed about the same from 1950 to 1970 and then it lost many people from 1970 to 1980.
   c. This city grew all the time from 1950 to 1980 but it grew more slowly after 1960.

Look Back What do you think the population of each of these cities is today?

Organized Listing

Paul and Tony are truck drivers. Paul's route takes him to St. Louis every 6th day. Tony is in St. Louis every 5th day. They had dinner together in St. Louis on May 1. They agreed to meet for dinner the next time both of them are in St. Louis together. What date will that be?

A list will often help you organize the facts in a problem and then help you to solve it.

Solving the Problem

Think   What is the question?

Explore   How often does Paul drive to St. Louis? How often does Tony drive to St. Louis? When was the last time they were in St. Louis together? Make a list of the days in May that Paul will be in St. Louis. Make a list for Tony.

Solve   When is the next time they will be in St. Louis together?

Look Back   How did the list help you to solve the problem?

Share Your Ideas

1. How much time will elapse between their dinners in St. Louis?

Extending Your Thinking

Solve. Use a calculator where appropriate.

CHOICES

Tim and Jerry are sightseeing in Madrid. They set their watches at 8:00 A.M. Tim's watch gains 5 minutes every hour. Jerry's watch gains 2 minutes every hour.

2. When are their watches 12 minutes apart?

3. When are their watches 21 minutes apart?

4. If it is 12 noon, what time will each of their watches show?

5. If they correct their watches at 3:00 P.M., what will each of them have to do?

THINK
EXPLORE
SOLVE
LOOK BACK

Mixed Strategy Review

6. Hana and Laura visited Nairobi for two weeks. It rained 4 days while they were there. How many days did it not rain?

7. Hana, Laura, and Tricia decided to share the cost of their dinner equally. The dinner cost $27. How much did each of them pay?

Use this information to solve 8–9.

Jerry and his mother rode a cab for 5 miles. The cab fare is $1.50 for the first mile and $.75 for each additional mile or part of a mile.

8. How much did the cab fare cost?

9. **What if** they gave the driver a $.75 tip? What was the total amount of money that they gave the driver?

JOURNAL WRITING

CREATE YOUR OWN

Write a problem that can be solved by making a list.

5° CENTENARIO DELLA NASCITA
DI LEONARDO DA VINCI 1452-1952

POSTE 25 LIRE
REPUBBLICA ITALIANA

The Granger Collection

Measuring in Centimeters and Millimeters

Many of Leonardo da Vinci's paintings are in the Louvre Museum, in Paris. This French postage stamp shows a portrait of da Vinci. The stamp is about 6 centimeters high.

▶ The **centimeter (cm)** is a unit of length in the metric system of measurement

A large paper clip is about 1 cm wide.

▶ The **millimeter (mm)** is another unit of length in the metric system.

10 millimeters = 1 centimeter

To the nearest centimeter, this pencil sharpener is about 3 cm long.

To the nearest millimeter, this pushpin is about 17 mm long.

Check Your Understanding

Measure each length to the nearest centimeter.

1.

2.

Measure each length to the nearest millimeter.

3.

4.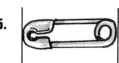

5.

Share Your Ideas Explain how you can find the length of an object in millimeters if you know its length in centimeters.

Measure each length to the nearest centimeter and to the nearest millimeter.

6.

7.

8.

9.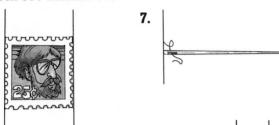

10.

11.

12. Trace the line below to make a map. Use the clues. Measure, then label each point.

- The Florist is 8 cm west of the Museum.
- The Park is 5 cm east of the Museum.
- The Hotel is between the Museum and the Florist.
- The Subway Stop is 4 cm west of the Park.
- The Bakery is west of the Museum.

Use your drawing to answer the questions.

13. How many centimeters are between the Bakery and the Museum?

14. How much farther is it from the Subway Stop to the Florist than from the Subway Stop to the Hotel?

15. If one centimeter stands for 2 kilometers, how many kilometers is it from the Bakery to the Park?

Think and Apply

Estimate in centimeters or millimeters. Then check by measuring. Use string where needed.

16. the width of your thumb

17. the length of your little finger

18. the width of your foot

19. the length of your foot

20. the distance from your elbow to your wrist

21. the distance around your wrist

Will a measurement in centimeters or millimeters be closer to the actual measure? Explain.

SHOW WHAT YOU KNOW

Estimating and Measuring Length

Independence Hall, in Philadelphia, Pennsylvania, is a popular tourist attraction. The doorway to Independence Hall is about 1 meter wide.

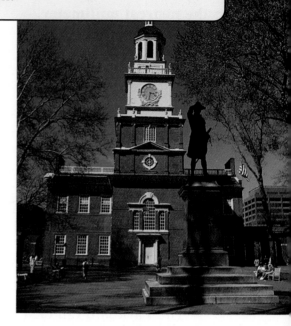

▶ The **meter (m)** is a unit of length in the metric system.

1 meter = 100 centimeters

▶ The **kilometer (km)** is a unit used to measure very long distances.

1 kilometer = 1,000 meters

▶ Another unit of length is the **decimeter (dm).**

1 decimeter = 10 centimeters
10 decimeters = 1 meter

To help you estimate length, think of these lengths.

The length of a baseball bat is about 1 meter.

The distance around a football field $2\frac{1}{2}$ times is about 1 kilometer.

Check Your Understanding

Would you choose centimeters, meters, or kilometers to measure each?

1. height of a ladder

2. length of the Missouri River

3. length of a crayon

4. length of an airplane

Share Your Ideas   Explain how to change a measurement from kilometers to meters.

Would you choose centimeters, meters, or kilometers to measure each?

5. height of a flagpole

6. width of a magazine

7. depth of a river

8. thickness of a slice of bread

9. width of a tennis court

10. height of a mountain

Complete.

11. 3 km = _____ m

12. 5 cm = _____ mm

13. 2 m = _____ cm

14. 7 dm = _____ cm

15. _____ km = 2,000 m

16. _____ m = 400 cm

17. 3 m = _____ dm

18. 0.5 km = _____ m

19. 1.2 m = _____ cm

**Complete the chart. First estimate each length.
Then measure to the nearest meter.**

	Distance	Estimate	Actual Measurement
20.	Length of chalk tray		
21.	Height of chalk tray		
22.	Distance around room		
23.	Length of desk		
24.	Width of desk		

Think and Apply

25. Eric walked 4 kilometers from his hotel to Independence Hall. Julie walked 2,800 meters to the hall. Who walked farther? How much farther?

26. Tessa went to see the Liberty Bell near Independence Hall and then returned to the hotel. She walked 1.6 kilometers each way. How many meters did she walk in all?

Mathematics and History
Ancient Egyptians used their arms, hands, and fingers to measure length.

- The digit was equal to the width of 1 finger.
- The palm was equal to 4 digits.
- The cubit was equal to 7 palms.

27. How many digits are equal to 5 cubits and 3 palms?

28. What is your height to the nearest cubit?

Explain how to change 4 kilometers to centimeters, using mental math.

SHOW WHAT YOU KNOW

> How can you find out which weighs more, 10 nickels or 10 dimes?

Estimating and Measuring Weight

United States mints are located in Denver and Philadelphia. Many tourists visit these mints to watch coins being made. A nickel weighs 5 grams.

▶ The **gram (g)** is a metric unit of weight.

The gram is used to measure the weight of light objects.

▶ The **kilogram (kg)** is used to measure the weight of heavy objects.

200 nickels together weigh 1 kilogram.

1 kilogram = 1,000 grams

To help you estimate weight, think of the weight of these objects.

A dollar bill weighs 1 gram.

This book weighs about 1 kilogram.

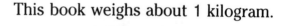

Check Your Understanding

Choose the best estimate.

1. A bicycle weighs about _____.   **a.** 13 g   **b.** 130 g   **c.** 13 kg

2. An apple weighs about _____.   **a.** 16 g   **b.** 160 g   **c.** 16 kg

3. An iron weighs about _____.   **a.** 10 g   **b.** 1 kg   **c.** 10 kg

4. A pencil weighs about _____.   **a.** 10 g   **b.** 1,000 g   **c.** 1 kg

Share Your Ideas If you know the weight of an object in kilograms, explain how you can find its weight in grams.

Would you choose grams or kilograms to measure each?

5.

6.

7.

8.

9.

10.

Choose the best estimate.

11. A skunk weighs about _____.   **a.** 700 g   **b.** 7 kg   **c.** 70 kg

12. A pair of shoes weighs about ____.   **a.** 1 kg   **b.** 10 kg   **c.** 100 kg

13. A bar of soap weighs about _____.   **a.** 10 g   **b.** 100 g   **c.** 10 kg

14. An automobile weighs about ____.   **a.** 125 g   **b.** 125 kg   **c.** 1,250 kg

Complete.

15. 3 kg = _____ g

16. 6,000 g = _____ kg

17. 9 kg = _____ g

18. 5,000 g = _____ kg

19. 2 kg = _____ g

20. 10,000 g = _____ kg

21. 7,000 g = _____ kg

22. 2.5 kg = _____ g

23. 4,500 g = _____ kg

Think and Apply

Use the chart and mental math or your calculator to solve.

CHOICES

24. What is the weight of 50 dimes?

25. A bag of pennies weighs 600 grams. How many pennies are in the bag?

26. How much more do 100 quarters weigh than 100 pennies?

27. How many dimes weigh 1 kilogram? how many nickels?

Weight of Coins to the Nearest Gram	
Penny	3 g
Nickel	5 g
Dime	2 g
Quarter	6 g

Explain two ways to find the answer for **26**.

SHOW WHAT YOU KNOW

Investigating Capacity

Capacity is the amount that a container can hold. See how well you can estimate the capacity of containers.

Working together

Materials: 5 containers of different sizes and shapes, water or a box of dried beans

A. Label the containers with the letters *A* through *E*.

B. Estimate which container has the greatest capacity, the next greatest, and so on. Record your estimates in a chart like the one shown.

C. Use water or beans to check your estimates. Record the actual order of the containers on your chart.

	Estimate	Actual
Greatest Capacity	B	C
Next Greatest		
Next Greatest		
Next Greatest		
Least Capacity		

Sharing Your Results

1. Before measuring, how did you estimate which container had the greatest capacity?

2. Describe how you used the water or beans to compare the capacities of different containers.

3. Does the tallest container always have the greatest capacity? Explain.

Extending the Activity

Work in a small group.

Materials: same containers from page 336, a box of dried beans, a piece of tagboard, Workmat 18

A decimeter cube holds 1 liter of water.

4. Use Workmat 18 to make a decimeter cube.

5. Fill one of the containers with beans. Estimate the number of decimeter cubes the container of beans will fill. Record your estimate in a chart like the one shown.

6. Empty the beans into the decimeter cube. Record the actual number of times you filled the decimeter cube.

7. Repeat steps **5** and **6** for each container. List the containers in order from least to greatest by capacity.

Containers	Number of Decimeter Cubes	
	Estimated	Actual
A		
B		
C		
D		
E		

8. Trade containers with another group. Repeat **5** through **7**.

Show What You Know

9. Which containers each hold about 1 decimeter cube of beans?

10. Which containers have capacities greater than 1 decimeter cube? less than 1 decimeter cube?

11. To estimate capacity, what dimensions of a container do you have to consider?

Estimating and Measuring Capacity

The Carroll family visited the famous San Diego Zoo. They saw newborn monkeys being given vitamins with an eyedropper. An eyedropper holds about 1 mL.

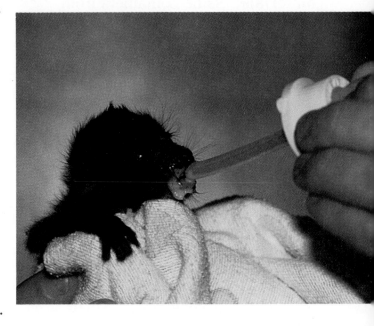

▶ The **milliliter (mL)** is a metric unit used to measure the capacities of small objects.

▶ The **liter (L)** is used to measure the capacities of large objects.

1 liter = 1,000 milliliters

To help you estimate capacity, think about the capacities of these objects.

A centimeter cube holds 1 mL.

1 cm
1 cm
1 cm

A decimeter cube holds 1 L.

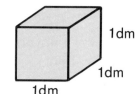
1dm
1dm
1dm

How many centimeter cubes will fit inside a decimeter cube?

A teaspoon holds about 5 mL.

A pitcher holds about 2 L.

Check Your Understanding

Would you choose milliliters or liters to measure each?

1. teacup   **2.** gasoline tank   **3.** milk carton   **4.** soup bowl

Share Your Ideas Explain how to change liters to milliliters and milliliters to liters.

Would you choose milliliters or liters to measure each?

5. water in a bathtub

6. juice in a lemon

7. milk in a glass

8. tea in a kettle

9. water in a pond

10. paint in a jar

Complete. Use mental math.

11. 3 L = _____ mL

12. 4,000 mL = _____ L

13. 7,000 mL = _____ L

14. 10 L = _____ mL

15. 1.6 L = _____ mL

16. 2,400 mL = _____ L

Choose milliliters or liters to complete each sentence.

17. The bird drank about 7 _____ of water.

18. The can holds about 750 _____ of hair spray.

19. The squeaky door needed about 2 _____ of oil.

20. The swimming pool holds about 90,000 _____ of water.

Think and Apply

Use the chart to answer the questions.

> 1 mL of water weighs 1 g.
> 1 L of water weighs 1 kg.

21. The camel drank 2,000 milliliters of water. What was the weight of the water in grams? in kilograms?

22. The water in the fish tank weighed 190 kilograms. How many milliliters of water were in the tank?

Name a container that holds about 1 L.
Name a container that holds more than 1 L.

Mixed Review

1. $\begin{array}{r} 5,304 \\ -879 \\ \hline \end{array}$

2. $\begin{array}{r} 3,876 \\ +605 \\ \hline \end{array}$

3. $\begin{array}{r} \$14.80 \\ -6.95 \\ \hline \end{array}$

4. $\begin{array}{r} \$27.58 \\ -9.79 \\ \hline \end{array}$

5. $\begin{array}{r} 652 \\ \times7 \\ \hline \end{array}$

6. $\begin{array}{r} 307 \\ \times5 \\ \hline \end{array}$

7. $\begin{array}{r} 843 \\ \times20 \\ \hline \end{array}$

8. $\begin{array}{r} 54 \\ \times40 \\ \hline \end{array}$

9. 68 × 79

10. 92 × 206

11. 4 × $8.06

12. 8 × $3.90

13. 56 × $7.58

14. 263 ÷ 8

15. 900 ÷ 6

16. 386 ÷ 7

17. 875 ÷ 4

18. 300 ÷ 5

SHOW WHAT YOU KNOW

339

Measuring Temperature

One day in Browning, Montana, the temperature dropped from 7°C to −49°C.

▶ The **degree Celsius (°C)** is a metric unit used to measure temperature.

To read the temperature, look at the number or mark beside the top of the red column.

- read   seven degrees Celsius
- write   7°C

The temperature on a cold day may be −5°C.

- read   five degrees below zero Celsius or minus five degrees Celsius
- write   −5°C

Which temperature is colder: −3°C or −5°C? How can you tell?

Thermometer scale labels:
- Water Boils, 100°C
- Hot Tap Water, 60°C
- Normal Body Temperature, 37°C
- Hot Day, 30°C
- Room Temperature, 20°C
- Water Freezes, 0°C
- Cold Day, −5°C
- Very Cold Day, −20°C

Check Your Understanding

Read and write each Celsius temperature shown.

1.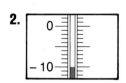

2.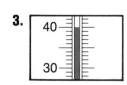

3.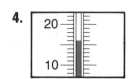

4.

Share Your Ideas   Look at the large thermometer above. Explain how to find the difference between the temperature on a hot day and the temperature on a very cold day.

Read and write the temperature in degrees Celsius.

5. ![thermometer showing between 10 and 20]

6. ![thermometer showing between 30 and 40]

7. ![thermometer showing between -10 and 0]

8. ![thermometer showing between -30 and -20]

Choose the most reasonable temperature.

9. boiling water
   a. 100°C **b.** 72°C

10. inside a refrigerator
   a. 60°C **b.** 5°C

11. temperature of a room
   a. 20°C **b.** 70°C

12. snowball
   a. 20°C **b.** −10°C

Use the thermometer on page 340 to help you find the rule. Then complete each table.

13. Rule   ?

Input	Output
14°C	9°C
14. 26°C	
61°C	56°C
15. 3°C	

16. Rule   ?

Input	Output
34°C	41°C
17. 18°C	
5°C	12°C
18. 0°C	

19. Rule   ?

Input	Output
2°C	12°C
20. 14°C	
⁻20°C	⁻10°C
21. ⁻18°C	

Think and Apply

22. This morning the temperature was 22°C. It rose 9°. What is the temperature now?

23. [DATA] Measure and record the outdoor temperature at your school for 5 days. Measure the temperature at the same time each day. Then make a line graph to show the data.

Visual Thinking

If you pull the ends of the string, will a knot form? Guess first. Then use a string to check.

24.

25.

26.

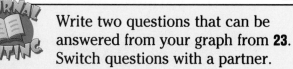

JOURNAL WRITING

Write two questions that can be answered from your graph from **23**. Switch questions with a partner.

SHOW WHAT YOU KNOW

Interview: Calculators and a Postal Clerk

Sue Malcom works at the United States Post Office in Glen Gardner, New Jersey. Sue has seen letters and packages mailed to just about every country in the world.

A. Sue said, "One customer mailed three packages. The postage on the packages was $4.57, $7.39, and $8.46. I used a calculator to figure out the total amount of postage."

The total amount of postage was $20.42.

B. What if the customer had only a $20 dollar bill and a $5 bill to pay for the postage? How much change would the customer receive? Explain how to use your calculator to find the amount of change.

Sharing Your Ideas

Use your calculator to solve. Estimate to check.

1. Ms. Herrick bought stamps for $6.26 and mailed two packages, one for $5.78 and one for $4.89. What was the total amount paid for postage?

2. Mr. Tibeson bought stamps for $9.25 and sent an express mail letter for $8.75. How much change did he receive from a $20 bill? Explain how you found your answer.

Extending Your Thinking

THINK
EXPLORE
SOLVE
LOOK BACK

Use your calculator to solve.

3. Mark mailed two packages. The postage was $4.10 for one package and $5.72 for the other package. Mark spent $2.50 insuring both packages. How much did Mark spend in all?

4. Sam mailed three packages. The postage on each package was $3.67. What was the total postage?

Use your calculator. Find the missing values. Estimate to check.

5. U.S. Postal Service

Item	Cost
1	$ .60
2	$1.45
3	$8.27
Total	_____

6. U.S. Postal Service

Item	Cost
1	$4.38
2	$ .92
3	$3.84
4	$7.28
Total	_____

7. U.S. Postal Service

Item	Cost
1	$4.29
2	$8.03
3	( )
4	$6.27
Total	$22.00

8. U.S. Postal Service

Item	Cost
1	$6.17
2	$2.30
3	$4.95
4	$3.83
5	( )
Total	$19.30

Show What You Know

9. Dara mailed three packages, **A**, **B**, and **C**. The postage for **A** was $3.50 more than the postage for **B**. The postage for **B** was $2.38 less than the postage for **C**. The postage for **C** was $4.72. What was the postage for **A**?

343

B.R. - BEFORE RULERS

WORKING TOGETHER

Ancient Egyptians used their arms, hands, and fingers to measure length. The *digit* was equal to the width of 1 finger. The *palm* was equal to 4 digits. The *cubit* was equal to 4 palms.

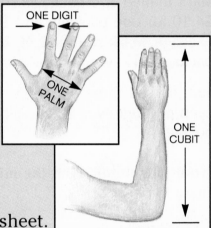

1. Work in groups. Choose ten objects to measure with a group partner.

2. Before measuring, make a recording sheet.

Object	Egyptian Measurement	Metric Measurement

3. Measure each object to the nearest digit or cubit. Write your results on your recording sheet.

4. Measure the objects again using a centimeter ruler or a meter stick. Measure to the nearest centimeter or meter. Write your results on your recording sheet.

5. Compare the recording sheets with your group. Talk about the following questions.

   • When you used Egyptian units to measure the objects, did everyone have the same results? Why?

   • When you used metric units to measure the objects, did everyone have the same results? Why?

6. Present your results to the class. Talk about these questions.

   • Which system is easiest to use?

   • Which gives the most accurate results?

CHAPTER REVIEW/TEST

Write each decimal.

1. 9 tenths

2. 9 hundredths

3. 7 and 6 tenths

Compare. Use >, <, or = for ⬤.

4. 8.32 ⬤ 82.3

5. 1.67 ⬤ 1.8

6. 1.5 ⬤ 1.50

7. 5.2 ⬤ 52

8. 0.6 ⬤ 0.64

9. 8.0 ⬤ 8

Add or subtract. Write zeros where needed.

10. 45.8 + 3.76

11. 5.66 − 2.3

12. 53 + 5.3

13. 2 − 0.2

14. 6.53 + 3.56

15. 54.37 − 2.68

Complete.

16. 3 L = _____ mL

17. 800 mm = _____ cm

18. _____ kg = 3,000 g

19. 3 m = _____ cm

20. _____ mm = 4 m

21. 7 km = _____ m

Choose the best estimate.

22. A whale weighs about _____.

    a. 90 g **b.** 90 kg **c.** 90,000 kg

23. A letter weighs about _____.

    a. 5 g **b.** 50 g **c.** 5 kg

Solve.

24. A door measures 175 centimeters high. Does a tourist 153 centimeters tall, wearing an 18.4 centimeter hat, need to stoop to fit through the door?

25. Jack, Sue, and Betty had a race. Make a list to find out how many different ways they could finish.

Think David has a bag that will hold 2.5 kilograms without breaking. He put the following items in the bag: a 500 gram ball, 1.5 kilograms of camping gear, and a 250 gram can of soup. Will the bag break?

The Meters Add Up

Play this metric measurement game in small groups.

Materials: centimeter tape measure, 1 set of cards cut from Workmat 19

Follow these steps to play the game.

1. Place the *Start Here* card anywhere you wish on the floor. Place the other cards from Workmat 19 in a pile face down. Take turns.

2. Pick a number card. Measure the distance shown on the card starting from the circle on the *Start Here* card. You can measure in any direction you wish. Replace the number card at the bottom of the deck.

3. Measure any object you find at the new location. Record the name of the object and its length, width, or height on a piece of paper.

4. Continue taking turns picking cards, measuring out distances, and measuring objects. Keep a running total of the measurements of your objects. The first person who has measured a total of 10 meters is the winner.

HOME CONNECTION

Your child has been working with division, fractions, decimals, and geometric shapes in Chapters **7–10**. This game will challenge everyone to quickly recognize the shape of a square, a hexagon, and a circle.

Enjoy playing the game together.

Stretch to Shape

Materials: small index cards, 8 of each shape; 36 large index cards, 12 of each shape; masking tape

There are 2 or 3 players plus 1 director.

Tape the 36 large shape cards onto the floor in this pattern.

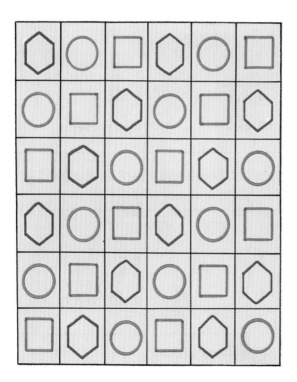

Rules:

1. The director shuffles the deck of small cards and turns the deck face down.

2. For each turn, the director picks a card from the deck. The director calls out the shape on that card.

3. Each player must put a hand or a foot on a free shape matching the one called out.

4. Once a hand or foot is on a shape, it cannot be moved during the first four turns. After that, only one hand or foot is moved on each turn.

5. If the same shape is called twice in a row, it is ignored the second time.

6. A player who falls is out. The winner is the last player remaining on the mat.

CUMULATIVE REVIEW

Choose the correct answer. Write A, B, C, or D.

1. $6{,}300 \div 9 = n$

  A 70   **C** 7,000

  B 700   **D** not given

2. Estimate $347 \div 4$.

  A 8,000   **C** 40

  B 800   **D** 80

3. $6\overline{)897}$

  A 149 R3   **C** 157 R5

  B 146 R1   **D** not given

4. Find the average. 12, 18, 21

  A 51   **C** 17

  B 13 R2   **D** not given

5. $355 \div 7 = n$

  A 5 R5   **C** 50 R5

  B 57 R6   **D** not given

6. $379 \div 20 = n$

  A 13 R19   **C** 19 R19

  B 18 R19   **D** not given

7. Name the shape.

  A square   **C** triangle

  B pentagon   **D** not given

8. Name the figure.

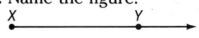

  A $\overleftrightarrow{XY}$ **C** $\overrightarrow{XY}$

  B $\overline{XY}$ **D** not given

9. Name the pair of lines.

  A obtuse   **C** parallel

  B segments   **D** not given

10. Name the diameter.

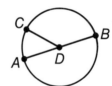

  A $\overline{AB}$ **C** $\overline{DB}$

  B $\overline{CD}$ **D** not given

11. What fractional part is shaded?

  A $\frac{1}{6}$ **C** $\frac{5}{6}$

  B $\frac{1}{6}$ **D** not given

12. Find $\frac{3}{5}$ of 25.

  A 25   **C** 12

  B 15   **D** not given

Choose the correct answer. Write A, B, C, or D.

13.

$$\frac{2}{3} = \frac{\square}{9}$$

A 4   **C** 8

B 6   **D** not given

14. Write a mixed number for $\frac{7}{4}$.

A $1\frac{1}{4}$ **C** $1\frac{3}{4}$

B $2\frac{1}{4}$ **D** not given

15. Write the fraction for 0.6.

A $\frac{6}{10}$ **C** $\frac{60}{10}$

B $\frac{6}{1,000}$ **D** not given

16. Write the decimal for 5 and 2 tenths.

A 5.2   **C** 2.5

B 5.02   **D** not given

17. What unit would you use to measure the thickness of a penny?

A kilometer   **C** centimeter

B meter   **D** not given

Solve.

Gail bought a squash for $1.29. She also bought 2 heads of lettuce for $.99 each and 3 cucumbers for $.39 each.

18. What was the total cost of the vegetables?

A $2.67   **C** $3.66

B $4.83   **D** not given

19. If she paid with a $5 bill, what was her change?

A $.56   **C** $.27

B $1.27   **D** not given

Choose the correct operation to solve.

20. Mrs. Parsons ordered crayons for the art classes. The crayons are sold in cartons of 12 boxes each. If there are 72 students, how many cartons must she order?

A divide   **C** subtract

B multiply   **D** not given

21. If there are 16 crayons in each box how many crayons are in a carton?

A multiply   **C** divide

B subtract   **D** not given

Perimeter, Area, and Volume

Sharing What You Know
Do you enjoy amusement parks? Many people do! Think about an amusement park you have visited. What kinds of rides and games did it have? Were there also special areas for food stands and parking? Why might amusement park planners need to know about area and perimeter?

Using Language
Amusement parks are often planned with special areas in mind. An **area** is a section of space that has a certain use — such as a picnic area. In mathematics, **area** is the number of square units needed to cover a region. Discuss these meanings of **area**. How are the meanings alike? How are they different?

Words to Know: perimeter, length, width, area, faces, edge, vertex, volume

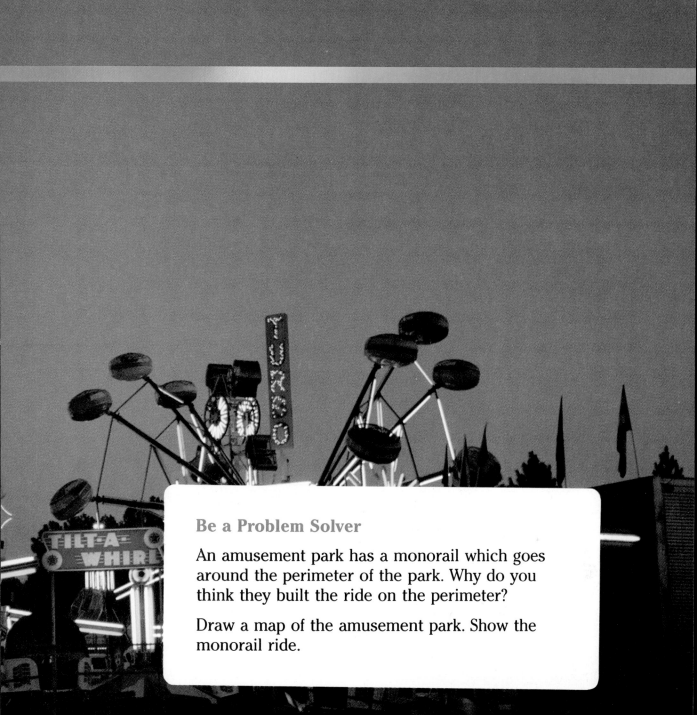

Be a Problem Solver

An amusement park has a monorail which goes around the perimeter of the park. Why do you think they built the ride on the perimeter?

Draw a map of the amusement park. Show the monorail ride.

> **What if** you walk around your school building? How many meters would you walk? Explain how you can find out.

Estimating and Finding Perimeter

The haunted house is a popular attraction at the amusement park. The base of the house forms a rectangle, 40 meters long and 30 meters wide. What is the perimeter of the base of the house?

▶ **Perimeter** is the distance around a figure.

You can estimate the perimeter of a rectangle.

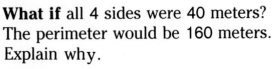

40 m

30 m   30 m

40 m

What if all 4 sides were 30 meters? The perimeter would be 120 meters. Explain why.

What if all 4 sides were 40 meters? The perimeter would be 160 meters. Explain why.

So, the perimeter of the base of the house is between 120 meters and 160 meters.

To find the actual perimeter, add the lengths of the sides.

30 + 40 + 30 + 40 = 140

The perimeter of the base of the house is 140 meters.

Check Your Understanding

Find the perimeter of each polygon.

1.

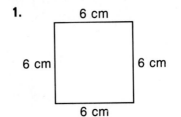

6 cm

6 cm   6 cm

6 cm

2.

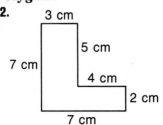

3 cm

5 cm

7 cm

4 cm

2 cm

7 cm

3.

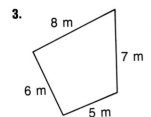

8 m

7 m

6 m

5 m

Share Your Ideas Look back at **1**. Describe two ways to find the perimeter.

Find the perimeter of each polygon.

4.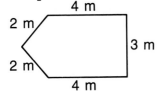

5.

6.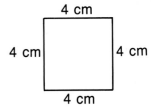

7.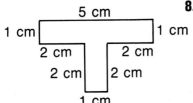

8.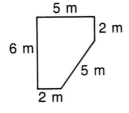

9.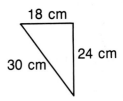

Use estimation. Match each figure with its description.

10.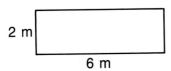

11.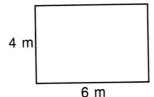

12.

a. The perimeter is between 16 m and 24 m.

b. The perimeter is between 28 m and 36 m.

c. The perimeter is between 8 m and 24 m.

Think and Apply

13. The rectangular door to the haunted house is 2 meters wide and 3 meters high. What is the perimeter of the door?

14. The perimeter of each square window in the haunted house is 12 meters. What is the length of each side of a window?

15. Choose something in your classroom that is shaped like a rectangle or a square. Measure its sides and find its perimeter.

16. If you know the perimeter of a rectangle and the length of one of the sides, how can you find the width of the rectangle?

How many rectangles can you draw with a 24 cm perimeter if each side is a whole number of centimeters?

SHOW WHAT YOU KNOW

Finding Area

The board at the ball toss booth is 4 meters by 3 meters. What is the area of the board?

▶ The **area** of a region is the number of square units needed to cover it.

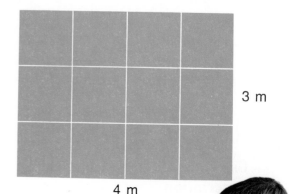
3 m

4 m

You can find the area by counting the number of square units. There are 12 square meters on the board.

The board is a rectangle. So, you can also find the number of square meters by multiplying.

There are 3 rows.
Each row has 4 square meters.
$3 \times 4 = 12$ square meters

▶ Area = length × width

Check Your Understanding

Find the area of each region.

1.
4 cm
4 cm

2.
5 cm
3 cm

3.
4 cm
8 cm

Share Your Ideas Use a piece of grid paper. For each polygon in **1** through **3**, draw a different shape that has the same area. Compare your drawings with those of a classmate.

Find the area of each region. Tell the number of square units.

4.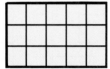

5.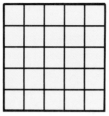

6.

7.

8.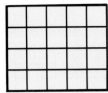

9.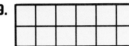

Use grid paper.

10. Draw three different rectangles, each with a perimeter of 12 units. Which of the rectangles has the greatest area?

11. Draw a rectangle that has a perimeter of 8 units and an area of 4 square units.

Think and Apply

12. The area of a rectangle is 20 square meters. The length of one side of the rectangle is 4 meters. What is the perimeter of the rectangle?

13. The perimeter of a square is 28 centimeters. What is its area? Explain how you know.

 JOURNAL WRITING How many rectangles can you draw with an area of 36 square units if each side is a whole number of units?

SHOW WHAT YOU KNOW

355

A figure is made using two rectangles. If you know the area of each rectangle, how can you find the area of the new figure?

Working with Area

At the movie theme park, Mary looked at a drawing of a western movie set. What is the floor area of the hotel on the drawing?

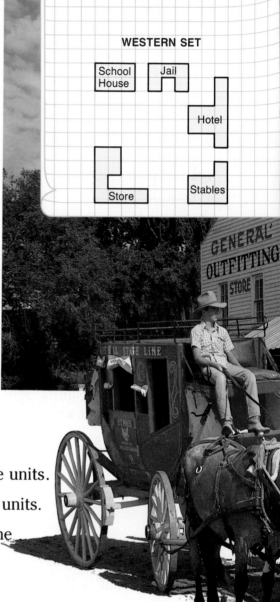

WESTERN SET

You can separate the figure into two rectangles. Then find the area of each rectangle.

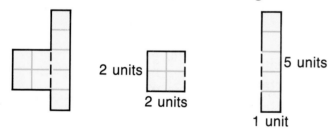

2 units

2 units

5 units

1 unit

$2 \times 2 = 4$ square units and $1 \times 5 = 5$ square units.

The floor area of the hotel is $4 + 5 = 9$ square units.

Can you separate the figure a different way? Is the total area the same?

Check Your Understanding

Use the drawing above. Find the area of each region.

1. store   **2.** jail   **3.** school house   **4.** stables

Share Your Ideas   Show two ways to separate the figure in **4** to find the area.

Find the area of each figure by separating it into rectangles.

5.

1 cm
2 cm
4 cm
3 cm
2 cm
4 cm

6.

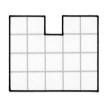

4 m
1 m
3 m
1 m
2 m
3 m

7.

4 m
2 m
2 m
4 m
2 m
2 m

8.

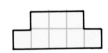

9.

10.

11.

12.

13.

Think and Apply

Use the figure at the right.

14. What is the length of side *B*?

15. Explain how to find the length of side *A*.

16. Describe two ways to find the area.

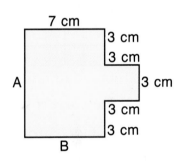

7 cm
3 cm
3 cm
A
3 cm
3 cm
3 cm
B

4 cm
2 cm
2 cm
4 cm

17. What is the area of the figure?

a. 8 square meters **b.** 8 square centimeters **c.** 8 centimeters

18. What is the perimeter of the figure?

a. 12 square centimeters **b.** 12 meters **c.** 12 centimeters

Draw two rectangles each with an area of 18 square centimeters. Compare the perimeters.

SHOW WHAT YOU KNOW

CHECKPOINT

Find the perimeter of each polygon. pages 352–353

1.
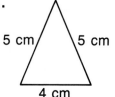
5 cm 5 cm
4 cm

2.
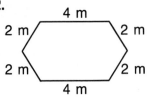
4 m
2 m 2 m
2 m 2 m
4 m

3.
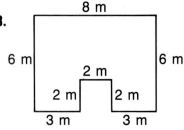
8 m
6 m 6 m
2 m
2 m 2 m
3 m 3 m

Find the area of each region. pages 354–355

4.
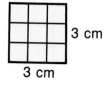
3 cm
3 cm

5.
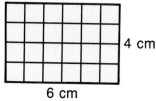
4 cm
6 cm

6.
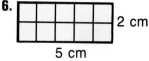
2 cm
5 cm

Find the area of each figure by separating it into rectangles. pages 356–357

7.
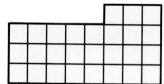

8.
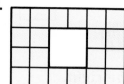

9.
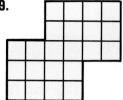

Choose the correct word to complete each sentence.

10. The distance around a figure is called the _____.

11. The number of square units needed to cover a region is called the _____.

12. The area of a rectangle is equal to its _____ times its _____.

Words to Know
area
length
perimeter
width

Solve.

13. In the fun house, the moving floor is 8 meters long and 4 meters wide. What is the perimeter of the floor? What is the area?

14. The area of a square is 36 square centimeters. What is the perimeter of the square?

What Shape Would You Make?

You are making the boundaries for a game of catch. You have 200 feet of rope to mark the boundaries. Sometimes there will be two players, sometimes three, four, or five players.

Thinking Critically

What type of boundaries can you make with the 200-ft rope?

Analyzing and Making Decisions

1. **What if** you wanted to make a long narrow field for two players? How long and how wide would you make the field?

2. **What if** you had 3 players? What kind of field would you make? Draw a diagram. About how long would you make each side?

3. Make a field for 4 players. Draw and label the boundaries. Now do the same for 5 players.

Look Back **What if** you could not change the boundaries? Sometimes two players would be inside, sometimes three, four, or five. What field would you make? Why?

Guess and Test

Jenny rode the Whirlwind Ferris Wheel and the Super-Dooper-Over-Looper. Altogether, she rode them 12 times. Each Ferris Wheel ride cost 3 tickets, and each Over-Looper ride cost 2 tickets. If she used 29 tickets for the 12 rides, how many times did she go on each ride?

Sometimes you can solve a problem by making a guess. Test your guess. If it is not the answer, make a better guess. Keep a record of your guesses to help you solve the problem.

Solving the Problem

Think What is the question?

Explore What facts are given? Guess how many times she rode each ride. How can you check to see if your guess is right? If your guess is not right, decide if it is too high or too low. Use that information to help you make a better guess. Keep guessing and testing until you solve the problem.

Solve How many times did Jenny go on each ride?

Look Back How would you change your guess if Jenny used only 27 tickets?

Share Your Ideas

1. How can making a list of your guesses help you solve a problem?

Extending Your Thinking

Solve. Use a calculator where appropriate.

CHOICES

2. Lonnie and Jody combined their money to buy 2 tickets. Each ticket cost 50 cents. Jody spent 10 cents more than Lonnie. How much did each of them spend?

3. Lenny worked at a booth. He placed 51 prizes on the shelves. He placed 19 more dinosaurs than elephants. How many of the prizes were dinosaurs? How many were elephants?

Use this information to solve 4–5.

Ralph was playing Hit the Numbers. The board had the numbers 1 to 20 on it.

4. To win a prize, he had to hit two whole numbers that are consecutive and have a sum of 35. What are the numbers?

5. For the grand prize, he had to hit two numbers whose product is 72 and whose sum is 22. What are the numbers?

Mixed Strategy Review

6. A train goes around the edge of a rectangular park. The park is 1,000 yards wide and 1,400 yards long. How long is the train ride?

7. An all-day pass for the amusement park costs $8.00. After 2:00 P.M. an all-day pass costs $5.00. Which costs less? Which is the better buy?

8. To win at the bottle toss, Sam must knock down all 12 bottles with 3 throws of the ball. He knocked down 4 bottles with each of 2 throws. How many bottles does he need to knock down on his last throw?

CREATE YOUR OWN

Write a problem about being at an amusement park.

How many different shaped food containers can you name?

Space Figures

At the Moon Munchie stand, food is sold in unusual containers with these shapes.

cube   **rectangular prism**   **pyramid**   **cylinder**   **cone**   **sphere**

The cube, rectangular prism, and pyramid all have flat sides or **faces**. Two faces meet at an **edge**. Two edges meet at a **vertex**.

A rectangular prism has 6 faces, 12 edges, and 8 vertices.

A cylinder has 2 flat faces and no vertices.

How many flat faces and vertices does a cone have? a sphere?

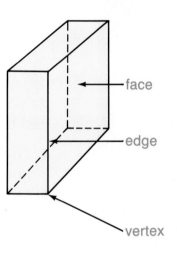

face

edge

vertex

Check Your Understanding

Name the space figure suggested by each object.

1.

2.

3.

4.

Share Your Ideas   Look at the cube and the pyramid at the top of the page. How are they alike? different?

Name the space figure suggested by each object.

5.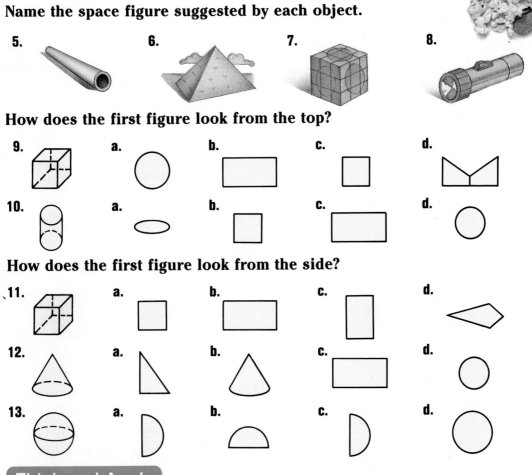

6.

7.

8.

How does the first figure look from the top?

9.   a.   b.   c.   d.

10.   a.   b.   c.   d.

How does the first figure look from the side?

11.   a.   b.   c.   d.

12.   a.   b.   c.   d.

13.   a.   b.   c.   d.

Think and Apply

**Name the shapes of all the faces of each
space figure.**

14. cube

15. pyramid

16. rectangular prism

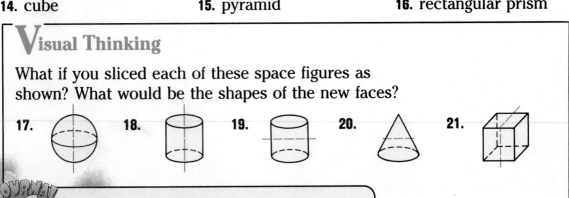

Visual Thinking

What if you sliced each of these space figures as
shown? What would be the shapes of the new faces?

17.   18.   19.   20.   21.

Why do you think most food packages
are rectangular prisms?

SHOW WHAT YOU KNOW

Investigating Volume

Volume is the number of cubic units a figure contains. You can explore volume by making rectangular prisms.

Working together

Materials: 24 centimeter cubes, Workmats 20, 21, 22

6 cubes

4 cubes

A. Build a rectangular prism like the one shown. Count the number of cubes to find its volume. Record its length, width, height, and volume on a chart like the one below or on Workmat 20. Then build other rectangular prisms, using all 24 cubes. Complete the chart.

B. Make as many different rectangular prisms as possible, using 7 centimeter cubes. Record the length, width, height, and volume of each in a chart like the one below or on Workmat 21.

C. Make as many different rectangular prisms as possible, using 12 centimeter cubes. Record the length, width, height, and volume of each in a chart like the one below or on Workmat 22.

RECTANGULAR PRISMS, USING 24 CUBES			
Length in Units	Width in Units	Height in Units	Volume in Cubic Units
6	4	1	24

Sharing Your Results

1. How many different rectangular prisms did you make using 24 cubes? 7 cubes? 12 cubes?

2. **Look back** at your charts. Describe how you can use the length, width, and height of a rectangular prism to find its volume.

Extending the Activity

▶ Volume = length × width × height

Work with a partner.

Materials: centimeter cubes, 3 boxes
of various sizes,
Workmat 23

3. Use centimeter cubes to help you estimate the
number of cubic centimeters each of your three
boxes will hold. Record each estimate in a chart
like the one below or on Workmat 23.

4. Measure the length, width, and height of the 3
boxes to the nearest centimeter. Find the actual
volume of each box by multiplying the length,
width, and height. Then complete the chart.

5. Compare each estimate with the actual volume.

Box	Estimated Volume	Height	Length	Width	Actual Volume
1					
2					
3					

Show What You Know

**Look back at your data to answer
these questions.**

6. Which box has the greatest volume? the least?

7. For which box was your estimated volume
closest to the actual volume?

8. The volume of which box was the most difficult
to estimate? Why?

9. Explain what is wrong with this statement:
"The tallest box always holds the most."

THINK AND SHARE Copy these dots. Draw a square around the third dot in the second row.

• • •
• • •
• • •

Ordered Pairs

A sign at the entrance to Ocean World shows the location of some of the exhibits.

To see the seals, go to the point with the ordered pair (3,4).

Follow these steps to locate the point with the ordered pair (3,4).

- Start at 0.
- Move 3 spaces to the right.
- Move 4 spaces up.

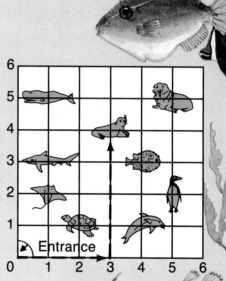

Another Example

What is the ordered pair that locates the dolphins?

- Start at 0.
- Move 4 spaces to the right.
- Move 1 space up.

The ordered pair for the dolphins is (4,1).

Check Your Understanding

Use the grid above to answer each question. Give an ordered pair that locates each exhibit.

1. Whales   **2.** Sting rays   **3.** Sharks   **4.** Walrus

Which exhibit does each ordered pair locate?

5. (0,0)   **6.** (2,1)   **7.** (4,3)   **8.** (5,2)

Share Your Ideas   The turtles are at point (2, 1). The stingrays are at point (1, 2). How are the points the same? different?

366

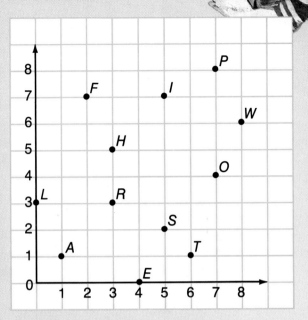

Use the grid above to answer each question.
Which point does each ordered pair locate?

9. (0,3) **10.** (3,5) **11.** (7,4)

12. (5,7) **13.** (8,6) **14.** (4,0)

Give an ordered pair to name each point.

15. *A* **16.** *S* **17.** *P*

18. *F* **19.** *T* **20.** *R*

Think and Apply

Use the grid above. Identify the ordered pairs to
spell the word.

21. WATER **22.** SEA

23. SHELL **24.** FISH

Explain why the order of numbers in
an ordered pair is important. Give
examples from the grid on page 366.

Graphing Ordered Pairs

At the games arcade, Tia and Pedro played Get the Point.

- Each player secretly placed 7 points on a 6-by-6 grid and labeled the points **A** through **G**.
- The players then took turns naming ordered pairs. The first player to name all the ordered pairs of the opponent's points won the game.

To graph the point for the ordered pair (1,5), follow these steps.

- Start at 0.
- Count 1 space to the right.
- Then count 5 spaces up.
- Make a dot.
- Write the letter **A** to name the point.

Can you name the ordered pairs for other points on Pedro's graph?

Check Your Understanding

Graph each point on grid paper.

1. *A* (7,0)　　**2.** *B* (5,5)　　**3.** *C* (1,6)　　**4.** *D* (3,5)　　**5.** *E* (4,2)

Share Your Ideas If you change the order of the numbers in an ordered pair, does it always change the location of the point? Explain.

Graph each point on grid paper.

6. *A* (2,4)   **7.** *B* (5,4)   **8.** *C* (5,2)   **9.** *D* (3,0)   **10.** *E* (2,2)

Use your graph. What if you connect the points in order? What polygons would you form?

11. *ABCDEA*   **12.** *ABDA*   **13.** *ABCDA*   **14.** *ABCEA*   **15.** *ADEA*

Follow each rule. Write the ordered pairs.

Rule: Move 2 spaces to the right on the grid.

	Input	Output
16.	(0,3)	
17.	(1,2)	
18.	(8,4)	

Rule: Move 1 space down on the grid.

	Input	Output
19.	(0,6)	
20.	(4,1)	
21.	(7,5)	

Think and Apply

22. Graph three ordered pairs with the same first number. Connect the points. Describe the position of the line segment.

23. Graph three ordered pairs with the same second number. Connect the points. Describe the position of the line segment.

24. Follow the rules on page 368 and play Get the Point.

Logical Thinking

25. Follow the one-way streets. How many different routes are there from *A* to *Z*? Record the routes.

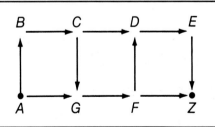

Graph 4 ordered pairs that will form a square when they are connected. List the 4 ordered pairs.

SHOW WHAT YOU KNOW

Map the Amusement Park

Alicia and Tim want to make a map of the amusement park. They have made a grid to show the location of the rides. They will put a dot at the entrance to each ride.

Materials: Workmat 1

A. Copy and finish the map. Put the letters for each ride or place in the correct location.

B. Alicia and Tim entered the park. They rode the Airplane and the Ferris Wheel. They played Knock Down Pins. They also bought food and ate at the Picnic Area, where they stayed. Use a colored pencil to draw a line that shows how they might have walked. (They wanted to walk the shortest distance.) How many blocks did they walk?

C. Make a list of what you would like to see. Use another colored pencil to make a line to show how you would walk the shortest distance when going to the sites. How many blocks in all would you walk?

Location of Places in the Park	
A Park Entrance	0,0
B Roller Coaster	2,9
C Ferris Wheel	8,4
D Rocket Twirl	6,7
E Fun House	2,5
F Saucer	5,2
G Airplanes	3,7
H Food	1,3 and 4,1
I Ring Toss	8,1
J Knock Down Pins	7,9
K Picnic Area	9,6

Sharing Your Ideas

1. The Fun House is at (2,5), and the Saucer is at (5,2). Which is closer to the Roller Coaster? to the entrance?

2. Explain the ordered pair that locates the Park Entrance?

Extending Your Thinking

You will need Workmat 1 for these activities.

3. Alicia and Tim said that some things could be improved at the park. "When we bought our food, we had to walk too far to the Picnic Area," said Alicia. "I wanted to play a different game after I played Knock Down Pins, but there was no other game nearby."

a. Make a plan for rearranging the park. Do not map it. Make a list of the rides and mark the new location (ordered pair) next to the rides. (The Roller Coaster, the Rocket Twirl, and the Fun House are the three most popular rides.) You may add three new rides of your own if you wish.

b. Exchange your list with a partner. Make a map of your partner's park. Show your work to your partner.

c. Pick five rides to visit at your park. Write them down. Have your partner draw a line that shows the directions that someone might walk to visit the rides and then tell how far it is.

Show What You Know

4. How did you change the amusement park? Explain why you made your changes.

5. Do you think ordered pairs are a good way to locate points on a grid? Explain.

AFRICAN GAME PRESERVE

Zimbabwe is a country in Africa. Hwange National Park is Zimbabwe's largest game park. It has an area of 5,600 square miles. Find Hwange National Park on the map.

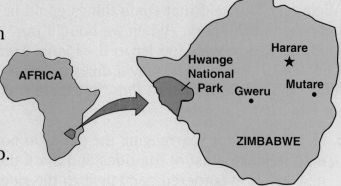

AFRICA

Harare ★
Hwange National Park ✕ Gweru • Mutare •
ZIMBABWE

WORKING TOGETHER

1. Work with a partner. Use base-ten blocks to model the area of Hwange National Park. Let each block stand for 100 square miles. Copy your model onto grid paper.

2. Now use the blocks to make any kind of polygon with an area of 5,600 square miles. Each partner should make his or her own polygon. Consider the following as you work.

   • Is your polygon a rectangle? If so, in how many ways could you arrange the blocks?

   • If your polygon is not a rectangle, how many sides does it have?

   • Copy your polygons onto grid paper.

3. Share your models with the class. Discuss these questions.

   • How are all the models alike or different?

   • How many different polygons were made for Exercise 2 above? How many different rectangles were made?

CHAPTER REVIEW/TEST

Find the perimeter and area of each polygon.

1.
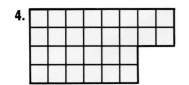
2 m
8 m

2.
3 cm
7 cm

3.
5 cm
4 cm
6 cm
2 cm
2 cm
3 cm

Find the area of each polygon.

4.

5.

6.

Name the space figure suggested by each object.

7.

8.

9.
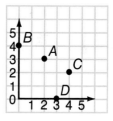

Give an ordered pair to name each point.

10. *A*　　　　**11.** *B*　　　　**12.** *C*　　　　**13.** *D*

5
4 B
3   • A
2   • C
1   D
0 1 2 3 4 5

Graph each point on grid paper.

14. *E* (3,2)　　**15.** *F* (0,5)　　**16.** *G* (6,3)　　**17.** *H* (5,0)　　**18.** *I* (4,2)

Solve.

19. The area of a floor is 20 square meters. The length of the floor is 5 meters. What is the width?

20. John has 6 coins that are worth a total of 61¢. What are the coins?

Think The area of a rectangle is 12 square centimeters. The length of the rectangle is three times as long as the width. What is the perimeter of the rectangle?

Tangrams

A **tangram** is a Chinese puzzle. You can use tangram pieces to form different shapes and designs.

Materials: Workmat 1, a set of tangram pieces or Workmat 24

1. Use your tangram pieces to make the large triangle shown below.

2. Find the area of the large triangle.
   - Count the complete squares inside the triangle.
   - Combine parts of squares that add up to a complete square.
   - Find the total number of squares.

3. Now use all your tangram pieces to make a large square that has the same area as the large triangle. Trace your completed square on Workmat 1.

4. Finally, use your tangram pieces to make designs. Trace each design on another copy of Workmat 1. Have a friend find the area of each design. Check that the areas are correct.

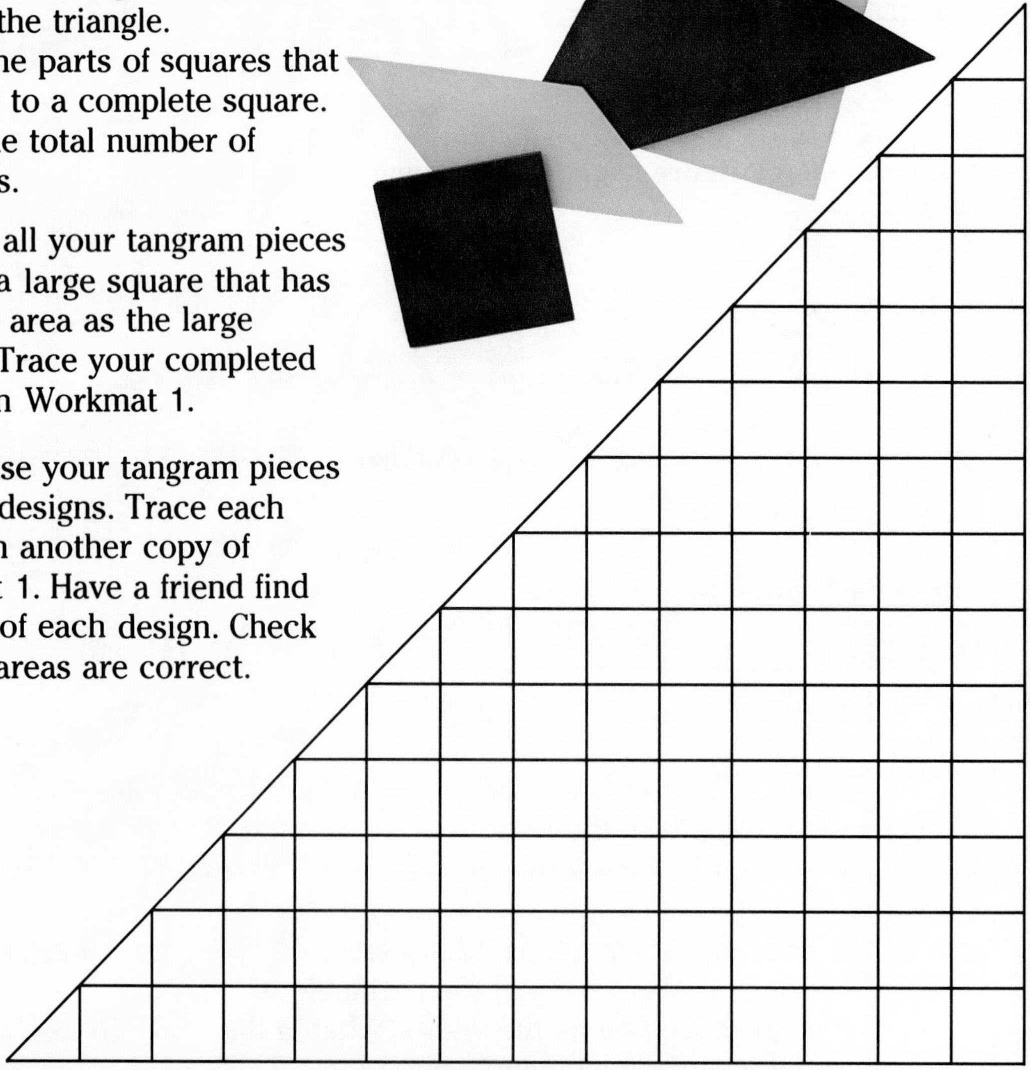

MAINTAINING SKILLS

Choose the correct answer. Write A, B, C, or D.

1. $\frac{1}{4}$ of 20

   A 6   **C** 5

   B 4   **D** not given

2.

   $$\frac{3}{3} = \frac{\square}{7}$$

   A 3   **C** 5

   B 7   **D** not given

3. Write $\frac{9}{4}$ as a mixed number.

   A 2   **C** $4\frac{1}{2}$

   B $2\frac{1}{4}$ **D** not given

4. Write the decimal for $\frac{23}{100}$.

   A 0.023   **C** 2.3

   B 0.23   **D** not given

5. Compare. 4.02 ⬤ 4.1

   A $<$ **C** $=$

   B $>$ **D** not given

6. Find $8.9 - 2.4$.

   A 6.3   **C** 6.5

   B 7.5   **D** not given

7.   8.63
      $+4.92$

   A 12.55   **C** 12.31

   B 13.55   **D** not given

8. Find the perimeter.

   3 in.   5 in.   6 in.

   A 12 in.   **C** 11 in.

   B 14 in.   **D** not given

9. Find the area.

   A 14 square units   **C** 9 square units

   B 8 square units   **D** not given

Solve.

10. Adam, Carl, and Janet are sitting on a park bench. How many different ways can they all sit together on the bench?

    A 4   **C** 6

    B 5   **D** not given

11. Timmy is printing his name as many times as he can across the whole chalkboard. He can fit a total of 35 letters across the board. What will the last letter be?

    A T   **C** M

    B I   **D** not given

THEME Entertainment:
Behind the Scenes

Sharing What You Know

Have you ever been to a play? To the ballet? How about the circus? Maybe you have even performed in one of these! If so, you know there's much work to be done before the curtain rises. The performers must practice, then practice some more. Make-up, costumes, and scenery must look real. Lights and music must be ready to go. How might being prepared affect the success of the show?

Using Language

The better prepared everyone in a show is, the more likely it is that the show will be a success. A hit show's **outcome**, or end result, is usually due to hard work. In mathematics, an **outcome** is one possible result of a probability experiment, such as flipping a coin. How are the two meanings of **outcome** alike? How are they different? Could chance ever affect the outcome of your school play?

Words to Know: mixed numbers, like fractions, unlike fractions, outcome, prediction, probability

Be a Problem Solver

You are about to watch an hour of TV. How might you predict the number of commercials you will see? What things might affect the outcome of your study?

Write about whether you think there are too many or not enough commercials on TV. Give reasons to support your opinion.

Use two congruent pieces of paper. Fold and tear one piece in two. Is each torn piece $\frac{1}{2}$ of the original piece? Explain.

Estimating Fractions

Boyd uses about $\frac{1}{2}$ yard of felt to make each hand puppet. He used $\frac{7}{10}$ yard of felt to make a frog puppet. Is $\frac{7}{10}$ about $\frac{1}{2}$?

You can use drawings to help you estimate.

One drawing shows tenths. The other shows halves.

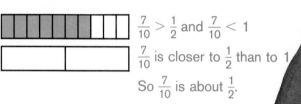

$\frac{7}{10} > \frac{1}{2}$ and $\frac{7}{10} < 1$

$\frac{7}{10}$ is closer to $\frac{1}{2}$ than to 1.

So $\frac{7}{10}$ is about $\frac{1}{2}$.

More Examples

Choose 0, $\frac{1}{2}$, or 1 for the best estimate.

a.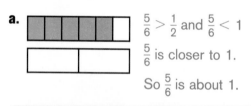

$\frac{5}{6} > \frac{1}{2}$ and $\frac{5}{6} < 1$

$\frac{5}{6}$ is closer to 1.

So $\frac{5}{6}$ is about 1.

b.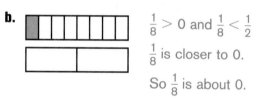

$\frac{1}{8} > 0$ and $\frac{1}{8} < \frac{1}{2}$

$\frac{1}{8}$ is closer to 0.

So $\frac{1}{8}$ is about 0.

Check Your Understanding

Write the fraction for each shaded drawing. Then choose 0, $\frac{1}{2}$, or 1 for the best estimate.

1. **2.** **3.**

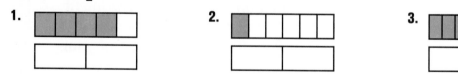

Share Your Ideas Explain why there are two acceptable estimates for this shaded drawing.

Write the fraction for each shaded drawing. Then choose 0, $\frac{1}{2}$, or 1 for the best estimate.

4.

5.

6.

7.

8.

9.

Write 0, $\frac{1}{2}$, or 1 for the best estimate of each fraction. Use drawings to help you if you wish.

10. $\frac{4}{10}$ 11. $\frac{7}{8}$ 12. $\frac{3}{5}$ 13. $\frac{2}{12}$ 14. $\frac{2}{3}$ 15. $\frac{26}{100}$

Think and Apply

Use the information in the chart for 16 and 17.

16. Estimate the fractional part of all the puppets that is alligators. Write 0, $\frac{1}{2}$, or 1.

17. Estimate the fractional part of all the puppets that is not monkeys. Write 0, $\frac{1}{2}$, or 1.

18. Boyd made 12 hand puppets one week. He said, "About $\frac{1}{2}$ of them were raccoons." About how many raccoon puppets could Boyd have made? Explain.

Types of Puppets	Number
Frog	5
Monkey	3
Alligator	1

Visual Thinking

19. Which puzzle piece fits?

a.   b.   c.   d.

How can you tell by looking at a numerator and denominator that a fraction is about 0? about $\frac{1}{2}$?

SHOW WHAT YOU KNOW

379

THINK AND SHARE Draw two congruent rectangles. Show $\frac{3}{5}$ of one. How would you shade the other to show the same area in tenths?

Comparing and Ordering Fractions

The school's play of *Peter Pan* has $\frac{3}{10}$ of the scenes in the Darling's house and $\frac{7}{10}$ of the scenes in Never-Never Land. Where do more scenes take place?

Compare $\frac{3}{10}$ and $\frac{7}{10}$.

▶ **Like fractions** have the same denominators

$\frac{3}{10}$ ▮▮▮☐☐☐☐☐☐☐ $\frac{7}{10}$ ▮▮▮▮▮▮▮☐☐☐

$$3 < 7 \text{ so } \frac{3}{10} < \frac{7}{10}$$

| To compare like fractions, compare the numerators. |

More scenes take place in Never-Never Land.

Compare $\frac{3}{4}$ and $\frac{5}{8}$.

▶ **Unlike fractions** have different denominators.

$\frac{3}{4}$ ▮▮▮☐ $\frac{5}{8}$ ▮▮▮▮▮☐☐☐

$\frac{6}{8}$ ▮▮▮▮▮▮☐☐ $\frac{5}{8}$ ▮▮▮▮▮☐☐☐

$$\frac{3}{4} = \frac{6}{8}; \ 6 > 5, \text{ so } \frac{6}{8} > \frac{5}{8}, \text{ so } \frac{3}{4} > \frac{5}{8}$$

To compare unlike fractions, find equivalent fractions with the same denominators. Then compare the numerators.

Check Your Understanding

Compare. Write > or < for 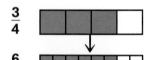. Use drawings to help you if you wish.

1. $\frac{4}{6} ⬬ \frac{3}{6}$ 2. $\frac{2}{3} ⬬ \frac{8}{9}$ 3. $\frac{3}{6} ⬬ \frac{2}{3}$ 4. $\frac{1}{6} ⬬ \frac{3}{12}$ 5. $\frac{2}{4} ⬬ \frac{3}{8}$

Share Your Ideas Make drawings to compare $\frac{2}{5}$ and $\frac{3}{10}$.

380

Compare. Write > or < for . Use drawings to help you if you wish.

6. $\frac{4}{8}$ ⬬ $\frac{7}{8}$ 7. $\frac{2}{4}$ ⬬ $\frac{1}{8}$ 8. $\frac{4}{10}$ ⬬ $\frac{1}{2}$

9. $\frac{3}{4}$ ⬬ $\frac{7}{8}$ 10. $\frac{7}{10}$ ⬬ $\frac{3}{5}$ 11. $\frac{7}{12}$ ⬬ $\frac{9}{12}$

12. $\frac{7}{12}$ ⬬ $\frac{1}{12}$ 13. $\frac{2}{5}$ ⬬ $\frac{3}{5}$ 14. $\frac{1}{2}$ ⬬ $\frac{1}{4}$

15. $\frac{4}{6}$ ⬬ $\frac{1}{3}$ 16. $\frac{2}{3}$ ⬬ $\frac{2}{4}$ 17. $\frac{1}{2}$ ⬬ $\frac{1}{3}$

Use < to write the fractions in order from least to greatest.

18. $\frac{3}{8}, \frac{1}{8}, \frac{7}{8}$ 19. $\frac{1}{6}, \frac{4}{6}, \frac{2}{6}$

20. $\frac{1}{4}, \frac{5}{8}, \frac{1}{8}$ 21. $\frac{4}{5}, \frac{3}{10}, \frac{1}{2}$

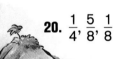

Think and Apply

22. Wendy told stories to $\frac{1}{4}$ of the lost boys. John played games with $\frac{5}{12}$ of the lost boys. Did more lost boys listen to stories or play games?

23. **What if** the numerators of two fractions are the same? How can you tell which fraction is greater just by looking at the denominator? Make up a rule. Use your rule to order these fractions from least to greatest: $\frac{1}{10}, \frac{1}{4}, \frac{1}{6}$.

Write fractions greater than $\frac{1}{2}$. Describe what is the same and different about them.

Mixed Review

1. $20.5 + 0.66$

2. $\begin{array}{r} 345.92 \\ + 8.43 \\ \hline \end{array}$

3. $\$7.03 - \$.96$

4. $\begin{array}{r} 7{,}324 \\ -4{,}888 \\ \hline \end{array}$

5. $\begin{array}{r} 273 \\ 18 \\ +846 \\ \hline \end{array}$

6. $8.3 - 2.48$

7. $7\overline{)376}$

8. $3.81 + 5.7$

9. $43.20 - 4.53$

10. $\begin{array}{r} 400.63 \\ -72.62 \\ \hline \end{array}$

11. $\begin{array}{r} 608 \\ \times78 \\ \hline \end{array}$

Write the value of the digit 4 using the word name.

12. 240

13. 2.047

14. 0.4

15. 74

16. 942,596

SHOW WHAT YOU KNOW

Investigating Adding Fractions

You can add fractions by using fraction pieces.

Working together

Materials: Workmat 25, 6 congruent strips of different colored paper or fraction pieces

A. Make 1 set of fraction pieces. Fold and cut the strips to show 1 whole, 2 equal pieces, 4 equal pieces, 3 equal pieces, 6 equal pieces, and 12 equal pieces. Label each piece.

B. Cut the cards from Workmat 25. Place them face down in a stack.

C. Take turns picking the top card. Show each fraction using fraction pieces. Then lay the fraction pieces end-to-end on the 1 whole. What is the sum of the two fractions?

D. Record your work on a piece of paper. The example $\frac{2}{6} + \frac{3}{6}$ is shown at the right. Repeat **C** until all the cards have been used.

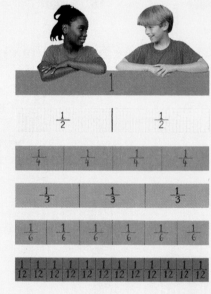

Sharing Your Results

1. Explain how you decided what numbers to use to record the total length of the fraction pieces.

2. What if you use your fraction pieces and add two fractions with the same denominator? What is the greatest possible sum? the least possible?

Extending the Activity

Work with a partner. Use the fraction pieces from page 382.

3. Pick 2 fraction pieces with different denominators. Lay them end-to-end on 1 whole piece. Find the total length of the fraction pieces by matching their length with one or more fraction pieces. The matching fraction pieces can have a different denominator.

4. Record the fraction pieces and their length. The example $\frac{1}{2} + \frac{1}{3}$ is shown at the right. Repeat the activity at least 3 times.

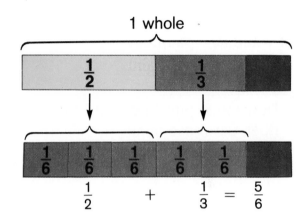

$$\frac{1}{2} + \frac{1}{3} = \frac{5}{6}$$

Find each sum. Use fraction pieces to help you.

5. $\frac{3}{6} + \frac{1}{6}$ **6.** $\frac{1}{4} + \frac{1}{3}$ **7.** $\frac{2}{3} + \frac{1}{12}$

8. $\frac{1}{4} + \frac{2}{4}$ **9.** $\frac{3}{12} + \frac{5}{12}$ **10.** $\frac{3}{12} + \frac{2}{6}$

Show What You Know

11. Explain how you decided what numbers to use to record the total length when the fractions had different denominators.

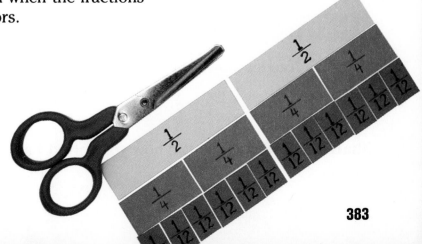

Draw a rectangle and divide it into eighths. Shade $\frac{2}{8}$ of the rectangle red and $\frac{3}{8}$ of it blue. How much of the rectangle is shaded?

Adding Fractions

Carol is a make-up artist. To make up a clown, she uses $\frac{2}{6}$ of a tube of pink face paint, $\frac{1}{6}$ of a tube of white face paint, and $\frac{1}{12}$ of a tube of blue face paint.

How much pink and white face paint does Carol use in all?	How much face paint does Carol use in all?
Find $\frac{2}{6} + \frac{1}{6}$.	Find $\frac{3}{6} + \frac{1}{12}$.
Use fraction pieces to help you.	Find equivalent fractions with the same denominator. Then add the numerators.

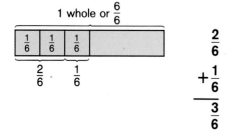

$$\begin{array}{r} \frac{2}{6} \\ + \frac{1}{6} \\ \hline \frac{3}{6} \end{array}$$

Think:

$$\begin{array}{r} \frac{3}{6} \\ + \frac{1}{12} \\ \hline \frac{7}{12} \end{array} \qquad \begin{array}{r} \rightarrow \frac{6}{12} \\ + \frac{1}{12} \\ \hline \frac{7}{12} \end{array}$$

Carol uses $\frac{3}{6}$ of a tube of pink and white face paint.

Carol uses $\frac{7}{12}$ of a tube of face paint in all.

Check Your Understanding

Add. Use fraction pieces or a drawing if you wish.

1. $\frac{3}{12} + \frac{4}{12}$
2. $\frac{1}{2} + \frac{2}{6}$
3. $\frac{1}{3} + \frac{2}{3}$
4. $\frac{1}{3} + \frac{3}{6}$

Share Your Ideas   Explain how you solved **4** above.

Find equivalent fractions. Then add.

5.

$$\frac{3}{5} + \frac{1}{5}$$

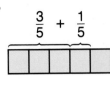

6.

$$\frac{3}{8} + \frac{1}{4}$$

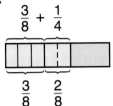

$$\frac{3}{8} \qquad \frac{2}{8}$$

7.

$$\frac{1}{3} + \frac{2}{4}$$

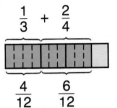

$$\frac{4}{12} \qquad \frac{6}{12}$$

8. $\frac{1}{5}$
$+\frac{1}{5}$

9. $\frac{5}{9}$
$+\frac{3}{9}$

10. $\frac{5}{10}$
$+\frac{2}{5}$

11. $\frac{1}{5}$
$+\frac{2}{5}$

12. $\frac{4}{6}$
$+\frac{1}{6}$

13. $\frac{2}{7}$
$+\frac{4}{7}$

14. $\frac{1}{4}$
$+\frac{2}{8}$

15. $\frac{3}{9}$
$+\frac{4}{9}$

Find each missing number.

16. $\frac{\square}{5} + \frac{3}{5} = \frac{4}{5}$

17. $\frac{\square}{8} + \frac{2}{8} = \frac{6}{8}$

18. $\frac{7}{12} + \frac{2}{6} = \frac{\square}{12}$

19. $\frac{2}{10} + \frac{\square}{10} + \frac{4}{10} = \frac{9}{10}$

Think and Apply

Use the information in the chart.

Types of Faces	Monster	Pumpkin	Cat
Tubes of Face Paint	$\frac{1}{2}$	$\frac{2}{3}$	$\frac{1}{4}$

20. How many tubes of face paint are needed for a monster face and a cat face?

21. How many tubes of face paint are needed for a cat face and a pumpkin face?

22. How many tubes of paint are needed to make 2 cat faces and a monster face?

Use unlike fractions. Write an example for which the sum is $\frac{3}{4}$.

Mixed Review

1. $45,609 + 5,782$

2. $5.37 - 2.9$

3. 253×47

4. $91.2 - 38.7$

5. 39×89

6. $477 \div 25$

7. $3.73 + 2.92$

8. $42\overline{)840}$

9. $3.7 - 2.8$

10. $228.81 - 39.25$

11. 8×26

12. $99.53 + 57.52$

13. $269.5 - 6.1$

14. $\$7.29 \times 92$

15. $26 - 3.49$

16. $4.2 + 7.4$

17. $51\overline{)938}$

18. $3.25 + 4.3$

19. $38 + 215$

20. 4×68

SHOW WHAT YOU KNOW

385

Investigating Subtracting Fractions

You can compare fractions using fraction pieces.

Materials: Workmat 26, fraction pieces from page 382

A. Cut cards from Workmat 26. Place cards face down in a stack. Take turns.

B. Pick the top card. Show each fraction with fraction pieces. Place the pieces for the greater fraction on the 1 whole. Cover the pieces showing the greater fraction with pieces showing the lesser fraction. Compare the lengths. How much longer is the greater fraction piece than the lesser fraction piece?

C. Record your results in a chart like the one below. The example $\frac{2}{3} - \frac{1}{3}$ is shown at the right. Repeat **B** at least 6 times.

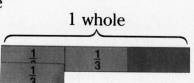

1 whole

Greater Fraction		Lesser Fraction		Difference
$\frac{2}{3}$	−	$\frac{1}{3}$	=	$\frac{1}{3}$

Sharing Your Results

1. Explain how you would use fraction pieces to compare $\frac{8}{12}$ and $\frac{5}{12}$ to find their difference.

2. **What if** you use your set of fraction pieces and pick two pieces with the same denominator? What would the difference be?

Extending the Activity

You can subtract fractions with different denominators.

Work with a partner. Use your fraction pieces.

3. Pick 2 fraction pieces with different denominators. Cover the greater fraction piece with the lesser fraction piece. Be sure the left sides are lined up.

4. Find one or more fraction pieces of one color that will cover up the rest of the bottom piece.

5. Record your results in a chart like the one on page 386. The example $\frac{1}{3} - \frac{1}{4}$ is shown at the right. Repeat the activity at least 4 times.

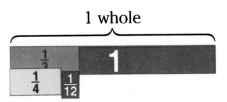

Subtract. Use fraction pieces to help you.

6. $\frac{1}{2} - \frac{1}{4}$ 7. $\frac{3}{4} - \frac{2}{4}$ 8. $\frac{3}{12} - \frac{1}{6}$

9. $\frac{7}{12} - \frac{5}{12}$ 10. $\frac{1}{3} - \frac{3}{12}$ 11. $\frac{5}{6} - \frac{5}{6}$

Show What You Know

12. **What if** you choose to compare $\frac{1}{3}$ and $\frac{1}{6}$? Describe two ways to cover the rest of the bottom piece.

13. Explain how to use fraction pieces to find $\frac{1}{2} - \frac{1}{6}$. Write two possible subtraction number sentences.

Name three equivalent fractions for each.

$$\frac{1}{2} \quad \frac{1}{3} \quad \frac{1}{4} \quad \frac{1}{5}$$

Subtracting Fractions

One half of the brass instruments are trumpets, $\frac{2}{6}$ are trombones, and $\frac{1}{6}$ are tubas.

How much larger is the trombone section than the tuba section?

Find $\frac{2}{6} - \frac{1}{6}$.

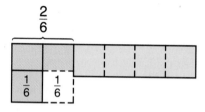

The trombone section is $\frac{1}{6}$ greater than the tuba section.

How much larger is the trumpet section than the tuba section?

Find $\frac{1}{2} - \frac{1}{6}$.

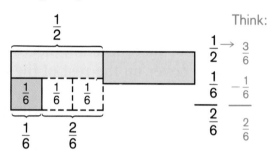

Think:

$$\frac{1}{2} \rightarrow \frac{3}{6}$$
$$\frac{1}{6} \quad -\frac{1}{6}$$
$$\frac{2}{6} \quad \frac{2}{6}$$

The trumpet section is $\frac{2}{6}$ greater than the tuba section.

Check Your Understanding

Subtract. Use fraction pieces or a drawing if you wish.

1.

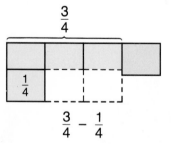

$$\frac{3}{4} - \frac{1}{4}$$

2.

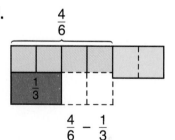

$$\frac{4}{6} - \frac{1}{3}$$

3.

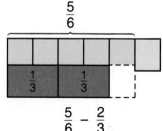

$$\frac{5}{6} - \frac{2}{3}$$

Share Your Ideas   Look back at your answer for **1**.
Write an equivalent fraction for your answer.

Subtract. Use a drawing if you wish.

4. $\dfrac{1}{4}$
$-\dfrac{1}{8}$

5. $\dfrac{5}{6}$
$-\dfrac{2}{6}$

6. $\dfrac{8}{9}$
$-\dfrac{2}{9}$

7. $\dfrac{1}{2}$
$-\dfrac{1}{8}$

8. $\dfrac{9}{12}$
$-\dfrac{4}{12}$

9. $\dfrac{4}{8}$
$-\dfrac{1}{4}$

10. $\dfrac{5}{8}$
$-\dfrac{2}{8}$

11. $\dfrac{7}{12}$
$-\dfrac{3}{6}$

12. $\dfrac{7}{10}$
$-\dfrac{3}{5}$

13. $\dfrac{8}{9}$
$-\dfrac{4}{9}$

14. $\dfrac{11}{12}$
$-\dfrac{2}{3}$

15. $\dfrac{7}{10}$
$-\dfrac{3}{10}$

16. $\dfrac{9}{10} - \dfrac{1}{2}$

17. $1 - \dfrac{1}{4}$

18. $\dfrac{1}{2} - \dfrac{1}{3}$

Follow the rule to find each output.

Rule: Subtract $\dfrac{1}{6}$.

	Input	Output
19.	$\dfrac{1}{2}$	
20.	$\dfrac{1}{3}$	
21.	$\dfrac{5}{12}$	

Rule: Subtract $\dfrac{5}{12}$.

	Input	Output
22.	$\dfrac{1}{2}$	
23.	$\dfrac{7}{12}$	
24.	$\dfrac{5}{6}$	

Rule: Subtract $\dfrac{1}{3}$.

	Input	Output
25.	$\dfrac{3}{6}$	
26.	$\dfrac{1}{3}$	
27.	$\dfrac{5}{12}$	

Think and Apply

28. Three eighths of the woodwind section is clarinets, and $\dfrac{1}{8}$ is oboes. How much greater is the clarinet section than the oboe section?

29. One half of the string section is violins, $\dfrac{1}{6}$ is string basses, and $\dfrac{1}{4}$ is cellos. How much greater is the violin section than the string bass section? than the cello section?

Common Error

30. How can estimation help you to know that the answer below is incorrect? Find the correct answer.

$$\dfrac{3}{4} - \dfrac{2}{8} = \dfrac{1}{8} \longleftarrow \text{incorrect}$$

The difference of 2 fractions is $\dfrac{1}{2}$. One fraction is $\dfrac{1}{4}$. Explain what the greater fraction must be.

SHOW WHAT YOU KNOW

CHECKPOINT

Write 0, $\frac{1}{2}$, or 1 for the best estimate of each fraction. pages 378–379

1. $\frac{1}{3}$ 2. $\frac{1}{5}$ 3. $\frac{4}{5}$ 4. $\frac{5}{9}$ 5. $\frac{2}{3}$ 6. $\frac{2}{6}$

Compare. Write > or < for ⬤. pages 380–381

7. $\frac{4}{7}$ ⬤ $\frac{2}{7}$ 8. $\frac{1}{2}$ ⬤ $\frac{3}{4}$ 9. $\frac{5}{6}$ ⬤ $\frac{2}{3}$ 10. $\frac{2}{12}$ ⬤ $\frac{3}{6}$ 11. $\frac{7}{9}$ ⬤ $\frac{5}{9}$

Add or subtract. pages 382–389

12. $\frac{3}{5}$ $+\frac{1}{5}$

13. $\frac{3}{5}$ $+\frac{3}{10}$

14. $\frac{5}{6}$ $-\frac{1}{6}$

15. $\frac{1}{12}$ $+\frac{1}{2}$

16. $\frac{3}{4}$ $-\frac{1}{2}$

17. $\frac{3}{5}$ $-\frac{2}{5}$

18. $\frac{2}{7}$ $+\frac{4}{7}$

19. $\frac{1}{3}$ $-\frac{2}{9}$

20. $\frac{1}{2}$ $+\frac{3}{8}$

21. $\frac{5}{6}$ $-\frac{1}{2}$

22. $\frac{1}{9}$ $+\frac{4}{9}$

23. $\frac{1}{2}$ $-\frac{3}{10}$

24. $\frac{2}{3} + \frac{1}{6}$

25. $\frac{2}{3} - \frac{1}{12}$

26. $\frac{1}{4} + \frac{1}{2}$

Choose the correct word to complete each sentence.

27. _____ have the same denominator.

28. _____ have different denominators.

Words to Know
Like fractions
Unlike fractions
Mixed numbers

Solve.

29. Cindy is painting a pumpkin face. She uses $\frac{1}{5}$ tube of green paint and $\frac{4}{5}$ tube of orange paint. How much more orange paint does she use than green paint?

30. Joe made 11 puppets. Some were elephants and some were giraffes. He made 3 more giraffes than elephants. How many of each kind did he make?

PROBLEM SOLVING

What Are the Spinner's Chances?

You are making a spinner to determine what prize someone will win in a game. You have 20 whistles, 60 buttons, 30 cars, and 10 stuffed animals. The spinner should help you give away the correct number of each prize. The chart at the right shows what prize will be given away when the spinner stops at each color.

Win a Prize	
Stop at	**Win**
Yellow	Whistle
Blue	Giant Button
Red	Toy Car
Green	Stuffed Animal

Thinking Critically

How would you design the spinner? Use paper, a straightedge, and Workmat 27.

Analyzing and Making Decisions

1. How many times as many buttons as whistles are there? How many times as many buttons as toy cars are there? How many times as many buttons as stuffed animals are there?

2. Should the four colors take up the same amount of space on the spinner or different amounts of space? Explain.

3. Which color should take up the most space? Should you have only one space for each color or several spaces? Explain.

4. Make a circle and color in the spaces for your game. Make it into a spinner and try it about 20 times. Record the number of times it stops at each color. Is your spinner a good one? Explain.

Look Back **What if** your spinner breaks before your game starts? How else can you play it?

391

Simulation

Sarah and her family went to the ballgame. Her favorite team was at bat and no one was on base. She hoped that the team would get someone on base. She asked herself, "How many different ways can runners be on the three bases?" Help Sarah find out the number of different ways.

Sometimes you cannot actually experiment to do the problem. But you can simulate or draw the action to find the answer.

Solving the Problem

Think What do you need to find out?

Explore Draw the 3 bases. Show 1 runner on base. List the different ways that 1 runner can be on the 3 bases.

Draw the three bases again. Show 2 runners on base. List the different ways that two runners can be on the three bases.

In how many ways can 3 runners be on base? List them.

Solve How many different ways can you find for runners to be on the bases?

Look Back How does testing with one runner first, then two runners, and then three runners, help you find the correct answer?

Share Your Ideas

1. How could you tell if you could jump over a puddle without actually jumping over it?

Extending Your Thinking

Solve. Use a calculator where appropriate.

CHOICES

2. Which set of letters shows a simulation of the following problem?

Four girls are standing in line at a movie theater. Carolyn is between Betsy and Valerie. Laurie is last in line next to Betsy.

a. B-C-V-L
b. V-C-B-L
c. B-L-C-V

3. Marbles the clown can cut a log into 3 pieces in 12 minutes. At the same rate, how long should it take Marbles to cut the log into 6 pieces?

4. The Flying Robinsons use 3 trapezes in their act. The red trapeze is 10 meters high. The blue trapeze is one half as high as the red trapeze. The gold trapeze is three times as high as the blue trapeze. How high is each trapeze?

5. In a three-person relay, Isabel ran her leg of the run in 90 seconds. Gwen ran her leg in 10 seconds less than Isabel. Marti ran her leg in 10 seconds less than Gwen. How many minutes did it take the relay team to finish the race?

Mixed Strategy Review

6. Pat needs to fence off a 20-meter square exhibition area. How many meters of fencing does she need?

7. Look at your answer for **6.** Fencing costs $17 a meter. How much will it cost to fence the area?

8. Mary worked at a lemonade stand during the fair. She sold 10 glasses of lemonade for 75 cents a glass. How much money did she receive?

CREATE YOUR OWN

Write a problem where the problem can be solved by simulating the action.

What if you press one key on your calculator? What numbers could you get?

Listing Outcomes

Richard works at Bird World. He uses one red, one blue, and one yellow ball in the parakeet show. **What if** Richard chooses one ball without looking? What is the chance that he will choose a red ball?

Choosing a ball without looking is an experiment. There are 3 **possible outcomes.**

The **chance** of choosing a red ball is 1 out of 3.

The chance of choosing a blue ball is 1 out of 3.

What is the chance of choosing a yellow ball?

Check Your Understanding

Use the letter cards at the right to answer each question.

1. How many outcomes are possible if you choose one card?

2. What are the possible outcomes? Make a list.

3. What is the chance of choosing the *C*?

4. What is the chance of choosing the *D*?

A	B
C	D
E	F

Share Your Ideas What if the letter *F* were changed to an *E*? What would the chance of choosing an *E* be then? Explain.

What if you choose one coin from the box below without looking?

5. How many possible outcomes are there?

6. List all the possible outcomes.

7. What is the chance of choosing a dime?

8. What is the chance of choosing a nickel?

9. What is the chance of choosing a coin worth more than 10¢?

10. What is the chance of choosing a coin worth more than 50¢?

11. What is the chance of choosing a coin worth less than 60¢?

> ## Think and Apply

What if there are **3** red counters, **3** green counters, and **2** blue counters in a bag? You choose one counter without looking.

12. List all the possible outcomes.

13. What is the chance of choosing a blue counter?

14. What is the chance of choosing a red counter or a green counter?

15. What is the chance of choosing a counter that is not red?

What if you have a bag of red and blue counters? What chance is there of choosing a red counter? a blue counter? Explain.

SHOW WHAT YOU KNOW

Investigating Making Predictions

This experiment will help you learn how to make good predictions.

Materials: letter cube, with faces labeled *X, X, Y, Y, Z, Z;*
Workmat 28

A. Copy the chart below or use Workmat 28.

- Record all possible outcomes.

- Record the chance of each outcome occurring for 1 toss.

- Predict the number of times you think each outcome will occur for 3 tosses, then for 30 tosses.

B. Toss the cube 30 times. Use tally marks to record your results. Compare your results with your predictions.

C. Compare your predictions and results with those of other groups.

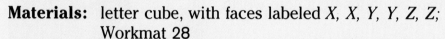

Possible Outcomes	Chance of Outcome for 1 Toss	Predictions for 3 Tosses	Predictions for 30 Tosses	Results for 30 Tosses

Sharing Your Results

1. What are the chances that *Z* will appear on top? that a letter other than *Z* will appear on top?

2. How many times did you predict that *X* would appear on top in 30 tosses? How many times was *X* on top?

3. Which letter appeared on top most often? least often?

4. Describe how you made your predictions.

Extending the Activity

Work in a small group.

5. Try another experiment.

   - Make a new letter cube. Label the faces *X, Y, Y, Y, Z, Z.*

   - Find the chance of each outcome occurring in 1 toss.

   - Predict the number of times each letter will appear on top in 30 tosses. Record your predictions.

   - Toss the cube 30 times. Record your results.

6. What is the chance that *X* will be on top in a single toss? Is it more likely that *X* will appear on top than *Z*? Explain.

7. Does *Z* have less of a chance of appearing on top than *Y*? Explain.

8. Which letter did you predict would be on top most often? How many times? How many times did it actually appear in 30 tosses?

Show What You Know

9. Combine your results with those of other groups. Then find the average results. Look at the average results and your group's results. Which are closer to the predictions? Why do you think this happened?

10. Explain how listing outcomes and chances can help you make better predictions.

ACTIVITY

Investigating Probabilities

At the magic show, ten people in the audience get to pick one card each. The cards are numbered from 1 through 10. If the card shows a multiple of 5 on it, the person wins a prize. What is the probability of winning?

▶ **Probability** is the chance of something happening.

There are *10* possible outcomes:
1, 2, 3, 4, 5, 6, 7, 8, 9, 10.
There are *2* multiples of 5: 5, 10.

There are 2 *chances in 10* of getting a multiple of 5.
The probability can be written as a fraction: $\frac{2}{10}$.

Working together

Materials: 10 blank cards, such as index cards

A. Write a different number on each card. Choose from the numbers 1 through 100.

B. Look at the numbers you chose. Find the probability of picking an even number. Record the probability on a sheet of paper.

C. Pick a card without looking. Record whether it is an even number or not. Return the card to the deck. Take turns until each person has picked a card 5 times. Record your results.

D. Repeat **B** and **C** for picking
  • a multiple of 3.
  • a prime number.

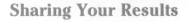

Sharing Your Results

1. How did you find the probability for picking an even number? a multiple of 3? a prime number?

2. How did your results compare with the probabilities in each case?

Extending the Activity

Work with a partner.

Conduct a hair-color survey in your classroom. Make a tally mark for each person. Find the total number of your classmates with each hair color.

Hair Color	Tally	Total
Brown		
Black		
Blond		
Red		

3. What is the probability that a person in your class will have
   a. brown hair?   **b.** blond hair?
   c. black hair?   **d.** red hair?

4. What if you pick one marble from the dish without looking? What is the probability of getting

   a. a red marble?
   b. a yellow marble?
   c. a black marble?
   d. a green marble?
   e. any color but yellow?
   f. a black or a green marble?

Show What You Know

5. The magician has a bag of fruit containing peaches, plums, and apricots. There are 12 pieces of fruit in the bag. If he picks one piece of fruit without looking, the probability of getting a plum is $\frac{1}{2}$. The probability of getting a peach is $\frac{1}{3}$.

   a. How many plums are in the bag? how many peaches?

   b. What is the probability of picking an apricot? Explain how you know.

ACTIVITY

Investigating Arrangements

The chorus members are getting ready for their spring concert. They are planning to sing three songs: "Oh, Susanna," "America, the Beautiful," and "Clementine."

They can sing these songs in any order. In what different ways can the songs be arranged?

Do this activity to find out.

Working together

A. Write the name of each song on a separate piece of paper.

B. Move the papers around to show all the arrangements with "Oh, Susanna" first. Make a list of the arrangements.

C. Do the same with "America, the Beautiful" first. Repeat with "Clementine" first.

"Oh, Susanna"

"America, the Beautiful"

"Clementine"

Sharing Your Results

1. How many different arrangements did you find with "America, the Beautiful" first?

2. How many different arrangements are there in all?

Extending the Activity

How many different arrangements of these cards can there be with *A* as the first card?

A tree diagram can help you find all the arrangements.

| A | B | C | D |

First letter ⟶

Second letter ⟶

Third letter ⟶

Fourth letter ⟶

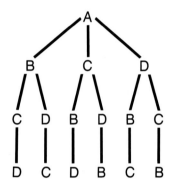

When *A* is the first letter, what could be the second?

Then if *D* is the second letter, what could be the third?

Then if *C* is the third letter, what must be the fourth?

Read down each branch to find the arrangements.

Arrangements: ABCD   ABDC   ACBD   ACDB   ADBC   ADCB

3. Use tree diagrams to find all the arrangements when *B, C,* and *D* are the first letters.

4. How many different arrangements are there when *B* is first? when *C* is first? when *D* is first?

5. How many different arrangements of all four letters are there, including those starting with *A?*

Show What You Know

6. Barry, Jill, and Nancy stand in the front row of the chorus. List the different ways they can arrange themselves in the row.

7. Eric is arranging four photographs in a row on his wall. How many different arrangements can he make?

The Fraction Estimation Game

The objective of this game is to win the game by correctly estimating whether a fraction is closer to 0 or to 1.

Working together

Play the Fraction Estimation Game with a partner.

Materials: 9 index cards with the digits 1 through 9 written on them, grid paper, Workmat 29

Follow these rules as you play the game.

A. Player A draws 3 cards and picks 2 of the 3 digits to form a fraction less than 1. Then player A writes the fraction on a piece of paper.

B. Player B estimates whether the fraction is closer to 0 or 1.

C. Player B then checks the estimate by making a drawing of the fraction on grid paper or by using a number line on Workmat 29.

D. A player wins 1 point for each correct estimate. The game is over when one person has 10 points.

Sharing Your Ideas

1. How did you determine whether the fraction was closer to 0 or to 1?

2. What fraction should the player who picks the 3 cards try to make?

3. **What if** you had to estimate whether $\frac{3}{6}$ is closer to 0 or to 1? What would you say?

Extending Your Thinking

4. Two people can play the *Fraction Order Game.*
The objective is to put the most fractions in order.

Materials: 16 index cards with the following fractions written on them:

$\frac{1}{2}$, $\frac{1}{6}$, $\frac{2}{6}$, $\frac{4}{6}$, $\frac{5}{6}$, $\frac{1}{12}$, $\frac{2}{12}$, $\frac{3}{12}$, $\frac{4}{12}$, $\frac{5}{12}$, $\frac{6}{12}$, $\frac{7}{12}$, $\frac{8}{12}$, $\frac{9}{12}$, $\frac{10}{12}$, $\frac{11}{12}$ and Workmat 29

Follow these rules:

a. Pick the fraction $\frac{1}{2}$ from the index cards and place it face up on the table. Turn all the other cards face down.

b. Player A draws 2 cards and decides whether or not to use only fractions less than $\frac{1}{2}$ or only fractions greater than $\frac{1}{2}$. If Player A decides to use fractions greater than $\frac{1}{2}$ he or she will place them to the right of $\frac{1}{2}$. Player B would then place fractions less than $\frac{1}{2}$ to the left of the fraction $\frac{1}{2}$.

c. Player B draws 2 cards and decides whether to play or to pass. Players may pass or must pass if they draw fractions they cannot use.

d. Continue taking turns. If you are using fractions less than $\frac{1}{2}$, each one must be less than the last. If you are using fractions greater than $\frac{1}{2}$, each one must be greater than the last.

e. Each player has five turns. The player with the most cards in order wins.

f. Use the number lines on Workmat 29 to check the order of the fractions.

Show What You Know

5. What strategy did you use for this game?

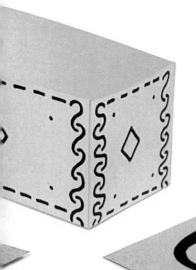

FRACTIONS WITH TANGRAMS

A tangram is a seven-piece Chinese puzzle. Each tangram piece is shaped so that it can be a part of a whole square. It is believed that tangrams were named after Tan, a legendary Chinese scholar.

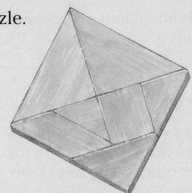

WORKING TOGETHER

1. Work in small groups. Look at your tangram set. The list below assigns a fractional value to each tangram piece. Notice that the sum of all seven pieces equals one whole.

Shape	Fractional Value
large triangle	$\frac{1}{4}$
large triangle	$\frac{1}{4}$
medium triangle	$\frac{1}{8}$
small triangle	$\frac{1}{16}$
small triangle	$\frac{1}{16}$
square	$\frac{1}{8}$
parallelogram	$\frac{1}{8}$

2. Label each tangram piece with its fractional value. Then lay the correct pieces on top of each other to answer these questions.

   • How many small triangles equal one medium triangle?

   • How many medium triangles equal one large triangle?

   • How many small triangles equal one parallelogram?

   • How many small triangles equal one square?

3. Now use your tangram pieces to create three designs, one with a sum of $\frac{3}{8}$, one with a sum of $\frac{5}{8}$, and the last with a sum of $\frac{3}{4}$. Tell how you reached each sum. Then trace each of your designs.

CHAPTER REVIEW/TEST

Compare. Write > or < for ⬤.

1. $\frac{7}{10}$ ⬤ $\frac{6}{10}$

2. $\frac{2}{3}$ ⬤ $\frac{7}{9}$

3. $\frac{5}{8}$ ⬤ $\frac{1}{2}$

4. $\frac{4}{6}$ ⬤ $\frac{1}{3}$

Add or subtract.

5. $\frac{3}{8}$
   $+\frac{1}{4}$

6. $\frac{2}{5}$
   $+\frac{2}{5}$

7. $\frac{5}{8}$
   $-\frac{1}{4}$

8. $\frac{7}{8}$
   $-\frac{1}{2}$

9. $\frac{1}{3}$
   $+\frac{3}{12}$

10. $\frac{4}{5} - \frac{1}{10}$

11. $\frac{1}{3} + \frac{2}{9}$

12. $\frac{1}{6} + \frac{2}{3}$

13. $\frac{3}{12} + \frac{6}{12}$

14. $\frac{4}{7} - \frac{3}{7}$

15. $\frac{4}{8} - \frac{1}{4}$

Use the spinner to answer each question.

16. List the possible outcomes of a spin.

17. What is the chance of each outcome occurring in 1 spin?

18. What is the probability of the spinner stopping on *A* or *C?*

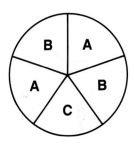

Solve.

19. Two thirds of the percussion section of the orchestra is drums. One sixth is cymbals. What fraction is drums and cymbals?

20. Mimi is building a tower of blocks. She is using one red, one blue, and one green block. List the different ways the blocks can be arranged.

Think   Donna has $\frac{1}{3}$ tube of blue face paint and $\frac{1}{2}$ tube of yellow paint. She mixes them together to make green paint. If she uses $\frac{1}{6}$ tube of the green paint, how much paint does she have left?

COMPUTER

Fraction Strips

MathProcessor™ can be used to explore fractions.

You can use **Fraction Strips** and **Number Spaces** to model $\frac{5}{8}$. Choose $\frac{0}{8}$ from the **Fraction Strips** catalog. Click on the increase button or click on unshaded segments of the $\frac{0}{8}$ **Fraction Strip** until $\frac{5}{8}$ is shaded.

MathProcessor™ Tools:

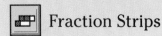 Fraction Strips

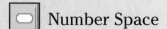 Number Space

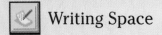 Writing Space

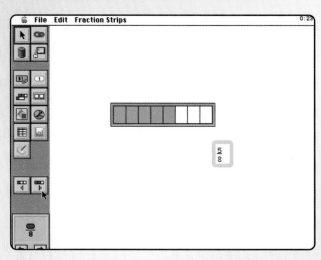

Doing the Computer Investigation

A. Use **Fraction Strips** to model $\frac{3}{4}$ and $\frac{1}{4}$. Which fraction is greater?

INVESTIGATION

B. Use **Fraction Strips** to compare $\frac{2}{3}$ and $\frac{5}{6}$. Which fraction is greater?

C. Tanesha and Carlos are running a marathon. Tanesha has finished $\frac{7}{10}$ of the distance. Carlos has run $\frac{7}{12}$ of the distance. Who has run a longer distance? Open a **Writing Space**. Explain your answer.

Sharing Your Results

1. Compare $\frac{1}{2}$ and $\frac{2}{4}$. How many other **Fraction Strips** can you make that are equal to $\frac{1}{2}$? to $\frac{1}{3}$? to $\frac{3}{4}$?

2. Share your results with your classmates.

Extending the Computer Investigation

Can you find two fractions with different denominators that have a sum of one? How many different pairs can you find? Open a **Writing Space** and describe your strategy.

Creating Disguises

Work with a partner.

Materials: 19 index cards, crayons, pencil

1. Draw one item on each card.
   - 4 different types of hats: western, baseball, sailor, helmet
   - 3 different types of sunglasses: round, square, triangular
   - 2 different types of mustaches: droopy and straight

2. Use the cards to make disguises. A disguise consists of one hat, one pair of sunglasses, and one mustache.

3. How many *different* disguises can you make? You may want to use a tree diagram to help you. Record the different disguises.

4. How many different disguises have
   a. western hats?
   b. sailor hats?
   c. round sunglasses?
   d. droopy mustaches?
   e. baseball hats and square sunglasses?
   f. helmets, round eyeglasses, and straight mustaches?

5. Design a set of disguise cards. Draw one item on each card.
   - 3 different types of hair
   - 2 different types of noses
   - 2 different types of mouths
   - 3 different types of bow ties

   How many different disguises can you make?

6. **Look back** at **5.** How can you use multiplication to find the number of different disguises in each case?

MAINTAINING SKILLS

Choose the correct answer. Write A, B, C, or D.

1. Write the decimal for three and five hundredths.

 A 3.05   **C** 5.3

 B 3.5   **D** not given

2.   621.5
   +327.8

 A 949.3   **C** 1,049.3

 B 948.3   **D** not given

3. 4,000 g = _____ kg

 A 40   **C** 4

 B 3   **D** not given

4. Find the perimeter.

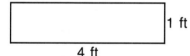

    4 ft

 A 4 ft   **C** 5 ft

 B 10 ft   **D** not given

Use the graph to answer 5–6.

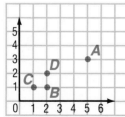

5. Give an ordered pair to name *A*.

 A (3, 5)   **C** (4, 2)

 B (5, 3)   **D** not given

6. What point does (2, 2) locate?

 A *D*   **C** *C*

 B *B*   **D** not given

7. $\frac{7}{8}$ is closest to what whole number?

 A 0   **C** 1

 B $\frac{1}{2}$ **D** not given

8. Compare.

$\frac{2}{3}$ ⬤ $\frac{1}{6}$

 A $<$ **C** $=$

 B $>$ **D** not given

Use guess and test to solve.

9. Sue bought pencils for $.30 each, pens for $.45 each, and rulers for $.40 each. If she spent $1.85, how many pens did she buy?

 A 1   **C** 3

 B 2   **D** not given

10. There were 12 children on the roller coaster. There were 4 more girls than boys. How many boys were on the roller coaster?

 A 5   **C** 4

 B 6   **D** not given

Customary Measurement

Sharing What You Know

Have you ever visited the seashore? Have you stared out at the huge ocean? Have you held a seashell in your hand, or studied a tiny grain of sand? What if you want to know how deep the ocean is, or how much that seashell weighs? How would you find out?

Using Language

How deep? How heavy? How much does it hold? How warm? Questions about size or temperature are best answered with **measurement**. This part of the ocean is 14 feet deep. That seashell weighs 3 ounces. This bucket can hold 1 quart of water. The ocean temperature is 65 degrees Fahrenheit. Feet, ounces, pints, and degrees Fahrenheit are all **customary units of measurement**. Why do you think measurement is important in our world?

Words to Know: measurement, customary units of measurement, inch, foot, yard, mile, ounce, pound, ton, capacity, cup, pint, quart, gallon, degree Fahrenheit

Be a Problem Solver

Meg used her feet, end-to-end, to measure the width of a beach blanket. It measured 10 of her feet. Tim measured the width of the same blanket. It measured 8 of his feet. Who has bigger feet?

List things you find at the seashore that you would measure in inches. List other things that you would measure in feet.

What are some objects in your classroom that are about an inch long? a foot long?

Measuring in Inches and Feet

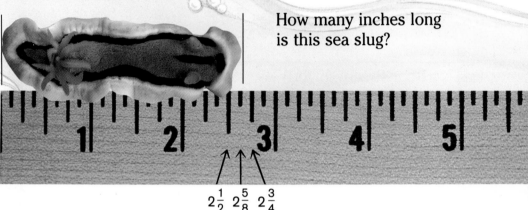

How many inches long is this sea slug?

$2\frac{1}{2}$ $2\frac{5}{8}$ $2\frac{3}{4}$

To the nearest inch, the sea slug is 3 inches long.

To the nearest $\frac{1}{2}$ inch, the sea slug is $2\frac{1}{2}$ inches long.

To the nearest $\frac{1}{4}$ inch, the sea slug is $2\frac{3}{4}$ inches long.

To the nearest $\frac{1}{8}$ inch, the sea slug is $2\frac{5}{8}$ inches long.

The **foot** is another unit of length. It is used to measure longer lengths.

1 foot (ft) = 12 inches (in.)

▶ To change from feet to inches, multiply by 12.

2 ft = _____ in.
2 × 12 = 24
2 ft = 24 in.

▶ To change from inches to feet, divide by 12.

36 in. = _____ ft
36 ÷ 12 = 3
36 in. = 3 ft

Check Your Understanding

Measure to the nearest inch, $\frac{1}{2}$ in., $\frac{1}{4}$ in., and $\frac{1}{8}$ in.

1.

2.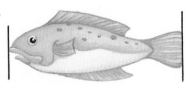

Share Your Ideas Explain how to find the length of an object in inches if you know its length in feet.

Measure to the nearest inch, $\frac{1}{2}$ in., $\frac{1}{4}$ in., and $\frac{1}{8}$ in.

3.

4.

5.

Complete.

6. 4 ft = _____ in.   **7.** 60 in. = _____ ft   **8.** 108 in. = _____ ft

9. 6 ft 2 in. = _____ in.   **10.** 4 ft 24 in. = _____ ft

Think and Apply

Use the clues and measure. Who drew each polygon?

11. Joan: "The perimeter of my polygon is 5 inches."

12. Theo: "The perimeter of my polygon is 4 inches."

13. Sara: "The perimeter of my polygon is 6 inches."

A

B

C

Common Error

What is wrong with this measurement?

14. The length of the arrow is $1\frac{5}{8}$ inches. ← incorrect

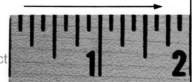

Is measuring to the nearest inch or nearest $\frac{1}{8}$ inch closer to the actual measurement? Explain.

SHOW WHAT YOU KNOW

Estimating and Measuring Length

The Greens had a picnic at the beach. They brought a beach blanket 2 yards long and 1 yard wide. After lunch they walked along the beach. They walked about 1 mile in 20 minutes.

Inches and feet are **customary units of measurement** used to measure shorter lengths. **Yards** (yd) are used to measure longer lengths. **Miles** (mi) are used to measure very long lengths.

1 yard	= 36 inches
1 yard	= 3 feet
1 mile	= 5,280 feet
1 mile	= 1,760 yards

▶ To change to a smaller unit, multiply.

6 yd = _____ ft

Think   1 yd = 3 ft

6 × 3 = 18

6 yd = 18 ft

▶ To change to a larger unit, divide.

108 in. = _____ yd

Think   1 yd = 36 in.

108 ÷ 36 = 3

108 in. = 3 yd

Check Your Understanding

Would you choose inch, foot, yard, or mile to measure each?

1. height of a door

2. distance from Chicago to Denver

3. width of this page

4. height of a telephone pole

Share Your Ideas   Explain how to change a measurement from yards to inches and from inches to yards.

Would you choose inch, foot, yard, or mile to measure each?

5. length of a football field

6. length of the Mississippi River

7. height of an adult

8. length of a skateboard

Choose the best answer for each.

9. A piano bench is about _____ long.
   a. 10 ft   b. 1 yd   c. 17 in.

10. Larry rode his bicycle _____ in 20 minutes.
    a. 3 mi   b. 500 yd   c. 1,000 ft

11. The insect was about _____ long.
    a. 1 yd   b. 1 ft   c. 1 in.

Choose estimation, mental math, or paper and pencil to compare. Use >, <, or = for ⬤.

CHOICES

12. 5,280 ft ⬤ 2 mi   13. 14 ft ⬤ 4 yd

14. 90 in. ⬤ 3 yd   15. 5 yd 36 in. ⬤ 6 yd

> **Think and Apply**

Work with a partner.

DATA

16. Measure five of your walking steps. Then find the average length of each step. About how many steps would you take to walk 1 mile?

17. If a room is 10 feet long, about how many of your steps would it take to walk from one end to the other?

JOURNAL WRITING Explain how you found the answer to **17**.

Mixed Review

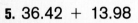

1. 87.46
   − 29.38

2. $4.85
   ×   93

3. 60)845

4. 20)395

5. 36.42 + 13.98

6. 4.6 + 3.9

7. 8.34 + 4.2

8. 96.4 − 81.35

9. $\frac{4}{8} + \frac{1}{2}$

10. $\frac{6}{8} - \frac{2}{4}$

11. $\frac{7}{6} + \frac{5}{6}$

12. $\frac{2}{3} - \frac{4}{9}$

List the numbers in order from least to greatest.

13. 238   328   283

14. 1,426   1,246   1,462

15. 4.6   4.62   4.26

16. 15.3   153.6   15.36

17. $\frac{1}{3}$ $\frac{1}{2}$ $\frac{1}{6}$

18. $\frac{2}{3}$ $\frac{1}{4}$ $\frac{1}{2}$

SHOW WHAT YOU KNOW

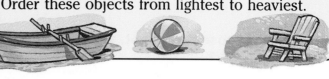

Estimating and Measuring Weight

Jack and Danielle built a giant sand castle. They used empty milk cartons to carry the sand. An empty milk carton weighs about 1 ounce.

The **ounce (oz), pound (lb),** and **ton (T)** are customary units of weight.

1 pound = 16 ounces
1 ton = 2,000 pounds

about 1 ounce

about 1 pound

about 1 ton

► To change to a smaller unit, multiply.

3 T = _____ lb

Think 1 T = 2,000 lb
2,000 × 3 = 6,000

3 T = 6,000 lb

► To change to a larger unit, divide.

32 oz = _____ lb

Think 16 oz = 1 lb
32 ÷ 16 = 2

32 oz = 2 lb

Check Your Understanding

Would you choose ounce, pound, or ton to weigh each?

1.

2.

3.

Share Your Ideas Explain the steps you would follow to change 6 pounds to ounces.

416

Would you choose ounce, pound, or ton to weigh each?

4. 5. 6.

Choose the best answer for each.

7. A rubber raft weighs about _____.
   a. 10 oz   **b.** 10 lb   **c.** 10 T

8. An adult whale weighs about _____.
   a. 4,000 oz   **b.** 400 lb   **c.** 40 T

9. An orange weighs about _____.
   a. 8 oz   **b.** 8 lb   **c.** 8 T

Choose estimation, mental math, or paper and pencil to compare. Use >, <, or = for ●.

CHOICES

10. 8,000 lb ● 3 T   11. 64 oz ● 4 lb

12. 30 lb ● 500 oz   13. 8 lb ● 120 oz

14. 5 lb 18 oz ● 6 lb   15. 2,002 lb ● 2 T 34 oz

Think and Apply

16. The largest sand castle on record was 5 stories high and was made with 48,384 tons of sand! How many pounds of sand were used to build the castle?

17. Write the steps to change from tons to ounces. Then find the number of ounces in 14 tons.

Logical Thinking

Choose weights from the right to make the scales balance.

23   37   40   65

18. 52   24

19. 26

Look back at **10**. Explain how you found the answer.

SHOW WHAT YOU KNOW

CHECKPOINT

Measure to the nearest inch, $\frac{1}{2}$ in., $\frac{1}{4}$ in., and $\frac{1}{8}$ inch pages 412–413

1.

2.

Choose the best answer for each. pages 414–417

3. A new baby weighs about _____.

   a. 7 oz   **b.** 7 lb   **c.** 7 T

4. A jogger runs about _____.

   a. 30 in.   **b.** 30 ft   **c.** 3 mi

5. A giraffe weighs about _____.

   a. 1 T   **b.** 1 oz   **c.** 1 lb

6. The moon is about _____ in diameter.

   a. 2,200 yd **b.** 2,200 in. **c.** 2,200 mi

Complete. pages 412–417

7. 4 lb = _____ oz

8. 84 in. = _____ ft

9. 2 mi = _____ ft

10. 3 T = _____ lb

11. 15 ft = _____ yd

12. _____ lb = 224 oz

Choose the correct words to complete each sentence.

13. Units of length in order from least to greatest are _____, _____, _____, and _____.

14. Units of weight in order from least to greatest are _____, _____, and _____.

Words to Know	
foot	pound
inch	ton
mile	yard
ounce	

Solve. pages 412–417

15. Craig needs 12 feet of fishing line. How many yards is that? how many inches?

16. The whale shark can grow up to 20 yards long and weigh up to 15 tons. How many feet long is that? how many pounds?

INVESTIGATING
PROBLEM SOLVING

THINK
EXPLORE
SOLVE
LOOK BACK

What's the Best Way to Mow?

At the entrance to the park is a lawn 20 ft by 24 ft. The lawn mower can cut a strip that is a little more than 3 ft wide.

Thinking Critically

What is the best way to mow this lawn? Work in a group and plan some patterns for mowing the lawn. You can use grid paper to help you.

Analyzing and Making Decisions

1. Draw at least two different patterns that you can use when mowing the lawn.
2. How far would you have to walk when using each pattern? Which pattern shows the shorter distance to walk?
3. Which pattern leaves your last strip closest to your starting point? Why might you want to finish close to where you started?
4. Which pattern for mowing would you choose? Explain.

Look Back Look at your different patterns. How many turns must you make in each one? What kind of turns are they? Would you change the way you would mow the lawn because of the turns? Explain.

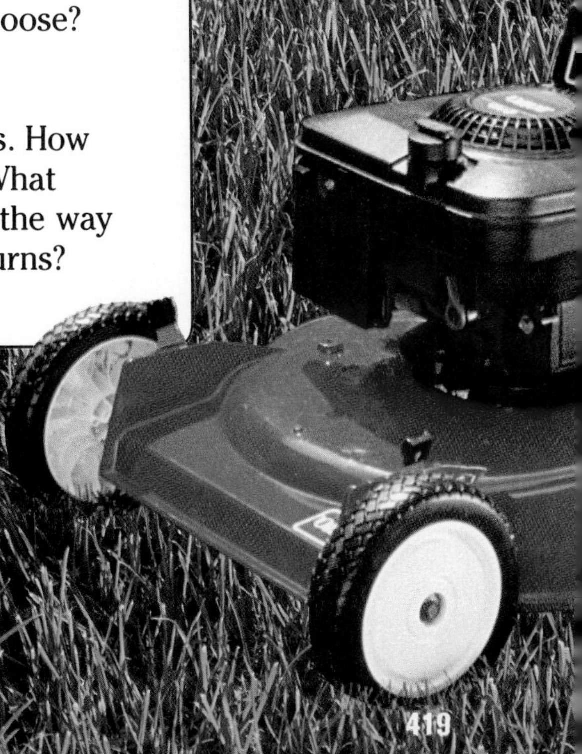

Alternate Solutions

In baseball, a pitch is usually called a strike if it crosses the plate above the batter's knees and below the midpoint of the batter's torso. The plate is 17 inches wide. Susy's strike zone is 22 inches long and 17 inches wide. Daryl's strike zone is 19 inches long and 17 inches wide. Susy's strike zone is how many more square inches than Daryl's?

You can often solve a problem several ways. You can use the numbers in different ways to solve it.

Solving the Problem

Think   What is the problem? What are the facts?

Explore   What is the area of Susy's strike zone? What is the area of Daryl's strike zone? How can you find out how much larger Susy's strike zone is?
How wide is each player's strike zone? How much longer is Susy's strike zone than Daryl's? What is another way you could find out how many more square inches Susy's strike zone contains?

Solve   Susy's strike zone is how many more square inches than Daryl's?

Look Back   What is different about the two methods of solving this problem?

Share Your Ideas

1. How large is your strike zone?

Extending Your Thinking

Solve. Use a calculator where appropriate.

CHOICES

2. Jeremy bought an old coin for 10 cents. He sold it to Louis for 20 cents. He bought it back from Louis for 30 cents. Then he sold it to Andrea for 40 cents. How much money did he make or lose?

Use this information to solve 3–5.

Timmy has 10 coins. He wants to arrange them in 3 piles so that none of the piles has the same number of coins.

3. Show the different ways he can arrange them.

4. What if one half of Timmy's coins are nickels and one half are dimes? What is the total value of his coins?

5. What if one arrangement has one coin in one pile, two in another, and seven in another? One pile is worth 60 cents. Which is it? How many nickels and dimes does the pile have?

Mixed Strategy Review

Use this information to solve 6–7.

David and Mark are sharing a bag of pennies.

David takes 1, Mark takes 2, David takes 3, and Mark takes 4. David takes 5, and Mark takes 6. They continue with this pattern until Mark takes the last pennies. He has 10 more coins than David.

6. How many pennies does each boy have?

7. How many pennies were in the bag when they started?

JOURNAL WRITING

CREATE YOUR OWN

Write a problem that can be solved in two ways.

Investigating Capacity

Cups, pints, quarts, and gallons are units of capacity. Find out how much each holds.

Working together

Materials: a measuring cup; 3 empty milk cartons: a pint, a quart, a gallon; a pail of water or a bag of beans; 5 containers of different shapes: some small and some large; Workmat 30

A. Place the 5 containers in order from least to greatest, according to how much you think they can hold. Label the containers 1 through 5.

B. Measure the capacity of each container. Use the measuring cup and the milk cartons with either water or beans. Record each measurement to the nearest cup, pint, quart, and gallon.

Container	Number of Cups	Number of Pints	Number of Quarts	Number of Gallons
1				
2				
3				

Sharing Your Results

1. How can you estimate the capacity in cups by looking at the capacity in pints?

2. How can you estimate the capacity in pints by looking at the capacity in quarts?

Extending the Activity

Work in a small group.

Material: same materials as used on page 422, Workmat 31

3. Exchange containers with another group. Measure the capacity of each new container to the nearest cup. Record the data in a chart like the one shown below or use Workmat 31.

4. Estimate the capacity of each container in pints, quarts, and gallons. Record your estimates.

5. Measure the capacity of each container. Record each measurement to the nearest pint, quart, and gallon. Compare the actual measurement with your estimate.

Container	Number of Cups	Number of Pints		Number of Quarts		Number of Gallons	
		Estimate	Actual	Estimate	Actual	Estimate	Actual
1							
2							

Show What You Know

6. Explain how you could use the cup measurements to estimate the other measurements.

7. If you know the capacity of a container in gallons, how can you find the capacity in quarts without measuring? in pints? in cups?

423

Order the units of measure from least to greatest.

cup   gallon   quart   pint

Estimating and Measuring Capacity

What if you wanted to measure the amount of water in a canteen? Which unit of measure would you use?

The **cup (c)**, **pint (pt)**, **quart (qt)**, and **gallon (gal)** are customary units used to measure liquid capacity.

2 cups = 1 pint
2 pints = 1 quart
4 quarts = 1 gallon

A canteen holds about 1 quart of water.

▶ To change to a smaller unit, multiply.

3 gal = _____ qt

Think   1 gal = 4 qt
            3 × 4 = 12

3 gal = 12 qt

▶ To change to a larger unit, divide.

16 c = _____ pt

Think   1 pt = 2 c
            16 ÷ 2 = 8

16 c = 8 pt

Check Your Understanding

Would you choose cup, pint, quart, or gallon to measure each?

1.   2.    3.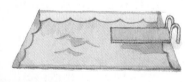

Share Your Ideas   Look back at **1**. Explain why using a gallon as the unit of measure would not be appropriate.

Would you choose cup, pint, quart, or gallon to measure each?

4.

5.

6.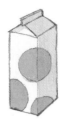

Complete.

7. 6 gal = _____ qt

8. 6 c = _____ pt

9. 8 qt = _____ gal

10. _____ gal = 16 pt

11. _____ qt = 32 c

12. _____ gal = 64 c

Follow the rule to find each output.

Rule: Add 3 cups.

	Input	Output
13.	1 pint	__cups
14.	1 quart	__cups
15.	1 qt 3 cups	__cups

Rule: Add 1 pint.

	Input	Output
16.	5 cups	__cups
17.	1 quart	__cups
18.	1 pint	__cups

Think and Apply

Use the information in the recipe.

19. How many cups of lime juice are needed for the punch?

20. How many more cups of club soda than lemonade are needed?

21. How many cups of fruit punch will the recipe make? How many pints?

22. **What if** you double the recipe? How many quarts of punch will you have?

Scouts' Fruit Punch
1 qt orange juice
1 pt lemonade
½ pt lime juice
2½ qt club soda
1 c cranberry juice

Explain how you found the answer to **20.**

SHOW WHAT YOU KNOW

Why is it important to know the outdoor temperature?

Measuring Temperature

The unit for measuring temperature in the customary system of measurement is **degree Fahrenheit** (°F).

To read the thermometer, look at the mark or number at the top of the red column.

On a warm day, the temperature might be 84°F.

- read   eighty-four degrees Fahrenheit

- write   84°F

On a very cold day, the temperature might be ⁻10°F.

- read   ten degrees Fahrenheit below zero, or minus ten degrees Fahrenheit
- write   ⁻10°F

What does each line on this thermometer stand for?

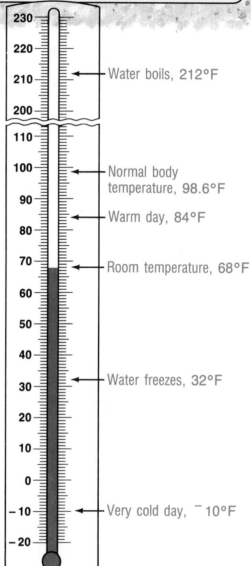

Water boils, 212°F

Normal body temperature, 98.6°F

Warm day, 84°F

Room temperature, 68°F

Water freezes, 32°F

Very cold day, ⁻10°F

Check Your Understanding

Read and write each Fahrenheit temperature shown.

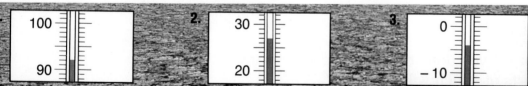

1. 100 / 90

2. 30 / 20

3. 0 / ⁻10

Share Your Ideas   Which temperature is colder, ⁻5°F or ⁻15°F? Explain.

Read and write each Fahrenheit temperature shown.

4.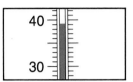

5.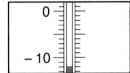

Choose the most reasonable temperature.

6. wearing a light sweater outdoors
 a. 90°F   **b.** 32°F   **c.** 64°F

7. building a snow fort
 a. 24°F   **b.** 49°F   **c.** 50°F

8. oven temperature for baking bread
 a. 78°F   **b.** 100°F   **c.** 325°F

9. boiling water
 a. 110°F   **b.** 200°F   **c.** 212°F

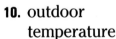
Think and Apply

DATA **Work in a small group. Estimate each temperature. Then use a Fahrenheit thermometer to measure. Read your estimates and the actual measurements.**

10. outdoor temperature

11. indoor temperature

12. temperature of hot tap water

13. temperature of cold tap water

14. temperature inside a refrigerator

15. temperature inside a freezer

16. What is the difference in degrees between the highest and lowest temperatures you found?

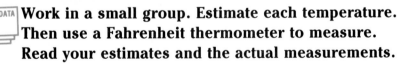

JOURNAL WRITING

If the temperature changes from 8°F to ⁻14°F, how many degrees did it fall? Explain.

1. $24.87
     + 39.42

2.   439
     × 39

3.   486
     254
    +395

4. 408 ÷ 7

5. 987 ÷ 32

6. 14.3 + 8.2

7. 9 − 0.5

8. 7.4 + 2.36

9. $\frac{3}{5} + \frac{1}{10}$

10. $\frac{1}{2} - \frac{1}{3}$

11. $\frac{1}{3} + \frac{3}{5}$

12. $\frac{8}{10} - \frac{4}{10}$

Write a fraction for each.

13. 0.9

14. 0.23

15. 0.02

16. 0.8

17. 0.10

18. 0.5

19. 0.2

SHOW WHAT YOU KNOW

Interview: Calculators and a Kite Maker

Carl Cleary is a kite maker in Tampa, Florida. He makes kites of different shapes and sizes. "I use a calculator to figure out how many square inches of material I will need. I also use a calculator to find the number of inches of framing string."

A. Kite **A** is made from a square piece of material, 17 inches on a side. To find the number of square inches of material needed, find the area of the kite.

Area = 17 in. × 17 in.
Area = 289 square inches

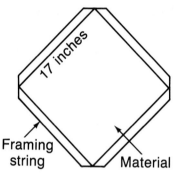

Framing string

Material

B. To find the number of inches of framing string, find the perimeter of the kite.

Perimeter = 17 in. + 17 in. + 17 in. + 17 in.
Perimeter = 68 in.

68 in. of framing string are needed.

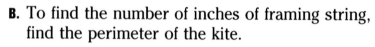

B.

16 inches

16 inches

10 inches

10 inches

C. Why are the measurements for perimeter and area different?

D. What does *perimeter* mean? What does *area* mean?

Sharing Your Ideas

Kite B is made from two squares. Use your calculator to solve.

1. What is the total number of inches of framing string that is needed for this kite?

2. How many square inches of material are needed for this kite?

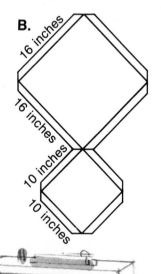

Extending Your Thinking

Kite C is a square that has two streamers. Each streamer is a rectangle. Use your calculator to solve.

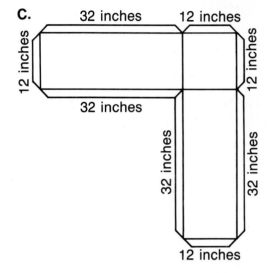

C.

3. How many square inches of material are needed for the square part of the kite?

4. How many square inches of material are needed to make the two streamers? to make the entire kite?

5. How many inches of framing string are needed for the kite? Explain how you found the answer.

This is a box kite. The boxes do not have tops or bottoms. Each side of the box is a square, 12 inches on a side.

6. What is the area of each side of the box?

7. How many square inches of material are needed to make each box? to make the kite?

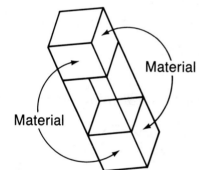

Show What You Know

8. What is a *perimeter?* What is an *area?* How can you use multiplication to find the perimeter of a square? to find the area of a square?

9. Which of these measures could be an area? Explain.
   a. 25 inches   **b.** 25 square inches

MEASURING TOOLS

Ghana is a country on the western coast of Africa. The Akan people of Ghana used brass weights to weigh things such as gold dust.

WORKING TOGETHER

1. Work in a small group. Use clay to make your own set of weights. Consider these questions as you plan.

   • How many weights should there be in the set?

   • What size should each weight be?

   • Should the weights be decorative or plain?

2. Select several objects in the classroom to weigh. Use a balance scale and your set of weights to weigh each object. Record the weight of each object in a chart.

3. Prepare a written or oral report about your group's set of weights. Be sure to explain the various weights you have included and the significance of any decoration.

4. Share your group's chart with the class. Discuss the following questions.

   • Did every group weigh the same objects?

   • If two groups weighed the same object, was the same amount recorded in each group's chart? Why or why not?

CHAPTER REVIEW/TEST

Measure to the nearest inch, $\frac{1}{2}$ in., $\frac{1}{4}$ in., and $\frac{1}{8}$ in.

1.

2.

Choose the best answer for each.

3. The living room is about _____ long.

   a. 20 ft   **b.** 20 yd   **c.** 20 in.

4. We ice skate outdoors in _____ weather.

   a. 85°F   **b.** 40°F   **c.** 20°F

5. The barbells weigh about _____.

   a. 12 lb   **b.** 12 oz   **c.** 12 T

6. The juice pitcher holds about _____.

   a. 1 c   **b.** 1 pt   **c.** 1 gal

Complete.

7. 14 lb = _____ oz

8. 8 c = _____ pt

9. _____ ft = 36 in.

10. 8,000 lb = _____ T

11. 4 yd = _____ ft

12. _____ gal = 16 qt

13. _____ yd = 216 in.

14. 5 gal = _____ qt

15. 3 mi = _____ yd

16. _____ in. = 5 ft

17. _____ lb = 112 oz

18. 6 T = _____ lb

Solve.

19. Fully clothed, Gary weighs 88 pounds. **What if** he puts on a 2 lb 8 oz winter coat and a 9 oz wool hat? How much does he weigh now?

20. Melissa uses 6 ounces of butter for 1 loaf of banana bread. How many loaves of bread can she make with 2 pounds of butter?

Think Carol is having a party for 24 children. She wants to have enough juice so that each child can drink 2 cups. How many gallons of juice should she buy?

Measure Up

A **ratio** is used to compare two numbers.

The ratio of **mouth to ears** is **1 to 2.**

The ratio of **fingers to hands** is **10 to 2.**

The ratio of **hands to fingers** is **2 to 10.**

Work with a partner.

Materials: customary tape measure, Workmat 32

1. Measure each of the following to the nearest inch. Then record the measurements as ratios on Workmat 32.

   a. your height to the length of your arm

   b. your height to the distance around your head

   c. the length of your arm to the distance around your wrist

   d. the distance around your neck to the distance around your wrist

   e. the distance around your thumb to the distance around your neck

   f. the length of your thumb to the length of your hand

   g. the length of your hand to the length of your arm

2. Compare your ratios with those of your partner. Which of the ratios were about the same? Which were different?

HOME CONNECTION

Your child has been learning about fractions, measurement, volume, area, and perimeter in Chapters **11–13**. Now you can help him or her use these concepts in a creative way.

Work together to design and make placemats with mosaic rectangles.

Mosaic Placemats

Materials: 4 sheets of grid paper, 2 pieces of 12 in. by 18 in. clear plastic with a sticky back, colored magazine pictures, tape, scissors

1. Tape together 2 sheets of graph paper to make one large sheet.

2. Draw a design for your placemat on the large sheet of paper. Use only rectangles.

3. Using another piece of graph paper, cut out rectangles for each part of your design. Now use these pieces as patterns to cut out rectangles from the colored magazine pictures.

4. Tape the graph paper design to your working surface. Over this, tape one sheet of the clear plastic with the sticky side up. Carefully place the colored rectangles on the stickly plastic over the design.

5. Carefully lay the second sheet of plastic over the first so that the sticky sides are together. Trim with scissors, if needed.

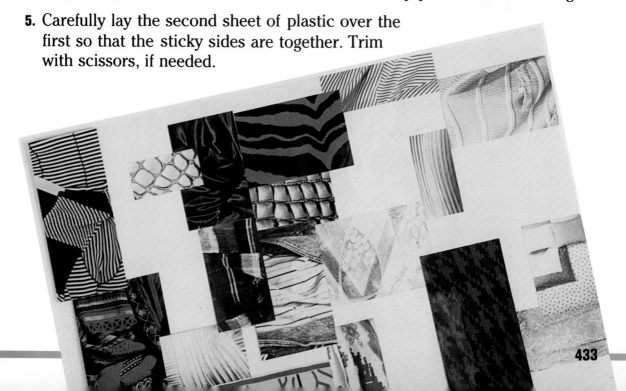

FINAL REVIEW

Choose the correct answer. Write A, B, C, or D.

1. Write 6,000 + 80 + 5 in standard form.

  A 685   **C** 6,085

  B 6,805   **D** not given

2.
$$\begin{array}{r} 90,038 \\ -25,634 \end{array}$$

  A 64,404   **C** 65,404

  B 75,604   **D** not given

3. Which month had the most rain?

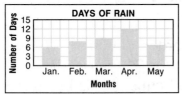

  A January   **C** May

  B March   **D** not given

4. $4 \times 9 = \square$

  A 32   **C** 36

  B 34   **D** not given

5. $56 \div 7 = \square$

  A 6   **C** 8

  B 7   **D** not given

6. $3,649 \times 8 = \square$

  A 29,192   **C** 28,822

  B 29,182   **D** not given

7.
$$\begin{array}{r} \$5.20 \\ \times \quad 30 \end{array}$$

  A $86.00   **C** $156.00

  B $15.60   **D** not given

8. $553 \div 60 = n$

  A 90 R13   **C** 9 R13

  B 8 R10   **D** not given

9. Name the angle.

  A straight   **C** obtuse

  B right   **D** not given

10. What fractional part is shaded?

  A $\dfrac{3}{7}$ **C** $\dfrac{3}{4}$

  B $\dfrac{4}{7}$ **D** not given

11.

$$\frac{4}{5} = \frac{\square}{10}$$

  A 8   **C** 10

  B 16   **D** not given

12. Compare. 8.02 ⬤ 8.1

  A $<$ **C** $=$

  B $>$ **D** not given

Choose the correct answer. Write A, B, C, or D.

13. Find the perimeter.

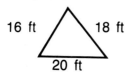

16 ft   18 ft

20 ft

A 44 ft   **C** 52 ft

B 54 ft   **D** not given

14. What point does (2,1) locate?

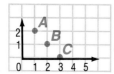

A A   **C** B

B C   **D** not given

15. □□□□□□   □□□

$$\frac{1}{6} + \frac{2}{3}$$

A $\frac{5}{6}$ **C** $\frac{4}{6}$

B $\frac{7}{6}$ **D** not given

16. What unit would you use to measure the length of a soccer field?

A gallons   **C** miles

B yards   **D** not given

17. 8 pt = _____ qt

A 2   **C** 6

B 4   **D** not given

Which fact do you need to solve?

18. Portia walks dogs for senior citizens. She walks 3 more dogs in the afternoon than she does in the morning. How many dogs does she walk in all?

A number of dogs   **C** number of dogs in the morning

B number all week   **D** not given

Solve.

John ordered a medium cup of yogurt for $1.85. He also bought 2 small cups for his brother and sister at $1.19 each.

19. How much did he spend on yogurt?

A $3.04   **C** $4.03

B $3.03   **D** not given

20. What was his change from $10.00?

A $6.23   **C** $6.77

B $5.77   **D** not given

Solve.

21. If 11 desks measure 66 feet and each desk is the same length, how long are 3 desks?

A 12 feet   **C** 6 feet

B 18 feet   **D** not given

Extra Practice

Add. pages 4–5

1. $4 + 7 = \square$ 2. $9 + 7 = \square$ 3. $6 + 5 = \square$ 4. $3 + 8 + 7 = \square$

5. $5 + 9 = \square$ 6. $8 + 6 = \square$ 7. $7 + 8 = \square$ 8. $9 + 5 + 1 = \square$

Subtract. Check by adding. pages 6–7

9. $\begin{array}{r} 12 \\ -\ 4 \\ \hline \end{array}$ 10. $\begin{array}{r} 8 \\ -5 \\ \hline \end{array}$ 11. $\begin{array}{r} 18 \\ -\ 9 \\ \hline \end{array}$ 12. $\begin{array}{r} 15 \\ -\ 7 \\ \hline \end{array}$ 13. $\begin{array}{r} 9 \\ -4 \\ \hline \end{array}$ 14. $\begin{array}{r} 11 \\ -\ 8 \\ \hline \end{array}$ 15. $\begin{array}{r} 12 \\ -\ 6 \\ \hline \end{array}$

Find each missing number. pages 8–9

16. $\square + 8 = 11$ 17. $\square - 4 = 6$ 18. $8 - \square = 2$ 19. $18 - 9 = \square$

20. $7 + 9 = \square$ 21. $5 + \square = 13$ 22. $\square - 7 = 7$ 23. $9 - \square = 6$

24. $15 - 7 = \square$ 25. $4 + 8 = \square$ 26. $17 - \square = 8$ 27. $7 + \square = 13$

Set B

Write each number in standard form. pages 14–19

1. $2,000 + 800 + 6$

2. one thousand, thirty-three

3. $40,000 + 7,000 + 900$

4. 981 thousand, seventy

5. sixty-one thousand, twelve

6. 12 million, 105 thousand

7. three hundred four million, sixteen thousand, nine hundred

8. six million, two hundred thousand, five hundred eighteen

Set C

Compare. Write >, <, or = for ⬤. pages 22–23

1. $205 \ ⬤ \ 209$ 2. $4,132 \ ⬤ \ 4,123$ 3. $7,856 \ ⬤ \ 8,856$

4. $73,456 \ ⬤ \ 74,356$ 5. $8,499 \ ⬤ \ 8,498$ 6. $6,127 \ ⬤ \ 6,127$

List these numbers in order from least to greatest. pages 22–23

7. 854   485   584

8. 638   583   683

9. 1,421   1,431   1,412

10. 4,099   4,090   4,900

Set A

Round to the nearest ten. pages 26–27

1. 682　　2. 347　　3. 707　　4. 844　　5. 198　　6. 176

Round to the nearest hundred dollars. pages 28–29

7. $8,106　　8. $4,249　　9. $7,068　　10. $6,827　　11. $5,555

Round to the nearest thousand. pages 28–29

12. 4,259　　13. 12,362　　14. 94,600　　15. 9,507　　16. 61,815

Set B

Estimate each sum two ways. pages 38–39

1.
$$\begin{array}{r} 82 \\ +39 \\ \hline \end{array}$$
2.
$$\begin{array}{r} 68 \\ +48 \\ \hline \end{array}$$
3.
$$\begin{array}{r} 279 \\ +564 \\ \hline \end{array}$$
4.
$$\begin{array}{r} 435 \\ +\ 87 \\ \hline \end{array}$$
5.
$$\begin{array}{r} \$2.19 \\ +\ 6.39 \\ \hline \end{array}$$

6. 73 + 64 + 56　　　7. 823 + 791　　　8. $5.83 + $.75

Estimate first. Then add. pages 40–43

9.
$$\begin{array}{r} 45 \\ +78 \\ \hline \end{array}$$
10.
$$\begin{array}{r} 39 \\ +80 \\ \hline \end{array}$$
11.
$$\begin{array}{r} 55 \\ +24 \\ \hline \end{array}$$
12.
$$\begin{array}{r} 97 \\ +42 \\ \hline \end{array}$$
13.
$$\begin{array}{r} 88 \\ +15 \\ \hline \end{array}$$

14.
$$\begin{array}{r} 61 \\ 14 \\ +23 \\ \hline \end{array}$$
15.
$$\begin{array}{r} 29 \\ 35 \\ +11 \\ \hline \end{array}$$
16.
$$\begin{array}{r} 85 \\ 44 \\ +91 \\ \hline \end{array}$$
17.
$$\begin{array}{r} 17 \\ 35 \\ +\ 8 \\ \hline \end{array}$$
18.
$$\begin{array}{r} 74 \\ 80 \\ +87 \\ \hline \end{array}$$

Set C

Add. Check by estimating or adding up. pages 44–47

1.
$$\begin{array}{r} 247 \\ +349 \\ \hline \end{array}$$
2.
$$\begin{array}{r} 672 \\ +846 \\ \hline \end{array}$$
3.
$$\begin{array}{r} \$3.64 \\ +\ \ .75 \\ \hline \end{array}$$
4.
$$\begin{array}{r} 903 \\ +849 \\ \hline \end{array}$$
5.
$$\begin{array}{r} 726 \\ +374 \\ \hline \end{array}$$

6.
$$\begin{array}{r} 8,247 \\ +3,859 \\ \hline \end{array}$$
7.
$$\begin{array}{r} 1,213 \\ +6,478 \\ \hline \end{array}$$
8.
$$\begin{array}{r} 44,293 \\ +17,842 \\ \hline \end{array}$$
9.
$$\begin{array}{r} \$72.83 \\ +\ 85.35 \\ \hline \end{array}$$
10.
$$\begin{array}{r} 93,842 \\ +49,259 \\ \hline \end{array}$$

11. 742 + 87 + 613 = ☐　　　　12. 1,434 + 23,703 + 92 = ☐

Extra Practice

Set A

Estimate each difference using rounding. pages 52–53

1.	93	2.	648	3.	407	4.	$6.93	5.	853
	−47		−390		−143		− 2.19		−835

Set B

Subtract. Check by adding. pages 54–57

1.	75	2.	81	3.	475	4.	842	5.	$6.50
	−62		−74		−203		−617		− 2.75

Subtract. Check by adding. pages 58–59

6.	708	7.	603	8.	500	9.	$4.05	10.	240
	− 49		−234		−317		− 3.89		−157

Subtract. Choose paper and pencil or a calculator. page 60–61

11.	4,738	12.	3,452	13.	1,001	14.	21,305	15.	$721.38
	−2,516		−1,826		− 99		−17,666		− 447.16

Set C

Write the value. pages 64–65

1. 3 quarters, 4 nickels

2. 4 dimes, 3 nickels, 7 pennies

3. 3 five-dollar bills, 2 one-dollar bills, 7 quarters, 3 dimes

---
Set D

Write each time using numbers. Then tell the time 1 h and 20 min later. pages 76–79

1.
2.
3.
4.

Estimate how much time has passed. pages 78–79

5. start 8:05 A.M.
   end 11:30 A.M.

6. start 1:54 P.M.
   end 2:28 P.M.

7. start 3:35 P.M.
   end 6:05 P.M.

Set A

Use the graph to answer each question. pages 84–85

1. What does the symbol ☂ mean?

2. Which month had the most rainy days?

3. Which month had the fewest rainy days?

4. How many more rainy days were there in April than July?

5. How many days did it rain during the 5 months?

NUMBER OF RAINY DAYS	
March	☂ ☂ ☂ ☂ ☂
April	☂ ☂ ☂ ☂ ☂
May	☂ ☂ ☂ ☂
June	☂ ☂ ☂
July	☂ ☂ ☂ ☂

Each ☂ stands for 2 days.

Set B

Tanya wrote on cards the number of shells she collected each day on vacation. pages 88–89, 94–99

1. Make a list with the days of the week in order. Start with Monday.

2. What type of graph would you use to display the data?

3. Use the data to make the type of graph you answered in **2**.

4. Which day had the greatest decrease from the previous day?

Tuesday 12	Wednesday 10
Thursday 16	Monday 15
Saturday 12	Friday 18

Set C

Multiply. pages 112–123

1. $\begin{array}{r}7\\ \times 2\end{array}$	**2.** $\begin{array}{r}9\\ \times 3\end{array}$	**3.** $\begin{array}{r}5\\ \times 4\end{array}$	**4.** $\begin{array}{r}3\\ \times 5\end{array}$	**5.** $\begin{array}{r}3\\ \times 0\end{array}$	**6.** $\begin{array}{r}2\\ \times 4\end{array}$	**7.** $\begin{array}{r}5\\ \times 6\end{array}$
8. $\begin{array}{r}6\\ \times 1\end{array}$	**9.** $\begin{array}{r}9\\ \times 2\end{array}$	**10.** $\begin{array}{r}3\\ \times 6\end{array}$	**11.** $\begin{array}{r}2\\ \times 8\end{array}$	**12.** $\begin{array}{r}8\\ \times 3\end{array}$	**13.** $\begin{array}{r}3\\ \times 4\end{array}$	**14.** $\begin{array}{r}4\\ \times 7\end{array}$

15. $6 \times 9 = \square$ **16.** $0 \times 8 = \square$ **17.** $7 \times 4 = \square$ **18.** $3 \times 8 = \square$

Extra Practice

━━━━━━━━━━━━━━━━━━━━━━━ **Set A** ━━━━━━━━━━━━━━━━━━━━━━━

Find each missing factor. pages 132–133

1. □ × 3 = 12   **2.** 7 × □ = 42   **3.** □ × 1 = 9   **4.** 5 × □ = 0

5. 8 × □ = 72   **6.** □ × 9 = 0   **7.** 6 × □ = 54   **8.** □ × 8 = 64

9. □ × 9 = 9   **10.** □ × 2 = 14   **11.** 9 × □ = 27   **12.** 4 × □ = 36

━━━━━━━━━━━━━━━━━━━━━━━ **Set B** ━━━━━━━━━━━━━━━━━━━━━━━

Find each quotient. pages 134–143

1. 2)‾16‾   **2.** 4)‾24‾   **3.** 6)‾42‾   **4.** 3)‾24‾   **5.** 4)‾16‾

6. 36 ÷ 6 = □   **7.** 18 ÷ 3 = □   **8.** 10 ÷ 2 = □   **9.** 0 ÷ 4 = □

Divide.

10. 5)‾40‾   **11.** 8)‾56‾   **12.** 10)‾10‾   **13.** 7)‾21‾   **14.** 9)‾36‾

15. 27 ÷ 9 = □   **16.** 49 ÷ 7 = □   **17.** 72 ÷ 8 = □   **18.** 80 ÷ 10 = □

━━━━━━━━━━━━━━━━━━━━━━━ **Set C** ━━━━━━━━━━━━━━━━━━━━━━━

Tell whether each answer is even or odd.
Then use pencil and paper or a calculator to find the answer. pages 144–145

1. 85 + 237   **2.** 490 − 152   **3.** 623 × 47

4. 2,364 − 985   **5.** 7,291 + 1,468   **6.** 94 × 89

━━━━━━━━━━━━━━━━━━━━━━━ **Set D** ━━━━━━━━━━━━━━━━━━━━━━━

Multiply. pages 154–155

1. 70   **2.** 80   **3.** 200   **4.** 500   **5.** 6,000
 × 6   × 3   × 9   × 7   × 4

6. 5 × 300 = □   **7.** 8 × 4,000 = □   **8.** 6 × 9,000 = □

━━━━━━━━━━━━━━━━━━━━━━━ **Set E** ━━━━━━━━━━━━━━━━━━━━━━━

Estimate each product. pages 156–157

1. 48   **2.** 21   **3.** 135   **4.** 872   **5.** 2,706
 × 7   × 6   × 8   × 5   × 9

6. 3 × 219   **7.** 4 × 366   **8.** 2 × 4,404

440

Set A

Estimate. Then find each product. pages 162–165

1. 82	**2.** 61	**3.** 26	**4.** 38	**5.** 96	**6.** 45
$\times\ 3$	$\times\ 5$	$\times\ 4$	$\times\ 7$	$\times\ 2$	$\times\ 6$

7. 212	**8.** 183	**9.** 605	**10.** 313	**11.** 491	**12.** 763
$\times\ \ 4$	$\times\ \ 2$	$\times\ \ 8$	$\times\ \ 7$	$\times\ \ 8$	$\times\ \ 3$

Estimate. Then multiply. pages 166–167

13. $6 \times 75 = \square$ **14.** $3 \times 204 = \square$ **15.** $7 \times 435 = \square$

16. $8 \times 638 = \square$ **17.** $5 \times 519 = \square$ **18.** $9 \times 187 = \square$

Set B

Use mental math, pencil and paper, or a calculator to multiply. Check each product with an estimate. pages 172–173

1. 4,183	**2.** 2,104	**3.** 4,321	**4.** 8,635	**5.** 7,909
$\times\ \ \ \ 4$	$\times\ \ \ \ 8$	$\times\ \ \ \ 2$	$\times\ \ \ \ 7$	$\times\ \ \ \ 9$

Estimate. Then multiply. pages 174–175

6. $3.25	**7.** $1.87	**8.** $30.89	**9.** $21.50	**10.** $10.99
$\times\ \ \ \ 5$	$\times\ \ \ \ 6$	$\times\ \ \ \ 4$	$\times\ \ \ \ 7$	$\times\ \ \ \ 3$

11. $9 \times \$4.89 = \square$ **12.** $2 \times \$7.95 = \square$ **13.** $8 \times \$1.39 = \square$

14. $4 \times \$11.25 = \square$ **15.** $6 \times \$22.02 = \square$ **16.** $5 \times \$35.47 = \square$

Set C

Find each product. pages 188–191

1. 28	**2.** 53	**3.** 81	**4.** 35	**5.** 142	**6.** 203
$\times 10$	$\times 30$	$\times 50$	$\times 60$	$\times\ 90$	$\times\ 80$

7. $60 \times 90 = n$ **8.** $49 \times 70 = n$ **9.** $650 \times 40 = n$

Estimate each product. pages 192–193

10. 72	**11.** 47	**12.** 89	**13.** 232	**14.** 666	**15.** 819
$\times 31$	$\times 42$	$\times 12$	$\times\ 57$	$\times\ 77$	$\times\ 38$

16. 68×73 **17.** 704×86 **18.** 557×19

Extra Practice

<hr>
Set A

Estimate first. Then multiply. pages 198–199

1. 83 ×21	**2.** 48 ×17	**3.** 70 ×32	**4.** 92 ×87	**5.** 44 ×65	**6.** 29 ×14
7. 61 ×97	**8.** 18 ×15	**9.** 67 ×76	**10.** 40 ×60	**11.** 37 ×29	**12.** 85 ×44

13. $12 \times 48 = n$

14. $75 \times 80 = n$

15. $52 \times 79 = n$

16. $93 \times 11 = n$

17. $66 \times 47 = n$

18. $43 \times 43 = n$

<hr>
Set B

Multiply. Estimate to be sure your answer makes sense. pages 204–205

1. 217 × 32	**2.** 340 × 28	**3.** 125 × 16	**4.** 805 × 43	**5.** 624 × 72	**6.** 447 × 29
7. 347 × 94	**8.** 602 × 45	**9.** 782 × 21	**10.** 961 × 86	**11.** 485 × 54	**12.** 700 × 36

Estimate. Then find each product. pages 206–207

13. $.81 × 17	**14.** $.65 × 20	**15.** $.49 × 36	**16.** $.17 × 82	**17.** $1.05 × 12	**18.** $2.40 × 24
19. $3.62 × 63	**20.** $4.27 × 52	**21.** $7.88 × 27	**22.** $1.98 × 45	**23.** $2.15 × 24	**24.** $8.09 × 96

<hr>
Set C

Estimate first. Then use mental math, paper and pencil, or a calculator to find each product. pages 208–209

1. 478 × 70	**2.** 1,426 × 35	**3.** 6,109 × 27	**4.** 9,830 × 72	**5.** 6,316 × 84
6. $3.98 × 20	**7.** $7.43 × 92	**8.** $10.49 × 36	**9.** $49.95 × 66	**10.** $72.09 × 75

Set A

Divide. Check by multiplying. pages 220–223

1. $6\overline{)45}$ 2. $8\overline{)37}$ 3. $9\overline{)72}$ 4. $4\overline{)21}$ 5. $3\overline{)19}$

6. $7\overline{)50}$ 7. $2\overline{)19}$ 8. $5\overline{)48}$ 9. $8\overline{)61}$ 10. $9\overline{)76}$

11. $3\overline{)120}$ 12. $6\overline{)540}$ 13. $2\overline{)160}$ 14. $7\overline{)350}$ 15. $8\overline{)6,400}$

16. $3,600 \div 4$ 17. $80 \div 9$ 18. $4,000 \div 5$ 19. $2,400 \div 3$

Estimate each quotient. pages 228–229

20. $3\overline{)52}$ 21. $8\overline{)184}$ 22. $6\overline{)250}$ 23. $4\overline{)903}$ 24. $9\overline{)797}$

25. $7\overline{)643}$ 26. $5\overline{)884}$ 27. $2\overline{)742}$ 28. $6\overline{)813}$ 29. $8\overline{)514}$

Set B

Divide. Check by estimating. pages 230–233

1. $4\overline{)87}$ 2. $3\overline{)75}$ 3. $6\overline{)97}$ 4. $9\overline{)49}$ 5. $7\overline{)88}$

6. $5\overline{)432}$ 7. $8\overline{)916}$ 8. $2\overline{)504}$ 9. $6\overline{)735}$ 10. $4\overline{)947}$

11. $612 \div 9$ 12. $777 \div 3$ 13. $340 \div 7$ 14. $78 \div 8$ 15. $671 \div 5$

Find each average. pages 238–239

16. 7, 9, 8, 6, 5 17. 98, 93, 85 18. 2, 3, 4, 6, 7, 8

Set C

Divide. Check by multiplying. pages 240–243

1. $4\overline{)414}$ 2. $7\overline{)851}$ 3. $8\overline{)879}$ 4. $5\overline{)600}$ 5. $9\overline{)943}$

6. $2\overline{)608}$ 7. $3\overline{)452}$ 8. $6\overline{)382}$ 9. $8\overline{)564}$ 10. $7\overline{)703}$

11. $5\overline{)\$4.85}$ 12. $4\overline{)\$.96}$ 13. $9\overline{)\$9.90}$ 14. $6\overline{)\$5.04}$ 15. $3\overline{)\$8.97}$

16. $\$6.50 \div 2$ 17. $\$6.36 \div 6$ 18. $\$4.55 \div 7$

Divide. Check by multiplying. pages 246–249

19. $20\overline{)88}$ 20. $10\overline{)42}$ 21. $30\overline{)205}$ 22. $50\overline{)417}$

23. $40\overline{)348}$ 24. $60\overline{)500}$ 25. $80\overline{)720}$ 26. $90\overline{)465}$

Extra Practice

Name each polygon. Write the number of sides and vertices.
pages 256–257

1.
2.
3.
4.
5.

Use the figures at the right. pages 258–265

6. Name two line segments that have *A* as an endpoint.

7. Name a ray with endpoint *J*.

8. Is ∠*BFG* acute, right, or obtuse?

9. Is ∠*QPR* acute, right, or obtuse?

10. Name two perpendicular lines.

11. Name a diameter.

12. Name three radii.

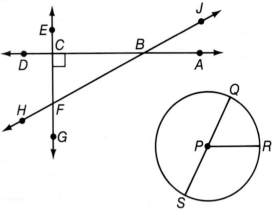

Set B

pages 270–273

a.
b.
c.
d.

1. Which pairs of figures are congruent?

2. Which pairs of figures are similar?

Set C

Is the dashed line a line of symmetry? Write *yes* or *no*. Then write the number of symmetry lines for the figure. pages 274–275

1.
2.
3.
4.
5.

Set A

Write the fraction that tells what part is blue. pages 290–293

1.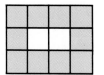

2.

3.

4.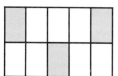

5.

6.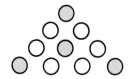

7.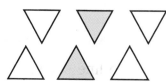

Find each missing number. pages 294–295

8. $\frac{1}{4}$ of 12 = n **9.** $\frac{3}{4}$ of 20 = n **10.** $\frac{3}{5}$ of 30 = n **11.** $\frac{3}{3}$ of 6 = n

12. $\frac{3}{10}$ of 70 = n **13.** $\frac{1}{6}$ of 54 = n **14.** $\frac{5}{8}$ of 24 = n **15.** $\frac{1}{2}$ of 18 = n

---

Set B

Write the equivalent fraction for each. pages 300–301

1. $\frac{2}{3} = \frac{2 \times 4}{3 \times 4} = \frac{\square}{12}$ **2.** $\frac{1}{5} = \frac{1 \times 2}{5 \times 2} = \frac{\square}{10}$ **3.** $\frac{3}{4} = \frac{3 \times 4}{4 \times 4} = \frac{\square}{16}$

4. $\frac{2}{3} = \frac{\square}{6}$ **5.** $\frac{3}{5} = \frac{\square}{20}$ **6.** $\frac{3}{4} = \frac{\square}{12}$ **7.** $\frac{5}{8} = \frac{\square}{16}$

Write a mixed number or whole number that tells what part is blue. page 302–303

8.

9.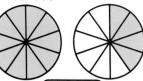

10.

Set C

Write a decimal for each. pages 314–317

1. $\frac{4}{10}$ **2.** $\frac{77}{100}$ **3.** $\frac{80}{100}$ **4.** $\frac{2}{10}$ **5.** $\frac{2}{100}$

6. $1\frac{3}{10}$ **7.** $3\frac{18}{100}$ **8.** $5\frac{5}{100}$ **9.** $6\frac{91}{100}$ **10.** $4\frac{60}{100}$

11. seven tenths   **12.** six and forty-one hundredths   **13.** nine hundredths

Extra Practice

Set A

Compare. Use >, <, or = for ⬤. pages 318–319

1. 0.6 ⬤ 0.8   **2.** 1.3 ⬤ 0.7   **3.** 4.9 ⬤ 0.49

4. 2.7 ⬤ 2.07   **5.** 6.59 ⬤ 6.95   **6.** 3.47 ⬤ 3.5

List these decimals in order from least to greatest. pages 318–319

7. 0.7, 0.9, 0.6   **8.** 1.01, 1.11, 1.10   **9.** 4.5, 0.45, 5.4

Set B

Add or subtract. pages 322–325

1. 6.8	**2.** 4.7	**3.** 9.4	**4.** 17.5	**5.** 46.3
+2.7	+8.2	−7.7	− 9.8	−34.8

6. 1.94	**7.** 18.3	**8.** 7.24	**9.** 12.02	**10.** 3.5
+4.21	+1.45	−4.18	− 9.9	+18.75

11. 2.3 + 7.8   **12.** 16.3 − 8.4   **13.** 40.7 − 13.9

14. 49.6 + 17.8   **15.** 40 − 29.3   **16.** 18.1 − 1.81

Set C

Choose cm, m, or km to measure each. pages 332–333

1. distance walked in 20 minutes   **2.** distance a train travels in 1 hour
3. length of your shoe   **4.** length of a school bus

Choose g or kg to measure the weight of each. pages 334–335

5. a pumpkin   **6.** a postcard   **7.** a potato

Choose mL or L to measure each. pages 338–339

8. bottle of cider   **9.** baby bottle   **10.** water in fish tank

Choose the most reasonable temperature. pages 340–341

11. glass of cold milk: **a.** 5°C   **b.** 15°C   **c.** 25°C

12. cup of hot chocolate: **a.** 20°C   **b.** 40°C   **c.** 80°C

Set A

Find the perimeter of each polygon. pages 352–353

1.
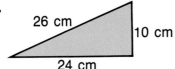
26 cm   10 cm   24 cm

2.
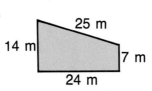
25 m   14 m   7 m   24 m

3.
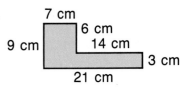
7 cm   6 cm   14 cm   9 cm   3 cm   21 cm

Find the area of each region. pages 354–357

4.

5.
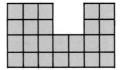

6.
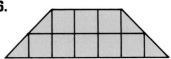

Name the space figure suggested by each object. pages 362–363

7.

8.

9.

10.

11.

Set B

What point does each ordered pair locate? pages 366–367

1. (2,1)   **2.** (6,5)   **3.** (4,5)

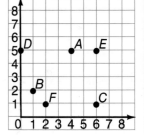

Give an ordered pair to name each point.

4. B   **5.** D   **6.** C

Graph the points on grid paper. Connect the points in order. Name the letter of the alphabet formed. pages 368–369

7. (2,3), (2,8), (5,3), (5,8)   **8.** (4,6), (1,6), (1,1), (4,1)

Set C

Write $0, \frac{1}{2},$ **or 1 for the best estimate of each.** pages 378–379

1. $\frac{5}{8}$ **2.** $\frac{9}{10}$ **3.** $\frac{1}{7}$ **4.** $\frac{3}{7}$ **5.** $\frac{11}{12}$

Compare. Write $>, <,$ **or** $=$ **for each** ⬤**.** pages 380–381

6. $\frac{3}{8}$ ⬤ $\frac{7}{8}$ **7.** $\frac{4}{5}$ ⬤ $\frac{2}{5}$ **8.** $\frac{5}{6}$ ⬤ $\frac{5}{7}$ **9.** $\frac{3}{5}$ ⬤ $\frac{6}{10}$ **10.** $\frac{5}{8}$ ⬤ $\frac{3}{4}$

Extra Practice

Set A

Add or subtract. pages 382–389

1. $\frac{3}{5} + \frac{1}{5} = \square$

2. $\frac{4}{7} + \frac{2}{7} = \square$

3. $\frac{5}{8} - \frac{1}{8} = \square$

4. $\frac{7}{9} - \frac{4}{9} = \square$

5. $\begin{array}{r} \frac{1}{3} \\ + \frac{1}{6} \end{array}$

6. $\begin{array}{r} \frac{7}{8} \\ - \frac{1}{4} \end{array}$

7. $\begin{array}{r} \frac{3}{4} \\ - \frac{1}{2} \end{array}$

8. $\begin{array}{r} \frac{11}{12} \\ - \frac{2}{3} \end{array}$

9. $\begin{array}{r} \frac{3}{10} \\ + \frac{1}{2} \end{array}$

Set B

Eight marbles—4 red, 3 white, and 1 blue—are placed in a bag. A marble is drawn from the bag without looking. pages 394–401

1. List the three possible outcomes.

2. What is the probability of each color?

3. Find the probability of drawing a blue or white marble.

4. What other event has the same probability?

5. List the different orders that Anna, Barry, and Carlos can be lined up in the lunch line.

6. Dottie joins the line but is not first. List the possible orders of the line.

Set C

Choose inch, foot, yard, or mile to measure each. page 412–415

1. height of a tree

2. length of your shoe

3. width of an envelope

4. distance across Atlantic Ocean

Choose ounce, pound, or ton to measure each. pages 416–417

5. weight of an apple

6. weight of a subway car

7. your weight

8. weight of bucket of sand

Set D

Complete. pages 422–425

1. 2 gal = _____ qt

2. 10 c = _____ pt

3. 1 qt = _____ c

Read and write each Fahrenheit temperature. pages 426–427

4.

448

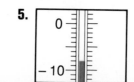

5.

6.

Extra Problem Solving

Set A

Solve. Use a calculator where appropriate. pages 11–13, 24–25

1. How many footballs are shown? soccer balls? baseballs?

2. Which kind of ball is the smallest?

3. How many more baseballs than footballs are there?

4. How many balls are there in all?

5. **What if** 2 more balls of each kind are added to the picture? How many balls of each kind will there be?

6. **What if** 3 more balls of each kind are added to the picture? How many more baseballs than footballs will there be?

Set B

Solve. Use a calculator where appropriate. pages 49–51, 62–63

1. Willie has 82 baseball cards in his collection. Alice has 45 cards. Kathy has 53 cards. Which girl has more cards? How many more?

2. Ellen scored 53 points in a board game. Pedro scored 12 more points than Ellen. The person with the lowest score wins. Who won?

3. Tracy and her father traveled 34 miles to the stadium. The game lasted 3 hours. Then they drove 34 miles home. How many miles in all did they travel?

4. During the summer, Suzu read 23 books in 8 weeks. Yoko read 17 books in 6 weeks. How many books in all did the 2 girls read?

Baseball cards are packaged in groups of 15, 50, and 75 cards each.

5. Ian bought 5 packages and had 265 cards. Which packages did he buy?

6. Mr. Dietz bought 4 packages and had more than 150 cards. What is the least number of cards he could have bought?

Extra Problem Solving

Set A

Solve. Use a calculator where appropriate. pages 91–93, 100–101

John has a paper route. He collects money each week.

MONEY COLLECTED FROM PAPER ROUTE	
Monday	$4.50
Tuesday	$7.25
Wednesday	$6.50
Thursday	$4.25
Friday	$5.75

1. How much money was collected for the entire week?

2. **What if** John needed to collect $32.00? How much more does he need to collect?

3. By which day had John collected at least half of the $32.00 that he needs to collect?

4. On which day did he visit the most customers?

5. John said that he collected more money on the 2 days that he collected the most than he collected during the rest of the week. Is he right? Explain.

6. One week John collected $32 in four days. He collected the same amount each day. How much did he collect each day?

Set B

Solve. Use a calculator where appropriate. pages 125–127, 144–145

1. Tickets to the Central Zoo are $3.00 for adults and $1.00 for children. How much did Mr. Cho pay for 2 adults and 3 children?

2. The keepers put 18 pounds of feed in the monkey cage each day. How many pounds of feed does each monkey get each day?

3. It costs $3 for a bag of bird food. How much did Pang Cho pay for 3 bags?

4. A kangaroo is 4 feet taller than a lion. How tall is a kangaroo?

5. Which example has a sum that is an even number? Explain how you know.

   a.   43   **b.**   72   **c.**   35
      + 14   + 19   + 53

6. Which example has a product that is an odd number? Explain how you know.

   a.   13   **b.**   25   **c.**   18
      × 6   × 3   × 7

Solve. Use a calculator where appropriate. pages 169–171, 178–179

Number of Tickets	Price per Ticket
1	$2.00
2	$1.90
3	$1.80
4	$1.70
5	——
6	——
7	——

1. The chart shows ticket prices for the Model Railroad show. What is the pattern?

2. If the pattern continues, what is the price of each ticket if you buy 5 tickets? 6 tickets?

3. The lowest price per ticket is $1.00. How many tickets do you have to buy to get that price?

4. What is the total cost if you buy 6 tickets?

5. If you have $10.00, will you be able to buy 7 tickets? Explain.

6. For $10 you can buy a special pass for 8 people. How much is saved by buying the pass instead of 8 individual tickets?

7. What is the total cost if you buy 10 tickets? 11 tickets? Compare your answers.

Solve. Use a calculator where appropriate. pages 201–203, 210–211

1. First-class postage is $.25 for the first ounce and $.20 for each additional ounce. What is the postage on a 4-ounce letter?

2. Parcel Post to Salem is $1.97 for up to 2 pounds. Each additional pound or part of a pound costs $.22. How much will it cost to send a 7-pound package?

3. Parking in the Park 'n Shop lot costs $.25 an hour for up to 3 hours, and $.50 an hour after 3 hours. How much will the Tylers pay for parking 4 hours?

4. Paula bought seven 25-cent stamps, two 20-cent stamps, and four 15-cent stamps. How much change did she get if she gave the clerk a $5.00 bill?

5. At the newstand, the *All News* magazine costs $1.75 each week. A one-year subscription costs $55. How much is saved by buying a subscription for one year?

6. To raise money, the choir had a music marathon for 5 hours. Tom had pledges of $6.20 per hour. Jim had pledges of $5.65 per hour. How much money did each raise?

Extra Problem Solving

Set A

Solve. Use a calculator where appropriate. pages 235–237, 244–245

1. Basketball shoes cost $34.75 a pair. Uniforms are $21.25 each. How much do 4 pairs of shoes cost?

2. The Mustangs basketball team has 9 players. How much will it cost for a uniform and shoes for one player?

3. Five players scored a total of 65 points. Each scored the same number of points. How many points did each player score?

4. The Mustangs scored 72 points in a game and won by 16 points. How many points did the other team score?

5. Manuel scored 17, 14, 19, and 18 points in his first four games. What was his point average for a game?

6. The Ace Sports Shop will supply 9 uniforms for the Mustangs for $180. How much less will each cost if they buy from Ace Sports Shop instead of paying $21.25 each?

Set B

Solve. Use a calculator where appropriate. pages 267–269, 280–281

1. From Building A, you walk 2 blocks east, 3 blocks south, 1 block west, 4 blocks south, 2 blocks east, and 7 blocks north. How far are you from Building A?

2. An elevator operator starts on the ground floor and goes 26 floors up, 4 floors down, 3 floors down, 9 floors up, and 2 floors up. On what floor is the elevator?

3. Mrs. Webb, Dr. Cruz, Ms. Green, and Mr. Elia have offices in the same building. Ms. Green is on a lower floor than Mrs. Webb. Dr. Cruz is on a higher floor than Mrs. Webb. Mr. Elia's office is on a floor between Ms. Green and Dr. Cruz. Whose office is on the highest floor?

4. Ben, Luisa, Karen, Dena, and Mike have desks in the same row. Ben is next to Karen. Luisa is between Karen and Dena. Mike is the farthest from Ben. Whose desk is in the middle?

5. Use dot paper. Draw a square for which the outline touches 12 dots.

6. Use dot paper. Draw a rectangle for which the outline touches 10 dots.

452

Solve. Use a calculator where appropriate. pages 297–299, 304–305

There are 16 boys and 24 girls in the school chorus.

1. One half of the boys are present. One half of the girls are present. Are there more girls or more boys present?

2. One fourth of the singers were absent from chorus practice. How many were absent? How many boys were absent? How many girls were absent?

There are 20 women and 30 men in the orchestra.

3. One half of the women are present for practice. One third of the men are present. Are there more men or women present, or are there the same number of men and women present? Explain.

4. On another day, one fifth of the orchestra members were absent from practice. How many members were present? How many women were present? Explain your answer.

5. Ms. Ruiz is designing a piece of cloth with red, white, and blue stripes. The middle stripe is white and on each side of it is a blue stripe. The next stripes in each direction are red, then white, then blue, and so on. There are 15 stripes in all. How many stripes are there of each color?

6. Fifteen cups are placed in a row. Each cup has one marble in it. Tanya starts at the beginning of the row and puts a marble in every second cup. Dan starts at the beginning and takes a marble from every third cup. How many cups now contain 2 marbles? 1 marble? 0 marbles?

Mr. Linden is putting tiles on a floor that is exactly 8 feet wide and 9 feet long.

7. How many tiles 1 foot by 1 foot, will Mr. Linden need to cover the floor? **What if** he used smaller tiles? Would he need more or fewer tiles?

8. One half of the tiles that he needs are white. The rest are green. How many 1 foot by 1 foot tiles of each color does he need?

9. Jack is very hungry. His mother said that he could have $\frac{1}{4}$ of pizza *A* or $\frac{1}{3}$ of pizza *B*. From which pizza should he take a piece if he wants the larger piece? Make a tracing of the pizzas on grid paper to check your answer.

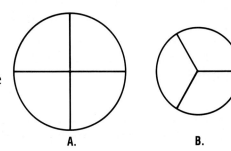

A.　　　　B.

Extra Problem Solving

Set A

Solve. Use a calculator where appropriate. pages 327–329, 342–343

1. You have one nickel, one dime, and one quarter in your pocket. You take out only one coin. How many different amounts of money could you take out of your pocket?

2. Paul, Yvonne, Tony, and Sonya like to hike in the woods. For safety, they hike only in pairs. How many different pairs of hikers are possible?

3. Mr. Cho mailed three packages. The postage was $2.40, $3.54, and $3.29. He had a $20 bill. How much did he have left for buying stamps?

4. Martha mailed four packages. The postage on each one was $2.40. The postage on a fifth package was $4.32. What was the total postage?

Eva's watch gains 3 minutes every hour. Flo's watch loses 2 minutes every hour.

5. Eva and Flo both set their watches at 12:00 noon. What time will each watch show at 2:00 P.M.?

6. At 3:00 P.M., Eva sets her watch back 10 minutes. What time will each watch show at 4:00 P.M.?

Set B

Solve. Use a calculator where appropriate. pages 359–361, 370–371

1. Benjamin paid $1.48 for a soda and an ice cream bar at the refreshment stand. The soda cost $.10 more than the ice cream bar. How much did the soda cost?

2. To ride the Space Chase, a person needs 9 tickets. Carrie had 4 more tickets than Lisa. Together they had just enough tickets so that both could ride. How many tickets did Carrie have?

3. In a ring–toss game, the pegs were labeled 1, 3, 6, and 10 points. Taro tossed 3 rings and scored 15 points. What pegs did he ring?

4. In the arcade, the electronic games cost $.25 and $.35. Maria spent $1.55 to play 5 games. How many 35–cent games did she play?

On grid paper, put X at (**1,0**) and Y at (**1,8**).

5. If Z is at (**7,4**), is Z closer to X or to Y, or is it the same distance from each?

6. T is at (**4,7**). W is at (**3,3**). Is T closer to Y than W is to X? Explain.

Set A

Solve. Use a calculator where appropriate. pages 391–393, 402–403

1. Brian is taller than Emily. Lee is shorter than Emily. Jason's height is between that of Emily and Lee. Who is tallest?

2. Susan walked 40 meters east and 30 meters south. Then she walked 30 meters west and 20 meters north. How many more meters does she have to walk to get back to her starting place?

3. Mr. McNamara put 4 fence posts along a side of his garden that is 6 meters long. If he keeps the same space between posts, how many posts will be needed to extend that side of his garden to 12 meters?

4. Teresa has 8 nickels and other coins. The number of quarters is one half the number of nickels. The number of dimes is three times the number of nickels. How much money does Teresa have?

5. Which of these fractions are closer to 1 than to 0?

$$\frac{2}{3}, \frac{2}{5}, \frac{3}{8}, \frac{3}{4}, \frac{4}{8}, \frac{5}{12}, \frac{5}{8}$$

6. I am thinking of a fraction that is closer to 0 than to 1. The denominator is 10. What numbers could the numerator be?

Set B

Solve. Use a calculator where appropriate. pages 419–421, 428–429

1. Carter bought 4 packages of stamps for $.75 each. Each package contained 2 new and 3 used stamps. How many stamps did he buy?

2. While playing a board game, Ginger moved ahead 6 spaces and back 4 spaces in each turn. How far ahead is Ginger after the three turns?

3. Find the sum of these numbers in two different ways.
$$3 + 4 + 5 + 6 + 7$$
Explain each way.

4. A Target Board has spaces marked 5, 3, 1, and 0. Tony scored 14 in 4 throws. What spaces did he hit?

5. Terry made a kite from two square pieces of material. One piece is 24 inches on a side. The other piece is 12 inches on a side. What is the total area of the kite?

6. Bill made a smaller version of the kite described in **5**. The side of each square is $\frac{1}{2}$ as long. What is the total area of the smaller kite?

Skill Hints

When reading or writing numbers look for commas.
They help you locate the repeating pattern of
hundred, tens and ones.

One hundred sixty-two thousand , three hundred fifty-one

162 , 351

Write each number in standard form.

1. 3,000 + 200 + 8

2. fourteen thousand, thirty-nine

3. 60,000 + 8,000 + 700

4. 425 thousand, twenty-one

5. eighty-two thousand, nine

6. 19 million, 402 thousand

7. three hundred six million, fifty-eight thousand,
two hundred seven

8. nine million, seven hundred thousand, three
hundred eleven

When comparing or ordering numbers, match the
place values starting with the greatest place value.

4,3**6**7

4,3**8**2

8 tens > 6 tens so 4,382 > 4,367

Compare. Write >, <, or = for ⬤.

9. 813 ⬤ 803

10. 1,781 ⬤ 1,981

11. 5,341 ⬤ 3,341

12. 2,116 ⬤ 2,118

13. 73,421 ⬤ 73,500

14. 3,400 ⬤ 3,399

15. 58,168 ⬤ 58,141

16. 20,003 ⬤ 19,561

17. 2,162 ⬤ 2,162

ᴴⁱⁿᵗ When rounding, think of the number on a number line.

Round 439 to the nearest ten.

439 is between 430 and 440.
It is closer to 440.
439 rounds to 440.

Round 23,199 to the nearest thousand.

23,199 is between 23,000 and 24,000.
It is closer to 23,000.
23,199 rounds to 23,000.

Round to the nearest ten.

1. 49	**2.** 82	**3.** 56	**4.** 131	**5.** 786	**6.** 98
7. 263	**8.** 349	**9.** 1,142	**10.** 2,157	**11.** 8,497	**12.** 999

Round to the nearest hundred.

13. 648	**14.** 391	**15.** 729	**16.** 874	**17.** 3,449	**18.** 7,052
19. 12,587	**20.** 23,403	**21.** 73,976	**22.** 80,191	**23.** 15,401	**24.** 29,561

Round to the nearest ten dollars.

25. $56	**26.** $142	**27.** $278	**28.** $96	**29.** $1,402	**30.** $2,976

Round to the nearest thousand.

31. 1,003	**32.** 3,476	**33.** 8,541	**34.** 11,476	**35.** 42,951	**36.** 30,073

Skill Hints

HINT Estimate first when adding or subtracting. The estimate will help you recognize unreasonable answers.

Estimate by:

Rounding		Front end estimation	
68 → 70		68 → 60 + 40 = 100	
+ 48 → + 50		+ 48 8 + 8 gives another 10	
120 ← Estimate		110 ← Estimate	

68 + 48 = 116   116 is a reasonable result.

Estimate first. Then add.

1. 73
    + 29

2. 57
    + 63

3. 388
    + 655

4. 527
    + 92

5. $3.16
    + 7.42

6. 73 + 82 + 56 = ☐

7. 807 + 29 = ☐

8. $5.92 + $.68 = ☐

9. 102 + 39 + 8 = ☐

10. 47 + 298 + 3 = ☐

11. $1.04 + $.98 = ☐

12. 207
     + 339

13. 3,816
     + 7,572

14. $12.87
     +   3.94

15. 81,376
     + 72,058

16. 51,307
     + 48,783

Estimate first. Then subtract.

17. 92
     − 57

18. 539
     − 280

19. 506
     − 154

20. $6.83
     − 2.79

21. 762
     − 744

22. 703
     − 59

23. $4.00
     − 2.78

24. 22,401
     − 16,765

25. $738.42
     − 546.14

26. 7,003
     − 107

27. 75 − 36 = ☐

28. 239 − 84 = ☐

29. 481 − 265 = ☐

30. $5.65 − $2.19 = ☐

31. 2,436 − 1,956 = ☐

32. 9,768 − 939 = ☐

H
I
N
T

To estimate elapsed time, round each time to the nearest hour or half-hour. Then count the hours and half-hours from beginning time to ending time.

Estimate from 8:10 A.M. to 10:35 A.M.
8:10 A.M. is closest to 8:00 A.M. (nearest hour).
10:35 A.M. is closest to 10:30 A.M. (nearest half-hour).
8:00 to 10:30 is two and one-half hours.

Estimate the elapsed time.

1. Start   9:05 A.M.
   End   11:05 A.M.

2. Start   3:25 P.M.
   End   7:55 P.M.

3. Start   11:35 A.M.
   End   2:20 P.M.

4. Start   3:18 P.M.
   End   4:22 P.M.

5. Start   11:28 A.M.
   End   12:53 P.M.

6. Start   1:07 P.M.
   End   4:52 P.M.

Find each time.

7. 20 min after 9:15 A.M.

8. 10 min before 7:05 P.M.

9. $1\frac{1}{2}$ h after 5:00 P.M.

H
I
N
T

A bar graph best describes comparisons of data.
A line graph best describes how data changes over time.

Sally's Scores on Math Tests

1st week	78
2nd week	89
3rd week	93

Decide which type of graph you would use.

10. to show how milk prices have changed in the last 10 years

11. to compare your classmates favorite type of reading book

12. to show the average height of girls from ages 10 to 15

H
I
N
T
Use doubles to help remember multiplication facts.

$2 \times 8 = 16$ so $4 \times 8 = 32$

4 is the   32 is the
double   double
of 2   of 16

Multiply.

1. $\begin{array}{r} 6 \\ \times\ 2 \\ \hline \end{array}$	2. $\begin{array}{r} 6 \\ \times\ 4 \\ \hline \end{array}$	3. $\begin{array}{r} 5 \\ \times\ 3 \\ \hline \end{array}$	4. $\begin{array}{r} 5 \\ \times\ 6 \\ \hline \end{array}$	5. $\begin{array}{r} 4 \\ \times\ 5 \\ \hline \end{array}$	6. $\begin{array}{r} 4 \\ \times\ 10 \\ \hline \end{array}$
7. $\begin{array}{r} 7 \\ \times\ 4 \\ \hline \end{array}$	8. $\begin{array}{r} 7 \\ \times\ 8 \\ \hline \end{array}$	9. $\begin{array}{r} 9 \\ \times\ 2 \\ \hline \end{array}$	10. $\begin{array}{r} 9 \\ \times\ 4 \\ \hline \end{array}$	11. $\begin{array}{r} 7 \\ \times\ 3 \\ \hline \end{array}$	12. $\begin{array}{r} 7 \\ \times\ 6 \\ \hline \end{array}$
13. $\begin{array}{r} 3 \\ \times\ 4 \\ \hline \end{array}$	14. $\begin{array}{r} 3 \\ \times\ 8 \\ \hline \end{array}$	15. $\begin{array}{r} 6 \\ \times\ 5 \\ \hline \end{array}$	16. $\begin{array}{r} 6 \\ \times\ 10 \\ \hline \end{array}$	17. $\begin{array}{r} 9 \\ \times\ 3 \\ \hline \end{array}$	18. $\begin{array}{r} 9 \\ \times\ 6 \\ \hline \end{array}$
19. $\begin{array}{r} 9 \\ \times\ 8 \\ \hline \end{array}$	20. $\begin{array}{r} 8 \\ \times\ 4 \\ \hline \end{array}$	21. $\begin{array}{r} 4 \\ \times\ 7 \\ \hline \end{array}$	22. $\begin{array}{r} 5 \\ \times\ 8 \\ \hline \end{array}$	23. $\begin{array}{r} 3 \\ \times\ 9 \\ \hline \end{array}$	24. $\begin{array}{r} 5 \\ \times\ 5 \\ \hline \end{array}$
25. $\begin{array}{r} 3 \\ \times\ 6 \\ \hline \end{array}$	26. $\begin{array}{r} 8 \\ \times\ 7 \\ \hline \end{array}$	27. $\begin{array}{r} 8 \\ \times\ 8 \\ \hline \end{array}$	28. $\begin{array}{r} 6 \\ \times\ 9 \\ \hline \end{array}$	29. $\begin{array}{r} 5 \\ \times\ 7 \\ \hline \end{array}$	30. $\begin{array}{r} 4 \\ \times\ 9 \\ \hline \end{array}$

Find the missing factors.

31. $\square \times 5 = 10$ 32. $\square \times 5 = 20$ 33. $4 \times \square = 16$ 34. $4 \times \square = 32$

35. $3 \times \square = 18$ 36. $6 \times \square = 36$ 37. $9 \times \square = 45$ 38. $9 \times \square = 90$

39. $\square \times 4 = 12$ 40. $6 \times \square = 18$ 41. $\square \times 1 = 5$ 42. $6 \times \square = 0$

43. $7 \times \square = 21$ 44. $\square \times 8 = 24$ 45. $\square \times 8 = 0$ 46. $9 \times \square = 54$

Estimating the product will help you recognize
unreasonable results.

H
I
N
T
Use mental math where possible to get an exact
answer quickly.

$2 \times \$1.95 = \square$
Think: $2 \times \$2.00 = \$4.00$
$\$4.00 - \$.10 = \$3.90$

$3 \times 502 = \square$
Think: $3 \times 500 = 1,500$
$3 \times 2 = 6$
$1,500 + 6 = 1,506$

Estimate. Then multiply.

1.	38 $\times$ 7	**2.**	41 $\times$ 6	**3.**	136 $\times$ 7	**4.**	936 $\times$ 5	**5.**	2,804 $\times$ 3

6.	1,115 $\times$ 4	**7.**	306 $\times$ 7	**8.**	240 $\times$ 9	**9.**	81 $\times$ 7	**10.**	$5.40 $\times$ 7

11. $6 \times 57 = \square$ **12.** $3 \times 702 = \square$ **13.** $8 \times 1,050 = \square$

**Use mental math, pencil and paper, or a
calculator to find each product.**

14.	$3.98 $\times$ 4	**15.**	$15.05 $\times$ 3	**16.**	$2.89 $\times$ 3	**17.**	$22.02 $\times$ 6	**18.**	1,001 $\times$ 9

19.	3,104 $\times$ 7	**20.**	5,122 $\times$ 2	**21.**	4,183 $\times$ 6	**22.**	7,802 $\times$ 5	**23.**	9,173 $\times$ 6

24. $2 \times \$8.95$ **25.** $7 \times 4,128$ **26.** $8 \times 2,004$ **27.** $3 \times \$6.95$

Skill Hints

HINT When multiplying by 10 or a multiple of 10 the product will have a 0 in the one's place value.

$$
\begin{array}{r}
87 \\
\times\ 10 \\
\hline
87\underline{0}
\end{array}
$$

$$
\begin{array}{r}
54 \\
\times\ 21 \\
\hline
54 \\
1{,}080 \\
\hline
1{,}134
\end{array}
$$

1,080 ← 20 × 54 = 108\underline{0}

HINT Remember to estimate!

Multiply.

1. $\begin{array}{r} 32 \\ \times\ 10 \\ \hline \end{array}$
2. $\begin{array}{r} 67 \\ \times\ 10 \\ \hline \end{array}$
3. $\begin{array}{r} 43 \\ \times\ 20 \\ \hline \end{array}$
4. $\begin{array}{r} 15 \\ \times\ 70 \\ \hline \end{array}$
5. $\begin{array}{r} 132 \\ \times\ 10 \\ \hline \end{array}$
6. $\begin{array}{r} 506 \\ \times\ 30 \\ \hline \end{array}$

7. $40 \times 30 = n$
8. $38 \times 60 = n$
9. $230 \times 40 = n$

10. $\begin{array}{r} 83 \\ \times\ 42 \\ \hline \end{array}$
11. $\begin{array}{r} 60 \\ \times\ 48 \\ \hline \end{array}$
12. $\begin{array}{r} 82 \\ \times\ 97 \\ \hline \end{array}$
13. $\begin{array}{r} 33 \\ \times\ 65 \\ \hline \end{array}$
14. $\begin{array}{r} 39 \\ \times\ 14 \\ \hline \end{array}$
15. $\begin{array}{r} 51 \\ \times\ 92 \\ \hline \end{array}$

16. $\begin{array}{r} 226 \\ \times\ 32 \\ \hline \end{array}$
17. $\begin{array}{r} 840 \\ \times\ 27 \\ \hline \end{array}$
18. $\begin{array}{r} 215 \\ \times\ 26 \\ \hline \end{array}$
19. $\begin{array}{r} 621 \\ \times\ 62 \\ \hline \end{array}$
20. $\begin{array}{r} 437 \\ \times\ 38 \\ \hline \end{array}$
21. $\begin{array}{r} 600 \\ \times\ 42 \\ \hline \end{array}$

22. $\begin{array}{r} \$.72 \\ \times\ 17 \\ \hline \end{array}$
23. $\begin{array}{r} \$.56 \\ \times\ 30 \\ \hline \end{array}$
24. $\begin{array}{r} \$1.05 \\ \times\ 14 \\ \hline \end{array}$
25. $\begin{array}{r} \$3.20 \\ \times\ 32 \\ \hline \end{array}$
26. $\begin{array}{r} \$4.17 \\ \times\ 43 \\ \hline \end{array}$
27. $\begin{array}{r} \$1.98 \\ \times\ 54 \\ \hline \end{array}$

28. $\begin{array}{r} 1{,}326 \\ \times\ 34 \\ \hline \end{array}$
29. $\begin{array}{r} 5{,}108 \\ \times\ 23 \\ \hline \end{array}$
30. $\begin{array}{r} 9{,}730 \\ \times\ 63 \\ \hline \end{array}$
31. $\begin{array}{r} 6{,}814 \\ \times\ 95 \\ \hline \end{array}$
32. $\begin{array}{r} \$10.51 \\ \times\ 27 \\ \hline \end{array}$
33. $\begin{array}{r} \$72.09 \\ \times\ 68 \\ \hline \end{array}$

The remainder of each subtraction in a division
H problem must be less than the divisor.
I
N
T Write 0 in the quotient when there is not enough in a
place value to divide.

$$\begin{array}{r} 3 \\ 6\overline{)19} \\ \underline{18} \\ 1 \end{array}$$ 1 < 6

$19 \div 6 = 3R1$

$$\begin{array}{r} 104 \\ 5\overline{)520} \\ \underline{5\downarrow\downarrow} \\ 020 \\ \underline{20} \\ 0 \end{array}$$

Think
$$\begin{array}{r} 0 \\ 5\overline{)2} \end{array}$$
Not enough tens to
divide. Write
0 in the quotient.

Find each quotient.

1. $6\overline{)49}$ 2. $8\overline{)45}$ 3. $9\overline{)71}$ 4. $4\overline{)25}$ 5. $3\overline{)23}$

6. $7\overline{)60}$ 7. $2\overline{)17}$ 8. $5\overline{)38}$ 9. $8\overline{)77}$ 10. $9\overline{)67}$

11. $6\overline{)130}$ 12. $6\overline{)480}$ 13. $2\overline{)120}$ 14. $7\overline{)420}$ 15. $8\overline{)5,600}$

16. $3,200 \div 4$ 17. $70 \div 8$ 18. $3,000 \div 5$ 19. $2,100 \div 7$

Estimate. Then divide.

20. $4\overline{)424}$ 21. $3\overline{)622}$ 22. $2\overline{)619}$ 23. $6\overline{)651}$ 24. $4\overline{)804}$

25. $5\overline{)380}$ 26. $7\overline{)307}$ 27. $9\overline{)491}$ 28. $8\overline{)296}$ 29. $6\overline{)146}$

30. $5\overline{)\$6.05}$ 31. $3\overline{)\$.69}$ 32. $9\overline{)\$9.63}$ 33. $7\overline{)802}$ 34. $4\overline{)871}$

35. $776 \div 3$ 36. $339 \div 7$ 37. $613 \div 9$ 38. $\$7.50 \div 2$

Skill Hints

H I N T
When naming an angle, the vertex point is the middle letter.

Identify angles by comparing them to a right angle.

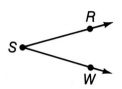

S is the vertex
This is angle *RSW*
or angle *WSR*

∠ *PQT* is acute
It fits inside a
right angle

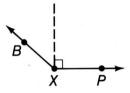

∠ *BXP* is obtuse
A right angle will
fit inside ∠ *BXP*.

Name each angle. Then identify it as right, acute, or obtuse.

1.

2.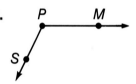

3.

4.

5.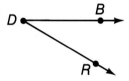

6.

7.

8.

Use the figure at the right.

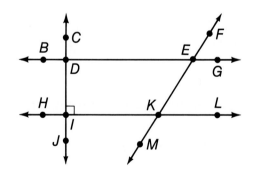

9. Name a right angle.

10. Name an acute angle.

11. Name an obtuse angle.

12. Name a line parallel to $\overleftrightarrow{BD}$.

13. Name two perpendicular lines.

14. Name two lines which intersect at *E*.

15. Are lines $\overleftrightarrow{CD}$ and $\overleftrightarrow{EK}$ parallel or intersecting?

The denominator of a fraction shows the number of equal parts in a region or the number of parts in a group.

9 equal parts
2 parts shaded

$\frac{2}{9}$ of the square
is shaded.

3 shapes in all
2 shapes shaded

$\frac{2}{3}$ of the shapes
are shaded

Write a fraction which tells what part is shaded.

1.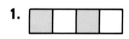

2.

3.

4.

5.

6.

7.

8.

Find each missing number.

9. $\frac{1}{3}$ of 12

10. $\frac{1}{5}$ of 30

11. $\frac{1}{2}$ of 20

12. $\frac{1}{10}$ of 40

13. $\frac{2}{3}$ of 18

14. $\frac{3}{5}$ of 15

15. $\frac{2}{2}$ of 16

16. $\frac{5}{8}$ of 24

Write an equivalent fraction for each.

17. $\frac{1}{4} = \frac{1 \times 3}{4 \times 3} = \frac{\square}{12}$

18. $\frac{3}{5} = \frac{3 \times 2}{5 \times 2} = \frac{\square}{10}$

19. $\frac{3}{8} = \frac{3 \times 4}{8 \times 4} = \frac{\square}{32}$

Skill Hints

HINT When comparing decimals write zeros to make the decimals have the same number of places.

Compare 0.24 and 0.2

0.24

0.20

$4 > 0$ so $0.24 > 0.2$

Compare. Write $>$, $<$, or $=$ for ●.

1. 0.5 ● 0.3

2. 0.16 ● 0.5

3. 0.87 ● 0.8

4. 2.36 ● 2.37

5. 5.4 ● 3.8

6. 0.8 ● 0.80

7. 3.2 ● 3.02

8. 5.1 ● .51

9. 7.62 ● 76.2

HINT When adding or subtracting decimals, line up the decimal points. Write zeros where needed. Remember the decimal point in a whole number is to the right of the one's place value.

$$\begin{array}{r} 2.80 \\ +\ .17 \\ \hline 2.97 \end{array}$$

$$\begin{array}{r} \overset{9}{\underset{}{3\ \cancel{10}10}} \\ 1\,4.0\,0 \\ -\ \ \ 3.7\,5 \\ \hline 1\,0.2\,5 \end{array}$$

Add or subtract.

1. $\begin{array}{r} 3.4 \\ +\ 2.7 \\ \hline \end{array}$

2. $\begin{array}{r} 5.8 \\ +\ 6.2 \\ \hline \end{array}$

3. $\begin{array}{r} 13.7 \\ -\ 4.8 \\ \hline \end{array}$

4. $\begin{array}{r} 9.43 \\ +\ 2.4 \\ \hline \end{array}$

5. $\begin{array}{r} 18.76 \\ -\ 8.53 \\ \hline \end{array}$

6. $\begin{array}{r} 5.87 \\ -\ 4.34 \\ \hline \end{array}$

7. $\begin{array}{r} 7.3 \\ +\ 1.87 \\ \hline \end{array}$

8. $\begin{array}{r} 3.24 \\ -\ 1.68 \\ \hline \end{array}$

9. $\begin{array}{r} 14.6 \\ -\ 8.73 \\ \hline \end{array}$

10. $\begin{array}{r} 2.8 \\ +\ 13.57 \\ \hline \end{array}$

11. $14 - 2.6$

12. $0.7 + 3.2$

13. $18.3 - 1.25$

H I N T   To choose an appropriate unit of measurement think of objects you already know.

Would you measure the height of a flagpole in centimeters, meters, or kilometers?

You would measure the height in meters.

Think: My fingernail is about 1 centimenter long.

The width of the classroom is about 10 meters.

When I ride in a car I measure the distance in kilometers.

Would you choose cm, m or km to measure each?

1. length of your foot

2. the distance a plane flies in 1 hour

3. the height of your house

4. the length of a jump rope

5. the length of a pencil

6. the distance from New York to California

Would you choose g or kg to measure the weight of each?

7. a strawberry

8. a 9 year old boy

9. your teacher

10. a thumb tack

11. a sandwich

12. an airplane

Would you choose mL or L to measure each?

13. a tea cup

14. a bathtub

15. a medicine dropper

Choose the most reasonable temperature.

16. snowy day   **a.** 0° C   **b.** 20° C   **c.** 32° C

17. a cup of hot soup   **a.** 20° C   **b.** 40° C   **c.** 80° C

Skill Hints

HINT When finding the area of a polygon separate it into rectangles.

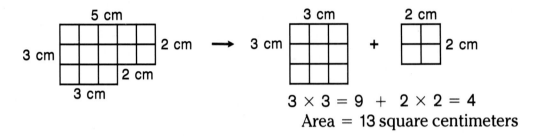

$3 \times 3 = 9 + 2 \times 2 = 4$

Area = 13 square centimeters

Find the area of the following figures.

1.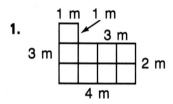

2.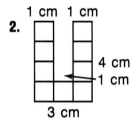

3.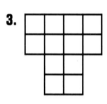

4.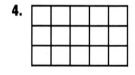

5.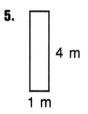

6.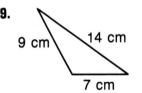

7. A rectangle that is 10 cm long and 17 cm wide.

Find the perimeter of the following figures.

8.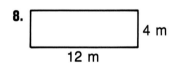

9.

10.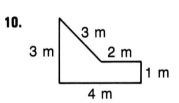

11. A rectangle 5 cm wide and 11 cm long

12. A triangle with all 3 sides 7 cm long

H I N T Use drawings to help you estimate fractions.

Is $\frac{6}{10}$ closer to 0, $\frac{1}{2}$, or 1?

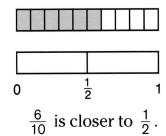

$\frac{6}{10}$ is closer to $\frac{1}{2}$.

Write 0, $\frac{1}{2}$, or 1 for the best estimate of each fraction. Use drawings to help you.

1. $\frac{3}{4}$ **2.** $\frac{3}{8}$ **3.** $\frac{5}{6}$ **4.** $\frac{5}{12}$ **5.** $\frac{7}{8}$

6. $\frac{1}{8}$ **7.** $\frac{2}{10}$ **8.** $\frac{11}{12}$ **9.** $\frac{9}{10}$ **10.** $\frac{8}{20}$

H I N T When comparing fractions find equivalent fractions with the same denominator. Then compare the numerators.

$\frac{2}{3}$ and $\frac{5}{6}$

$\downarrow$ $\downarrow$ 4 is less than 5.

$\frac{4}{6}$ $\frac{5}{6}$ $\frac{4}{6} < \frac{5}{6}$

Compare. Write >, <, or = for 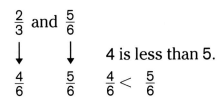.

11. $\frac{5}{6}$ ⬤ $\frac{3}{6}$ **12.** $\frac{2}{3}$ ⬤ $\frac{5}{12}$ **13.** $\frac{3}{4}$ ⬤ $\frac{1}{8}$ **14.** $\frac{7}{10}$ ⬤ $\frac{2}{5}$

15. $\frac{1}{2}$ ⬤ $\frac{3}{6}$ **16.** $\frac{3}{4}$ ⬤ $\frac{4}{12}$ **17.** $\frac{2}{3}$ ⬤ $\frac{4}{6}$ **18.** $\frac{1}{6}$ ⬤ $\frac{5}{18}$

Skill Hints

$\begin{smallmatrix} H \\ I \\ N \\ T \end{smallmatrix}$ Before you add or subtract fractions be sure the fractions have the same denominator.

$$\begin{array}{r} \frac{2}{6} \\ +\frac{3}{6} \\ \hline \frac{5}{6} \end{array} \qquad \begin{array}{r} \frac{3}{4} \\ -\frac{1}{3} \\ \hline \end{array} \rightarrow \begin{array}{r} \frac{9}{12} \\ \frac{4}{12} \\ \hline \frac{5}{12} \end{array}$$

Add. Use fraction pieces or a drawing if you wish.

1. $\begin{array}{r} \frac{1}{4} \\ +\frac{1}{4} \\ \hline \end{array}$ **2.** $\begin{array}{r} \frac{2}{3} \\ +\frac{1}{3} \\ \hline \end{array}$ **3.** $\begin{array}{r} \frac{3}{6} \\ +\frac{1}{6} \\ \hline \end{array}$ **4.** $\begin{array}{r} \frac{3}{8} \\ +\frac{2}{8} \\ \hline \end{array}$ **5.** $\begin{array}{r} \frac{2}{10} \\ +\frac{3}{10} \\ \hline \end{array}$

6. $\begin{array}{r} \frac{1}{3} \\ +\frac{1}{6} \\ \hline \end{array}$ **7.** $\begin{array}{r} \frac{2}{4} \\ +\frac{2}{8} \\ \hline \end{array}$ **8.** $\begin{array}{r} \frac{1}{2} \\ +\frac{2}{10} \\ \hline \end{array}$ **9.** $\begin{array}{r} \frac{2}{5} \\ +\frac{1}{10} \\ \hline \end{array}$ **10.** $\begin{array}{r} \frac{1}{2} \\ +\frac{1}{6} \\ \hline \end{array}$

Subtract.

11. $\begin{array}{r} \frac{7}{8} \\ -\frac{1}{8} \\ \hline \end{array}$ **12.** $\begin{array}{r} \frac{5}{6} \\ -\frac{1}{6} \\ \hline \end{array}$ **13.** $\begin{array}{r} \frac{8}{10} \\ -\frac{5}{10} \\ \hline \end{array}$ **14.** $\begin{array}{r} \frac{3}{4} \\ -\frac{1}{4} \\ \hline \end{array}$ **15.** $\begin{array}{r} \frac{1}{2} \\ -\frac{1}{4} \\ \hline \end{array}$

16. $\begin{array}{r} \frac{6}{8} \\ -\frac{1}{4} \\ \hline \end{array}$ **17.** $\begin{array}{r} \frac{2}{3} \\ -\frac{3}{6} \\ \hline \end{array}$ **18.** $\begin{array}{r} \frac{4}{5} \\ -\frac{2}{10} \\ \hline \end{array}$ **19.** $\begin{array}{r} \frac{3}{4} \\ -\frac{1}{2} \\ \hline \end{array}$ **20.** $\begin{array}{r} \frac{6}{12} \\ -\frac{1}{4} \\ \hline \end{array}$

21. $\frac{7}{10} - \frac{1}{2}$ **22.** $1 - \frac{1}{3}$ **23.** $\frac{2}{3} - \frac{1}{6}$

HINT To change from smaller units of measure to larger units, divide.
To change from larger units to smaller units, multiply.

24 in. = _____ ft
Inches are smaller than feet.
$24 \div 12 = 2$
24 in. = 2 ft

3 gal = _____ qt
Gallons are larger than quarts.
$3 \times 4 = 12$
3 gal = 12 qt

Complete.

1. 3 ft 5 in. = _____ in.   **2.** 6 ft = _____ yd   **3.** 48 oz = _____ lb

4. 3 T = _____ lb   **5.** 20 qt = _____ gal   **6.** 1 qt 1 pt = _____ pt

7. 6 c = _____ pt   **8.** 2 lb 10 oz = _____ oz   **9.** 3 mi = _____ ft

HINT To estimate measures compare them to easily remembered examples.

Is a full tank of gasoline in a car about 20 quarts or 20 gallons?
Think, milk comes in quarts and a small fish tank is about 5 gallons.
The car's tank is more likely 20 gallons.

Choose the best measure for each.

10. The length of a pencil   **a.** inch   **b.** foot   **c.** mile

11. The weight of a watermelon   **a.** ounce   **b.** pound   **c.** ton

12. The capacity of a swimming pool   **a.** cup   **b.** quart   **c.** gallon

13. The temperature for ice skating   **a.** $-10°F$ **b.** $28°F$ **c.** $72°F$

14. The distance to the moon   **a.** inch   **b.** foot   **c.** mile

Glossary

A.M. Used to show the time between midnight and noon.   p. 76

acute angle An angle less than a right angle. p. 260
Example:

addends The numbers that are added.   p. 2
Example: 7 + 8 = 15
The addends are 7 and 8.

addition An operation on two or more numbers to find the sum.   p. 2
Example: 4 + 2 + 3 = 9
The sum is 9.

angle Two rays with a common endpoint.   p. 260
Example:

area The number of square units needed to cover a region.   p. 354

average The sum of the addends divided by the number of addends.   p. 238

bar graph A graph with bars of different lengths to show information.   p. 85

capacity The amount of liquid a container can hold.   p. 336

centimeter (cm) A standard unit in the metric system to measure length.   p. 330

chance A possibility or probability.   p. 394

circle A closed plane figure. All the points of a circle are the same distance from a point called the center.   p. 264

circle graph A graph that shows how a total amount has been divided into parts.   p. 100

composite number A whole number greater than 1 that has more than two factors.   p. 131
Example: 8 is a composite number. Its factors are 1, 2, 4, and 8.

cone A space figure with one circular flat surface and one vertex.   p. 362

congruent figures Figures that have the same size and shape.   p. 270

cube A space figure with six square faces.   p. 362

cup (c) A unit of volume in the customary system equal to 8 ounces.   p. 424

customary system A measurement system that measures length in inches, feet, yards, and miles; capacity in cups, pints, quarts, and gallons; weight in ounces, pounds, and tons; and temperature in degrees Fahrenheit. *See* Table of Measures.   p. 414

cylinder A space figure with two bases that are congruent circles.   p. 362
Example:

data Information that is gathered.   p. 94

decimal A number with one or more places to the right of a decimal point.   p. 314
Examples: 0.7, 1.8, 2.06

decimal point The dot used to separate dollars from cents and ones from tenths.   p. 44
Examples: $1.54, 1.3

degree Celsius (°C) A unit for measuring temperature in the metric system.   p. 340

degree Fahrenheit (°F) A unit for measuring temperature in the customary system.   p. 426

denominator The number below the fraction bar in a fraction.   p. 290
Example: $\frac{2}{5}$
The denominator is 5.

diameter A line segment that passes through the center of a circle and has both endpoints on the circle.   p. 264

difference The answer in subtraction.   p. 6
Example: 9 − 4 = 5
The difference is 5.

digit Any of the symbols used to write numbers: 0,1,2,3,4,5,6,7,8 and 9.   p. 14

dividend The number to be divided.   p. 134
Example: 6)36 or 36 ÷ 6
The dividend is 36.

divisible A number is divisible by another number if the remainder is 0 after dividing. p. 252

division An operation on two numbers that results in a quotient.   p. 134

divisor The number by which another number is to be divided.   p. 134
Example: 7)28 or 28 ÷ 7
The divisor is 7.

472

dollar sign ($) A symbol used to represent dollars. p. 44
Example: $2.35

edge The segment where two faces of a space figure meet. p. 362
Example: edge

elapsed time The amount of time that has passed. p. 78

endpoint A point at the end of a line segment or ray. p. 258

equivalent fractions Fractions that name the same number. p. 300
Example: $\frac{1}{2}$ and $\frac{2}{4}$

estimate To give an approximate rather than an exact answer. p. 36

even number A whole number that is divisible by 2. p. 3

expanded form A number written as the sum of the values of its digits. p. 14
Example: 200 + 80 + 7 is the expanded form of 287.

experiment To carry out a plan in order to test a prediction. p. 298

face A flat surface of a space figure. p. 362

fact family Related facts using the same numbers. p. 8
Example: 2 + 3 = 5   5 − 3 = 2
3 + 2 = 5   5 − 2 = 3

factor pair A pair of numbers to be multiplied together to form a given product. p. 129

factors The numbers that are multiplied to give a product. p. 112
Example: 3 × 5 = 15
The factors are 3 and 5.

flip To pick up and turn over. p. 278

foot (ft) A unit of length in the customary system equal to 12 inches. p. 412

fraction A number that names part of a group or part of a region. p. 290
Examples: $\frac{1}{2}$ $\frac{2}{3}$ $\frac{6}{6}$

front digit The digit in the greatest place, used for estimation. p. 38

gallon (gal) A unit of volume in the customary system equal to 4 quarts. p. 424

gram (g) A unit in the metric system used to measure the mass/weight of light objects. p. 334

graph A drawing used to show information. p. 84

greater than (>) The symbol used to compare two numbers when the greater number is written first. p. 22
Examples: 7 > 3, 9 > 6

grouping property of addition The way in which numbers are grouped does not change the sum. p. 2
Example: 2 + (4 + 5) = (2 + 4) + 5

grouping property of multiplication The way in which numbers are grouped does not change the product. p. 116
Example: 2 × (3 × 5) = (2 × 3) × 5

hexagon A polygon with six sides and six vertices. p. 256

hour (h) A unit of time equal to 60 minutes. p. 76

inch (in.) A standard unit in the customary system to measure length. p. 412

intersecting lines Lines that cross at one point. p. 262

inverse operations Two operations that are opposite in effect. Addition and subtraction are inverse operations. Multiplication and division are inverse operations. p. 147

kilogram (kg) A unit in the metric system used to measure the mass/weight of heavy objects. p. 334

kilometer (km) A unit in the metric system used to measure long lengths. p. 332

length The distance from one end of an object to the other end. p. 330

less than (<) The symbol used to compare two numbers when the lesser number is written first. p. 22
Examples: 3 < 7, 6 < 9

Glossary

like fractions Fractions that have the same denominator.   p. 380

Example: $\frac{3}{4}$ and $\frac{1}{4}$

line The collection of points along a straight path that goes on and on in opposite directions. A line has no endpoints.   p. 258

line graph A graph used to show changes over a period of time.   p. 86

line of symmetry A line that divides a figure into two congruent parts.   p. 274
Example:

line segment A part of a line drawing having two endpoints.   p. 258

liter (L) A unit in the metric system used to measure amounts of liquid.   p. 338

meter (m) A unit of length in the metric system equal to 100 centimeters.   p. 332

metric system A measurement system that measures length in millimeters, centimeters, meters, and kilometers; capacity in milliliters and liters; mass in grams and kilograms; and temperature in degrees Celsius. *See* Table of Measures.   p. 330

mile (mi) A unit of length in the customary system equal to 5,280 feet, or 1,760 yards.   p. 414

milliliter (mL) A unit in the metric system used to measure small amounts of liquid.   p. 338

millimeter (mm) A unit of length in the metric system: 10 millimeters equals 1 centimeter.   p. 330

minute (min) A unit used to measure a short amount of time.   p. 76

mixed number A number written as a whole number and a fraction.   p. 302

Example: $3\frac{4}{5}$.

multiple The product of a whole number and any other whole number.   p. 122
Example: 0, 3, 6, and so on, are multiples of 3.

multiplication An operation on two or more numbers, called factors, to find a product.   p. 112
Example: $4 \times 5 = 20$
The product is 20.

number line A line that shows numbers in order.   p. 26
Example:

number sentence A fact written in horizontal form.   p. 2
Example: $3 + 4 = 7$

numerator The number above the fraction bar in a fraction.   p. 290

Example: $\frac{2}{5}$
The numerator is 2.

obtuse angle An angle greater than a right angle.   p. 260
Example:

octagon A polygon with eight sides and eight vertices.   p. 256

odd number A whole number that is not divisible by 2.   p. 3

order property of addition The order in which numbers are added does not change the sum.   p. 2
Example: $9 + 3 = 3 + 9$

order property of multiplication The order in which numbers are multiplied does not change the product.   p. 116
Example: $3 \times 2 = 2 \times 3$

ordered pair A pair of numbers used to locate a point in a plane.   p. 366

ounce (oz) A unit of weight in the customary system.   p. 416

outcome A possible result in a probability experiment.   p. 394

P.M. Used to show the time between noon and midnight.   p. 76

palindrome A word or number that reads the same forward and backward.   p. 72
Examples: toot, 737

parallel lines Lines that never cross.   p. 262

parenthesis ( ) A symbol that shows grouping.   p. 2
Example: $(2 + 3) + 4 = 9, 5 + 4 = 9$

partial product When multiplying 2 two-digit numbers, the product after multiplying by ones or the product after multiplying by tens.   p. 195

pentagon A polygon with five sides and five vertices. p. 256

perimeter The distance around a polygon. p. 352

period A group of three digits of a number, separated from other digits by a comma. p. 18

perpendicular lines Two lines that meet to form right angles. p. 262

pictograph A graph that shows number information by using picture symbols. p. 84

pint (pt) A unit of volume in the customary system equal to 2 cups. p. 424

place value The value of a digit determined by its position in a number. p. 14
Example: In 562, the digit 5 means 5 hundreds, the digit 6 means 6 tens, the digit 2 means 2 ones.

plane figure A geometric figure whose points are all in one plane. p. 256

point An exact location in space. p. 258

polygon A closed plane figure with straight   es sides called line segments. p. 256

pound (lb) A unit of weight in the customary system equal to 16 ounces. p. 416

predict To make a reasonable statement about what might happen. p. 396

prime factors The lowest numbers which can be multiplied together to form a given product. p. 150
Example: $2 \times 2 \times 3 = 12$.
2, 2, and 3 are the prime factors for 12.

prime number A whole number greater than 1 with only two factors—itself and 1. p. 131
Examples: 5, 7, 11, and 13 are prime numbers.

probability The relation of favorable outcomes to possible outcomes of an experiment. p. 398

product The answer in multiplication. p. 112
Example: $4 \times 8 = 32$
The product is 32.

property of one for division Any number divided by 1 is that number. Any number except 0 divided by itself is 1. p. 142
Examples: $6 \div 1 = 6$
$3 \div 3 = 1$

property of one for multiplication The product of any number and 1 is that number. p. 116

pyramid A space figure whose base is a polygon and whose faces are triangles with a common vertex. p. 362

quadrilateral A polygon with four sides and four vertices. p. 256

quart (qt) A unit of volume in the customary system equal to 4 cups, or 2 pints. p. 424

quotient The answer in division. p. 134
Example: $24 \div 3 = 8$ or $3\overline{)24}^{\,8}$
The quotient is 8.

radius A line segment with one endpoint on the circle and the other endpoint at the center. p. 264

ratio A comparison of two quantities. p. 432
Example: 3 to 5

ray A part of a line that has one endpoint and goes on and on in one direction. p. 258

rectangle A polygon with four sides and four right angles. p. 256

rectangular prism A space figure whose faces are all rectangles. p. 362

regroup To use 1 ten to form 10 ones; 1 hundred to form 10 tens; 12 ones to form 1 ten 2 ones, and so on. p. 40

remainder The number that is left over after dividing. p. 220
Example: $42 \div 8 = 5$ R2
The remainder is 2.

right angle An angle that has the shape of a square corner. p. 260
Example:

rounding Expressing a number to the nearest ten, hundred, thousand, and so on. p. 26
Example: 43 rounded to the nearest ten is 40.

similar figures Figures that have the same shape. They are not the same size. p. 272

Glossary

slide To move without picking up. p. 278

space figure A geometric figure whose points are in more than one plane. p. 362

sphere A space figure shaped like a round ball. p. 362

square A polygon with four equal sides and four right angles. p. 256

subtraction An operation on two numbers to find the difference. p. 6

sum The answer in addition. p. 2
Example: 8 + 7 = 15
The sum is 15.

tally mark A mark made to keep count. p. 94

ton (T) A unit of weight in the customary system equal to 2,000 pounds. p. 416

triangle A polygon with three sides and three vertices. p. 256

turn To move around a point in a circular motion. p. 278

unlike fractions Fractions that have different denominators. p. 380

vertex The point where two rays meet. The point of intersection of two sides of a polygon. The point of intersection of three edges of a space figure. p. 256

volume The number of cubic units that fit inside a space figure. p. 364

yard (yd) A unit of length in the customary system equal to 36 inches, or 3 feet. p. 414

zero property of addition The sum of any number and 0 is that number. p. 2
Example: 3 + 0 = 3

zero property of division 0 divided by any number except 0 is 0. You cannot divide a number by 0. p. 142
Example: 0 ÷ 5 = 0

zero property of multiplication The product of any number and 0 is 0. p. 116
Example: 5 × 0 = 0

zero property of subtraction When 0 is subtracted from any number, the difference is athat number. When a number is subtracted from itself, the difference is 0. p. 6
Examples: 7 − 0 = 7
12 − 12 = 0

Computer Terms

button A picture that, when clicked, performs a command.

click Press the mouse button once.

click-and-drag Press and hold the mouse button while moving the mouse.

delete Remove information from the screen and memory.

double-click Press the mouse button twice quickly

Frames In MathProcessor™, a collection of squares or objects used to represent numbers.

Geometry Workspace A geoboard in MathProcessor™.

link In MathProcessor™, connects two or more things so that any change in one will change the other.

Manipulative Workspace In MathProcessor™, a window that contains counters, money, or blocks.

MathProcessor™ An interactive set of mathematics tools.

menu List of command choices.

mouse A hand-held moving device that guides the cursor or pointer.

Number Space In MathProcessor™, a window that acts as a counter and calculator.

Probability Workspace In MathProcessor™, number cubes or a spinner.

select To choose an item with a mouse or a keystroke.

window A visual workspace on the screen.

Writing Space In MathProcessor™, a place to write; also called a text window.

Measures

Metric

Length

1 centimeter (cm) = 10 millimeters (mm)
1 meter (m) = 100 centimeters
1 kilometer (km) = 1,000 meters

Mass/Weight

1 kilogram (kg) = 1,000 grams (g)

Capacity

1 liter (L) = 1,000 milliliters (mL)

Customary

Length

1 foot (ft) = 12 inches (in.)
1 yard (yd) = 36 inches, or 3 feet
1 mile (mi) = 5,280 feet, or 1,760 yards

Weight

1 pound (lb) = 16 ounces (oz)
1 ton (T) = 2,000 lb

Capacity

1 pint (pt) = 2 cups (c)
1 quart (qt) = 2 pints
1 gallon (gal) = 4 quarts

Time

1 minute (min) = 60 seconds (s)
1 hour (h) = 60 minutes
1 day (d) = 24 hours
1 week (wk) = 7 days
1 month (mo) = 28 to 31 days, or about 4 weeks
1 year (yr) = 12 months, or 52 weeks, or 365 days

Money

1 nickel = 5 cents (¢)
1 dime = 10 cents, or 2 nickels
1 quarter = 2 dimes and 1 nickel
1 half-dollar = 2 quarters
1 dollar ($) = 4 quarters

Symbols

=	is equal to	65¢	sixty-five cents
>	is greater than	$2.10	two dollars and ten cents
<	is less than	°C	degree Celsius
. . .	and so on	°F	degree Fahrenheit

$\overleftrightarrow{AB}$ line AB
$\overline{AB}$ line segment AB
$\overrightarrow{AB}$ ray AB
$\angle ABC$ angle ABC

Formulas

$P = a + b + c + d$ Perimeter of a quadrilateral
$A = l \times w$ Area of a rectangle
$V = l \times w \times h$ Volume of a rectangular prism

Credits

484